Contents

Preface xiii

1 The Environment of Texas Politics 1

Political Behavior Patterns 2
Political Culture in Texas 3
Texas's Frontier Experience 3

Texas and Texans: Land and People 4
Land: The Politics of Geography 4
People: Numbers and Distribution 8
People: Ethnic Groups 11

Some Social and Economic Policy Issues 14
Immigration: Federal and State Problems 14
Texas's Changing Economy 16
Texas in the Course of National Affairs 18

Notes 20
Key Terms and Concepts 21

Selected Readings

1.1 Changes in Texas's Hispanic-Black Population *(Juan R. Palomo)* 22

2 Federalism and the Texas Constitution 25

The American Federal Structure 26
The Distribution of Powers 26
An Evolving Process 28

The Texas Constitution: Politics of Policymaking 30
Historical Developments 31
Today's Texas Constitution: After a Century of Usage 33

Constitutional Revision and Amendment 34
A Major Reform Effort 35
The Amendment Process 37

The Texas Constitution Today: A Summary 38
The Bill of Rights 38
The Powers of Government 39
Suffrage 39

Local Government 40
Other Articles 40

Notes 40
Key Terms and Concepts 41

Selected Readings

2.1 Time to Write a New Constitution for Texas 42
2.2 Amending the Constitution of Texas: Article XVII as Amended in 1972 43

3 Local Governments 44

Municipal Governments 45
Legal Status of Municipalities 45
Forms of Municipal Government 46
Municipal Politics 48
Municipal Services 49
Financing Municipal Government 51

The County 53
Structure and Operation 54
County Finance 57
Reform Areas 59

Special Districts 60
School Districts 60
Junior or Community College Districts 61
Nonschool Districts 61
The Politics of Special Districts 63

Metropolitan Areas 63
Councils of Governments 64
Stopgap Approaches 64
Future Alternatives 65

Conclusion 66
Notes 66
Key Terms and Concepts 67

Selected Readings

3.1 David vs. Goliath: A Neighborhood Challenges City Hall
(James Ragland) 68

4 The Politics of Elections and Parties 71

The Politics of Elections 72
The Texas Voter 72

PRACTICING
TEXAS POLITICS

PRACTICING TEXAS POLITICS

A BRIEF SURVEY / Third Edition

Eugene W. Jones

Angelo State University

Joe E. Ericson

Stephen F. Austin State University

Lyle C. Brown

Baylor University

Robert S. Trotter, Jr.

*El Centro College of the Dallas County
Community College District*

Eileen M. Lynch

*Brookhaven College of the Dallas County
Community College District*

HOUGHTON MIFFLIN COMPANY   BOSTON

Dallas   Geneva, Illinois   Palo Alto   Princeton, New Jersey

Printed in the U.S.A.

Library of Congress Catalog Card Number: 89-80946

ISBN: 0-395-35943-0

CDEFGHIJ-MP-96543210

Primary Elections 77
General Elections 79
Special Elections 82
Administration of Elections 82

The Politics of Parties 84
Party Structure: Temporary Organization 84
Party Structure: Permanent Organization 87

The Quest for Political Democracy 88
Republicans and Democrats 88
A Question of Party Realignment 90
Women in Texas Politics 93
Ethnic Politics 94

Some Election Issues: Campaigns and Money 95
Financing Campaigns 97
Giving and Spending 98
Government Regulation of Campaigns 100

Notes 102
Key Terms and Concepts 103

Selected Readings

4.1 The Gender Barrier Is Coming Down *(Sam Attlesey)* 104

5 *The Politics of Interest Groups* 107

Interest Groups in the Political Process 108
What Is an Interest Group? 108
Interest Groups and Political Parties 109
Interest Groups in American Politics 109

Organization of Interest Groups 111
Membership in Interest Groups 111
Leadership in Interest Groups 111

Classification of Interest Groups 111
Economic Groups 112
Professional Groups 113
Ethnic Groups 113
Public Interest Groups 113
Public Officer and Employee Groups 114
Texas Power Groups 114

Interest Group Activities and Techniques 114
Group Activities 115
Techniques of Interest Groups 115

Interest Group Power and Public Policy 118
    Interest Groups and Public Policy in Texas 119
    Interest Group Power Linkage 120

Hazardous Waste Disposal Policies and Interest Group Activity 121
    Disposal of Radioactive Waste 121
    Disposal of Nonradioactive Hazardous Waste 123
    Hazardous Waste: A Continuing Problem? 126

Pinpointing Political Power 126
Notes 127
Key Terms and Concepts 127

Selected Readings

5.1 A Case of Textbook Lobbying *(Wayne Slater)* 128
5.2 Legislator Defends Free Perks *(Mike Ward)* 131

6 *The Legislature* 134

A Preliminary View 135

Legislative Framework 136
    Composition 137
    Election and Terms of Office 137
    Sessions 137
    Districting 137
    Compensation 139

Membership 140
    Qualifications of Members 140
    Characteristics of Members 140

Powers and Immunities 143
    Nonlegislative Powers 143
    Legislative Powers 145
    Immunities 146

Organization and Procedure 147
    Formal Organization 147
    Caucuses 151
    Procedure: A Bill Becomes a Law 154

Influences in the Legislative Environment 159
    The Governor's Influence 159
    Influence of the Courts, the Attorney General, and the Comptroller of
        Public Accounts 160
    Influence of Lobbyists 160

Prospects for Legislative Reform 162
Notes 163
Key Terms and Concepts 164

Selected Readings

6.1 AIDS: A Big Issue in the 71st Legislature *(Kaye Northcott)* 165

7 The Executive 168

Overview of the Governorship 169
  Qualifications and Term of Office 171
  Election and Compensation 171
  Succession 172
  Removal from Office 172
  Staff 173

Powers of the Governor 174
  Executive Powers 174
  Legislative Powers 177
  Judicial Powers 178
  Informal Powers 179

The Plural Executive 179
  Lieutenant Governor 180
  Attorney General 180
  Commissioner of the General Land Office 181
  Commissioner of Agriculture 181
  Comptroller of Public Accounts 182
  Treasurer 183
  Secretary of State 183

The Bureaucracy and Public Policies 183
  Personnel 184
  Public Education Policy Issues 184
  Higher Education 185
  Human Services 186
  Health 188
  Mental Health and Mental Retardation 188
  Employment 189
  Major Areas of State Economic Regulation 189
  Other Important Areas of State Economic Regulation 191
  Certification in Trades and Professions 192
  Promotion of Commerce and Economic Development 192
  Conservation of Wildlife and Plant Resources 192
  Coping with the Problem of Bureaucratic Proliferation 193

Conclusion 193
Notes 194
Key Terms and Concepts 194

Selected Readings

7.1 Agriculture Commissioner Hightower: The Popular Populist
(Curtis Wilkie) 195

8 *Law, Courts, and Justice* 200

An Introduction to Texas's Justice System and Its Problems 201

State Law in Texas 202
    Code Revision 203
    Criminal Law 203

Courts, Judges, and Lawyers 207
    Minor Trial Courts 207
    County-Level Trial Courts 210
    District-Level Trial Courts 211
    Appellate Courts 213
    Lawyers 215

Juries 216
    The Grand Jury 216
    The Trial Jury 217

Judicial Procedures 218
    Civil Trial Procedure 218
    Criminal Trial Procedure 220

Correction and Rehabilitation Policies 222
    The Texas Department of Criminal Justice 222
    Institutions of Correction 223
    Community-Based Programs 225

Problems and Reforms: Implications for Public Policy 227
    Rights of Crime Victims 227
    Coping with Crowded Dockets 228
    Disciplining and Removing Judges and Justices 229
    Selecting Judges 230

Notes 232
Key Terms and Concepts 232

Selected Readings

8.1 Compensation for Crime Victims in Texas *(John Forshee)* 234

8.2 Judicial Oversight in Texas: The Case of Judge Jack Hampton
   (Jeffrey E. Key) 236

9 *Revenues, Expenditures, and Fiscal Policy* 241

Fiscal Crises of the 1980s 242
   The Texas Economy in Transition 242
   Demands for Services 243
   The 1990–1991 Budget 244

Traditional Fiscal Policies 244
   Budget Policy 245
   Taxing Policy 245
   Spending Policy 245

Politics of Budgeting and Fiscal Management 246
   Budgeting 246
   Tax Collection 247
   Investment of Public Funds 247
   Purchasing 248
   Accounting 248
   Auditing 248

Politics of Revenue and Debt Management 249
   The Politics of Taxation 250
   Nontax Revenues 253
   The Public Debt 254

Politics of Spending 255
   Spending to Purchase Services 256
   Spending to Perform Services 262

Fiscal Forecast 262
Notes 263
Key Terms and Concepts 264

Selected Readings

9.1 Health Spending Could Boost Texas's Share of Federal Grants 265
9.2 No New Taxes 267

Selected Bibliography 271

Glossary 285

Index 295

Preface

The authors of *Practicing Texas Politics* believe that Texas politics ought to be portrayed as practiced. Students need to know how government actually functions within Texas's complex social order. To pursue this principle, it is essential that information be as up-to-date as possible. Rapid changes occur as new policies are formulated, adopted, and administered. In the face of a rapidly changing social order, Texas government daily becomes more complex. Especially evident are population changes resulting from immigration and natural growth, historic developments in political party competition, restructuring of Texas's economy following a crippling oil crisis, court-ordered changes in public school financing, and overhauling of the state's prison system. Students need to be informed fully of fundamental changes affecting governmental policy decisions.

As with the longer edition, this brief survey is prepared for a variety of classroom needs. For example, some instructors prefer a shorter textbook that permits students to have more time for other reading assignments. In addition, most Texas colleges and universities combine in one course the study of Texas government with that of American national government. This means that the subject of Texas government must be covered in a shorter period of time than if it were taught separately. Furthermore, most students in these combined courses are not political science majors. For these reasons, a more concise text is preferable, but one that includes all essential information related to the practice of Texas politics.

It is important to note that in this brief edition we reduced detail but retained the topics covered in the longer edition. The *Brief Survey*, therefore, is a more concise text with fewer charts, tables, photos, cartoons, and readings. On first mention, key terms and concepts are italicized for emphasis and then listed at the end of the text portion of each chapter. A bibliography at the end of the text lists over two hundred titles of books and articles found in most college and university libraries. Entries in the bibliography are recent publications, many published in 1989. Finally, an index covers all chapters, including readings.

Concerned with political developments that extended into November 1989, this third edition of *Practicing Texas Politics: A Brief Survey* contains up-to-date coverage of the 1988 presidential election, the 71st session of the Texas Legislature (1989), significant changes in the comparative strengths of Texas's two major political parties, further consequences of the oil crisis of 1985, new developments in the state's education crisis (including court-ordered changes in public school financing), election upheavals in the Texas Supreme Court, painful legislative decisions on taxation and spending, the growing crime rate connected to drug trafficking, and the state's complex prison problems.

As in previous editions, many persons assisted in the preparation of this *Brief Survey.* They include journalists, newspaper editors, state and local government officials, librarians, and professors—especially colleagues in our own departments. The following reviewers read all or part of the manuscript and provided many useful comments and suggestions for which we are grateful:

Elizabeth Flores, *Del Mar College*
John Forshee, *Dallas County Community College District*
Robert Peters, *Tyler Junior College*
Candy Smith, *Texarkana College*

Last, we dedicate *Practicing Texas Politics: A Brief Survey,* Third Edition, to those Texas college and university students and instructors who, we hope, will be the chief beneficiaries of our work.

Eugene W. Jones
Joe E. Ericson
Lyle C. Brown
Robert S. Trotter, Jr.
Eileen M. Lynch

Chapter 1

The Environment of
Texas Politics

Reprinted by permission, Tribune Media Services

*T*exas is a former republic that became a big state—big in area and population, and big in various economic activities, for example, farming, ranching, and
mineral production. Because of unique historical and geographic characteristics,
Texans tend to brag about their state. In addition, as cartoonist Fred Wagner
suggests, they are apt to think of other states in terms of distance from Texas.

The focus of this book is on Texas *politics,* although references are made to
other states, to the U.S. government, and to neighboring Mexico. In describing
and analyzing state and local governmental institutions and policies affecting
residents of the Lone Star State today, the authors have sought to help readers
understand political action and to prepare them for more active political participation

Through the process of politics, *public policy* is formulated, adopted, and implemented. Political scientist David Easton relates politics and public policy as
follows: "Political life concerns all those varieties of activity that influence significantly the kind of authoritative policy adopted for a society and the way it is
put into practice."[1] The term *authoritative* refers to the power to enforce obedi-
ence. Political decisions must be authoritative in order to allocate values. By
public policy we mean governmental response or lack of response of authoritative decision makers (legislative and administrative bodies) to a public issue.
At the state level of government, public policy is a governmental response to
politics featuring conflict among legislators, between legislators and the governor, within the courts, and among various other governmental bodies, lobby
groups, and citizens. Each policy is adopted by government to meet a particular
need or demand.

For example, a policy to conserve Texas water resources could be formulated
by a government agency such as the Texas Water Development Board or by a
nongovernmental body such as the Sierra Club, an organization dedicated to
environmental protection. To be adopted as public policy, the proposed plan would
need to be submitted to the Texas Legislature by a state senator or representative.
There, at public sessions, the plan would be debated before legislators, interest
group lobbyists, and citizens. When a bill containing the conservation program
is passed by the Legislature and signed into law by the governor, the policy is
officially adopted. Then the new public policy must be implemented or put into
operation. This responsibility might be assigned by law to the Texas Water Commission or to some other government agency specially prepared to administer
the conservation program. Then the new policy measure may be challenged in
the courts; and the judiciary may uphold all or part of the legislation or nullify
it completely.

Political Behavior Patterns

The attitudes, habits, and general behavior patterns that shape a state's politics
and ultimately its policy formulation and adoption is called *political culture.*

According to political scientist Daniel Elazar, "these culture patterns give each state its particular character and help determine the tone of its fundamental relationships."[2] Political culture is always in flux, with changes occurring constantly but with influences continuing over time. The aggregate of political patterns that today give Texas political behavior its unique quality stems from both remote and recent experiences of all Texans.

Political Culture in Texas

Texas's political foundations were laid and developed under the flags of six nations: Spain, France, Mexico, the Republic of Texas, the Confederacy, and the United States. Texas's political and cultural foundations have been fashioned only in part, however, by the experiences of its past. These foundations have been shaped also by the state's geographic location and rugged terrain, and by the pioneering efforts of people representing different cultures who all came to be known as Texans.

According to Daniel Elazar, the *political culture of Texas* is strongly individualistic and traditionalistic. He identifies Texas traditionalism with economic and social conservatism, strong support of personal politics, distrust of political parties, and minimization of parties' importance. Elazar notes that a majority of Texans are descendants of immigrants from Southern states with traditions of conservatism, elitism, and one-party (Democratic) politics. Although a recent influx of people from other states and countries is changing the origins of Texas's population, the traditionalistic *influence of the Old South* still lingers. Many Anglo Texans have inherited Southern racist attitudes that for decades were reflected in state laws that discriminated against blacks in voter registration, party membership, and voting. Lingering conservatism may also be discerned among many Mexican-American Texans who are descendants from a traditionalistic political culture that was characterized by the elitist *patrón* (protector and political boss) system. Democratic party dominance, however, is giving way in the Lone Star State as Republicans struggle successfully to achieve a place in the Texas sun.

Texas's Frontier Experience

In addition to the influences of the Old South and other traditionalistic culture patterns, the *frontier experience* has had an equal if not greater impact on the molding of Texas political culture. Unlike their Spanish predecessors, Anglos entering Texas in the 1820s were looking for land rather than for gold and silver. Discovery of Texas's "black gold" (rich oil deposits) did not occur for another hundred years. In the meantime, most Anglo Texans earned their meager livelihood from farming and ranching. Pushing the frontier westward was slow; by 1870, no more than a third of the huge land mass of Texas was settled.

Beyond the coastal areas, hard soil and dry climate limited agricultural production but were not alone responsible for the snail's pace conquest of the Texas frontier by Anglo settlers. Violent and bloody warfare added to the burden of home building. After independence was proclaimed in 1836, Mexicans continued to threaten the lives and safety of Texas farmers and ranchers, at times supporting the Indians in their struggle against determined Texans. Thousands of Anglos and Indians—men, women, and children—perished on the Texas frontier from 1836 to the time of the American Civil War; settlers and Indians continued to die at each other's hands until the mid-1870s. This period of frontier warfare lasted longer than it did in any other state.

After the Texas frontier was secured, there remained the task of bringing law and order to the relatively lawless land. Range wars, cattle rustling, and other forms of violence continued to menace law-abiding citizens. From the Texas Revolution that ended in 1836 to the mid-1870s, war and other forms of violence had been a way of life for Texas families. As a result of these experiences, Texans grew accustomed to the use of force in settling disputes and in struggling for survival. This hardship and suffering of nearly a half-century on the Texas frontier had its effect on succeeding generations. As a result, Texans today may be more independent and self-reliant than most Americans.

Although the influences of both the Old South and the frontier experience have been significant in shaping Texas's political culture, we need to be reminded that the structuring of political attitudes is a never-ending process. Consequently, the Lone Star State's political culture continues to be affected by population growth, urbanization, communication, and education, along with other national and even international developments.

Texas and Texans: Land and People

Texas is endowed with mountains and plains, marshlands and arid regions, seacoasts and offshore islands, farms and ranches, petroleum and natural gas deposits, big cities and small towns, and an Anglo majority together with Mexican-American and black minorities. All these elements of physical and human geography—and more—continue to affect the state's economy, to mold its political institutions, and to determine the policies of its units of government from state capitol to county courthouse and city hall.

Land: The Politics of Geography

The political attitudes of Texans have been greatly influenced by the *state's physical geography*, including its climate, soil, mineral resources, and vast size.

Size The large area of Texas, which is second in size to Alaska, has helped to shape its politics. Covering more territory than most countries of the world, the Lone Star State occupies about 7 percent (over 267,000 square miles) of the total land and water area of the United States. Texas could squeeze within its borders all the original 13 states except Georgia. Traveling in a straight line between Brownsville on the Mexican border and the Oklahoma boundary in the Panhandle region, one must cover 800 miles, and the distance between the Louisiana border and El Paso is almost as great. In fact, Texarkana is closer to Chicago than to El

Paso. One state senatorial district in Texas has a greater area than any one of 30 states of the Union, ranking just below the state of Washington in size.

Chiefly because of the state's vast area and *regional diversity*, Texans early came to see its five major areas—North, South, East, West, and Central—as five potentially separate states. In fact, the congressional resolution by which Texas was admitted to the Union in 1845 specifies that up to four states "in addition to said state of Texas" may be formed out of the territory and that each "shall be entitled to admission [to the Union]." Subsequently, scores of plans for carving Texas into separate states have been proposed to the Texas Legislature, none of which has been taken seriously by that body.

Since the Texas Revolution that ended in 1836 with Texas independence from Mexico, the long Texas-Mexico boundary line has been the source of an immigration problem. This boundary issue has included the flow into Texas of *undocumented Mexican aliens* and the related controversy over employing them and providing free public education and other social services for their children.

Size has also given rise to political issues concerning road building and compliance with a nationwide speed limit of 55 miles per hour (raised in 1987 to 65 miles per hour on rural sections of interstate highways). For decades, too, the *state's size* has influenced the politics of its major industries, the first being the cattle industry.

Cattle, Cotton, and Oil   The origin of the *Texas cattle industry* can be traced to Francisco Vásquez de Coronado, the Spanish explorer who brought livestock into Texas in the mid-sixteenth century. Adapting readily to the open range, Spanish cattle developed into the now-famous Texas longhorns. Plentiful land and the relative absence of government interference encouraged establishment of huge cattle empires by determined, enterprising men like Henry Lawrence Kinney, Richard King, Mifflin Kenedy, and George W. Littlefield. By 1876, an estimated 5 million cattle ranged over Texas's nearly 160 million acres of land. As the cattle business expanded, Texas governors and legislators became aware of the industry as a source of tax revenue. They did what they could to keep the range open, and when fences were built, judges rarely convicted fence cutters. In time, the cattle business as a political and economic force leveled off in the wake of farming and newly emerging industries.

In the 1820s, cultivated cotton was first grown in East and Central Texas, where crop conditions most resembled those in the Old South. As more frontier land was opened, *cotton production* moved westward and increased in volume. When cotton prices declined and farmers' incomes shrank accordingly, Texas farmers formed the Farmers Alliance. By 1887, it had become a national political organization with over a million members.

Perhaps the most spectacular increase in cotton production came with its mid-twentieth-century introduction into the Texas Panhandle and South Plains region. An average of 4.3 million acres of Texas land produces nearly 4 million bales of cotton annually and 1.6 million tons of cottonseed. Each year the value of the Texas cotton crop is close to $1 billion.

West Texas ranching in the 1890s. (Courtesy Golda Foster, San Angelo.)

Long the state's leading industry, oil began to affect Texas politics when the world's most famous gusher, *Spindletop,* came in near Beaumont in 1901. Thirty years later, Columbus M. "Dad" Joiner discovered in East Texas the richest oil field in the state's history. Thereafter Texas oil boomed into a multibillion-dollar industry with powerful political ties. By 1928, Texas was the leading oil-producing state in the nation. After major discoveries in East Texas, oil wells spread to the Permian Basin (where the cities of Midland and Odessa are located) and then into the tidelands and offshore regions of the Gulf of Mexico. With large amounts of oil revenue flowing into the treasury, Texas government could hardly escape the *oil industry's political influence,* especially whenever proposed legislation involved petroleum and natural gas. In 1947, the chair of the Texas Democratic Executive Committee could state, "It may not be a wholesome thing to say, but the oil industry is in complete control of state politics and state government."[3] At its peak in the early 1980s, the Texas petroleum industry employed a half-million workers who earned over $11 billion annually; but by 1989 only 185,000 petroleum workers were employed in the Lone Star State.

In 1985, because of a developing worldwide oil surplus, crude oil prices in Texas and elsewhere began a sharp decline. Texas state government, which for over 60 years had reaped abundant measures of revenue from the petroleum industry, began to feel the pinch of reduced income from that source. This worldwide plunge in oil prices adversely affected the entire Texas economy, resulting in increased unemployment, numerous bank failures, and a major financial crisis in state government operations. Whereas oil and gas taxes accounted for 27 percent of the state government revenue for fiscal year 1983 (beginning September 1, 1982, and ending August 31, 1983), for fiscal year 1991, those taxes were expected to make up only 7.8 percent of total state revenue.

Regionalism In a sense, Texas may be considered a land where the United States either begins or ends. Three major geological regions of the United States—the Rocky Mountains, the Great Plains, and the Gulf Coastal Plains—come together in Texas. (See Figure 1.1.)

The *Coastal Plains of East Texas* constitute an extension of the Gulf Coastal Plains of the United States, which stretch from the Atlantic to beyond the Mexican border. In Texas the belt is about 200 miles wide and extends from the Red River on the Oklahoma border to the Rio Grande on the Mexican border. This huge land mass constitutes a third of the total area of Texas and contains most of the state's population, its most fertile soil, and its largest cities. The region produces the bulk of Texas's oil and petrochemicals, lumber, vegetables, and citrus fruit; it also

FIGURE 1.1 Texas Geographic Regions

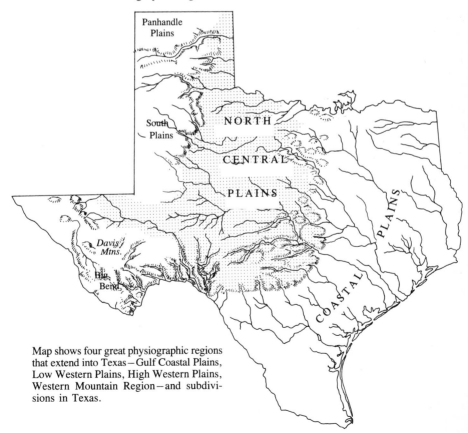

Map shows four great physiographic regions that extend into Texas—Gulf Coastal Plains, Low Western Plains, High Western Plains, Western Mountain Region—and subdivisions in Texas.

supplies a major portion of the state's cotton and cattle. A wide variety of manufacturing and service industries operate along the western edge of the East Texas Coastal Plains. Chief cities are Houston, San Antonio, Beaumont, Corpus Christi, and Brownsville.

Texas's *North Central Plains* are a southern extension of the Great Plains region of the United States. The Texas portion of that vast territory is bounded by the Blacklands Belt on the east, the Cap Rock Escarpment on the west, the Red River on the north, and the Colorado River on the south. Farming and ranching are important enterprises of this prairie country. Many industries operate in the two leading cities of Dallas and Fort Worth.

Immediately west of the North Central Plains and rising to much higher altitudes, the *Texas Great Plains* are a southern extension of the Great High Plains of the United States. Entering Texas at the northern boundary of the Panhandle, this region extends to the Rio Grande. The Panhandle and South Plains portion of the area is known principally for its large-scale production of cotton and grain sorghum. These irrigated crops draw their water from the world's largest underground lake, the *Ogallala Aquifer.* Formed a million years ago by runoff from the Rocky Mountains, this rapidly depleting aquifer (underground water-bearing rock formation) extends from Texas to North Dakota and underlies parts of eight states.

Texas's only mountainous area is an extension of the Rocky Mountain range. This rugged triangle forming the westernmost part of the state is a popular vacation area that includes the Davis Mountains and Big Bend National Park.

Although geographic factors do not directly determine political differences, geography does greatly influence the economic pursuits of a region's inhabitants, which in turn largely shape political interests and attitudes. Geography has encouraged population growth, urbanization, and industrialization in East Texas; in arid West Texas, it has decreed a sparsely populated, rural, and agricultural environment.

People: Numbers and Distribution

According to the federal census of 1980, the Texas population of 14,228,383 was the third largest among the 50 states. Only California and New York had more people in 1980 than did the Lone Star State. Texas's population of over 14 million in 1980 represented a doubling of the state's population since 1950.

Population Growth Projections Following the 1980 census, *Texas's population* continued its rapid growth. Although the economic recession of the mid-1980s slowed the flow of newcomers to Texas, a population of 17,809,000 is projected for the 1990 census count and over 20 million by the year 2000. Between 1990 and 1995, Texas is expected to pass New York and become the nation's second most populous state. The Metroplex (Dallas–Fort Worth) and the Central Corridor (Waco–Austin–San Antonio) have been the fastest-growing regions. Texans are moving into urban areas three times faster than is true of the nation as a whole. (See Table 1.1.)

TABLE 1.1 Population, 1980, Estimated Population, 1986, and Projected Population, 1990–2025 by Race/Ethnicity for State of Texas

Year	Total	Anglo	Black	Hispanic	Other
1980	14,229,191	9,350,297	1,692,398	2,985,824	200,672
1986	16,682,000	10,666,882	2,018,156	3,753,112	243,850
1990	17,809,286	11,102,184	2,145,978	4,306,031	255,093
1995	19,215,664	11,647,825	2,340,428	4,949,228	278,183
2000	20,682,019	12,186,070	2,545,747	5,649,160	301,042
2005	22,245,373	12,735,526	2,769,050	6,416,749	324,048
2010	23,999,093	13,337,567	3,015,846	7,298,050	347,630
2015	25,870,713	13,937,851	3,254,767	8,307,243	370,852
2020	27,723,601	14,438,580	3,475,241	9,417,745	392,035
2025	29,555,821	14,865,119	3,678,007	10,601,389	411,306

Source: Texas Department of Commerce, *The Texas State Population Estimates and Projections Program* (Austin, December 1988).

Texas's population is younger than that of the rest of the United States. Despite a slight decline in the under-25 age group during the first half of the 1980s, the Lone Star State still has a larger percentage of young people than does the nation as a whole. Lower rates of birth and death have raised the median age throughout the United States. Yet both migration of young families to Texas and the state's above-average birthrate have tended to keep the population of Texas younger than the rest of the country. Another factor in low median age is the high percentage of blacks and Hispanics, who tend to have relatively higher birth rates and shorter life spans than Anglos.

Population Distribution Texas's geography makes the state a land of great contrasts; so does the distribution of its inhabitants. Densely populated eastern areas contrast with vast sparsely populated regions in the west. At one extreme is Dallas County, with over 2,000 people per square mile; at the other is Loving County, with a population density of 0.14 people per square mile. Thirty-six of Texas's 254 counties have more than 100 people per square mile; of these, 20 have over 200 per square mile. Bexar County has over 900 people per square mile, and Harris, Dallas, and Tarrant counties have from 1,000 to 3,000 per square mile. With a total of over 7 million residents in 1986, these four Texas counties had a larger combined population than the five eastern states of Maine, New Hampshire, Vermont, Rhode Island, and Delaware, with a combined population of slightly over 4 million. But there are also over a hundred Texas counties with fewer than ten people per square mile.

Population Changes A million new Texans have migrated from other states since the 1970 census. Some of these migrants came from California in the early 1970s. Later waves, extending into the 1980s, came from other Sunbelt states, the Northeast, and the Midwest. Though migrants entering Texas from other states have added significantly to the state's population increase, illegal immigrants from other countries have also contributed measurably to the growth pattern. (The subject of Texas's illegal immigration problem is considered in more detail later in this chapter.)

Urbanization and Metropolitanization *Urbanization* features migration of people from rural regions to growing cities. Urban areas are composed of one or more large cities and surrounding suburban communities. A *suburb* is a relatively small town or city, usually incorporated but outside the corporate limits of a central city. Suburbanization on a large scale results in the development of *metropolitan areas.*

For a century after statehood, Texas remained primarily rural. Then came urbanization that progressed at an accelerated pace. Whereas Texas was 80 percent rural at the beginning of the twentieth century, after 70 years it was 80 percent urban. By 1980, almost half of the state's people were living in six metropolitan counties (Harris, Dallas, Bexar, Tarrant, El Paso, and Travis); and according to the U.S. Bureau of the Census, three Texas cities (Houston, Dallas, and San Antonio) were among the ten most populous cities in the nation.

Texas, like most states, is experiencing *metropolitanization.* This process concentrates large numbers of people into urban centers, which become linked in a single geographic entity, a metropolitan area. Although socially and economically integrated, a metropolitan area is composed of separate units of local government, including counties, cities, and special districts.

Since 1910, federal agencies have defined metropolitan areas for census purposes. In 1950, a set of standard metropolitan statistical areas (SMSAs) was developed composed of groups of urbanized counties. In 1983, these areas were redefined. The word *standard* was dropped and three new area classifications based on population were adopted:

1. *Metropolitan statistical areas (MSAs):* the basic unit, comprising a free-standing urbanized area with a total population of at least 50,000
2. *Primary metropolitan statistical areas (PMSAs):* composed of two or more MSAs and with a total population of 100,000 or more
3. *Consolidated metropolitan statistical areas (CMSAs):* a megalopolitan area composed of two or more PMSAs and comprising a total population of 1 million or more

There are within the United States 261 MSAs, with 22 in Texas; 71 PMSAs, with 7 in Texas; and 20 CMSAs, with 2 in Texas. Each of the Dallas and Fort Worth urbanized areas is designated a PMSA; combined they form a CMSA. The only other CMSA in Texas is composed of the Houston PMSA, the Galveston–Texas City PMSA, and the Brazoria PMSA.

With an estimated population of 3,655,300 in July 1986, the Dallas–Fort Worth metropolitan area is the eighth most populous metropolitan area in the nation. Between 1980 and 1986, the area grew 25 percent for a gain of 725,000 people as it became the most populous area in the state. During the same period, the Houston-Galveston-Brazoria metropolitan area (population 3,634,300) grew by 17 percent to become second in population.

Cities are anxious to retain their federal statistical designations because many federal appropriations are made accordingly. For example, to qualify for urban mass transit system funds, an area must be an MSA. The business community in turn uses data on population concentrations for market analysis and advertising.

Texas's rate of population growth is consistently greater in the MSAs than throughout the state as a whole. Most of these population concentrations are in the eastern part of the state. Texas's MSAs contain 80 percent of the state's population but include only 53 of the 254 counties. It is politically significant that these 53 counties potentially account for four out of every five votes cast in statewide elections. Thus, makers of governmental decisions are answerable primarily to people living in one-fifth of the state's counties. The remaining four-fifths, constituting the bulk of the state's area, have only 20 percent of the people. Urban voters, however, are rarely of one mind at the polls; they do not tend to overwhelm rural voters by taking opposing positions on all policy issues.

People: Ethnic Groups

Approximately 99 percent of Texas's population includes three major ethnic groups: *blacks, Mexican Americans,* and *Anglos.* In 1980, one Texan in three was non-Anglo, that is, a member of a racial or ethnic minority. The national ratio was one in five. By 1985, minorities constituted 38 percent of the Texas population, compared with only 22 percent for the nation. In 1990, prior to the census of that year, an estimated 11.9 percent of the Texas population was black and 28 percent was Hispanic.

Though members of ethnic groups tend to be concentrated in their own respective communities and neighborhoods throughout the state,* *racial intolerance* among blacks, Hispanics, and Anglos may be on the decline in the Lone Star State. In 1986, a poll conducted by researchers at Texas A&M University revealed that racial prejudice involving these three groups had declined dramatically over the last two decades. For instance, the poll indicated that Anglos and Hispanics in 1986 maintained a higher degree of tolerance for blacks than in 1968, when a statewide Belden Poll (a Texas polling agency based in Dallas during the 1960s and 1970s) was conducted on the subject. Blacks, in turn, indicated more tolerance for both Anglos and Hispanics. Results of the 1986 poll were based on degree of mutual acceptance among the three ethnic groups in work and school situations, living next door to each other, and using the same public swimming pool.

Indians   American Indians (often called native Americans) no longer constitute a significant element of the state's population, but the Anglo-Indian frontier warfare of the nineteenth century had a strong influence on development of the state's political culture.

As Joe B. Frantz has written, "Once Texas was a great empty land, a world of animals and birds and insects and fish and nature."[4] Then came people. First to

---

*Reasons for this demographic situation include majority opposition to minority residents and differences between minority and majority family incomes.

arrive were the Indians. Most anthropologists and historians believe that American Indians are of Asiatic Mongoloid stock and may have begun crossing the Bering Strait into North America sometime after the end of the Ice Age. Today, Indians constitute less than 1 percent of the state's residents; but the *Indian population of Texas* was never large.

One Indian tribal group gave Texas its name. The *Caddo Indians* in East Texas were accustomed to referring to one another as *Tayshas,* meaning "friends." When the Spaniards arrived, they were greeted by the Caddo Indians with this word. Then the term evolved into the Spanish word *Tejas* and finally into the English word *Texas.* The Caddo Indians were only one of many tribes that the Spaniards encountered in Texas. Today there are approximately 62,000 Indians in Texas, of whom about 4 percent live on tribal reservations. About 2,000 Indians, the remainder of the *Alabama and Coushatta tribes,* live on a 4,351-acre reservation in Polk County in East Texas. Across the state near El Paso is a 100-acre reservation set aside for the *Tigua Indians.* About 1,000 Tiguas live there, practicing their native arts and crafts chiefly for the tourist trade and striving to maintain their tribal culture. Until 1987, the Alabama-Coushatta and the Tigua reservations were supervised by the Texas Indian Commission. In that year, Congress granted federal trust status to the two tribes. This gave the Indians federal protection of their lands and assured survival of their tribal governments. Another Indian tribe lives on the Texas-Mexico border at Eagle Pass. It is the *Kickapoo Indian tribe,* of approximately 600 members, who wander back and forth between Eagle Pass, Texas, and Nacimiento, Coahuila, Mexico, still following centuries-old migration customs while they struggle to preserve sacred burial grounds across the Rio Grande. In 1983, the United States granted the Kickapoo legal tribal status. In 1989, the 71st Texas Legislature permitted the Texas Indian Commission to be "sunsetted" (terminated). This left Texas's nonreservation Indians without a state government agency.

Blacks   In the sixteenth century, blacks first entered Texas as slaves of Spanish explorers. Three centuries later, larger numbers of black slaves from the United States were brought into Texas by Anglo settlers. In addition, a few free blacks entered Texas chiefly from the northern states. By 1847, blacks accounted for one-fourth of the state's population, and in 1880 they numbered about 400,000. According to a 1989 Census Bureau estimate, Texas in 1985 had 1.9 million blacks, about 12 percent of the state's population. This was the third largest black population in the nation; New York and California were first and second, respectively. The great bulk of Texas's black population is located in Southeast and North Central Texas, where in 21 counties blacks constitute one-fifth or more of the population.

Like most Texans, blacks have largely abandoned farms and rural villages and have moved into the state's urban areas. Their search for employment and their desire for a higher standard of living have been moving forces behind the *black migration cityward.* Today over half of the state's black population resides in and around the cities of Houston, Dallas, Fort Worth, San Antonio, and Beaumont.

Mexican Americans   Near the middle of the sixteenth century, about 100 years before the Pilgrims landed in New England, Spanish explorers moved northward into Texas from Mexico. This began nearly 300 years of Spanish exploration, occupation, and colonization. These years of Spanish rule left Texas a rich heritage. Spanish culture gave Texas its homestead and community property laws, its 10½-mile offshore limits, and its laws extending equal rights to illegitimate and adoptive children. Present-day symbols of the Lone Star State—the longhorn, the horse, and the cowboy—were *Spanish gifts to the Texas heritage.*

Until 1836, Texas history was a part of the history of Spain and Mexico. After the Texas Revolution of that year, Mexican immigration to Texas all but ceased; it then resumed after 1900, especially during the decade of the Mexican Revolution that began in 1910.

In 1988, Texas Hispanics numbered about 4 million, or 25 percent of the state's population. An overwhelming majority—92 percent—were of Mexican origin. Before 1950, Mexican Americans were heavily concentrated in the 60 counties bordering, or near, the Rio Grande from Brownsville to El Paso; since World War II, however, they have been migrating cityward. With a population that is 97.9 percent Hispanic, Laredo, on the Rio Grande, is the nation's most Hispanic city. Nearly all of these Hispanics are of Mexican descent. Mexican-American majorities are found in both San Antonio and El Paso, the largest cities in the United States with such majorities. Blacks and Mexican Americans together constitute over 50 percent of the population in Corpus Christi; over 40 percent in Dallas, Houston, Beaumont, Galveston, and Port Arthur; and over 25 percent in Austin, Fort Worth, Midland, Odessa, San Angelo, and Temple. The economic strength and political clout of Texas's Mexican Americans, who are younger than the Anglo population (median age of 22 compared with 28 for Anglos) and have larger households, are on the increase. Demographers estimate that the Mexican-American population in Texas will double in 20 years, compared with 33 years for blacks and 50 years for Anglos. (See Reading 1.1.)

Anglos   Over 60 percent of the Texas population is composed of Anglos. Federal census data include in the Anglo group all whites except Hispanic Americans. The term *Anglo,* therefore, is not restricted to those of Anglo-Saxon lineage. Although the first non-Spanish-speaking immigrants to Texas were largely of English ancestry (hence the term *Anglo*), other immigrant groups have included German, French, Scandinavian, and East European people, together with a scattering of Greeks and Asians.

In 1821, when Spain opened Texas's doors to immigrants from the United States, only a handful of Anglos resided in Texas. By 1836, there were an estimated 30,000 Anglos in Texas; and when the first census was taken in 1847, following statehood, Anglos numbered 90,000 in a total population of 135,775. At the beginning of the 1980s, there were around 9 million Anglos in Texas. Thus, for nearly three centuries before any English-speaking settlers arrived in Texas, a relatively sparse Spanish-speaking population occupied the region; then, within 15 years after the arrival of the first significant group of settlers from the United States, Texas became predominately Anglo in population and has remained so to the present.

Some Social and Economic Policy Issues

Since the time of the philosopher Aristotle of ancient Greece, the impact of social and economic forces on government and politics has been recognized. Harold Lasswell of Yale University described politics as the science of "who gets what, when, how"[5]; Samuel C. Patterson of the University of Iowa observed a close relationship between the civic culture and economic prosperity. "As affluence increases," Patterson wrote, "interpersonal trust increases, political partisanship takes on a different meaning, class awareness relaxes and class voting by racial minorities is facilitated, and political alienation declines."[6]

Immigration: Federal and State Problems

Due largely to Mexico's depressed economy, millions of undocumented Mexican immigrants entered the United States in the 1980s. In 1986, Commissioner of the U.S. Immigration and Naturalization Service (INS) Alan C. Nelson said, "We are seeing the greatest surge of people in history across our southern border."[7] The INS arrested close to 2 million such aliens in 1986. Yet for every one arrested upon entry, two or three would avoid detection. With the enlarged influx of illegal aliens, some Texas border communities—particularly El Paso, McAllen, and Laredo—were burdened with a rising crime rate, increasing unemployment, and overcrowded hospitals and schools. A U.S. Supreme Court decision mandates that all undocumented children who live in the United States are entitled to a free education.

Immigration Control   After 14 years of debate and controversy, Congress enacted and President Ronald Reagan signed into law the *Immigration Reform and Control Act of 1986.* This federal statute is designed to restrain the flow of illegal immigrants into the United States by penalizing employers who knowingly hire undocumented workers and by appropriating funds to provide more enforcement personnel for the Immigration and Naturalization Service. Congress was impelled to take this action in view of dramatic increases in arrests of illegal immigrants.

Amnesty   The 1986 immigration law provided *amnesty* to those aliens who had lived continuously in the United States since before January 1, 1982. This provision offered millions of illegal immigrants living in Texas the opportunity to end their underground existence and eventually become U.S. citizens. Starting May 5, 1987, and ending May 4, 1988, immigrants were permitted to apply for temporary residence status; 18 months after receiving temporary status, they were eligible to apply for permanent residence. Then, after five years, they may apply for U.S. citizenship. Amnesty application centers were opened in 1987 in nine Texas cities.

With no guarantee that they would be eligible for resident status, however, many immigrants were reluctant to apply and thereby admit their illegal status. Some were unsure that they had sufficient documentation to prove they had lived in the United States before January 1, 1982. By May 4, 1988, the INS had received 1.7 million applications nationally under the general amnesty program; about 300,000 applications were received from Texas.

To help states absorb any additional health, education, and welfare costs resulting from legalizing immigrants, Congress appropriated $4 billion to be distributed over four years starting October 1, 1987. Texas, California, New York, Illinois, and Florida were to be the major recipients of the funds.

Seasonal farm workers who live and work in this country during harvest seasons only and who could not meet the law's continuous residence requirement for amnesty had until November 30, 1988 (instead of May 4, 1988) to apply for amnesty under the Seasonal Agricultural Worker program. The law also provides that sanctions against hiring illegal aliens would not be imposed against those agricultural employers until December 1, 1988; sanctions against all other employers began on June 1, 1988. By November 30, 1988, under the Seasonal Agricultural Worker program, the INS had received 1.3 million applications nationally; about 130,000 of these applications came from Texas.

Employer Sanctions   Penalties are imposed against employers who knowingly hire unauthorized aliens, that is, those immigrants who are in the United States illegally or who are here legally but are not authorized to work. To prove compliance, employers must sign and retain for each employee an INS form I-9 stating that the employee has submitted documentation proving legal residence and *employment authorization*. Fearing that criminalizing the hiring of undocumented workers could lead to discrimination against ethnic minorities, Congress included in the immigration law a provision that prohibits employers from discriminating against documented residents on the basis of national origin or citizenship status.

Immediately following passage of the 1986 immigration law, the employer sanctions clause was severely criticized as discriminatory and unworkable. Theodore M. Hesburgh, former chair of the Select Commission on Immigration and Refugee Policy, responded to the criticism by defending the law. He contended that to make it illegal for an alien to work and not also make it illegal for an employer to hire an alien would be contradictory and self-defeating. Hesburgh stated: "The only way that one could realistically do anything about illegal immigration was to somehow control employment, and say to employers that if you insist on hiring illegals, you are going to be caught by the law, and you will pay a fine or go to jail or both. I do not know any other way of solving the problem."[8] Eleven months after the amnesty applications period ended, fines had been imposed on 1,668 employers nationally for hiring illegal immigrants. In that period, 63 cases involving $232,000 in fines were filed in the Houston area.

According to a study released in July 1989 by the Urban Institute and Princeton University, sanctions against employers who hire undocumented alien workers have materially slowed the rate of illegal immigrants across the Mexican border.

No less than 71 percent of the decline in apprehensions along the U.S.-Mexican border seems due to the employer sanctions clause in the 1986 Immigration Reform and Control Act. Officials of the Urban Institute indicated that the employer sanctions are the only deterrent in the law.

Impact After Amnesty   The inflow of illegal aliens, though materially reduced after passage of the immigration law, has continued despite uncertainty of employment and grave dangers encountered en route to the United States. Most of those attempting illegal entry know that they risk bodily injury, robbery, and even death by armed assailants who roam the border areas. On July 2, 1987, the bodies of 18 Mexican nationals were found in a sealed railroad boxcar near the town of Sierra Blanca, Texas, 80 miles southeast of El Paso. Locked within the boxcar by their *bollero* (smuggler), with temperatures inside the car reaching 130° Fahrenheit, the men died of asphyxiation. But with the minimum *daily* wage in Mexico less than the minimum *hourly* wage in Texas, many Mexican laborers choose to face the risks involved with illegal entry.

Texas's Changing Economy

Landownership accounted for the earliest of the many *economic influences on Texas politics.* The importance of land as an economic asset led in turn to the politics of cattle, followed in succession by the politics of cotton and then of oil. Today, economic influences on Texas politics include all of these and more: manufacturing, trade, banking, insurance, transportation, construction, service industries, tourism, and a host of lesser economic activities. (Chapter 5 contains information on the variety and strength of economic forces bearing directly upon Texas political processes through lobbying activity and political campaign financing.) The image of a state once identified in the popular mind with cattle barons and oil millionaires has long since changed. Texas has merged into middle-class America with its share of professionals and businesspeople associated with varied enterprises: law firms; universities; federal, state, and local government offices; real estate and insurance brokerages; wholesale and retail sales firms; and manufacturing, communication, and transportation industries.

Industry: A Search for New Direction   For more than a half-century, oil with its related enterprises led in Texas's industrial development. Then, devastated by plunging oil prices in the second half of the 1980s, the entire Texas petroleum industry declined sharply. Following the slump, thousands of experienced workers and managers left the industry and the number of college students studying geology and petroleum engineering declined sharply. By the middle of 1987, the Texas economy seemed to hit bottom. Though oil prices strengthened somewhat, the economy remained sluggish throughout the year. By the middle of 1988, however, the state comptroller could report that the Texas economy was on the road to recovery. More Texans were working, retail sales had climbed encouragingly, and for the first time in five years Texas's petrochemical industry was operating at full capacity. While the state's overall economy continued to recover in 1989, the real estate, construction, and finance industries still struggled to overcome problems resulting from overbuilding in the early 1980s and the oil price collapse of 1986.

As the last decade of this century begins, a series of Texas's fastest-growing industries are pacing the state's emerging post–oil depression economy. These industries represent an economy that is moving away from reliance on energy to a much healthier economic diversity that emphasizes manufacturing, services, and trade. For Texas, the 1980s began with an oil boom, but at midpoint of the decade, the boom had become a bust. Yet from 1983 to the end of the decade, a number of Texas industries experienced a healthy expansion without being involved in oil and gas operations. These two dozen industries include high technology manufacturing firms and various service industries.

High technology refers to companies involved in the research, development, manufacturing, and marketing of a seemingly endless line of electronic products: computers, calculators, digital watches, microwave ovens, telecommunications devices, automatic bank tellers, aerospace guidance systems, aircraft equipment, medical instruments, and even industrial robots. Fastest-growing of the high-tech firms were those engaged in computer programming and software services. The defense build-up of the 1980s stimulated the manufacturing of guided missiles and other space vehicles. Texas aircraft manufacturing also prospered from higher defense spending. In the last half of the decade, these high-tech manufacturing firms had an annual average growth rate of 6 to 10 percent. During the 1983–1990 period, five of Texas's high-tech firms created nearly 40,000 new jobs; in 1988, average annual wages paid by these companies exceeded the state average ($20,608) by $10,000.

Most of the two dozen Texas firms that prospered during the oil-related depression period of the 1980s were service-producing companies. A myriad of services are provided by these industries: hospital, health, and medical; employment; computer programming; domestic; legal; banking; management consulting; investment; day-care; rental and leasing; janitorial; accounting and auditing; insurance; detective and protective. Seven of these service-related companies paid average annual wages of $35,500 in 1988; they created over 80,000 new jobs in the 1983–1990 period. Highest paid among these service firms were employees of security brokers and dealers, whose average annual salary for 1988 was $76,000.

Meanwhile, Texans are playing a major role in establishing a new industry, *biotechnology*. This new venture on the Texas industrial horizon is based on development and use of microorganisms or biochips, which may become more useful than the silicon chip, the technical foundation of the high-tech industry. Including any technique that uses living organisms to make or modify products, improve plants and animals, or provide treatment for human diseases, biotechnology promises to involve Texans in both new businesses and new jobs.

In 1985, the Texas Legislature established the Advanced Technology Research Program, appropriated $35 million for high-tech research, and earmarked 35 percent of the fund for specific biotechnology projects. In that same year, striving to take the lead in biotechnology development, San Antonio adopted plans for a $23 million Institute for Biotechnology to be located in the city's Texas Research Park. Work on such a long-range project will extend well into the 1990s. During that time, San Antonio will need to continue lobbying at the local and state levels for money to complete construction and for funding of the University of Texas Health Science Center. On the national level, the city will need to compete for additional research funds.

With a $100 million fund and a gift of 250 acres of land to finance biotechnology development, another Texas city, Houston, also has sought a leadership position in the field. Houston's Texas Medical Center and the Houston Area Research Center could jointly provide that city with the resources needed to take a commanding lead in biotechnology research and development. Keys to Texas's future growth in biotechnology include a strong network of universities cooperating with industry, together with research-oriented faculty members capable of teaching highly motivated students.

Agriculture   *Texas agriculture* leads the 50 states in total acreage and numbers of farms and ranches, as well as in cattle, wool, mohair, cotton, and grain sorghum production. Endowed with a favorable climate, productive soil, good transportation and export facilities, and an abundant supply of labor, the state is well situated for high productivity in agriculture. But farm surpluses, low prices for farm products, the high cost of chemicals and farm machinery, depletion of the water supply for irrigation, and declining export of American agricultural products have tended to increase the risks faced by Texas farmers and ranchers. Nevertheless, with cash receipts amounting to $11 billion, Texas's gross agricultural income for 1988 was slightly higher than that for the previous year. With a total of 156,000 farms that average 846 acres per farm, Texas's total farm assets (such as land, buildings, machinery, crops, and livestock) totaled $78 billion in 1988.

Family-owned farms in Texas are giving way to large corporate agricultural units, a trend that began in the mid-1930s. According to a 1986 survey by the Texas Department of Agriculture, 9,000 Texas farmers were driven out of business in 1985, and 49,000 Texas farms had failed since 1981. In 16 of the 22 major farming regions of the state, farmers were unable to make enough money at the marketplace to cover costs of production. This decline in farm units parallels the rate of decline nationally.

In 1984, Texas farm employees—of whom about 60 percent are Mexican Americans—won a significant legislative victory in the form of a new *Texas workers' compensation law* that makes workers' compensation available to all farm and ranch laborers who are injured on the job. In 1985, the Legislature brought farm and ranch laborers under the Texas Unemployment Act. This legislation makes unemployment compensation benefits available to seasonal and migrant workers as well as to those employed year-round. In 1987, the 70th Texas Legislature enacted a farm workers' minimum wage law and a law that gives farm workers the right to be informed about health hazards related to use of crop pesticides.

Texas in the Course of National Affairs

Since statehood, Texas has occupied a prominent place among the states in determining the course of national affairs. In the twentieth century, the state's wealth in natural resources, its growing population and formidable strength in Congress, and its contribution to national legislative and executive leadership all have given Texas a strong voice in Washington, D.C.

Beginning with the 100th Congress, Texan Lloyd Bentsen, Jr., became chair of the powerful Senate Finance Committee. In the 101st Congress (1989–1990), three Texans chaired committees in the House of Representatives: Kika de la Garza of McAllen, Agriculture; Jack Brooks of Beaumont, Judiciary; and Henry B. Gonzalez of San Antonio, Banking, Housing, and Urban Affairs. Following his 1988 election as president, Texan George Bush appointed Texans James A. Baker III to head the cabinet as secretary of state, Lauro Cavazos (former president of Texas Tech University and son of a King Ranch cowhand) as secretary of education, and Houston millionaire businessman Robert Mosbacher as secretary of commerce. Then in 1988 the federal Department of Energy announced that Texas had been chosen for the location of the $5.9 billion superconducting super collider. This scientific laboratory is to be contained in a 53-mile underground tunnel surrounding the city of Waxahachie in Ellis County south of Dallas.

With 27 members in the House (third among the states) and counting Texas's two U.S. senators, the Lone Star State is apportioned 29 electoral votes in presidential elections, the third highest among the states. Following the 1990 federal census, Texas's population growth may cause its number of electoral votes to increase to 32, effective for the rest of this century. This electoral vote increase, however, may hinge on the outcome of a case pending in federal courts. The federal judiciary will decide whether illegal aliens are to be included in the apportionment of representatives among the states following the federal census. The decision is important to Texas for two reasons. First, Texas could gain four additional seats (instead of three) in the U.S. House of Representatives if all "free persons" (U.S. Constitution, Art. I, Sec. 2), including illegal aliens living in Texas in 1990, are included in the apportionment process. Second, the federal government requires that states provide illegal aliens with a variety of services, including free education for their children. Federal funds for these services would be lost to Texas if the state's estimated 1 million undocumented residents are not included in the census count.

As it enters the last decade of the century, Texas will be increasingly affected by public policy decisions concerning its economy and its entire social order. The most important of these policy decisions will relate to the continued restructuring of public and higher education, to technological changes in the state's industries, and to the burdening of Texas's ecological system. An urgent need to improve and strengthen the state's public and higher education system, considered in detail in Chapter 7, continues to gain public support. Success in this long-range task is an important key to Texas's ability to compete nationally and internationally in technological and cultural advancement. A recent study by the Washington-based Sunbelt Institute ranked Texas 47th among the states in literacy of its citizens. With 33 percent of its adult population being illiterate, according to the study, one out of every three Texans over 18 years of age cannot read or write well enough to fill out an employment application form. The Texas Department of Commerce estimates that because the state's many adult illiterates have low incomes and generate little tax revenue, Texas loses $17 billion annually in revenue.

Aside from the problem of illiteracy, Texas ranks at the bottom of the fifty states in (1) amount paid out in aid to families with dependent children (AFDC), (2) per capita spending for housing and community services, (3) per capita expenditures for alcohol and drug abuse control (Texas spends $1.67 per capita compared with California's $8.18 and New York's $25.34), (4) care for the state's mentally ill, (5) control of land and air pollution, and (6) expenditures for the arts. These revealing statistics stand out even more sharply when set against Texas's tax policy that shows Texans as the lowest taxed citizens in the United States. It would seem, therefore, that the surest way for Texas to raise its rank among the states in providing needed human services would be through increased tax revenue.

Because the petroleum industry is not expected to recover its former leading role, restructuring of the state's economy has begun—largely outside the realm of oil and gas. In performing this task, Texans must plan a new industrial program within the context of rapidly changing national and international economic environments. This need comes at a time when U.S. dominance of the international economy, which began after World War II, is fading. Faced with the unprecedented growth of competing industries in Western Europe, Japan, South Korea, Taiwan, and Singapore, the United States is no longer the world's leading exporter. Long surpassed by Japan in growth of worker productivity, in 1986 the United States for the first time ran a trade deficit in the high-tech industry. Moreover, the United States has been losing ground in corporate profitability, education and research advancements, and shares of world markets. In Texas especially, the closing of banks and savings and loan institutions was particularly critical in 1988.[9]

As the long-term process of rebuilding a highly diversified business and industrial base proceeds, some of Texas's cherished values are being sorely tried. In an age of unprecedented popular interest in business, Texans will encounter increasingly critical environmental problems (including pollution of air, water, and soil) while experiencing a diminishing water supply. In addition, the state must face a rising level of poverty complicated by an expanding and aging population.

Growth also exerts new pressures on land use, educational facilities, and service capacities of local governments. Care must be taken to encourage distribution of investment and opportunity among industries, occupations, local areas, and social groups. As growth pressures are revealed, policy initiatives by state and local governments should assure that private interests adopt growth patterns most beneficial to all Texans. The ability to cope successfully with public problems in the years ahead will depend largely on how well Texas prepares a new generation of citizens through education to meet the demands of today and tomorrow.

Notes

1. David Easton, *The Political System* (New York: Knopf, 1953), p. 128.
2. Daniel Elazar, *American Federalism: A View from the States* (New York: Crowell, 1972), p. 119.
3. Quoted in Robert Engler, *The Politics of Oil: A Study of Private Power and Democratic Directions* (Chicago: University of Chicago Press, 1961), p. 354.

4. Joe B. Frantz, *Texas: A Bicentennial History* (New York: Norton, 1976), p. 3.
5. Harold Lasswell, *Politics: Who Gets What, When, How* (New York: McGraw-Hill, 1936).
6. Samuel C. Patterson, "The Political Cultures of the American States," *Journal of Politics* 30 (February 1968), 206, citing Robert E. Lane, "The Politics of Consensus in an Age of Affluence," *American Political Science Review* 50 (December 1965), 874–895.
7. Quoted by James Reston in a nationally syndicated newspaper column, March 2, 1986.
8. House Research Organization, *The New Federal Immigration Law* (Austin: Texas House of Representatives, February 12, 1987), p. 17.
9. For details on the S&L crisis, see Stephen Rizzo, Mary Fricker, and Paul Muolo, *Inside Job: The Looting of America's Savings and Loans* (New York: McGraw-Hill, 1989).

Key Terms and Concepts

politics
public policy
political culture
political culture of Texas
influence of the Old South
frontier experience
state's physical geography
regional diversity
undocumented Mexican aliens
state's size
Texas cattle industry
cotton production
Spindletop
oil industry's political influence
Coastal Plains of East Texas
North Central Plains
Texas Great Plains
Ogallala Aquifer
Texas's population
urbanization
suburb
metropolitan area
metropolitanization
metropolitan statistical area
  (MSA)
primary metropolitan statistical
  area (PMSA)

consolidated metropolitan
  statistical area (CMSA)
blacks
Mexican Americans
Anglos
racial intolerance
Indian population of Texas
Caddo Indians
Tayshas
Alabama and Coushatta tribes
Tigua Indians
Kickapoo Indian tribe
black migration cityward
Spanish gifts to the Texas
  heritage
Immigration Reform and Control
  Act of 1986
amnesty
employment authorization
economic influences on Texas
  politics
high technology
biotechnology
Texas agriculture
Texas workers' compensation law

Selected Readings

1.1 Changes in Texas's Hispanic-Black Population

Juan R. Palomo

According to this article from the Houston Post, *the continued migration into Texas from Mexico and Central America and the high birth rate among Hispanics may soon cause the Hispanic population in Houston to eclipse that of blacks. Congressional redistricting following the 1990 census may give both Houston and Dallas congressional districts with black-Hispanic majorities. In 1985, only five other counties in the nation had more blacks than Harris County, Texas. Texas's 3.7 million Hispanics in 1985 ranked second among the states. Together, Texas and California contain 55 percent of the Hispanic population in the United States.*

The continued steady migration from Mexico and Central American countries in recent years has pushed the Houston area's Hispanic population to the brink of eclipsing blacks as the city's largest minority group, according to figures released Tuesday [June 20, 1989] by the U.S. Census Bureau. If, as expected, the early figures are reinforced by the official population count to be taken next April, they are almost certain to be used as ammunition by Hispanic politicians in their battle to create a new congressional district by 1992 in the Harris County area where a Hispanic would have a chance of winning.

"It helps make a strong case," said State Rep. Al Luna of Houston. "Assuming that the Harris County area gains another congressional district, you could make a very very strong argument that one district should be drawn with at least a greater percentage of Hispanics than any other group."

Most experts predict Texas will get at least two, and possibly three, additional congressional districts—with at least one going to the Houston area—through redistricting after new population figures are released. Of the county's five congressmen, only one, Rep. Mickey Leland, D-Houston, belongs to a minority group.* Dallas blacks and Hispanics are also expected to push for a minority congressional district and political observers predict they will get one. A number of them have said that the decision by Rep. John Bryant, D-Dallas, to seek the state attorney general's post instead of re-election was due primarily to his realization that his district would be a prime candidate to be turned into a minority district.

From *The Houston Post,* June 21, 1989, pp. A-1, A-10. Juan R. Palomo is a reporter in the *Houston Post's* Washington Bureau. Copyright 1989, The Houston Post. Reprinted by permission.

Editors' note: On August 7, 1989, Rep. Leland was killed in a plane crash over Ethiopia, Africa. In a called special election on November 7, 1989, to fill the vacant congressional seat, none of the four black candidates won a majority. A later run-off election was scheduled to decide a winner from the two top candidates: state senator Craig Washington and Houston city councilman Anthony Hall, both Democrats.

The bureau figures show that while the Houston area's black population grew by an estimated 77,000 between 1980, when the last census was taken, and 1985, the proportion of the city's black population during that time dropped slightly, from 18.2 percent to 18 percent. Houston's Hispanic population, on the other hand, grew by more than a third during that same time period, from 400,200 to 538,800, and it made up 16.7 percent of the area's population, compared to only 14.4 percent in 1980. The question in Harris County is whether a new predominantly Hispanic district is formed by taking Hispanic voters from Leland's 18th District and Rep. Mike Andrews' 25th, making both less safe for the incumbents.

Texas A&M population expert Steven Murdock—who said the Texas Department of Commerce also projects a Hispanic population slightly larger than the area's black population by 1990—said the Hispanic increase is due not only to the large migrations from Latin American countries, but also because Hispanics have a higher birth rate than other groups, including blacks.

Among other statistics contained in the bureau figures:

1. Texas ranks third—behind New York and California—among states with more than 1 million blacks despite the fact that the proportion of blacks to the general population dropped from 12 percent to 11.8 percent during those five years. The state, which had close to 2 million blacks in 1985, moved ahead of Illinois, which was No. 3 in 1980. Houston's black population increased by 77,000, from 564,000 in 1980 to 641,000 in 1985. Only Florida and California had a larger net in-migration of blacks than Texas and the number of blacks migrating to Texas from other states was almost as high as those moving to California.
2. Houston's minority population—blacks, Hispanics, Asians and others—grew from 34.8 percent to 38.2 percent.
3. Only five other counties in the country had more blacks than Harris County: Cook County (Chicago), Los Angeles, Wayne County (Detroit), Kings County (Brooklyn) and Philadelphia.
4. Texas' estimated 1980–1985 growth rate for people listed by the bureau under the "other races" category ranked first among states. The growth, put at 67.1 percent, was due primarily to the migration of Southeast Asians to the Houston and Dallas areas. That rapid growth placed the state fourth—behind California, Hawaii, and New York—in the number of people belonging to the other races category, with 315,000, compared to only 188,000 in 1980.
5. Most new immigrants to Texas settled in the Houston area, whose other races population more than [almost] doubled during that period, from 67,000 to 125,000. Nationwide, only the Dallas area, with an 88.3 percent growth rate, outpaced the Houston area (87.2 percent) in this category.
6. Nationwide, Hispanics accounted for 7.3 percent of the population, up from 6.3 percent in 1980. Hispanics accounted for one-quarter of the nation's population gain during that period. One-third of the country's Hispanics live in California. The estimated 5.8 million Hispanic population in that state exceeded the total population in 38 states.
7. Texas, with 3.7 million Hispanics in 1985, ranked second among states in Hispanic population. Together, California and Texas contain 55 percent of the Hispanics

in the country. California's Hispanic population is estimated to have increased by more than 1.3 million (29.4 percent), while Texas registered an increase of nearly 700,000 (23.1 percent).

8. The Houston area eclipsed San Antonio for the No. 6 spot in Hispanic population. In 1980, San Antonio had 485,000 Hispanics, compared to 446,000 for Houston. By 1985, however, Houston's Hispanic population had grown to 595,000 and San Antonio's to only 568,000. While Dallas's Hispanic population is much smaller in number than that of Houston, the former grew by a higher percentage, 40.5 percent—the highest in the nation.

The ten states with the largest Hispanic population in 1985 are as follows:

1.	California	5,873,000
2.	Texas	3,690,000
3.	New York	1,879,000
4.	Florida	1,102,000
5.	Illinois	755,000
6.	New Jersey	573,000
7.	New Mexico	551,000
8.	Arizona	533,000
9.	Colorado	384,000
10.	Pennsylvania	159,000

Chapter 2

Federalism and the
Texas Constitution

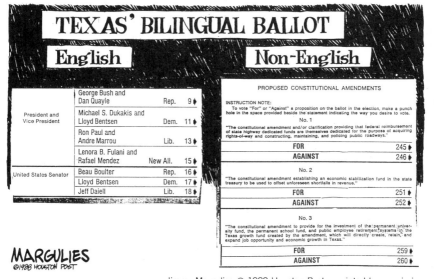

Jimmy Margulies © 1989 Houston Post, reprinted by permission

*A*lthough the U.S. Constitution is brief, readable, and seldom amended, the Texas Constitution is long, difficult to read, and frequently amended. Even the wording of amendment propositions appearing on Texas election ballots is sometimes so confusing that cartoonist Jimmy Margulies has labeled this wording "Non-English." The two basic sources of policymaking power in the Lone Star State are the state's membership and participation in the American Federal Union and Texas's Constitution. In this chapter, we examine these two sources, beginning with the American federal structure.

The American Federal Structure

A federal structure of government is characterized by a division of powers between a general government and associated regional governments. Federal government in the United States is marked by a division of powers between the national government, its seat in Washington, D.C., and the governments of each of the 50 states. Federal government in the United States, prescribed by the national Constitution since 1789, is 200 years old. Described by North Carolina's former governor Terry Sanford as "a system of states within a state," American federalism has survived two centuries of stresses and strains, including the Civil War (1861–1865), which almost dismembered the Union.

The Distribution of Powers

Division of powers and functions between the national government and state governments was accomplished simply by spelling out in the U.S. Constitution the powers of the central government and by adding the *Tenth Amendment.* The latter asserts: "The powers not delegated to the United States by the Constitution, nor prohibited by it to the States, are reserved to the States, respectively, or to the People." Although the Tenth Amendment may seem to endow the states with powers comparable with those delegated to the national government, we should be reminded that Article VI of the Constitution contains the following terse statement: "This Constitution, and the laws of the United States which shall be made in pursuance thereof; and all treaties made, or which shall be made, under the authority of the United States, shall be the supreme law of the land; and the judges in every State shall be bound thereby, anything in the Constitution or laws of any State to the contrary notwithstanding." This *National Supremacy Clause* emphasizes that the U.S. Constitution and the laws and treaties made under it prevail over the constitutions and laws of the states.

Limitations on the States   As members of the Federal Union, Texas and the other states are constrained by limitations imposed by Article I, Section 10, of the U.S. Constitution. They may not enter into treaties, alliances, or confederations, or, without the consent of Congress, participate in interstate or foreign compacts. Furthermore, they are forbidden to levy import duties on another state's products and must accept the Constitution, laws, and treaties of the United States as the supreme law of the land. From the Civil War and the U.S. Supreme Court's landmark ruling in *Texas* v. *White* (1869), Texans learned that states cannot secede from the Union. In the *White* case, the court ruled that the national Constitution "looks to an indestructible union, composed of indestructible states." Neither Texas nor any other state may deny anyone the right to vote because of race, sex, failure to pay a poll tax, or age (if the person is 18 years of age or older). Furthermore, no state is permitted to deny anyone the equal protection of the laws or the privileges and immunities of citizens of the United States; neither may any state deprive persons of life, liberty, or property without due process of law.

Guarantees to the States   The U.S. Constitution provides all states with an imposing list of constitutional guarantees. For example, Texas may be neither divided nor combined with another state without the consent of both states. At the same time, the state is entitled to protection against invasion and domestic violence and is guaranteed a republican form of government (that is, representative government). In addition, Texas may have its own militia (National Guard units) and is assured that trials by federal courts for crimes committed in Texas will be conducted in Texas. Each state is guaranteed that it will have equal representation with the other states in the U.S. Senate and will have at least one member in the House of Representatives. In fact, each state has two senators in Washington. After the 1980 census, Texas was apportioned 27 representatives; the 1990 census was expected to give the Lone Star State three or four more House seats. Finally, Texas and the other states participate in approving or disapproving proposed amendments to the U.S. Constitution.

Interstate Relations   Article IV states: "Citizens of each state shall be entitled to all *privileges and immunities* of citizens in the several states." In 1823, the U.S. Supreme Court defined privileges and immunities broadly as follows: protection by government, enjoyment of life and liberty, right to acquire and possess property, right to egress and ingress (to leave or enter), and right to use of courts. Although corporations are legal persons, they are not included under the privileges and immunities clause.

Article IV of the Constitution also states that "*full faith and credit* shall be given in each State to the public acts, records, and judicial proceedings of every other State." This means that any legislative enactment, state constitution, deed, will, marriage, divorce, or court decision of one state must be officially recognized and honored in every other state. This clause does not apply to criminal cases. A person convicted in Texas for a crime committed in Texas is not punished in another state to which that person has fled. Such cases are handled through extradition, whereby the person is returned to Texas at the request of the governor of Texas.

State Powers   Nowhere in the U.S. Constitution is there a listing of state powers. Instead, according to the Tenth Amendment as quoted above, all powers not delegated to the national government are reserved to the states. The *reserved* *powers* of the states are therefore undefined. No attempt is made here to define or list a state's reserved powers; however, political scientists have broadly identified them in four categories:

1. Police power (protection of the health, morals, safety, and conveniences of residents)
2. Taxing power (raising revenue to pay for the costs of government)
3. Proprietary power (public ownership of property such as airports, energy-producing utilities, and parks)
4. Power of eminent domain (taking private property for public use at a fair price)

Needless to say, states today have imposing powers, responsibilities, and duties. States, for example, are responsible for all the nation's public elections—national, state, and local. There are no nationally operated election facilities. State courts conduct most trials, both criminal and civil; states operate the public and higher education systems; and states maintain most of the nation's prisons. One must be cautious in attempting to identify state powers or mark the boundary line between state and national powers. The reason is that since the establishment of the American federal system, states have operated within a constitutional context that has allowed considerable fluctuation in the relative authority of national and state governments.

An Evolving Process

In creating a federal republic, the framers of the U.S. Constitution sought to provide for national and state governments a workable balance of powers that would sustain the Union indefinitely. That the American federal system has endured for over 200 years of stresses and strains attests to their wisdom and foresight. In the early years of the federal republic, there was an assumption that each government would operate within its own policymaking sphere, separate and distinct and without interference from the other. With the passing of time, however, powers have continuously been debated and many fluctuations have occurred in the national government–state government relationship.

Cooperative Federalism   Following adoption of the Sixteenth Amendment in 1913, a federal income tax provided Congress with enough revenue to entice the states through federal grants of money to participate in policy programs initiated in Washington. One of the earliest of such enactments by Congress was the Federal Road Act of 1916, which offered money to the states to build a network of federal-state highways. By accepting the money and participating in the highway program, Texas and the other states helped to implement policies that were not of their own making. This proved to be only the beginning of a long period of national-state relationships based on federal grants-in-aid and termed *cooperative federalism*. Through this arrangement, Congress initiated policy programs and then offered grants of money to the states to fund the programs. In all of these policy initiatives, and in scores of others, the states became active partners with the national government. Cooperative federalism resembled a marble cake in which national and state governments were swirled together; thus, almost any governmental activity within the national sphere revealed involvement of both levels of government.

Before 1930, only 10 *grant-in-aid programs* were adopted by Congress, and only 17 were adopted between 1931 and 1945. However, the 1960s witnessed an explosion of grants-in-aid to the states. As these federally initiated programs multiplied, the national policymaking sphere widened accordingly—with the loss of state control over many policy areas. With the Great Society initiated by President Lyndon Johnson in the mid-1960s, new *categorical grants* were introduced. These grants applied variously to health care, education, poverty relief, environmental protection, problems of the cities, agriculture, employment, law enforcement, and many other matters involving national-state-local government relationships. No longer were Washington-initiated programs designed merely to assist states in fulfilling their own goals. Increasingly, the national government arranged grant-in-aid ties directly with cities, counties, and districts; thus state governments were bypassed. Categorical grants, for example, require that state and local agencies of government submit detailed grant requests. Then, if the grant is made, state agencies are required to provide meticulous reports on how the grant money is spent. Categorical grant programs increased in number from 132 in 1960 to 530 in 1970, and total federal spending for these programs grew from $9 billion to $24 billion.

In the 1970s, the Nixon-Ford administrations developed two new forms of federal aid by way of grants: the *block grant system* and *revenue sharing*. Unlike categorical grants, block grants do not require details on how the money is spent. Federal money is given to state and local governments for spending in broad policy areas and is designed to combine a number of categorical grants. If block grants were awarded to state and local governments with fewer strings attached than in the case of categorical grants, then revenue sharing became available with still fewer strings. The revenue-sharing program permitted state and local governments to spend grant money for purposes of their own choosing. Both the block grant and the revenue-sharing plan would in their respective turns restore some policymaking powers to state and local officials, powers that were lacking under categorical grants.

Like his three predecessors (Nixon, Ford, and Carter), President Ronald Reagan in the 1980s was committed to reducing the nonmilitary portions of the federal budget. In the first year of the Reagan administration, Congress authorized nine new block grant programs that replaced 27 categorical grants. However, these block grants featured major reductions in federal funding. Although state and local governments were given more freedom to spend federal funds, they were granted less money to spend. This was especially true following the effective elimination by the Reagan administration of revenue sharing and by reduction in funding of the Community Development Block Grant program. As the 1980s drew to a close, evidence was clear that the states would need to assume more responsibility in formulating and funding their own programs. This likelihood became more certain in late 1987 when Congress adopted a $76 billion deficit-reducing budget package. With resumption of greater policymaking responsibilities by the states, the last decade of this century is likely to see major changes in the availability of some public services that many Texans desire.

The Texas Constitution: Politics of Policymaking

"Humbly invoking the blessings of Almighty God, the people of the state of Texas do ordain and establish this Constitution." These are the words of the preamble to the state Constitution that became Texas's seventh supreme law in 1876. By 1976, when Texans observed the 100th anniversary of this Constitution, it had been changed by 221 amendments; and 105 more amendments were added by the end of 1989. Cumbersome and outdated, the Texas Constitution is over six times the length of the U.S. Constitution. With more than 63,000 words, the Constitution of the Lone Star State is now the fourth longest state constitution in the nation. If the past rate of amendment continues to the year 2000, it will then have accumulated nearly 400 amendments.

Texas's seventh constitution has grown by amendment chiefly because its framers spelled out policymaking powers and limitations in minute detail. This in turn made frequent amendments inevitable as policy provisions had to be altered to fit changing times and conditions. Constitution makers ought not to attempt to solve specific policy problems; rather they should state clearly who is to solve them, both in the present and in the future. When this rule is followed, there will be no need for later generations to adopt numerous amendments. In the case of a state, it is the legislature's job to make specific statutory laws authorized by its constitution. For example, a constitution may provide for the election of government officials, but the legislature enacts the laws that schedule and regulate the elections. The great fault of the present Texas Constitution is its detailed length. For over a century, the document has continued to grow through an accumulation of amendments, most of which are essentially statutory in nature. The result is a constitution that more closely resembles a code of laws than a fundamental instrument of government.

Within the federal structure of government in the United States, the Texas Constitution is the *fundamental law* of the Lone Star State. This document establishes the government, defines governing powers, and imposes limitations thereon. It is subject only to the U.S. Constitution, federal laws, and treaties. The Texas Constitution is a product of history, an expression of political philosophy, a reflection of the moral and social principles of the people who adopted it and who later added amendments.

In spite of the idealistic sentiment commonly attached to constitutions (similar to the patriotic attachment to the flag), the task of drafting and amending a constitution is essentially political in nature. Less practical-minded people may see the political aspects of constitution making as involving shady operations carried out through secret, under-the-table deals. More realistic observers, however, view those who draft a constitution as pragmatic men and women. Each constitution under which Texans have been governed has reflected strongly the unique political situation that existed when the document was drafted. In this chapter we see this process at work as we examine the drafting of Texas's seven constitutions and the subsequent tasks of amendment and revision.

Historical Developments

Texas's constitutional history began over 150 years ago. The Lone Star State was governed under two constitutions before it joined the Union.

The First Six Constitutions After Mexico revolted from Spain in 1821, the former Spanish provinces of Texas and Coahuila became a single Mexican state. Each state within the federal union of Mexico adopted its own constitution. Thus, the *Constitution of Coahuila y Tejas,* which became effective in 1828, marked Texas's first experience with a state constitution. Political unrest among Texans, who wanted more representation than two seats in the 12-member Texas-Coahuila legislature, arose almost immediately. Finally, on March 2, 1836, at Washington-on-the-Brazos, a delegate convention of Texans issued a declaration of independence from Mexico and drafted the *Constitution of the Republic of Texas.* It was modeled largely on the U.S. Constitution.

In 1845, the Congress of the United States belatedly offered statehood to the young republic. Texas President Anson Jones then called a constitutional convention at which delegates drew up a new state constitution and agreed to accept the invitation to join the Union. In February 1846, after Texas voters ratified both actions of the constitutional convention, Texas became the 28th state of the United States. The *Constitution of 1845* lasted until the Civil War. During that war and until 1876 a prolonged and bitter period of constitution making occurred in Texas history. Three state constitutions were adopted to meet particular political demands related to the Civil War: the *Constitution of 1861,* to adjust to membership in the Confederacy; the *Constitution of 1866,* to provide for reinstatement in the Union; and the *Constitution of 1869,* to meet the demands of Reconstruction. The last of these three served the state until the present Constitution was adopted in 1876.

With the defeat of the Confederacy, Texas's Constitution of 1861 became null and void, and President Andrew Johnson appointed a provisional governor for Texas in June 1865. Following voter registration in 1866, a new constitution was adopted and President Johnson proclaimed that insurrection in Texas had ended. The Constitution of 1866 provided for black equality with whites before the courts and, in general, assured the former slaves more security than did the constitutions of other former Confederate states.

The relatively uncomplicated reinstatement of the Lone Star State into the Union ended abruptly when the *Radical Republicans* gained control of Congress in November 1866. Refusing to seat Texas's two U.S. senators and three representatives, Congress set aside the state's reconstructed government, enfranchised blacks, disfranchised leading whites, and imposed military rule across the state;

Washington-on-the-Brazos. This clapboard building at Washington-on-the-Brazos is the site where Texas declared independence from Mexico in 1836. (Courtesy *San Angelo Standard-Times.*)

federal military officers replaced civil authorities. Subsequently, to meet the demands of congressional Reconstruction, a constitutional convention drafted yet another constitution for Texas, and it was ratified in 1869. With elections supervised by the military, Radical Republicans gained control of the Texas Legislature and elected E. J. Davis, a former Union army general, governor of Texas.

Governor Davis imposed martial law in some places and used police methods to enforce his decrees. This administration, alleged to be one of the most corrupt in Texas history, has been described by historians as characterized by extravagant public spending, property tax increases to the point of confiscation, gifts of public funds to private interests, intimidation of newspaper editors, and control of voter registration by the military. Although the Constitution of 1869 is associated in Texas history with the unpopular administration of Governor Davis, the machinery of government it created was quite modern. This fundamental law called for annual sessions of the Legislature, a four-year term for the governor and other executive officers, and gubernatorial appointment of, rather than popular election of, judges. It abolished county courts and raised the salaries of public officials. These changes centralized more governmental power at Austin and weakened government at the grassroots.

The Davis rule survived from 1870 to 1874. In perhaps the most fraudulent election ever conducted in Texas, Davis was soundly defeated in December 1873 by Democrat Richard Coke. Democrats had gained control of the Legislature in 1872; two years later, they were able to wrest control of the state courts away from the Republicans. The next step was to rewrite the Texas Constitution.

Drafting the Constitution of 1876 In the summer of 1875, Texas voters elected 75 Democrats and 15 Republicans (six of whom were black) as delegates to a constitutional convention, but only 83 attended the gathering in Austin. One-half were members of the *Texas Grange,* a farm organization committed to the cause of economy and limited government. Its slogan of *"retrenchment and reform"* became the major goal of the convention. So strong, in fact, was the spirit of economy among the delegates that they refused to hire a stenographer or to allow publication of the convention proceedings. As a result, no official record was ever made of the convention that gave Texas its most enduring constitution. Delegates, as a body, represented the unreconstructed element of the state rather than those who had been sympathetic to the Davis regime.

In their zeal to undo Reconstruction policies, the delegates on occasion overreacted. Striking at Reconstruction measures that had given Governor Davis control over voter registration, the overwrought delegates inserted a statement providing that "no law shall ever be enacted requiring a registration of voters of this state." Within two decades, the statement had to be amended to permit voter registration laws.

Continuing to dismantle the Davis administration machinery, the determined delegates inserted numerous pages of specific policy provisions, making the document read like a legal code instead of a basic fundamental law. They reduced the governor's term of office (from four to two years), salary, and powers; made all executive offices (except that of secretary of state) elective for two-year terms; and tied the hands of legislators with biennial sessions, low salaries, and restricted legislative powers. All judges became popularly elected for relatively short terms of office. Public services were trimmed to the bone. As further concessions to taxpayers, the delegates lowered salaries of public officials, established racially segregated public education, and repealed the school attendance law. They limited the public debt and severely curbed the taxing and spending powers of the Legislature. Local government was stimulated by the establishment of justice of the peace courts, county courts, and district courts. In addition to prohibiting voter registration, the convention restored precinct elections and allowed only taxpayers to vote on city bond issues.

Texas's most enduring constitution was put to a vote in 1876 and was approved by more than a two-to-one majority. Although Texans in the state's largest cities— Houston, Dallas, San Antonio, and Galveston—voted against it, the much greater rural population voted for approval.

Today's Texas Constitution: After a Century of Usage

With all its shortcomings, the *Constitution of 1876* has endured for more than a century. The disadvantage of its *excessive length* is compounded by its *structural disarray* and confusion. The wordy document contains misnumbered sections, misspelled words, and articles left blank. One sentence contains 756 words. Some sections devoted to the same subject are scattered throughout the body of the Constitution rather than being grouped in a single article. (See Reading 2.1.) Chiefly because of its length, complete copies of the Texas Constitution are not readily available to the public. However, each edition of the *Texas Almanac,* published every other year by the *Dallas Morning News,* includes the complete text.

Sharing in the prevailing distrust of government, the framers of the Constitution of 1876 sought with a vengeance to limit and thus to control policymaking by placing many restrictions in the state's fundamental law. Prevailing opinion of that day held that a state government could exercise only those powers that were listed in the state constitution. Thus, instead of being permitted to exercise powers not denied by the national or state constitutions, for over a century Texas law-makers have been limited to those policymaking powers that are enumerated in the state's basic law. The inevitable result is a lengthy constitution that has grown longer with time. Amendments have been added in response to new policy de-mands resulting from changing circumstances. For example, delegates in 1875 saw fit to include pages of detail on government regulation of railroads. Ultimately, government supervision of railroads ceased to be of prime importance and the regulatory detail was largely amended out in 1969. Today, more lawmaking atten-tion must be devoted to building highways and regulating the automobile and truck traffic thereon. The same is true of the changing policy needs of education, public health, crime control, and a wide variety of social services unforeseen in 1875.

It was inevitable that filling the Texas Constitution with statutory detail in 1875 would soon require constitutional amendments in order to move the state into and through the twentieth century. Urbanization, industrialization, revolution in communication, population explosion, growing demands in education, and count-less needs for social services—all of these produced pressures for constitutional change. Most, if not all, policy issues arising in a rapidly changing state may be resolved only after adoption of a constitutional amendment. But most of Texas's 326 amendments have applied to policy issues that should have been resolved by statute alone. Instead, an often uninformed and usually apathetic electorate has decided the fate of each policy issue involved. A sample of the utter absurdity of policymaking by constitutional amendment is provided by the 25 proposals on the ballot in 1987. One of the proposed amendments called upon Texas voters statewide to decide whether or not county treasurers were needed in Gregg, Fayette, and Nueces counties. Other policy issues on the lengthy ballot involved tax exemptions for some groups, raising taxes for others, creating more special districts, and increasing the number of justice of the peace offices in some counties.

Constitutional Revision and Amendment

Attempts to revise the Texas Constitution of 1876 began soon after its adoption. A legislative resolution calling for a constitutional revision convention was introduced in 1887 and was followed by many more, but none was implemented until 1972. However, in 1969, some positive gains were realized when 56 obsolete provisions were removed by an amendment.

A Major Reform Effort

The most comprehensive movement in the state's history to achieve constitutional revision began in 1971; but like earlier attempts, it failed to produce a revised basic law for Texas. The 62nd Legislature began the process with a resolution that proposed an amendment authorizing the appointment of a study commission and naming the members of the 63rd Legislature as delegates to a constitutional convention. Submitted to the voters in 1972 as a proposed constitutional amendment, the resolution was adopted by a comfortable majority. With 49.7 percent of the registered voters voting on the resolution, it was approved by a margin of 1,549,982 to 985,282.

Constitutional Revision Commission   Under authority of the 1972 amendment, a 37-member Constitutional Revision Commission was selected by a six-member committee composed of the governor, the lieutenant governor, the speaker of the House, the attorney general, the chief justice of the Texas Supreme Court, and the presiding judge of the Court of Criminal Appeals. After these selections were approved by the Legislature, the commission prepared a draft constitution or working model. It was based on opinion and information gathered at public hearings and from various authorities on constitutional revision. Only one-fourth the length of the present Constitution, the completed draft was submitted to the Legislature on November 1, 1973.

Legislative Constitutional Convention   On January 8, 1974, members of both houses of the Texas Legislature met in Austin as a constitutional convention. Previous Texas constitutions had been drafted by delegates popularly elected for that purpose. Adoption of the basic constitutional framework recommended by the revision commission gave the convention a head start. With this advantage, some observers believed that the convention would complete its task well within the time allowed by the 1972 amendment. When the entire document was considered on July 11, however, the two-thirds majority vote needed for final approval could not be obtained. Attempts to reach compromises on controversial issues, chiefly those related to public education and the inclusion of a *right-to-work law*,[1] proved futile, and the remaining days of the convention passed. Then, following a last-minute, cliff-hanging drama that ended at midnight on July 30, the convention adjourned. By a final vote of 118 to 62, the convention failed by three votes to attain the necessary two-thirds majority of the 181 delegates to adopt a draft constitution for submission to the Texas voters.

Perhaps there has been no better demonstration in Texas of constitution making as a political process than the *1974 constitutional convention*. First, the convention was hampered by lack of positive political leadership. Governor Dolph Briscoe maintained a hands-off policy throughout the convention, and Lieutenant Governor Bill Hobby similarly failed to provide needed political leadership. The retiring speaker of the House and president of the convention, Price Daniel, Jr.—presumably to enhance his credibility as an impartial presiding officer—in effect impaired his leadership role by announcing that he was not a candidate for any public office in 1974. On the other hand, the legislator-delegates were concerned about their prospects for nomination and re-election to the House and Senate, which influenced their voting positions on major issues before the convention. House members were distracted also by the campaign for the office of speaker for the next legislative session. After an April recess to allow campaigning for the May primaries, it was difficult for delegates to pick up the major convention issues that had been left unresolved.

A prime reason the convention failed by a razor-thin margin to agree on a proposed constitution was the paper tiger issue of the right-to-work law. With a statutory law already in effect, adding this provision to the constitution would not have strengthened the legal hand of employers to any significant degree. Nevertheless, conservative, antilabor forces insisted on the provision, and a prolabor minority vigorously opposed it. The controversy aroused much emotion, and at times the issue produced loud and bitter name-calling among delegates on the floor and spectators in the galleries.

Labor leaders and their supporters in the galleries used binoculars and movie cameras to record votes and identify delegates on the floor. Certain Mexican-American and black delegates, heavily dependent on the labor vote, sought to prove their support of labor's position on the right-to-work question. At one point Craig Washington, a black delegate from Houston, shouted to the president of the Texas AFL-CIO: "Harry Hubbard, wherever you are in the gallery, I know that you have misused my people, but I'm telling you from this convention floor now—don't forget who brung you. I'm bringing you today, baby, and I'll be back for mine."[2]

A Legislative Proposal   Before the sound of the gavel had faded at the conclusion of the convention, there was mounting public criticism of the delegates' failure to produce a constitution that could be offered to the voters in 1974. Most critics saw the convention's efforts as an exercise in futility—two years of lost effort and over $4 million of state money wasted. A statewide poll reported that about 80 percent of the voters were "shocked that the delegates had not produced."[3] Stung by this rebuke from constituents, the 64th Legislature resolved to submit a proposed constitution to voters.

In April 1975, a *constitutional revision resolution* was agreed upon. This resolution proposed a constitution composed of ten articles to be submitted to the Texas electorate in November of that year. Content of the articles was essentially the same as that of the final resolution the 1974 convention had failed to adopt by a margin of only three votes. The ten articles were contained in *eight propositions* to be placed on the ballot, the first three articles being consolidated into one proposition. Voters could vote on any or all of the eight propositions.

The People Decide   The eight propositions submitted to Texas voters in November 1975 represented a substantially revised state constitution. For the first time in a century, Texas voters had the opportunity to vote on a new fundamental law. The proposed revision represented years of work by men and women well informed on the subject of constitution making. Recognized constitutional authorities considered the concise and orderly document to be among the best-drafted state constitutions ever submitted to voters.[4] Although new and innovative in many respects, it did not discard all the old. In addition to retaining the Bill of Rights, the proposed constitution incorporated such basic principles as limited government, separation of powers, and bicameralism (a two-house legislature).

Nevertheless, Texas voters demonstrated a strong preference for their century-old Constitution by rejecting each proposition; voters in 250 of the state's 254 counties rejected all eight. Only 23 percent of the estimated 5.9 million registered voters cast ballots, which meant that only about 10 percent of the state's voting-age population participated in this important referendum. When asked to explain the resounding defeat of the proposals, Lieutenant Governor Hobby responded, "There's not enough of the body left for an autopsy."

Organized political support for the proposed constitution had come from the League of Women Voters, the Citizens for the Texas Constitution, and the lawyers' state bar association. Among elected officials voicing their support were the lieutenant governor, the speaker of the House, and the attorney general. Most big-city daily newspapers also were in favor of the proposals. In opposition were organized groups such as the Citizens to Preserve the Texas Constitution, led by Senator Peyton McKnight of Tyler. Governor Briscoe announced his opposition as the absentee voting period began. He ominously predicted that adoption was likely to result in enactment of a state income tax law, increased cost of state government, a too-powerful Legislature, and adoption of a Missouri Plan for selection of state judges (a process involving both appointment and popular election). Other reasons for defeat included popular ignorance of the issues and opposition to a constitutional convention made up of legislators.

Piecemeal Revision After the defeat of the proposed constitution, legislators sought to achieve some measure of revision by other means, including legislative enactments and piecemeal constitutional amendments. In 1977, for example, the 65th Legislature enacted into law two of the proposals defeated at the polls in 1975. One established a sunset procedure for reviewing state administrative agencies. The other law created a planning agency within the governor's office. In 1979, the 66th Legislature proposed six amendments designed to implement parts of the constitutional revision package rejected in 1975. Three were adopted by the voters and added to the Texas Constitution:

1. Establishing a single property tax appraisal district in each county
2. Giving criminal appellate jurisdiction to 14 courts of civil appeal that formerly had exercised civil jurisdiction only
3. Allowing the governor limited removal power of appointed statewide officials

The Amendment Process

Each of the 50 state constitutions contains means for changing the powers and functions of government. Without a provision for amendment, a constitution could not long survive. We have noted in this chapter how revision may produce a totally new constitution to replace an old one. A state legislature may also change a constitution by enactment of laws under authority granted by the constitution. Similarly, courts may alter constitutions by interpreting and ruling on their meaning. And finally, constitutions may be changed by *formal amendment,* which is the chief means whereby the Texas Constitution has been altered.

The procedure for amending the Texas Constitution, a relatively simple process, is specified in Article XVII, Section 1. (See Reading 2.2.) There are two steps involved. First, the Legislature may propose amendments by adopting a joint resolution at any regular session or, if requested by the governor, at a special session. To be valid, a proposed amendment must be approved by a recorded vote of two-thirds of the entire membership of each house. This means that at least 21 senators and 100 representatives must vote for the proposed amendment in the form of a joint resolution. The Legislature also decides when the registered voters—in a special election or in the November general election of every even-numbered year—will have an opportunity to ratify or reject a proposed amendment. If a simple majority of those voting on the proposed amendment votes in favor of a proposal, it is ratified and becomes a part of the Constitution. Then the governor, who has no veto power in this process, proclaims the amendment a part of the Constitution.

A proposed amendment must be officially publicized before it is submitted to the voters in a regular or special election. The secretary of state and the attorney general prepare a short explanation of each proposed amendment. This explanation is published twice in all Texas newspapers that print official state notices. A copy of the full text of every proposed amendment is posted in each county courthouse at least 30 days before the election.

The Texas Constitution Today: A Summary

For two reasons, the entire Texas Constitution is not included in this textbook. First, reprinting the 63,000-word document would require over 100 pages. Second, this textbook is based largely on the Texas Constitution; each chapter looks to the Texas basic law for its content. Nevertheless, so that the reader may be introduced to some details of the document's 17 articles, we provide the summary below.

The Bill of Rights

Eleven of the 29 sections of Article I, the *Bill of Rights,* provide protections for people and property against arbitrary governmental actions. Sections 3, 4, 7, 8, 12, 16–19, and 27 afford such guarantees as freedom of speech, press, religion, assembly, and petition. In addition, they prohibit the taking by law of property without just compensation and forbid impairment of the obligation of contract. These and other rights in the Texas Constitution are protected by the U.S. Constitution against impairment by the states. Thus, with their basic rights guaranteed in both national and state constitutions, Texans have a double safeguard against arbitrary governmental action. Thirteen sections (9–16, 19–22, and 28) relate to persons accused of crimes and to those convicted of crimes. For example, Section 11 guarantees the right of release on bail; Section 9 prohibits unreasonable searches and seizures; and Section 15 states that "the right to trial by jury shall remain inviolate."

Sections 1, 2, and 29 contain certain philosophical phrases that have no direct force of law. Still smarting from what was seen as the "bondage" years of Reconstruction, the angry framers of 1875 understandably began their work by inserting this terse statement: "Texas is a free and independent state, subject only to the Constitution of the United States."

The Powers of Government

Holding fast to the principle of limited government, in Article II the framers of 1875 firmly embedded into the new Constitution the familiar doctrine of *separation of powers;* they assigned the legislative, executive, and judicial powers of government to three separate branches—the legislative, executive, and judicial departments. Article II then adds unequivocally: "and no person, or collection of persons, being of one of these departments, shall exercise any power properly attached to either of the others except in the instances herein expressly permitted." Those expressly permitted include the governor's power to veto legislation and the legislative power to override the veto. In addition, the impeachment process (a judicial function) is assigned to the Legislature, and the Senate (a legislative body) is given the power to confirm certain appointments of the governor.

The Legislature is composed of a House of Representatives and a Senate. Article III, The Legislative Department, contains 65 sections, vivid testimony to over 100 years of amending. Article IV, The Executive Department, provides that the governor "shall be the Chief Executive Officer of the State" but then provides for the sharing of executive powers with five other popularly elected officers who are independent of the governor. With this and other forms of division of executive power in the Constitution, the Texas governor is little more than first among equals in the Executive Department. Through Article V, The Judicial Department, Texas joins Oklahoma as the only states in the Union with two courts of final appeal, one for civil cases and one for criminal cases. Below these two supreme appellate courts are intermediate appellate courts and trial courts of original jurisdiction. In a constitution with separation of powers, the ideal judicial article needs only to create a court system, name at least one court, and specify the mode of selection and tenure of judges. In contrast, Article V in the Texas Constitution, with a total of 28 sections, is heaped with technical verbiage addressed principally to lawyers and judges.

Suffrage

Article VI, *Suffrage,* is one of the shortest articles in the Texas Constitution. The term *suffrage* refers to voting in elections or the right to vote. Prior to 1870, states had definitive power to conduct elections. Since that time, the U.S. Constitution, Congress, and the Supreme Court have vastly diminished this power. Within the scope of current federal regulations, the Texas Constitution establishes voter qualifications, provides for registration of citizens for voting, and governs the conduct of elections.

Local Government

The most disorganized part of the Texas Constitution concerns units of local government: counties, municipalities, special districts, and school districts. Although Article IX is entitled Counties, county government is dealt with in parts of four other articles. To find all that is contained on the subject, one must read Article XI on Municipal Corporations, Article V on the Judiciary, Article VIII on Taxation and Revenue, Article XVI on General Provisions, and Article IX on Counties. Moreover, the basic structure of county government is defined, not in Article IX on Counties, but in Article V on the Judiciary. Article XI on Municipalities is equally disorganized and inadequate. Only three of the ten sections of this article relate exclusively to municipal government. Other sections concern county government, taxation, public indebtedness, and forced sale of public property. Along with counties and municipalities, the original Constitution of 1876 referred to school districts but not special districts. Authorization for special districts, however, crept into the Constitution with a 1904 amendment that authorizes the borrowing of money for water development and road construction by a county "or any defined district." Thereafter, special districts were created to provide a myriad of services, such as drainage, conservation, urban renewal, public housing, and those provided by hospitals and airports.

Other Articles

The nine remaining articles also reflect a strong devotion to constitutional minutiae. Titles are as follows: Education, Taxation and Revenue, Railroads, Private Corporations, Spanish and Mexican Land Titles, Public Lands and Land Office, Impeachment, General Provisions, and Mode of Amendment. The shortest of these is Article XIII, Spanish and Mexican Land Titles. All of its text was deleted by amendment in 1969. The longest of these, containing 67 sections, is Article XVI, General Provisions. This article, for example, provides for county poorhouses for the indigent, prohibits the charging of usurious interest rates, regulates the manufacture and sale of intoxicants, permits the use of convict labor to build public roads, and provides for pensions for retired Texas Rangers (not the baseball team!).

Notes

1. Passed by the U.S. Congress in 1947, the Taft-Hartley Act prohibits closed-shop labor contracts whereby nonunion workers cannot be hired. A later amendment to the law permits the states to adopt statutory or constitutional

right-to-work provisions that ban the union shop (that is, prohibit any employer-employee labor contract requiring an employee to join a union in order to keep a job). Texas has a right-to-work law that was enacted by the Legislature in 1974.

2. John Kamensky, "Six Hours—And No Reprieve," in Eugene W. Jones, Joe E. Ericson, Lyle C. Brown, and Robert S. Trotter, Jr., *Practicing Texas Politics*, 7th ed. (Boston: Houghton Mifflin, 1989). p. 72.
3. Felton West, "Shame Helped Pass Constitution," *Houston Post,* April 20, 1975.
4. See Janice C. May, "The Proposed 1976 Revision of the Texas Constitution," *Public Affairs Comment,* 21 (August 1975), 1.

Key Terms and Concepts

Tenth Amendment	Constitution of 1866
National Supremacy Clause	Constitution of 1869
privileges and immunities	Radical Republicans
full faith and credit	Texas Grange
reserved powers	"retrenchment and reform"
cooperative federalism	Constitution of 1876
grant-in-aid program	excessive length
categorical grant	structural disarray
block grant system	right-to-work law
revenue sharing	1974 constitutional convention
fundamental law	constitutional revision resolution
Constitution of Coahuila y Tejas	eight propositions
Constitution of the Republic of	formal amendment
Texas	Bill of Rights
Constitution of 1845	separation of powers
Constitution of 1861	suffrage

Selected Readings

2.1 Time to Write a New Constitution for Texas

This brief editorial from the Houston Post *is another of the many pleas by the Texas press and other media for a new state constitution. With scores of amendments added each year by direct vote of the people, Texas is more and more substituting direct lawmaking for the traditional statutory enactments by the people's representatives.*

More and more we're inclined to think Texas should have another constitutional convention. A state constitution that has to be revised a dozen or two dozen times about every two years is for the birds. But that's what's happening with our unwieldy, 113-year-old state charter.

Since it was first adopted in 1876, the Reconstruction-reaction constitution has been amended by the Legislature and voters 307 times. The voters have rejected 158 other proposed amendments submitted by the Legislature. More and more, as evidenced by the increasing number of amendments necessary, the long-winded, detailed old document becomes out of step with our times. Since 1932 there have been 15 different years in which the biennially meeting Legislature submitted at least a dozen amendments to the voters each time, not to mention hundreds of other amendments proposed by lawmakers that never got the two-thirds votes in both houses to make it to the voters.

Twenty-seven amendments were proposed by the Legislature in 1965, and the record of 28 was set in 1987. This year [1989] lawmakers have submitted another 20 to voters in an election next Nov. 7. All this is requiring far too many decisions by voters, especially when many of them involve boring and uninteresting subject matter. We cannot expect voters to show much interest in—or take very seriously—their basic charter of government when this is the case.

The last attempt to revise the constitution resulted in an abortive 1974 convention, whose delegates were our legislators, that failed to finally approve its own rewrite. Sitting as the Legislature, virtually the same people then submitted almost the same document to voters in eight individual amendments in 1975. Unfortunately, influenced by a governor who turned against the revision effort late in the process, Texans rejected the proposed new constitution.

Some member in the 1991 Legislature should propose another constitutional convention and try to get a revision effort going again.

2.2 Amending the Constitution of Texas: Article XVII as Amended in 1972

Proposals to amend the Texas Constitution may be submitted to the electorate by a two-thirds majority vote of each chamber of the Legislature. Any proposal is adopted as an amendment if a majority of the votes cast in a general or special election favor the proposal.

Section 1. The Legislature, at any regular session, or at any special session when the matter is included within the purposes for which the session is convened, may propose amendments revising the Constitution, to be voted upon by the qualified electors for statewide offices and propositions, as defined in the Constitution and statutes of this state. The date of the elections shall be specified by the Legislature. The proposal for submission must be approved by a vote of two-thirds of all the members elected to each House, entered by yeas and nays on the journals.

A brief explanatory statement of the nature of a proposed amendment, together with the date of the election and the wording of the proposition as it is to appear on the ballot, shall be published twice in each newspaper in the State which meets requirements set by the Legislature for the publication of official notices of officers and departments of the state government. The explanatory statement shall be prepared by the Secretary of State and shall be approved by the Attorney General. The Secretary of State shall send a full and complete copy of the proposed amendment or amendments to each county clerk who shall post the same in a public place in the courthouse at least 30 days prior to the election on said amendment. The first notice shall be published not more than 60 days nor less than 50 days before the date of the election, and the second notice shall be published on the same day in the succeeding week. The Legislature shall fix the standards for the rate of charge for the publication, which may not be higher than the newspaper's published national rate for advertising per column inch.

The election shall be held in accordance with procedures prescribed by the Legislature, and the returning officer in each county shall make returns to the Secretary of State of the number of legal votes cast at the election for and against each amendment. If it appears from the returns that a majority of the votes cast have been cast in favor of an amendment, it shall become a part of this Constitution, and proclamation thereof shall be made by the Governor.

Chapter 3

Local Governments

COW POKES
By Ace Reid

"I ain't gonna vote fer him no more. He had to
hammer this sign down with a Helicopter!"

Ace Reid

*W*hether grappling with sensitive issues, such as sex education in the public schools, or with day-to-day ones, such as constructing and maintaining rural roads (see the cartoon that opens this chapter), local officials are on the firing line as they provide services to residents, over 80 percent of whom are urban. As discussed in Chapter 2, however, state constitutional restraints continue to limit the effectiveness of *grassroots governments* in addressing issues that affect the quality of life for all Texans. Within Texas's system of government and politics, there is no sharper contrast than that between the local problems of the late twentieth century and the state's ancient constitution. Over 4,000 units of local government operate with outmoded constitutional structures fastened upon them.

Correction of constitutional defects, however, will not alone solve the complex problems of Texas government at the local level. What is required is more citizen involvement, whether at the ballot box or through interest group activity. Other opportunities for individual participation include securing signatures for *referendum* or *initiative* petitions. A voter-approved referendum forces a city council to rescind a local law known as an *ordinance.* Citizen-drafted initiatives, if approved at the polls, become law without city council approval. Working in voter registration drives, joining neighborhood associations of homeowners or renters, and assisting in election campaigns for local offices further enhance one's political clout.

How a decision is actually made at meetings of policymaking bodies (e.g., a city council, a commissioners court, or a school board) should not be beyond the understanding of any citizen who asks, "Why am I not getting more services for my taxes?" Answers to such questions require untangling the web of institutions that govern locally.

Municipal Governments

If an individual accepts the adage "You can't beat city hall," then apathy and frustration are obvious consequences that result from nonparticipation, such as failure to vote in a local election or refusal to attend a zoning commission meeting. Increasingly, however, special-interest groups (perhaps motivated by unpaved streets, increased crime rates, mistreated minorities, or raised taxes) have been able to affect the outcome of elections and to influence policy decisions. Thus individuals and groups are refuting the notion that city hall cannot be beaten. Before venturing into a local political arena, citizens should have a grasp of the organizational and legal framework within which they will be working.

Legal Status of Municipalities

Powers of city governments are restricted by municipal charters, state and national constitutions, and statutes. There are two legal classifications of cities in Texas: general-law cities and home-rule cities. The Texas Constitution stipulates that an area with a population of 5,000 or less may become a *general-law city* with a charter prescribed by a general law enacted by the Legislature. An area with more than 5,000 people may be incorporated as a *home-rule city* with a locally drafted charter that is adopted, amended, or repealed by majority vote in a citywide election. Once chartered, a general-law city does not automatically become a home-rule city just because its population rises above 5,000, nor does home-rule status change when a population declines to less than 5,000. Local voters would have to decide at the polls what the legal designation of their city would be.

Home-rule cities were first established in Texas under the Home Rule Enabling Act of 1913, which followed a constitutional amendment in 1912. There are now nearly 300 home-rule cities and about 800 general-law cities in Texas. The principal advantage of the former over the latter is that home-rule cities have greater flexibility in determining the structure and form of municipal government. Their citizens draft and adopt a city charter spelling out the procedure for passing ordinances and listing the powers, salaries, and terms of office for members of the city council. Also, the charter stipulates the powers, qualifications, and methods of selection and removal of the mayor and other city officials. Some cities, such as Austin, provide a process for removing elected officials through a popular vote. This procedure is referred to as *recall.*

Forms of Municipal Government

Four principal forms of municipal government are in operation in Texas and other states: strong mayor–council, weak mayor–council, commission, and council-manager. The council-manager form prevails in a majority of home-rule cities in Texas.

Strong Mayor–Council   Within the major cities of the United States, the *strong mayor–council form* continues as the predominant governmental structure. Among the nation's ten largest cities, only Dallas (council-manager) and San Antonio (council-manager) operate with a structure other than some variation of the mayor-council system. In New York, Chicago, Philadelphia, Detroit, Boston, and St. Louis, the mayor is the administrative head as well as the political head of the city. In Texas, except for Houston and El Paso, the strong mayor-council form of government has not been adopted in the more heavily populated cities. Perhaps this is due to disdain for so-called machine or ward-heeling politics, a style that once characterized the strong-mayor form in some Northern U.S. cities. In Texas, cities operating with the strong mayor-council form have the following characteristics:

1. A council composed of members elected from single-member districts
2. A mayor, elected at large, with the power to appoint and remove department heads
3. Budgetary power (e.g., preparation and execution) given to the mayor, with council approval needed in most cities before the budget is implemented
4. Veto power over council actions given to the mayor

Houston has implemented a variation of the mayor-council form that features a strong mayor assisted by a chief administrator and an elected comptroller who is responsible for the budget. Essentially, this type of municipal government allows the mayor to delegate much of the city's administrative work to an assistant, whom the mayor appoints and may remove.

Weak Mayor–Council As the term *weak mayor–council form* implies, this model of local government gives limited administrative powers to the mayor, who is popularly elected along with members of the city council, some department heads, and other municipal officials. The council has the power to override the mayor's veto. The mayor's position is weak because the office lacks appointive and removal power over municipal government personnel. Instead of being a chief executive, the mayor is merely one of several elected officials who are responsible to the electorate. Significantly, none of the ten largest cities in Texas now operates under the weak mayor–council form of municipal government. In other parts of the country, too, the trend is away from this form.

Commission As of 1990, only seven home-rule cities had chosen to operate under some variation of the *commission form* of municipal government. Essentially, this system does not provide a single executive but relies instead on elected commissioners who constitute a policymaking board. Individually, each commissioner administers a department (for example, public safety, finance, public works, welfare, legal). Most students of municipal government are critical of this form because it lacks a chief executive and has a dispersed administrative structure.

Council-Manager The most popular type of municipal government among Texas's home-rule cities is the *council-manager form* (sometimes termed commission-manager form). It has the following characteristics:

1. City council members elected at-large or in single-member districts
2. A city manager appointed and removable by the council and responsible for budget coordination
3. A mayor, elected at-large, who is the presiding member of the council

The principal advantage of the council-manager form is that it allows the city council to make policies after deliberation and debate on issues that confront cities—taxation, police protection, zoning ordinances, and the like. Once a policy is made, the city manager's office directs its implementation by the appropriate office.

As the policymaking arm of municipal government, the city council is a sounding board for many of the grievances and issues that arise in a city. Weekly meetings are open to the public. Most city councils in Texas consist of from five to nine members serving either without pay or for only token compensation.

When Amarillo and Terrell adopted the council-manager form in 1913, a new era began in Texas municipal administration. The city manager is the key officer in Texas's largest central cities and growing suburban communities (with the exception of Houston and El Paso). Because the city manager is an appointed, professional administrator, the city council looks to the manager for preparation of the annual budget and for general advice and recommendations. Policy, however, is made by the council and is carried out by the city manager.

The most delicate relationship within the council-manager form is that between the manager and members of the council.[1] On occasion, a city manager may oppose a council policy and refuse to carry it out. Such situations produce a fairly rapid turnover of city managers. Competitive salaries, larger staffs, a need for city planning, and complex grant-in-aid programs financed by state and federal governments have combined to make the city manager's office the pivotal institution for effective municipal administration. This form of city government tends to separate politics and administration, but managers cannot divorce themselves completely from community politics because their superiors are the elected council members, who usually represent different factions. The fact that the manager is not elected gives the council-manager model an undemocratic image. Nevertheless, most Texas home-rule cities are governed under this form. Although a large majority of the state's city managers have been Anglos, black and Mexican-American city managers were hired in Dallas and Austin, respectively, in the 1980s.

Home-Rule Flexibility   One final point needs to be made about the structure or forms of municipal governments in Texas. A typical question from a citizen is "How do you explain the structure of municipal government in my town? None of the preceding models accurately depicts our government." The answer lies in the flexibility afforded home-rule cities. That is, a city might have a commission form, such as in Corpus Christi, but have an elected mayor. Any combination of the forms discussed here is possible, depending on the wishes of the voters, in a city operating under a home-rule charter.

Municipal Politics

All public policy decisions of municipal government officials are made within an environment of personal politics. Power plays among city council members, the mayor, administrators, and staff stem from inputs of neighborhood groups, ethnic minorities, businesses, and special-interest groups such as environmentalists and tax protesters.

City councils or commissions are the focal point of municipal politics, but voter turnout tends to be low. One may find council members whose election resulted from participation by less than 10 percent of the citizens that they represent. Texas municipal elections are *nonpartisan*. That is, candidates are not listed on the ballot by party label. Rather, aspirants to a city council or mayoral position are endorsed and supported by community groups. It follows that those groups whose candidates win the election have the best access to their respective council members or mayor.

In the 1980s, politics at the municipal level was influenced by two significant developments: emergence of single-member districts for city councils and rising expectations of blacks and Mexican Americans, particularly those living within the inner cities of Houston, Dallas, San Antonio, El Paso, Austin, and Fort Worth. When a city adopts *single-member districts* for electing council members, each voter casts a ballot for a candidate who resides within that voter's district. In the *at-large system,* council members are elected on a citywide basis. All the council members in San Antonio (ten), El Paso (six alderpersons), and Fort Worth (eight)

Houston Mayor Kathy Whitmire (right) confers with two members of the Harris County delegation, Representative Sylvester Turner (left) and Senator Gene Green (middle) on the floor of the Texas Senate during the 71st Legislature (1989). (Senate Media Services.)

are elected from single-member districts, whereas combination plans exist in Houston (nine single-member, five at-large members) and Dallas (eight single-member, two at-large).* In each of these cities the mayor is elected citywide (at-large) and presides at meetings of the council. Strong black and Mexican-American support has been credited with the mayoral victories of Houston's Kathy Whitmire and Dallas's Annette Strauss. Charters for Houston, Dallas, San Antonio, and Fort Worth allow the mayor to vote on any matter before the council, but El Paso's mayor has only a tie-breaking vote.

Some cities, such as Austin, operate a *place system.* Under this structure, city council candidates file for a numerically designated place, and those candidates who file for the same place run against each other. Council members are then elected on an at-large basis, with all voters in the city voting in each place contest. Austin's mayor is elected citywide. Voters in that city opted in 1985 to retain the place system.

Municipal Services

Nowhere is the linkage between politics and government more evident than in the delivery of services to city residents. Municipal administrators rely on council

*Dallas's 10-4-1 plan, approved by voters in a charter amendment election in 1989, was challenged by minority group plaintiffs in a federal lawsuit.

members to communicate needs and problems to them. With single-member districts representing a broad diversity of interests and producing divisive issues (for example, public housing, racial, transportation, and environmental issues), council meetings are often scenes of controversy and heated debate.

As a result of federal court decisions that have broken up many at-large electoral systems for city councils, monolithic business domination is no longer the rule in most Texas cities. In place of absolute control by business interests, one finds greater involvement of groups representing blacks, Mexican Americans, environmentalists, homeowners, and consumers. Ethnic or racial groups frequently are able to identify with and elect one or two council members who reside in their part of town. Where at-large seats still exist for council members, however, well-financed citywide campaigns usually bring about the election of candidates who are probusiness. At-large and place system methods of selection tend to dilute the voting strength of minority groups within a city and to increase significantly the cost of getting elected. On the other hand, single-member district selection raises the distinct possibility of "ward politics," whereby council members are more interested in problems of their own districts than in citywide issues.

Establishment power revolving around a city's major banks and business corporations persists in every large Texas city. Chambers of commerce will always have considerable clout in policy decisions affecting municipal services, particularly those relating to the city as a whole. Groups that are successful in obtaining favorable decisions from city councils, regulatory boards, and commissions are frequently those that have mastered the art of representing themselves and their causes in the most convincing manner. Such groups have also learned the procedures required for successful appeals. (See Reading 3.1.)

Although citizens express different opinions as to which city services are most important, there is general agreement that services should be delivered at the lowest possible cost to taxpayers. An overview of typical municipal services is provided by the following items of municipal expenditures outlined in a staff research report to the Texas Legislative Council:

1. *General administration:* expenses for the council, courts, manager (if any), legal department, planning, finance and personnel administration, conduct of elections, recording and reporting
2. *Police:* expenditures for the police department, custody of prisoners, and traffic control
3. *Fire:* cost of fire protection and prevention
4. *Streets:* operation and maintenance costs of alleys, sidewalks, curbs and gutters, and grade crossings
5. *Sewer:* sewage-disposal plant expense and cost of maintenance, and salaries for garbage-disposal workers
6. *Welfare:* assistance to needy persons and expenses of institutions for the needy
7. *Health:* expenses for the health department, clinics, and food and sanitary inspections

8. *Hospitals:* expenditures for city-owned hospitals, payments to other hospitals for municipal patients, and allocations to joint city-county hospitals
9. *Libraries, parks, and recreation*
10. *Contributions to trust funds:* retirement systems
11. *Debt service:* interest and sinking fund payments
12. *Utilities:* expenses of water, electric power, and natural gas
13. *Miscellaneous:* markets, warehouses, cemeteries, and airports

Ordinance-making power gives home-rule cities their greatest flexibility in providing services to their communities. Ordinances govern zoning restrictions, consumer affairs, traffic safety, pollution control, planning development, building safety, and other municipal services. City councils pass, repeal, or amend ordinances. Most cities have appointed boards and commissions that work in advisory capacities with municipal departments in the administration of municipal ordinances. However, constitutional restraints on municipal powers are numerous.

Financing Municipal Government

Of all the issues confronting Texas cities in the 1980s and 1990s, none has attracted more attention than taxing and spending. Although city hall has been a favorite target of angry taxpayers, the Texas Legislature has caught its share of heat because of strict statutory and constitutional limitations on cities.

Texas municipalities are constitutionally limited to raising funds from three tax sources: sales taxes, general property taxes, and miscellaneous occupation taxes. In addition, the Legislature may authorize new revenues, allocating funds from such nontax sources as license fees, permits, fines, and penalties. Also, cities receive a local share of certain state-collected taxes (e.g., the sales tax and the alcoholic beverages mixed-drink tax), as well as subsidies and other grants from federal and state governments. If these sources prove insufficient to meet capital expenditures (e.g., new buildings) and operating expenses (e.g., salaries of employees), municipal governments sell bonds or resort to other methods of borrowing.

Texas cities may charge a *franchise fee* based on the gross receipts of public utilities (e.g., telephone companies) operating within their jurisdictions. Texas courts have held that this is fundamentally a "street rental" or "alley rental" charge. Rates vary considerably, but the most common is a 2 percent levy on gross receipts from business conducted within a city; however, rates for TV cable companies have been increasing steadily. In addition, Texas municipalities may levy fees for issuing beer and liquor licenses and building and plumbing permits. Because cities are authorized to maintain municipal courts, revenues from these courts (e.g., court costs, fines, and forfeitures) are retained by the city. These revenues may be substantial, especially if vigorous enforcement of traffic regulations is followed. Fees derived from parking meters are designated as police regulatory fees rather than taxes; but under whatever guise, this is a substantial source of revenue for many of the larger cities. Some Texas communities levy so-called impact fees on builders for construction projects such as water and sewer facilities.

Texas municipalities have authority to own and operate water, electric, and gas utility systems. If a city decides to offer these services, it can collect fees large enough to permit profits, which are then transferred to general funds. Charges are also levied for services such as sewage disposal, garbage and trash collection, hospital care, and use of municipal recreation facilities. These services usually do not require subsidies from a city's general revenue fund.

Taxes and fees normally produce enough revenue for Texas cities to cover day-to-day operating expenses, but money for capital improvements (e.g., construction of new city facilities) and for emergencies must often be obtained through the sale of municipal bonds. The Texas Constitution allows municipalities to issue bonds in any amount, provided they assess and collect annually sufficient revenue to pay the interest and retire the principal without exceeding legal tax limits. Cities are authorized to issue general obligation bonds and revenue bonds. *General obligation bonds* are redeemed out of a city's general revenue fund. *Revenue bonds* are backed by and redeemed out of the revenues of the property or activity financed by selling the bonds. Money obtained from the sale of municipal bonds is used for such items as street improvements, storm sewers, water and sewer lines, airport expansion, municipal buildings, and recreation facilities.

Financial aid from state and federal governments has diminished as a source of municipal revenue. Some state aid is obtained for employee retirement programs and for the construction of expressways, but this source is not yet a significant factor in municipal revenue systems. Most state aid goes to local school districts.

The Texas Constitution authorizes general-law cities to levy a maximum ad valorem property tax of $1.50 for each $100 valuation of all property within city limits. It allows home-rule cities to increase that rate to a maximum of $2.50 for each $100 valuation. Like county governments, cities may tax any occupation already being taxed by the state government.

State statutes authorize municipal governments to levy two additional taxes: sales and franchise. By 1990, over 900 Texas cities had adopted a 1 percent sales tax through a favorable vote of their citizens. This local sales tax, along with the state's 6 percent sales tax, is collected by the comptroller of public accounts and distributed to cities monthly. A state constitutional amendment allows cities that are not within the boundaries of a transit authority to levy an additional 0.5 percent sales tax and to use the revenue to offset property taxes. As of January 1, 1990, over 50 cities had adopted the additional tax, after voter approval. A 2 percent cap on combined local sales taxes is another restraint of the Texas Constitution on local governments. Also, since 1985, the Legislature has allowed city councils to impose a 1 percent tax on utilities such as telephone service.

Faced with the dual dilemma of deteriorating inner-city neighborhoods and the need to attract new businesses, some Texas cities have opted for an innovative revenue-raising plan. The Legislature has authorized municipalities to create tax reinvestment zones (TRZ) that produce revenue through tax increment financing (TIF). Although there are some legal restrictions, funds can be raised and spent in these zones in the following ways:

1. Through its ordinance-making power, a city council or commission creates a TRZ by designating an area that is in need of investment capital.
2. Within that zone, property values are frozen (for accounting purposes) at their preproject levels.
3. When new projects are developed within the zone, increased property values are "captured" through reassessment.
4. The tax levy on the "captured assessed value" is placed in a fund that pays for the costs of the public investment.
5. The city council is responsible for spending fund money within the zone.[2]

Legal restrictions prevent a city from placing more than 15 percent of its taxable real property and more than 10 percent of its residential property in a TRZ. All revenue bonds issued by a city, applicable to a TRZ, must be approved by the Texas attorney general.

Given a severe reduction in local sales tax revenues in recent years (see Chapter 9), Texas cities have been forced to cut budgets and look for new revenue sources. Compounding the problem are difficulties in passing bond issues. The 1986 Federal Tax Reform Act prohibits cities and state governments from issuing tax-exempt industrial development bonds for private use if 10 percent or more of the proposed activity is for commercial business or trade.

City councils have been forced to opt for one or more of the following steps to relieve financially strapped budgets: creating new fees or raising current ones on such services as garbage collection, raising property taxes, imposing hiring and wage freezes, or cutting services that are especially important for poverty-stricken, inner-city populations. Unlike many big cities outside of the sunbelt, Texas municipalities levy neither personal nor corporate income taxes.

The County

Article IX of the Texas Constitution is entitled "The Counties." According to the Constitution, the *county* is an administrative arm of the state, created by the state to serve its needs and purposes. State supervision of county operations, however, is minimal. But as an agent of the state, each of the 254 Texas counties issues state automobile licenses, enforces state laws, registers voters, conducts elections, levies and collects some state taxes, and helps administer justice. In conjunction with state and federal governments, the county conducts health and welfare programs, maintains records of vital statistics (such as births and deaths), issues various licenses, collects fees, and provides a host of other public services.

Texans tend to regard the county's governmental functions as local rather than statewide in nature. Most people cannot distinguish between functions performed for the county and those conducted for the state. For example, the county sheriff and county judge enforce and administer state law. These officials are, therefore, state functionaries; yet they are elected by the voters of the county and are paid from the county treasury.

Counties vary in area size from Rockwall County, with 147 square miles (smaller than some ranches), to Brewster County, with over 6,000 square miles. In population, they range from less than 100 residents in Loving County to over 2 million inhabitants in Harris County.

Despite its rural image and provincial ways, the county remains a potent political and administrative force within the state. Nevertheless, county governments in Texas have been plagued with persistent problems, such as inadequate jail facilities and personnel systems based more on spoils (with jobs awarded to friends and supporters of elected officials) than on merit.[3] Bickering and power plays among county officials give rise to questions concerning the performance and effectiveness of county government. Citizens' lack of understanding about the structure and operation, however, is one of the underlying reasons public affairs are not conducted in a more efficient fashion at the county level.

Structure and Operation

The operation of county government in Texas is influenced by the Jacksonian principle of popular election of most county officers. Because of an already lengthy ballot, some people have questioned the desirability of this arrangement. Nevertheless, any structural change would require alteration of the Texas Constitution, because that document requires the election of many officials. Included among them are county commissioners, county and district attorneys, a county sheriff, a county clerk, a district clerk, a county tax assessor-collector, and a county treasurer, as well as court officials (county and district judges, justices of the peace, and constables). All elected county officials serve four-year terms.

Commissioners Court Policymaking is performed by many county officials, principal among whom is a body called the *commissioners court*. It comprises the county judge, who presides, and four elected commissioners. The latter serve staggered four-year terms—thus two commissioners are elected every two years.

Each commissioner is elected by voters residing in a commissioner's precinct. Boundary lines for a county's four commissioner precincts are set by its commissioners court, which is required to provide precincts of substantially equal population as mandated by the "one-man, one-vote" ruling of the U.S. Supreme Court in *Avery* v. *Midland County* (1968).

The term *commissioners court* is actually a misnomer because judicial functions are not involved. The court's major financial functions include adopting the county budget and setting tax rates. In performing these duties, the commissioners must observe state constitutional limitations on types of taxes and maximum tax rates. Power to decide how revenue will be used to finance functions prescribed by the state extends to building and maintaining county roads and bridges, operating a courthouse and a jail, and administering county health and welfare programs. Beyond this, a county is free to decide whether to enter other programs authorized but not required by the state. Within these limits, the commissioners court may establish and operate county hospitals, libraries, parks, airports, museums, and

Travis County Commissioners Court. Seated, left to right: Commissioners Henry Gonzalez and Pam Reed; County Judge Bill Aleshire; and Commissioners Bruce Todd and Samuel Biscoe conduct a weekly meeting in Austin, the county seat for Travis County. (Travis County Media.)

other public facilities. Increasing public demands for services rendered by these agencies impose on most counties an ever-expanding need for money.

Another major function of the commissioners court is the conduct of elections. The state leaves the administration (and expense) of virtually all general and special elections—national, state, and local—to the county; the exceptions are elections for municipal and special-district offices. Each county is divided into voting precincts by its commissioners court, which also canvasses or checks county election returns.

In addition to their collective responsibilities, members of a commissioners court have individual duties. Each commissioner serves as road and bridge administrator in a precinct, except in places where a county unit road system has been established. Frequently, money allotted for county roads and bridges is divided among the four precincts regardless of need. Lack of coordination and faulty administration are the inevitable result.

County Judge Major responsibility for administrative operations of the commissioners court is vested in a *county judge*, who is elected to a four-year term. Acting in an administrative capacity, the county judge presides over meetings of the commissioners court; in a judicial capacity, the judge hears cases in county court, but is not required to be a lawyer. (See Chapter 8 for information on county judges, justices of the peace, and constables.) The county judge is also the county budget officer unless the county has a population of 225,000 or more, in which case the county auditor performs that function or a budget officer is appointed by the commissioners court.

As a member of the election board, the county judge posts election notices, receives election returns from election judges in the precincts, presents these returns to the commissioners court for official canvassing, and then forwards the final results to the secretary of state. The judge also fills vacancies within the commissioners court, serves as a *notary public* (one who certifies documents, takes affidavits, and administers oaths), and is authorized to perform marriages.

County Attorney and County Sheriff The *county attorney* serves as legal adviser to county and precinct officers and represents the state in criminal cases. Some counties do not have a county attorney because the functions of that office are performed by a resident district attorney. The *county sheriff*, as chief law enforcement officer, is charged with keeping the peace of the county. In this capacity, the sheriff appoints deputies and is in charge of the county jail and its prisoners.

County Clerk and County Tax Assessor-Collector A *county clerk* keeps records and handles a variety of paperwork for both the county court and the commissioners court. In a county of fewer than 8,000 people, the county clerk may also be clerk of the district court when it is in session in that county. A county with a population of 8,000 or greater also has a district clerk, who is elected for a four-year term and works with the district courts in filing cases and scheduling trials. In addition, the county clerk is the recorder of legal documents (such as deeds, mortgages, and contracts) and the keeper of records of vital statistics (such as births and deaths). Responsibility for the administration of elections also extends to the county clerk, who certifies each candidate for a place on the general election ballot and prepares the ballot. Measured by the extent and variety of duties, the county clerk is one of the most important county officers.

The *tax assessor-collector* is primarily occupied with the collection of a county's general property tax. Beginning in 1982, the tax assessment function of this office was placed within a countywide tax appraisal district (defined on page 59) for each county. A county tax assessor-collector issues certificates of title and collects license fees for motor vehicles. Prior to 1977, voter registration was the exclusive responsibility of each tax assessor-collector; since then, however, a commissioners court may designate the county clerk as voting registrar or may appoint an election administrator. In counties of fewer than 10,000 people, duties of the tax assessor-collector and sheriff are combined in the latter's office, unless voters prefer to separate these offices.

County Treasurer and County Auditor The *county treasurer,* who is elected to a term of four years, receives and pays out all county funds authorized by the commissioners court. Payments are made by warrants signed by the treasurer and drawn on the county treasury. With constitutional amendments, the office of county treasurer has been abolished in Andrews, Bee, Bell, Bexar, Collin, El Paso, Fayette, Gregg, Nueces, and Tarrant counties. In these counties the treasurer's duties are now handled by other county officials designated by the commissioners court.

A county of 35,000 or more people with a county tax valuation in excess of $35 million must have a *county auditor,* who is appointed by the district court judge or, in a county having more than one district court, is selected by a majority of the total number of district judges in that county. In a county of 225,000 or more people, the auditor also serves as county budget officer. The auditing function involves checking account books and records of all county officials who handle county funds.

County Surveyor The *county surveyor* draws no salary but is paid for specific surveys of land within the county. In many counties, the office is not filled.

Appointed Officials Depending on the population of a county and the wishes of the voters and the commissioners court, several appointed officers are found in counties across the state. Whenever a county engages in activities authorized but not required by the Texas Constitution or state statutes, the commissioners court must appoint an administrative head to oversee the program. As an example, following enabling legislation by the Texas Legislature, Dallas County appointed a budget officer in 1977, the first office of this kind in the history of Texas county government. Federal grants-in-aid also involve the counties in programs requiring administrators for health, welfare, home demonstration, agricultural extension, and other programs.

County Finance

Just as the structure of county governments is frozen in the Texas Constitution, so is the county's power to tax and, to a lesser extent, its power to spend. The Constitution authorizes county governments to collect taxes on property and occupations. Although counties may constitutionally tax all property, they are restricted to taxing only those occupations already taxed by the state. Counties that are not part of a mass transit authority may levy a half-cent sales tax to supplement property taxes. As of January 1, 1990, more than 80 counties, after approval by the voters, had opted for this increase.

Each commissioners court determines annually the county tax rate for the fiscal year, which in Texas extends from September 1 to the following August 31. A commissioners court is limited to establishing the county's tax rate at a maximum of 80 cents for each $100 valuation. Money collected from this basic levy is distributed among general revenue, permanent improvement, road and bridge, and jury funds in each county treasury.

Additional property taxes may be imposed by a commissioners court, but only after approval by a majority of the county's qualified voters. A special road and bridge tax of 15 cents for each $100 valuation may be levied for maintenance of public roads, and a levy of 30 cents may be imposed for construction and maintenance of ranch- and farm-to-market roads and flood control facilities.

Revenues All forms of property are subject to ad valorem taxation (that is, taxation in proportion to value). Nearly $2.5 billion in property tax revenue went into Texas county treasuries in 1987–1988. Although state constitutional restrictions limit the categories of taxable property, the definition of valuation has been broadened since 1978. In that year Texas voters approved a tax relief amendment that mandates certain changes and permits the Legislature to enact others. One significant change requires the valuation of farm and ranch land to be made on the basis of productivity rather than market value. All other *real property* (such as buildings, mines, minerals, and quarries) continues to be assessed at market value. Also subject to ad valorem taxation is *tangible personal property* (goods located in the state). Exempted from taxation are government-owned property; household goods and personal effects not used in the production of income, including boats, aircraft, and recreational vehicles; holdings of certain designated private, charitable, educational, and religious institutions; farm products in the hands of producers; and family supplies for farm and home use. Also, the 71st Legislature proposed a constitutional amendment exempting property in transit (e.g., warehouse products, airplanes) from all taxation by local governments. Voters approved the amendment in November 1989.

The Legislature may allow a county to issue bonds, subject to voter approval. Revenue from the sale of bonds is used for capital outlays, such as payment for a new county courthouse or county jail. County indebtedness is limited by the Constitution to 35 percent of a county's total assessed property valuation.

As additional sources of income, counties may impose fees for liquor, wine, and beer permits; they also receive a percentage of the state gross receipts tax on liquor. Texas statutes also allow counties to share in revenues obtained from state motor vehicle registration fees, motor fuel taxes, and fees for issuance of certificates of title for motor vehicles. Federal grants-in-aid form another important source of county revenues, but the Reagan and Bush administrations severely reduced these grants in the 1980s. Congress has generally made counties eligible to receive any and all aid extended to cities and towns. For example, federal aid is given to counties for construction of hospitals, airports, and public housing.

Despite these revenue sources, Texas counties, like other units of local government, are caught in an ever-tightening revenue squeeze. Demands for county services and the cost of administration continue to increase, but sources of tax revenue for counties have not expanded significantly in many years. By 1990, property taxes were producing about 60 percent of county revenue in Texas. However, dependence on property tax revenue is perhaps the most dangerous trend in local government finance across the nation. Given the public's growing opposition to property taxes, both county and other local government officials must seriously consider finding alternative sources of revenue.

Expenditures   Although county expenditures are restricted by legal requirements and state administrative directives, patterns of spending vary considerably from county to county. Although the county judge or the county auditor prepares the budget, the commissioners court is responsible for final adoption of the annual spending plan. Maintenance of county roads and bridges continues to be the item requiring the largest expenditures in counties throughout the state.

Counties do not have complete control over their spending because state statutes and administrative directives require that certain county services be furnished and that regulatory activities be conducted. Thus counties are required to raise and spend funds for some purposes dictated by the state, not by county commissioners. Examples of such expenditures include welfare and mental health programs.

Property Tax Issue   Heavy reliance on the ad valorem tax on personal and business property brought many communities to the brink of a taxpayers' revolt in the late 1970s and early 1980s. In the 1980s, Texas cities with populations over 50,000 were levying property taxes totaling over $5 billion. All business and residential properties within each Texas county are now being assessed for tax purposes by the *countywide tax appraisal district.*

Now, as the result of a constitutional amendment, each of the 254 counties is required to operate with a single appraisal district per county. All tax-levying units of government within a county appoint representatives to the appraisal district board. To offset somewhat the jolt of higher taxes arising from reappraisals, local governments (including cities) may grant homeowners a 40 percent homestead exemption (reduction in tax assessment value of a home). In addition, the Texas Supreme Court has held that voters can force local governments to roll back property tax rates whenever the rates exceed an 8 percent increase from the previous year.[4] Submitting a petition of 10 percent of the registered voters in a county, municipality, or special district forces that government to call a rollback election within 90 days. A majority vote for or against a rollback proposition binds a local governing body to follow the voters' wishes.[5]

Reform Areas

Two basic problems underlie any organizational or power changes in county government: the governmental structure established in the Texas Constitution, and voter apathy about local governments in general and about county government in particular. The media can do much to overcome the latter problem. Whenever investigative reporting uncovers abuses of power and wrongdoing in county government, the activities of county officials should be held up to closer public scrutiny.

Ordinance-Making Power   There is consensus among Texas's county officials that their governments need ordinance-making power to regulate unincorporated areas outside city limits. Issues ranging from inadequate land development standards to social problems posed by massage parlors force counties to lobby the

Texas Legislature for local bills affecting only individual counties. But thus far, lawmakers have turned a deaf ear to the counties' alleged need for power to make their own local laws or ordinances.

Chief Executive Another change, as advocated by many students of county government, would entail establishing a single chief executive of the county. This proposal would go far toward eliminating lengthy ballots and would center administrative responsibility in a single chief executive elected directly by the people or appointed by a county commission. The county commissioners court could be renamed the county council, which would describe its present functions. Adoption of a county manager plan or county executive plan would require adding a county home-rule amendment to the Texas Constitution.

County Road System A third area of needed reform is the county road system, which in most counties is inefficient and uncoordinated. Wherever budgeted money for roads is divided four ways among precinct commissioners, the result is often a four-way struggle for power that sees commissioners concerned primarily with padding their individual road and bridge budgets to benefit political cronies. When each commissioner is free to carry out a road and bridge program on an individual basis, there is no guarantee that plans and operations of the four commissioners will be coordinated and that funds will be spent in a businesslike fashion.

Special Districts

Among units of government at the local level, the least known and least understood are *special-district governments.* They fall into two basic categories—school districts and nonschool districts. Junior or community college districts are special districts that provide services at the level of higher education. Created by act of the Legislature or in some cases by local ordinance (for example, a public housing authority), a special district usually has one function and serves a specific group of people in a particular geographic area. Special districts must be classified as units of government because they meet the following criteria:

1. Organized existence
2. Governmental character (for example, many exercise taxing power)
3. Substantial independence from other units of government

School Districts

For most Texans, the school district is the most important and visible special district. Currently, there are over 1,000 independent school districts in the state. These districts are headed by boards composed of nonsalaried members, usually elected for a three-year term. Given the nonsalaried status of the office, one may wonder why a citizen would seek membership on a school board. The answer lies in the many powers conferred on these boards by the Texas Legislature. Included among the more important powers are the following:

1. Setting personnel policy
2. Determining salary schedules
3. Providing for construction and maintenance of school buildings
4. Selecting textbooks from a list prepared by the State Textbook Committee
5. Setting the property tax rate for the district

In short, the local school board, working under guidelines established by state policy and federal mandates (such as court-ordered busing), sets the tone and direction for a community's schools.

Junior or Community College Districts

Another example of a special district is the junior college or community college district, which offers two-year academic programs beyond high school and provides various technical and vocational programs. Operated by 49 districts, Texas's 63 public junior or community colleges constitute the state's fastest-growing level of postsecondary education (see Table 3.1).

Unlike fully state-supported four-year colleges, universities, and technical institutes, most junior colleges are financed in part by local taxes. Approximately 17 percent of the financial support for junior colleges comes from local or district tax revenue; about 61 percent comes from state appropriations; another 15 percent comes from tuition and fees; and the remainder is obtained directly in the form of federal aid and miscellaneous sources, such as local scholarships. Principal financial responsibilities assumed by a junior college board include setting property tax rates, issuing bonds (subject to voter approval), and approving the annual budget.

Nonschool Districts

If 1,100 municipalities, over 1,000 school districts, and 254 counties were not enough local government for Texas taxpayers to bear, scores of other governments have been created. Each carries out a special function. Heading the list are over 1,300 water-related districts, followed by 416 housing authorities, 208 soil and water conservation districts, 117 hospital districts, 115 local fire prevention districts, 24 hospital authorities, 15 health districts, 11 mosquito control districts, 6 mass transit authorities (Houston, Dallas, San Antonio, Austin, Fort Worth, Corpus Christi), 5 noxious weed control districts, 3 emergency medical services districts, 2 municipal power agencies, 1 waste disposal authority, 1 ground water subsidence district, and 1 urban renewal agency (San Antonio).[6] Jail districts may also be created by counties. As authorized by a 1966 amendment to the Texas Constitution, airport authorities may be created by an act of the Legislature. Only one airport authority currently exists in Texas—the Dallas–Fort Worth (DFW) International Airport. Cities own and administer municipal airports. The Dallas–Fort

TABLE 3.1 Public Junior (Community) College Enrollment in Texas, Fall 1988

Enrollment Category	Institutions (in descending order of enrollment)
23,854	Houston Community
22,447	Alamo Community, San Antonio
21,470	Austin Community
15,272	El Paso Community (total for 3 campuses)
13,305	North Harris County Community
12,996	Dallas County Community, Richland
10,000–11,990	Tarrant County Junior, Northeast; Tarrant County Junior, South
8,000–9,999	San Jacinto, Central; Dallas County Community, Eastfield; Del Mar; Tyler Junior; Lee; Collin County Community
6,000–7,999	Dallas County Community, Brookhaven; Alamo Community, St. Philip's; Dallas County Community, North Lake
5,000–5,999	Amarillo; Dallas County Community, Mountain View; Dallas County Community, El Centro; Texas Southmost College; McLennan Community; Blinn; Central Texas*
4,000–4,999	Odessa; Tarrant County Junior, Northwest; Laredo Junior; Kilgore; Alvin Community; South Plains; San Jacinto, South; Trinity Valley Community
3,000–3,999	Midland; Brazosport; Texarkana; College of the Mainland; San Jacinto, North; Victoria; Grayson County; Dallas County Community, Cedar Valley; Alamo Community, Palo Alto; Galveston
2,000–2,999	Wharton County Junior; Angelina; Southwest Texas Junior; Temple Junior; Paris Junior; Cooke County; Bee County; Weatherford
1,000–1,999	Vernon Regional Junior; Cisco Junior; Northeast Texas Community; Hill Junior; Panola Junior; Howard County, Big Spring
100–999	Western Texas; Frank Phillips; Clarendon; Ranger Junior

*The 71st Legislature changed Central Texas College to a four-year institution that, if approved by the Texas Higher Education Coordinating Board, will begin operations by September 1, 1994.

Source: Higher Education Coordinating Board.

Worth airport is administered by a separate 11-member (7 from Dallas, 4 from Fort Worth) city council–appointed board with power to issue revenue bonds for airport operations. This special-district government is the result of a contract between Dallas and Fort Worth.

Creation of a special district stems from a combination of legislative, constitutional, economic, and governmental relationships. The objective of such an effort is to meet a special need of a particular locale, which may consist of two or more counties, part of one or more counties, or a single county. These special districts often overcome restrictions placed on municipalities and counties by the Texas Constitution. Therefore, many public hospitals, as an example, have been built by hospital districts because they operate on a multicounty basis, reaching beyond city limits and county lines.

The Politics of Special Districts

One of the most significant causes for the proliferation of nonschool districts lies in the cozy relationships among land developers, bankers, and legislators. Out of this axis of power have sprung hundreds of municipal utility districts (MUDs) around Texas's central cities. In the Houston area alone, over 500 MUDs have been created since 1969. A common practice is for a subdivision builder to finance a project with a bank loan at high interest rates, to lobby for state or local action creating a MUD that provides water or other services, to elect the governing board of the MUD from a handful of the builder's friends in the subdivision, and to conduct a bond election to pay off the loan. Retirement of the bonds will be fulfilled either by residents, most of whom move into the subdivision after the bond election has been held, or by the taxpayers of a neighboring city, if the subdivision is annexed. In either case, a new government has been added through one of the most undemocratic methods within the Texas political system.

Governments of most special districts have the power to raise revenue through property taxes or sales taxes. As examples, the Greater Houston Metropolitan Transit Authority (MTA) and the Dallas Area Rapid Transit Authority (DART) levy a 1 percent sales tax. Public pressure to relieve traffic congestion in these cities prompted a favorable vote to create MTA and DART. Thus, another unit of government was created for Houstonians, Dallasites, and residents of surrounding communities that voted to join within these metropolitan areas. Petitions, requiring signatures of at least 20 percent of the registered voters in a DART-served city, can force a withdrawal election. The cities of Flower Mound (Denton County) and Coppell (Dallas County) exercised this option and withdrew from DART in 1989. DART came under close scrutiny by the 71st Legislature, resulting in the requirement of periodic audits of its financial records by the state auditor beginning in 1990.

Metropolitan Areas

According to U.S. Census estimates, Texas will surpass New York before the year 2000 and become the nation's second most populous state. Of Texas's 16 million people, 80 percent live in metropolitan areas surrounding and including Dallas, Houston, San Antonio, Austin, El Paso, and Fort Worth. Ringing these and other Texas cities are rapidly growing suburban communities with municipal and special-district governments that further fragment local governance. An ever-tightening squeeze on property taxes underlies metropolitan problems more than any other issue. Furthermore, many critics question the wisdom of continuing to attack problems involving transportation, education, pollution, crime, and housing through the fragmenting approach of more and more special districts.

How will Texas's metropolitan areas be governed in the future? Given the complex legal and political impediments to any comprehensive overhaul of existing governmental structures, practical answers to these complex problems are needed.

Councils of Governments

Over the past two decades, the most widely used approach to the metropolitan problem has been the creation of *councils of governments* or, in some areas, planning commissions or planning associations. Commonly referred to as COGs, these organizations are composed of representatives from various units of local government within each of 24 regions.

Membership in a COG is voluntary. Furthermore, COGs do not attempt to usurp the local autonomy of any governmental unit. They perform regional planning activities and deliver other services that are requested by member governments. Stringent guidelines for federal grants to local governments have done much to encourage the growth and utilization of COGs. Through a "review-and-comment" procedure, local officials in cooperation with COGs draft and implement state- and federally funded programs. The term *review and comment* refers to a COG's evaluation function concerning grant proposals submitted by member governments. If, for example, a city wants to construct a new water treatment facility with federal or state funds, a COG would determine how the facility would affect other governments in the COG. Some critics of COGs argue that these regional forums are the first step toward *metro government*, which is currently in use in Toronto, Canada; Miami, Florida; Nashville–Davidson County, Tennessee; and on a smaller scale, Portland, Oregon. Metro government results in consolidation of existing local governments in an urban area under one umbrella authority. But COGs are not governments; they have neither taxing nor lawmaking authority.

Stopgap Approaches

Aside from the use of councils of governments, other means of coping with metropolitan problems tend to be Band-Aid solutions for serious illnesses. Three of the principal approaches are discussed below.

Municipal Annexation   In an attempt to provide statewide guidelines for cities grappling with suburban sprawl, the Texas Legislature passed a *municipal annexation law* in 1963. This statute allows Texas cities to annex territory beyond their corporate limits by following certain restrictions to protect the citizens involved:

1. Generally, territories annexed during a calendar year may not exceed 10 percent of a city's area as of January 1 and, depending on a city's population, must be within one-half mile to five miles of the city limit.
2. When the unincorporated area is annexed, the city must provide services (for example, water and sewage) for the area; otherwise residents of the annexed area can petition a state district court for deannexation.

3. An adjoining suburb of the central city may be annexed by the central city, but only after voter approval in both the central and suburban communities.

One of the most controversial features of the annexation law stems from the unilateral action taken by a city council when it passes an ordinance to annex an unincorporated area, thus depriving residents in the annexed area of an opportunity to vote on the proposal.

Intergovernmental Contracting Another trend in metropolitan areas is for local governments to contract for services when one government lacks funds to do the job alone. *Intergovernmental contracting* arrangements facilitate intergovernmental cooperation, but this is not a long-range solution to governing metropolitan areas.

Special Districts A special district may provide a service that otherwise would be missing. Two successful metropolitan special districts in Texas are the Dallas–Fort Worth Airport Authority, which provides air transportation facilities that service the North Texas area, and the Gulf Coast Waste Disposal Authority, which operates water pollution and industrial waste treatment facilities in three refinery-impacted counties—Harris, Galveston, and Chambers—on the Texas Gulf Coast.

Future Alternatives

Texas's basic conservatism leads to the conclusion that sweeping changes at the local level, including a proposal for any variation of metro government, are not feasible in the near future. Safer assumptions for the future, however, are threefold. First, because of the scope of its jurisdiction, the county could take the lead in providing more urban-oriented services; but urban counties must be freed from their constitutional chains before they can attack most problems that transcend municipal jurisdictions. Second, existing COGs are perhaps in the best position to provide expertise and leadership for member governments in working on metropolitan problems, particularly those related to transportation. Third, given cutbacks in federal funding, along with legislative redistricting that has resulted in increased representation for urban areas, the 1990s promise to see an expanded role for state government in dealing with Texas's urban problems.

Noteworthy, for example, is the Legislature's creation of the *Texas High-Speed Rail Authority* (THRA), responsible for connecting Texas cities with mass transit. Inspired by successful European rail systems, this state agency is governed by a nine-member board of directors. By statute, the board members serve six-year staggered terms, with four persons appointed by the governor, subject to Senate confirmation. One of the gubernatorial appointees must be a director for a regional transportation authority. Five directors head other governing bodies as chairmen of the State Highway and Public Transportation Commission, the Texas Turnpike Authority, the Railroad Commission, a regional transportation authority, and a metropolitan transit authority. Possessing neither taxing nor bond-issuance authority, THRA is empowered to plan, construct, operate, and maintain a high-speed rail facility with franchises awarded to private contractors. Emphasis is being placed on connecting Houston and Dallas with a "super train." What follows from this initial effort could be an innovative statewide program that could help local governments.

Conclusion

A difficult paradox persists in trying to understand Texas's local governments. On one hand, county governments, with their formidable legislative lobbying efforts, resist legislative attempts to overhaul their structures. On the other hand, most residents in metropolitan areas are demanding improved governmental services that place a heavy strain on available revenue sources.

Lord Bryce, a British scholar, concluded in 1889: "The government of cities is the one conspicuous failure of the United States."[7] One hundred years later, some critics believe that his observation applies to the Lone Star State's current urban scene. Solutions for problems of Texas's population centers will require intensive commitment from planners and policymakers alike. Action by an informed citizenry, however, remains the key catalyst in forcing changes that will modernize units of local government.

Notes

1. See Alan Beals, "Council-Manager Relations," *Texas Town & City*, May 1987, pp. 13, 23.
2. Paul Flynn and Charles Knerr, "Tax Increment Financing," paper presented at a meeting of the Southwestern Political Science Association, San Antonio, March 1986.
3. Charldean Newell, Laura L. Vertz, Linda Lohrke, and Michael Webb, "The Use of Professionalized Personnel Management Tools and Techniques in Texas County Governments," *The Municipal Matrix*, April 1987, pp. 1–4.
4. See *Ellis County* v. *Winborne* and *Vinson* v. *Burgess* in *Texas Supreme Court Journal*, 32 (May 31, 1989), pp. 418–424.
5. *Texas Tax Code Annotated*, 26.07, 26.08 (Vernon 1982), pp. 344–347.
6. This list is an updated (1989) extension of the compilation in Peggy Hamilton, *Special District Governments in Texas* (Austin: Texas Advisory Commission on Intergovernmental Relations, June 1977), pp. 5–14, as well as José Jorge Anchondo, *Special Districts: A Growing Form of Government in Texas Metropolitan Areas* (Austin: Texas Advisory Commission on Intergovernmental Relations, March 1985), pp. 1–10.
7. Quoted by Arnold P. Fleischmann, "Balancing New Skylines," *Texas Humanist*, January/February 1984, p. 31.

Key Terms and Concepts

grassroots governments
referendum
initiative
ordinance
general-law city
home-rule city
recall
strong mayor–council form
weak mayor–council form
commission form
council-manager form
nonpartisan
single-member district
at-large system
place system
ordinance-making power
franchise fee
general obligation bond
revenue bond
county
commissioners court

Avery v. *Midland County*
county judge
notary public
county attorney
county sheriff
county clerk
tax assessor-collector
county treasurer
county auditor
county surveyor
real property
tangible personal property
countywide tax appraisal district
special-district government
council of governments
review and comment
metro government
municipal annexation law
intergovernmental contracting
Texas High-Speed Rail Authority

Selected Readings

3.1 David vs. Goliath: A Neighborhood Challenges City Hall

James Ragland

Increasingly, Texas residents are affecting public policy through grassroots organizations. This reading exemplifies how residents in a Dallas neighborhood accomplished their goals by working with their homeowners' association.

Legs crossed, a young high school student sat attentively facing "the horseshoe," a semicircular dais around which 15 Dallas City Planning Commission members were discussing a controversial zoning case. After more than two hours of heated debate among commission members, the student cupped her face in her hands, let out a deep sigh and lazily leaned over to pose a question to a reporter. "Why," she asked, "don't they just let the guy build a shopping center on his land? It's a free country, isn't it?" Zoning cases often perplex observers of municipal politics. Such is the case that follows.

Background on Zoning

Dallas, as well as all other Texas cities and other municipalities, has the power to determine appropriate zoning for land within its borders. Zoning is employed to control how land is used and to limit the size and type of structures. Theoretically, zoning protects property owners by preventing conflicting land uses—such as building a factory in the middle of a neighborhood.

Changes in zoning can significantly affect property values. A rezoning that allows a shopping center to be built where an apartment complex once stood could dramatically increase land prices. And, on a smaller scale, permitting a two-story building instead of a one-story structure can make the difference between a profit or loss for a developer.

Municipal zoning is a process by which a city is carved up into districts which regulate the use of land. The city of Dallas, for example, has more than three dozen districts—each of which permits different land uses: heights for buildings, density of developments, and setbacks from adjoining properties. As clinical as it may sound, deciding the proper zoning for a tract of land is hardly ever a black-and-white issue of "what's best for the city." Politics is involved.

Land Developer's Case

On April 21, 1988, L. R. Taylor Interests, Inc., a group of investors led by its namesake, L. R. Taylor, went before the Dallas City Planning Commission seeking to change the

This reading was prepared especially for *Practicing Texas Politics*. James Ragland is a staff writer for the *Dallas Morning News*. Printed by permission.

zoning on a 14.6-acre site from "multifamily-1" to a "planned development district for community retail uses." Mr. Taylor did not own the land at the time, but intended to purchase the property from Federal Home Savings—if the zoning change were approved.

Under the multifamily zoning, Mr. Taylor was restricted to building apartments on the land. Apartments were already there, but they were unoccupied and many were dilapidated. Mr. Taylor proposed to demolish the vacant apartment complex and instead build a shopping center with an Albertson's supermarket and a pharmacy. To do that, he needed different and broader zoning provisions.

Mr. Taylor's task was to convince city zoning officials that his proposal represented an appropriate use of the land, a use that would not adversely impact surrounding properties. Mr. Taylor hired one of the city's foremost zoning experts, lawyer Kirk Williams, to state his case. Mr. Williams and Mr. Taylor cleared the first hurdle with relative ease, as the city planning staff recommended to the planning commission that the zoning change be approved: "The proposed use would not adversely impact the surrounding properties. The property to the north, across Skillman Street, remains undeveloped and is part of the former telephone training facility. The property to the east, across Larmanda Street, is developed with retail uses; therefore, the request is compatible with the area," the city planning staff concluded in its recommendation to the commission.

Armed with the planning staff's stamp of approval—and with overwhelming support from neighboring homeowners—Mr. Taylor and Mr. Williams appeared to be coasting to a zoning victory. But, as is normal in a zoning case, the opposition has an equal amount of time to state its case.

A Grocery Chain Enters

Leading the opposition was Neil Anderson, an attorney representing Cullum Companies, the parent company of Tom Thumb-Page and Simon David supermarkets. Mr. Anderson argued that the proposed zoning change should be denied because there were too many retail stores already in the area in question and that another major shopping center would cause traffic congestion. More community retail, Mr. Anderson contended, was not needed and was therefore not the best use of the land. Mr. Anderson urged that the 14.6-acre site remain zoned as multifamily.

In three months, Cullum Companies was scheduled to open a new supermarket at the intersection of Abrams Road and Skillman Street, about 1,000 feet from where the Albertson's would be built.

The Dilemma

The planning commission's job was to sift through the rhetoric and decide on the merits of the case; specifically, whether the proposed zoning change would represent an appropriate use of the land. Mr. Taylor's zoning request was narrowly rejected, ostensibly meaning that eight commission members believed that community retail would be an inappropriate use of the land, which was surrounded by a combination of residential and retail uses, a church, and undeveloped land.

But Mr. Taylor and Mr. Williams argued that politics, not land-use issues, swayed the planning commission. Mr. Taylor and Mr. Williams accused Cullum Companies of trying to block competition. They also questioned the presence of former Dallas Mayor Jack Evans at the commission meeting when the zoning case was decided. Mr. Evans, chief executive officer of Cullum Companies, Inc., did not address the commission, but Mr. Williams contended the former mayor's presence intimidated the commission.

A week later, the planning commission surprisingly decided to reconsider its decision. After a brief but heated debate, the commission voted 8–6 to reopen the public hearing on June 2 to once again review Mr. Taylor's request. Two commission members admitted that they voted against the zoning change for reasons other than appropriate land use. One member said she voted against the request because she thought there were tenants occupying the apartment complex that Mr. Taylor planned to demolish. Another commission member said she simply got caught in the crossfire as Tom Thumb's attorney argued with Mr. Williams and Mr. Taylor about the economic viability of the proposed Albertson's. The opposing attorney, she conceded after the April 28 meeting, succeeded in clouding the issue.

On June 2, the planning commission reversed its earlier decision and voted 9–4 for the zoning change; two commission members were absent. The planning commission's recommendation was then forwarded to the City Council, the body empowered to make the ultimate decision.

Homeowners Organize

About 125 neighboring residents packed the City Council chambers on July 13 to show their support for the zoning change. They presented a petition signed by 678 area residents—roughly 95 percent of the affected community. The Dallas Homeowners' League and the Merriman Park–University Manor Neighborhood Association also overwhelmingly endorsed the proposal. But the Texas Tenants Union opposed the zoning change because the group did not want the apartment complex destroyed. One black resident also testified in support of keeping the apartments.

The City Council voted 9–1 for the request. One black council member, Al Lipscomb, voted against it because he said he was concerned about destroying the apartments to make room for more retail. The other black council member, Deputy Mayor Pro Tempore Diane Ragsdale, voted with the majority.

Conclusion

Grassroots support for the zoning change ultimately was the deciding factor in this case study. Elected politicians were swayed by both the petition and the visible clout of residents who appeared *en masse* before the Dallas City Council. Through their neighborhood association, these Dallas activists challenged a major Dallas Corporation, Cullum Companies, and the clout of its chief executive officer, former Mayor Jack Evans. Furthermore, many residents who signed the petition and boarded the bus to appear at the Council meeting were senior citizens, who had lived in this neighborhood for 20 years or more. Once again, participating democracy refuted the notion that "you can't beat city hall."

Chapter 4

The Politics of Elections and Parties

Reprinted with special permission of King Features Syndicate, Inc.

*T*his chapter is about elections—Texas elections—and about the state's Democratic and Republican parties. To conduct elections, there must be voters, as suggested by the cartoon that opens this chapter. In order to attract voters, offices are needed together with candidates seeking election to those offices. If elections are free, political parties will be formed to select candidates and to influence the election outcome and the policy issues involved. Election laws are essential to ensure fairness and to guard against fraud. Geographic voting precincts must be established, ballots provided, and election officials selected and assigned to polling places. Eligible voters need to be informed of election dates and places, of candidates and parties. Money is needed by candidates for payment of election campaign expenses.

When Texas was a sparsely populated, primarily rural, one-party Democratic state, the conduct of elections was relatively simple. By the last decade of the twentieth century, however, the electoral process had become quite complex in an urbanized, industrialized Texas—the nation's third most populous state. For example, Texas election laws are detailed, and campaign policy issues require citizens' time and attention for adequate understanding. Because most candidates must use the electronic media to communicate with voters, campaigns are expensive at all levels of government. We begin our study of electoral processes by first examining the Texas voter.

The Politics of Elections

A basic prerequisite of democratic government is free elections (those scheduled at regular intervals with two or more parties and candidates competing and practically all adult citizens permitted to participate). Through the process of free elections, citizens in a representative democracy choose those who are to govern. At the ballot box, voters indirectly set public policies that affect their lives. For most Texans, voting is their principal participation in the political process. Exercise of the right to vote is a cherished civil right. The U.S. Supreme Court has declared voting to be the "preservative" of all other rights. Casting the ballot brings individuals and their government close together for a moment and reminds people anew that they are a part of that government.

The Texas Voter

Freedom of the ballot has not always been as widespread in the United States or in Texas as it is today. *Universal suffrage,* which means that almost all adults can vote, did not become a reality in Texas until about 25 years ago.

Democratization of the Ballot In America, obstacles to suffrage have been removed by successive waves of democratization. Adopted after the Civil War, the Fourteenth and Fifteenth Amendments to the U.S. Constitution were intended to prevent denial of the right to vote because of race. But for the next 100 years black citizens in Texas and other states of the Confederacy were prevented from voting by one barrier after another—legal and extralegal. For example, the white-robed Ku Klux Klan and other lawless groups used terrorist tactics to keep blacks from voting.

The so-called *white primary,* largely a product of Texas political and legal maneuvering, was designed to deny blacks access to the Democratic primary. That primary was the real election in predominantly one-party southern states where Democrats won the general elections. The Texas Legislature and the Texas Democratic party generally were able to keep blacks from voting in Democratic primaries from 1923 to 1944, when the practice was declared unconstitutional by the U.S. Supreme Court in *Smith* v. *Allwright.*[1]

A *poll tax* as a prerequisite for voting was also required in Texas, beginning in 1902. For the next 60 years, low-income people, including disproportionately large numbers of blacks and Mexican Americans, frequently failed to pay the poll tax during the designated four-month period from October 1 to January 31. This in turn disqualified them from voting during the following 12 months in either a party primary or the general election. With ratification of the Twenty-fourth Amendment to the federal Constitution in January 1964, the poll tax as a prerequisite for voting in national elections was abolished. Then, in *Harper* v. *Virginia State Board of Elections* (1966), the U.S. Supreme Court invalidated all state laws that made payment of a poll tax a prerequisite for voting in state elections.

To democratize the ballot even more, Congress added its weight to the effort with a series of election laws that culminated in the Voting Rights Act of 1965. These laws, together with federal court rulings, provide additional guarantees against denial of the right to vote. Included are safeguards that restrict the use of literacy tests, reduce the period of time required for residency in a state as a condition for voting, and require all states to provide for absentee voting. In addition, the services of federal administrative and judicial agencies have been made more directly available to persons whose voting rights are denied or abridged. This imposing body of congressional legislation, together with federal court orders, has removed almost every obstacle to exercising the right to vote. In practice, these new safeguards have been particularly applicable to situations involving minority groups.

Amendments to the U.S. Constitution have been equally impressive in expanding the American electorate. The Fifteenth Amendment, already mentioned, prohibits the denial of voting rights because of race; the Nineteenth precludes denial of suffrage on the basis of sex; the Twenty-fourth prohibits states from requiring payment of a poll tax as a condition for voting; and the Twenty-sixth forbids setting the minimum voting age above 18 years.

In Texas, as in all the states, the conduct of elections is essentially a state responsibility. All state election laws currently in effect in Texas are compiled into one body of law, the Texas Election Code. In administering this body of state election laws, voting rights guaranteed by federal law may neither be abridged nor denied to Texas voters.

Qualifications for Voting in Texas   As a result of federal expansion of the ballot by constitutional amendments, statutes, and judicial decisions, Texans now enjoy virtually universal suffrage. But to vote in Texas, a person must have the following qualifications:

1. Be a native-born or naturalized citizen of the United States
2. Be at least 18 years of age on or before election day
3. Be a resident of the state for at least 30 days immediately preceding election day, of the county for at least 30 days immediately preceding election day, and of the election precinct on election day
4. Be a registered voter for at least 30 days immediately preceding election day

The avowed purpose of *voter registration* is to help determine in advance whether those desiring to vote have all the qualifications prescribed by law. Most states, including Texas, use a permanent registration system today. Under this plan, voters register once and remain registered unless they change their permanent residential address and fail to notify the voting registrar of the new address. Currently, the Texas Election Code allows citizens to register in person at the office of the *county voting registrar,* who is the tax assessor-collector unless the county commissioners court designates the county clerk or appoints an elections administrator.

Registration by mail is also permitted by law; and a member of the same family (husband, wife, father, mother, brother, sister), if already registered, may in turn register for other members. Upon receipt by the registrar of a properly completed voter registration application form, an initial registration certificate is mailed to the voter. Thereafter, between November 1 and November 15 of each year in which no general election is held (each successive odd-numbered year), the registrar mails to every registered voter of the county a registration certificate effective for the succeeding two voting years. A certificate mailed to the address indicated on the voter's application form may not be forwarded by postal authorities to a different mailing address; it must be returned to the registrar and canceled. This process enables the county voting registrar to maintain an accurate and up-to-date list of names and mailing addresses of persons to whom voting certificates have been issued. Such a file is open to public inspection in the county voting registrar's office. From these county lists, a statewide registration file is maintained in Austin, where it is available to the public.

The color of voting certificate cards mailed to voters in November of each odd-numbered year and effective for the following two years is different from the color of those sent two years earlier. For example, cards mailed to voters in 1985 were yellow, those sent in 1987 were white, and cards mailed in 1989 (effective for 1990 and 1991) were pink. As the 1988 election approached, the Mexican-American Democrats (MAD) urged Texas voters to "Vote White in 88." Such a slogan had a twofold purpose. It warned that the yellow 1986–1987 certificate was no longer valid, and it urged white-card holders to vote. According to MAD president Ruben Bonilla, the Hispanic constituency is affected disproportionately by the biannual purging or updating of the registration rolls. He said that the Mexican-American community has comparatively more renters than homeowners and more younger members than are found within the Anglo voting population. The result is that a greater proportion of Hispanic voters fail to renew their registrations.

A person serving a jail sentence as a result of a misdemeanor is not disqualified from voting. The Texas Constitution, however, bars from voting anyone who is incarcerated, on parole, or on probation as a result of a felony conviction and anyone who is "mentally incompetent as determined by a court." Convicted felons may vote two years after completing their sentences or immediately following a full pardon. (See Table 8.1, pp. 204–205, for examples of misdemeanors and felonies.)

Two Trends in the Suffrage   From this overview of suffrage, we plainly see two trends emerging. First, there has been a steady expansion of voting rights to include virtually all persons of both sexes who are 18 years of age or older. Second, there has been a movement toward uniformity of voting policies among the 50 states. It is a fact, however, that the democratization of the ballot has been pressed upon the states largely by the federal government. States lagged in expanding the suffrage until prodded by federal action, because all voting—national, state, and local—is administered by the states. There is no national election machinery. Therefore, the states rather than the federal government have been more likely to engage in discriminatory election practices.

Voters and Nonvoters   Now that nearly all legal barriers hindering access to the ballot have been swept away, the road to the voting booth seems clear for rich and poor alike, for minority groups as well as for the majority, for those of all races, colors, and creeds. But universal suffrage has not resulted in a corresponding increase in *voter turnout,* either nationally or in Texas.

Just as voter turnout in the United States is below that in other countries with democratic forms of government, turnout in Texas is below that in the rest of the United States. Few people believe their vote will determine an election outcome. Yet with a million and a half votes cast in the Texas Democratic party's first primary in 1984, only 243 votes separated the two leading candidates for U.S. senator. The number of votes separating the top three candidates was so low that one more vote cast in each county could have reversed the Democratic nomination and possibly the ultimate election of a U.S. senator from Texas.

Decisions by the people to vote or not to vote are made in the same way that other decisions are made—on the basis of anticipated consequences. A strong impulse to vote stems from a sense of duty toward one's country, state, political party, interest group, candidate, or to oneself. Decisions to vote or refrain from voting are also made on the basis of cost measured in time, money, experience, information, job, or other resources. The easier it is to cast a ballot, the more likely a person is to vote. Voting, however, requires more than merely going to the polls and casting a ballot on election day. Persons must first register. Then they will need to decide on which candidates, party, and issues to support. These essentials require time, study, travel, and attention. Generally, the poor and uneducated find the cost of voting higher than do middle- and upper-income citizens. Those with greater resources can more easily bear the costs involved.

Of all the socioeconomic influences on voting, education is by far the strongest. Statistics clearly indicate that as educational level rises, people are more likely to vote if all other socioeconomic factors remain constant. The effect of education on voting is greatest for those with the least education. Schooling tends to reduce the cost of voting. For example, educated people usually have more income and leisure time for voting; moreover, education enhances one's ability to learn about political parties, candidates, and issues. Persons with education can better comply with voting regulations, learn how and when to register, understand instructions for filling out forms, and follow and interpret coverage of political campaigns by television, newspapers, and other media.

Though far less important than education, age and sex do relate to voting behavior. Women are slightly more likely to vote than men. The voting rate for females declines somewhat after age 40, but males continue to vote after age 65 at about the same rate as in middle age. Married people, both men and women, are more likely to vote than the unmarried, including those divorced, separated, or widowed.

Ethnicity, too, influences voter turnout. The turnout rate for blacks is still substantially below that for Anglos. Blacks tend to be younger, less well educated, and lower on the socioeconomic scale. When these deficiencies are removed, however, there seems to be no difference in turnout between the two racial groups. Like blacks, Mexican Americans also tend to be younger, less well educated, and poorer than Anglos. Though Hispanic voter turnout rates are below the state average in general elections, in Democratic primary contests Mexican-American turnout has exceeded the state average since 1980.

Weakness of party competition has contributed to low voter turnout in Texas, but this condition is becoming less significant. Since 1950, Texas Republicans have seriously challenged the long-dominant Democrats in statewide, district, and county electoral contests as well as in presidential elections. Additionally, prior to the 1980s, the large percentage of blacks and Mexican Americans in the state accounted in part for the low voter turnout. In the 1980s, however, both registration and voting by these two minority groups have increased sharply. Yet many blacks and Mexican Americans still are not assimilated into an electoral process that is overwhelmingly Anglo-dominated. For example, Anglo candidates are more likely than minority candidates to receive endorsements (that is, public statements by influential individuals or groups in support of a candidate). Anglo-related issues are generally emphasized more in campaigns by the two major political parties than are minority issues. Officeholding by blacks and Mexican Americans still is limited largely to local and district positions.

It is highly unlikely that low voter turnout produced by poverty and lack of education would be raised by laws designed to free the ballot and increase voter participation. Significant voting-rights legislation of the last two decades has had little or no effect on voter turnout. Until deep-seated social ills are materially improved in Texas, voter turnout is likely to remain below the level of the rest of the nation.

Another widespread belief concerning voting habits holds that the frustrating apathy and neglect of people who fail to vote can be traced to the trouble they encounter in registering. For example, many concerned citizens believe that a lengthy registration period prior to an election contributes significantly to low voter turnout. Persons wishing to vote in Texas must be registered 30 days prior to an election. This requirement has led voter analysts to advocate a so-called same-day registration plan that would allow registration on election day. Legislation considered by the U.S. Congress in 1989 would require states to permit registration and voting on the same day. Three states—Minnesota, Wisconsin, and Maine—allow same-day registration and voting. Those opposed to such permissive voting procedures hold that same-day registration invites abuse of the ballot, especially in big cities that are noted for widespread voting fraud. They point out that the reason for low voter turnout is that most nonvoters simply do not want to vote. Such apathy can be traced to myriad causes unrelated to registration.

Another voter registration plan, debated but not enacted into law by the 71st Texas Legislature, targets an estimated 4 million of the state's unregistered adults. This program would give all adult Texans who are doing business with a state agency an opportunity to register. For example, anyone applying for a driver's license, for food stamps, or for enrollment in a state university would be offered a voter registration application. Advocates of this registration plan estimate that no less than 400,000 unregistered Texans would register during the first year. These advocates also believe that if such a registration plan were adopted, it would be the first step toward automatic registration whereby a person could automatically become registered to vote—for example, by applying for a driver's license.

Primary Elections

Not all Texas elections are of the partisan type. For example, all municipal and public school elections are nonpartisan. This means that candidates for these offices are neither identified with nor nominated by a political party. On the other hand, all partisan elections are preceded by formal nominating procedures in which political parties choose candidates to run under a party label in the general election.

Direct Primary Although the convention method is still used for party nomination of candidates for president and vice president of the United States, every state now uses some form of the *direct primary* for nominating other candidates for public office. The direct primary is a unique product of American political ingenuity. It was designed to provide a nominating method that would avoid boss domination and allow wider participation by party members. This form of nomination permits party members to select their candidates directly at the polls on primary election day. For each office (except president and vice president of the United States), party members select by popular vote the person they wish to represent their party in the general election in which candidates of all parties compete. Texas adopted the direct primary in 1903 and, with subsequent revisions, has continued its use to the present.

In two-party states outside the South, the person receiving the most votes (a plurality) for a particular office becomes the party nominee. But in Texas and most southern states (except Virginia and Tennessee), an absolute majority (over 50 percent) is required for nomination. When the *first primary* does not produce such a majority, a *run-off primary* is held to allow party members to choose a candidate from the two top contenders in the first primary. While seeking the Democratic party's nomination in the presidential campaign of 1984, Jesse Jackson called for abolition of the run-off primary. He contended that a minority candidate, after receiving a plurality of votes in the first primary, usually cannot win a majority of votes over a white (Anglo) opponent in the run-off contest.

Three rather indistinct forms of the direct primary, determined by who is permitted to participate, have evolved on the American political scene. In the two states using the *blanket primary* (Washington and Alaska), no party identification of the voter is required. All eligible voters are given the same ballot on which are printed the names of all candidates and their party labels. Voters may vote for candidates regardless of party affiliation. A half dozen other states use the *open primary,* in which voters are not required to declare their party affiliation. Most states use some form of *closed primary,* in which party identification of the voter is required, either when registering or when voting in the primary. The Texas Election Code identifies the Texas variety as a closed primary. In essence, however, it is an open primary because there is no requirement of party identification at the time of registration. Registration certificates are stamped with the party label when voters participate in a primary. Texas law permits qualified voters to vote in the primary of any party, provided they have not already voted in another party primary. Persons who have voted in the first primary of one party may not vote in the second or run-off primary of another party.

According to the Texas Election Code, persons are considered members of a political party holding a primary election when they have voted in that party's primary or have participated in a convention of that party. While voting, a voter may read at the top of the ballot the following statement: "I am a Democrat (Republican) and understand that I am ineligible to vote or participate in another political party's primary election or convention during this voting year." Write-in votes are disallowed in primary elections except for party offices of precinct chair and county chair.

Bonds of party loyalty in Texas are loose at election time. Whether this is a result of the openness of the primary makes little difference. Since the early 1950s, it has been common practice in Texas for persons to participate in the primary of the Democratic party and then cross over to vote for one or more of the candidates of the Republican party in the general election. This practice of *crossover voting* is evidence of a long-term trend toward voter independence of traditional party ties. Frequently, Texas voting statistics have revealed instances wherein many votes were cast for candidates in the Democratic party primary while only a few votes were cast in the Republican primary. But in the general election of the same year, some Republican candidates defeated or almost defeated their Democratic opponents.

Texas voting behavior is changing, however. Election of a Republican governor in 1978 and 1986 and capture of the state by the Republican presidential–vice presidential ticket in six of the last ten presidential elections (1952–1988) have changed the face of the Texas Republican party. Throughout the 1980s, the state

GOP (Grand Old Party) increased its membership in the Texas Legislature while growing stronger at the county and precinct levels of government. As more local offices were won by Republicans, GOP voters became less tempted to vote in Democratic primaries and were more attracted to the primaries of their own party.

Administration of the Direct Primary Primaries are administered in most states by the political parties sponsoring them. Texas primaries are administered on the county level by the county executive committees of the political parties. The Texas Election Code requires parties receiving 20 percent or more of the vote in the preceding gubernatorial general election to nominate all their candidates in direct primaries. The first primary and a run-off primary, as needed, are conducted in even-numbered years. For several years prior to 1988, they were held on the first Saturdays in May and June respectively; but beginning in 1988, they have been held on the second Tuesdays in March and April.

Persons wishing their names to appear on a party primary ballot for a statewide office must file necessary papers with their party's state chair. A party state executive committee in turn certifies the names of such persons to the party's county chairs in counties in which the election is administered. Persons desiring to have their names placed on the primary ballot for a county or precinct office file with the county chair of their party. Anyone seeking nomination for a district office must file with each county chair in the district. The county executive committee prints the ballots, arranges for polling places in the precincts, provides voting equipment and supplies, together with the state executive committee determines the order of names of candidates on the ballot, appoints a presiding judge of elections in each precinct, and canvasses (that is, scrutinizes and certifies) the election returns.

Financing Primaries Major items of cost for administering party primaries include printing of ballots and compensation of clerks and judges who preside at the polling places. A maximum of 60 percent of primary expenses is covered by the state. The remainder is obtained from *filing fees* paid by candidates. For example, candidates for the office of U.S. senator pay $4,000, while those for all other statewide offices pay $3,000. Candidates for the Texas Senate and the Texas House of Representatives pay $1,000 and $600, respectively. In lieu of a fee, candidates may file a *nominating petition* containing a designated number of signatures of people eligible to vote for the office for which the candidate is running.

General Elections

Party primaries must be distinguished from *general elections,* which are public in nature and are conducted, financed, and administered by the state. Primaries are not strictly public elections in the sense that the voter officially determines who will hold public office. Rather, they are functions of political parties and are conducted for the purpose of allowing party members to choose candidates to run against opposing party candidates in general elections. This distinction is a valid one, even though the U.S. Supreme Court has ruled that primary elections are so necessary in the selection of candidates for election as to be subject to state regulation. Thus, even though the state may, and does, regulate party primary elections, they are still only party nominating devices. As we have seen, Texas primaries are conducted and partially financed by political parties. In short, primary elections are party functions that select candidates. General elections, however, are state functions that officially determine which candidates will hold public office.

General Election Schedules Throughout the United States, the date prescribed by law for congressional elections is the first Tuesday following the first Monday in November of even-numbered years. Presidential elections take place on the same day in November of every other even-numbered year (for example, 1988 and 1992). This schedule is followed in Texas for the election of state, district, and county officials. With few exceptions, general elections to fill municipal offices and special-district offices are held in odd-numbered years.

In general elections involving state, district, and county offices in Texas, the candidate who polls a plurality is the winner with or without obtaining a majority. Thus, when a majority is not obtained, a run-off election is not held. Elections for governor and other statewide officers serving terms of four years are scheduled in the off-year, that is, in November of the even-numbered years between presidential elections (for example, 1990 and 1994). Along with 32 other states, Texas follows this schedule to avoid the influence of presidential contests. Elections to offices with two-year terms or staggered six-year terms must be held in both off-years and presidential-election years.

General Election Ballot Forms Use of the paper or secret ballot in public elections may be traced in American history to 1629. Prior to the use of a secret ballot (with subjects on which to be voted written or printed on paper), voting was by voice (*viva voce*). Two basic forms of the paper ballot have emerged in American voting history, the party-column and the office-block. Texas uses the party-column ballot (also called the Indiana ballot because it originated there). In general elections, Texas uses the party-column ballot in three different ways: as paper ballots (now used mostly in rural, sparsely populated areas), as punch-card ballots, and as voting-machine ballots. (Figure 4.1 shows a sample punch-card ballot.) The party-column ballot encourages straight party ticket voting because the names of the candidates of each party are arranged in parallel columns with the name of the party at the top of each column. Voters may vote for all candidates of a party (straight party ticket voting) by placing a single X in the box at the top of the column (on paper ballots), by pulling a lever (on voting machines), or by punching a hole opposite the party designation (on punch-card ballots).

Offices to be filled are listed in the first column on the left. National offices (president and vice president and members of Congress) are listed first and are followed by state, district, county, and precinct offices in that order. Names of corresponding party candidates are aligned to the right of each office. The Texas Election Code provides that the party obtaining the highest number of votes in the previous gubernatorial election will be assigned the first party column on the left for paper ballots or at the top of the list of party candidates on punch-card

FIGURE 4.1   General Election Ballot, Punch-Card Type, 1988, Nacogdoches County

SAMPLE BALLOT

GENERAL ELECTION
NACOGDOCHES COUNTY, TEXAS
NOVEMBER 8, 1988

VOTING FOR CANDIDATES AND PROPOSITIONS

1. Vote for the candidate of your choice in each race by making a punch hole in the space provided adjacent to the name of that candidate.

2. You may cast a straight-party vote (that is, cast a vote for all the nominees of one party) by making a punch hole in the space provided adjacent to the name of that party. If you cast a straight-party vote for all the nominees of one party and also cast a vote for an opponent of one of that party's nominees, your vote for the opponent will be counted as well as your vote for all the other nominees of the party for which the straight-party vote was cast.

3. WRITE-IN VOTING: Write in the name of the candidate and the office for whom you wish to vote on the ballot-card stub or write-in envelope where indicated. Only votes for the candidates whose names appear on the list of Declared Write-In Candidates will be counted.

GENERAL ELECTION
NACOGDOCHES COUNTY, TEXAS
NOVEMBER 8, 1988

Page A-01

Straight Party	Republican	(Rep)	1 ▶
	Democrat	(Dem)	2 ▶
	Libertarian	(Lib)	3 ▶
	New Alliance	(New)	4 ▶
President and Vice President	George Bush /Dan Quayle	(Rep)	5 ▶
	Michael S. Dukakis /Lloyd Bentsen	(Dem)	6 ▶
	Ron Paul /Andre Marrou	(Lib)	7 ▶
	Lenora B. Fulani /Rafael Mendez	(New)	8 ▶
United States Senator	Beau Boulter	(Rep)	9 ▶
	Lloyd Bentsen	(Dem)	10 ▶
	Jeff Daiell	(Lib)	11 ▶
United States Representative, District 2	Charles Wilson	(Dem)	12 ▶
	Gary W. Nelson	(Lib)	13 ▶

ballots. Strategically, these are the most favored positions because it is assumed that uninformed voters are apt to vote for candidates in the first party column on the left or at the top of a list of party candidates. For over a century, the Democratic party occupied this favored position, but the Republican victory in the 1978 gubernatorial election reserved that column on the ballot for the GOP in 1980 and 1982. The Democrats reoccupied the position on the left following Governor Mark White's victory in 1982 only to lose the coveted position again to the Republicans with Bill Clements's victory over White in 1986.

Parties whose gubernatorial candidates finished second or lower in number of votes received in the preceding gubernatorial general election are ranked in succeeding columns. Parties that are not organized in Texas but have national candidates are listed next, followed by columns for independent candidates. Finally, the column farthest to the right is reserved for write-in candidates. On punch-card ballots, space for names of write-in candidates is provided on a detachable portion of the ballot card. Beginning with the general election in 1978, the only authorized names of write-in candidates on any ballot for state, district, and county offices are of those who have, prior to the election, filed a declaration of write-in candidacy with proper officials (secretary of state for state and district offices, county judge for county offices). A list of such candidates is then posted in each precinct polling place on election day.

Absentee Voting   Qualified voters who expect to be absent from the county of their residence on election day, who will be 65 years of age or older on election day, or who are unable "because of sickness, physical disability, confinement in jail, or religious belief" to appear at the precinct polling place on the day of election are permitted by law to vote an absentee ballot by mail at any election—primary, general, special, or municipal. Any qualified voter may vote an absentee ballot by personal appearance at the office of the appropriate voting registrar (county, municipal, special district) prior to an election; a statement of cause is not required. The county clerk's office (or office of elections administrator if one has been established in the county) conducts absentee balloting for all elections and party primaries except municipal and special-district elections. In more populous counties, the county clerk's office accommodates voters by maintaining branch offices during the period for absentee voting. In municipal elections, absentee voting is conducted by the city clerk or city secretary and in special-district elections by a clerk designated by the district governing board. The period for absentee voting in person or by mail begins on the twentieth day and continues through the fourth day preceding the election.

Special Elections

In Texas, *special elections* are held to fill vacancies in state legislative and congressional offices, to consider proposed amendments to the Texas Constitution, to vote on local bond issues, and on occasion to elect members of city councils and school boards. If no candidate obtains a majority in the special election, a run-off contest between the top two contenders must be conducted in order to obtain a winner. Vacancies in state judicial and executive offices are filled by gubernatorial appointment.

Administration of Elections

The Texas Constitution empowers the Legislature to provide for conducting elections. Aside from making the secretary of state the chief election officer of the state, the Legislature leaves most administrative duties to the counties.

Voting Precincts   The basic unit for conducting national, state, district, and county elections is the *voting precinct.*Created by the county commissioners court, these relatively small geographic areas in 1988 numbered 6,546 in Texas's 254 counties. In total number, they will vary slightly from year to year to accommodate population changes. Generally, the Texas Election Code requires that a precinct shall have no less than 100 and no more than 2,000 voters, but exceptions are permitted on the bases of population of a county and the use of voting machines. There must be at least one voting precinct in each of the four county commissioners precincts from which commissioners are elected. Election precincts for municipal and special-district elections are designated by the governing body of the city or special district.

Election Officials Various county and political party officials participate in conducting elections. The county clerk or elections administrator prepares general- and special-election ballots based on the certification of state and district candidates by the secretary of state. Local candidates are certified and their names are placed on the ballot by the county clerk or elections administrator. The *county election board* consists of the county judge, county clerk or the election administrator, sheriff, and chairs of the two major political parties. It selects polling places, prints ballots, and provides supplies and voting equipment. The county commissioners court (the county judge and four elected commissioners) determines boundary lines of voting precincts according to population, appoints one election judge and one alternate judge to administer the election in each voting precinct, and officially canvasses election returns. In turn, each election judge selects clerks needed to assist in conducting general and special elections. The Texas Election Code prescribes that, where practicable, clerks shall be selected from different political parties. Federal law requires that county commissioners courts submit maps of voting precinct boundaries to the U.S. Department of Justice to ascertain that there is no discrimination against a protected class of voters. The county commissioners court pays the cost of general and special elections.

Vote Counting and Recounting Many precincts continue to use paper ballots, which must be counted by hand. This manual counting operation, when compared with use of mechanical or electronic voting devices, requires more clerks, is more subject to error, and is more likely to delay reporting of election returns. Voting machines automatically count each vote as the ballot is cast. If the punch-card device is used, ballots can be electronically counted as soon as the polls close. Purchase and storage of mechanical and electronic voting equipment are expensive, but their use can reduce the cost of conducting elections. A candidate for nomination or election to an office may upon request obtain a recount of ballots if conditions meet the provisions of the Texas Election Code, which provides detailed procedures for settlement of disputed elections.

Bilingual Requirements The Texas Legislature anticipated the intent of Congress to amend the Voting Rights Act of 1965 by including Spanish-speaking citizens in the act's coverage and to extend such coverage to Texas. Thus, in 1975, the state's lawmakers enacted a bilingual voting law. The statute requires that registration and election materials be printed in both English and Spanish.

The Politics of Parties

When Texas entered the Union in 1845, party government in the United States was nearly 50 years old. To most Americans, a democracy without political parties is inconceivable. Such organizations are an integral part of the total political system in Texas as in the other states. Parties serve as essential instruments for selecting public officials. In the pursuit of their major objective—obtaining control of the government through popular elections—parties must inform people about issues and candidates. A basic characteristic of democratic societies is freedom of political party organization and operation, and this above all else sets democracies apart from more authoritarian systems of government.

American political parties are structured on four levels: national, state, county, and precinct. In part, this is in response to the federal arrangement of government in the United States. Each major party is loosely joined so that units (state and local) are relatively free to decide what position to take on all party issues. However, the two national party organizations have influential financial resources and are able to withhold money and technical aid from state and local organizations that openly oppose declared national party policies. In Texas, a party's rules are adopted by its state executive committee; precinct and county units, in turn, have little or no alternative to acceptance of these rules. Also, a county delegation may be denied official seating at a state convention. In practice, however, each higher level organization must try to maintain cooperation at lower levels without resorting to heavy pressure or penalties.

Texas political parties are part of the loose, nonhierarchical structure that sharply distinguishes American parties from those of other countries. Until the middle of the twentieth century, party identification had been primarily Democratic, but since 1950 Texas has moved toward a two-party system similar to that of most other states.

Party Structure: Temporary Organization

Texas's two major parties are alike in organizational structure. Each has a permanent and a temporary organizational pattern. (See Figure 4.2.) The *temporary party organization* is composed of primaries and conventions. It comes into being for a few hours or a few days and then is dismantled until called into existence two years later, in a manner depending on the level of government involved. The direct primary, for example, is organized for one day (two days if there is a run-off primary) to enable a party to nominate its candidates. Conventions, on the other hand, are used generally on state and local levels to select party leaders and determine party policy. In presidential-election years, conventions on all levels can be used also to select delegates to the national convention, where candidates are chosen for president and vice president of the United States.

Precinct Conventions At the bottom of the temporary party structure is the *precinct convention,* which in Texas occurs every even-numbered year on the first primary day, the second Tuesday in March. Both the Democratic and Republican parties hold conventions in almost all the voting precincts in the state. Although

FIGURE 4.2 Texas Political Party Organization

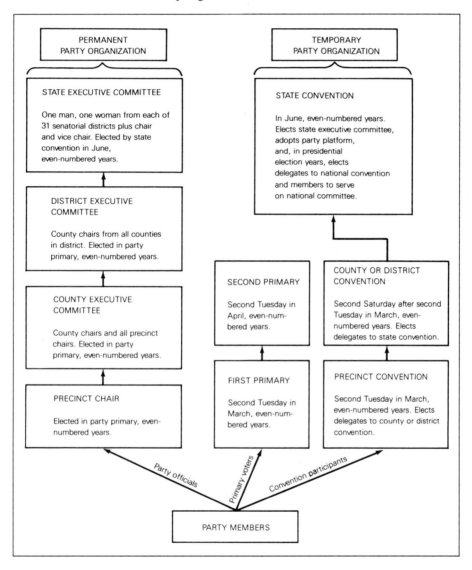

all party members who reside in a precinct and who have voted in the party primary are eligible to participate, only a small percentage of each precinct's registered voters usually attends precinct conventions. The main business of this convention is to elect delegates to the next higher party organization, which assembles 11 days later. This is the *county convention* or, in heavily populated counties such as Harris, Dallas, Tarrant, and Bexar (each of which has more than one state senatorial district), the *district convention*.

County and District Conventions   Delegates elected to the county or district convention assemble in March on the second Saturday after the first primary. Depending on how sharply the issues are drawn between liberal and conservative factions within a party, delegates at county or district conventions tend to represent the views of the majority faction within the precinct convention. In Texas, internal factionalism has applied more to the Democratic party than to the Republican party, though in the mid-1980s, conservative and moderate factions began to divide the Republican party. Generally, when factional issues are heated, bitter internal party battles may erupt in conventions at any level.

If such a factional division occurs at the precinct level, it is usually based on a statewide or national issue and will therefore carry upward into the county, district, and state conventions. County and district conventions elect delegates to the state convention. Each party's state executive committee sets the exact ratio for selection of delegates to the state convention (one delegate for each 300 to 600 votes cast in each county for that party's candidate for governor in the last gubernatorial election).

State Conventions   In June of even-numbered years, each Texas political party holds a biennial *state convention* to conduct party business, including the following:

1. Certifying to the secretary of state the names of party members nominated in the March and April primaries for Texas elective offices
2. Drafting and adopting a party platform
3. Selecting members of the party's state executive committee

In presidential election years, the June convention also conducts the following business:

1. Elects delegates to the national presidential nominating convention, the number for Texas calculated under national party rules
2. Elects members from Texas to serve on the party's national committee
3. Elects a slate of potential presidential electors to cast Texas's electoral votes if the party's ticket wins a plurality of the state's popular presidential vote

Beginning with the 1984 presidential election, Texas has been allowed 29 electoral votes—one for each of its members of Congress (27 representatives and two senators).

Texas Presidential Primary-Caucus   In a *presidential preference primary*, rank-and-file party members are permitted to vote directly for the presidential candidates of their choice. In Texas, each party conducts its own primary. Voters participating have their registration certificates stamped with the name of the party conducting the primary. Based on the results of the primary vote, delegates to each party's national convention are chosen. At the respective national conventions, Democratic and Republican party candidates for president and vice president are chosen.

Another plan currently in use in many states for selecting delegates to national conventions is the caucus (conference). By this method, party members assemble in caucuses at respective precinct, county, and state levels; and they choose national convention delegates who are either pledged to support a particular presidential candidate or who are uncommitted.

For the 1988 presidential candidate selection process, the Texas Legislature provided a unique system combining primary and caucus. By this method, parties were free to employ both methods and to apply their own rules governing the entire process. On March 8, Democrats and Republicans, voting in their separate primaries, indicated their choices for presidential candidates as well as candidates for state and local offices, all on each party's single ballot.

In selecting the March date, Texas joined 19 other states (11 being southern states) to hold presidential primaries or caucuses on the same *"Super Tuesday"* in 1988. Such a regional primary was designed to give the South greater influence in the selection of a nominee for the White House. Supported in the Legislature by both parties, the early regional primary was supposed to provide a special benefit to the Lone Star State. Of the three most populous states in the nation (California, New York, and Texas), Texas had the earliest presidential primary. Employing both the primary and the caucus, Texas sent 197 delegates to the Democratic party's national convention in Atlanta and 111 delegates to the Republican party's national convention in New Orleans.

At their June state convention in Houston, Texas Democrats selected 60 percent of their delegates (119 out of 197) on the basis of the March 8 primary balloting. Another 14 delegates were chosen from uncommitted elected and party officials. Selection of the remaining 64 delegates was based on choices indicated in precinct caucuses and county conventions.

Texas Republicans were somewhat more direct in choosing their national convention delegates. The Texas GOP selected all of their 111 national convention delegates based on the March 8 primary balloting. The Republican state convention selected 81 delegates by choosing three from each of the state's 27 congressional districts and 30 on a statewide basis. However, rules of the Texas Republican party permitted any candidate who won over 50 percent of the primary vote in a district to take all three delegate openings; similarly, any candidate who won over 50 percent of the state's primary vote was awarded all 30 of the statewide delegates.

Party Structure: Permanent Organization

Each of the two major political parties in the United States consists of thousands of virtually autonomous party committees at local, state, and national levels. For both parties, these committees nationwide are linked only nominally. On the highest level, each party has a national committee. In Texas, the precinct chair (there is no precinct committee) together with the county, district, and state executive committees form the *permanent party organization* of the state Democratic and Republican parties.

Precinct Chair   The basic party official in both the temporary and the permanent party structures in Texas is the *precinct chair*, who is elected by precinct voters in the party primaries for a term of two years. If both parties are evenly matched in strength at the polls, the precinct chairs' respective positions become more vital at the grassroots level. Precinct chairs in most counties do little more than conduct the precinct convention, serve as election judge at general and special elections, and conduct party primaries. The precinct chair also arranges for the precinct convention and serves on the county executive committee.

County and District Executive Committees   Each party organization at the county level is headed by a *county executive committee* composed of all the precinct chairs and the *county chair*, who is elected on a countywide basis by party members in the primaries. The county executive committee conducts primary elections and arranges for the county convention. In practice, these duties normally are performed by the county chair, who is the key party official at the local level and usually is the person best informed on party affairs. The Texas Election Code also provides for a *district executive committee* composed of the county chairs from each county in a given state senatorial district. These committees are supposed to perform party primary duties related to district offices, but few are functional. Most such committees prefer to leave their duties to county committees within the districts.

State Executive Committee   The highest permanent party organization of the state is the *state executive committee*, composed of one man and one woman from each of the 31 state senatorial districts plus a chair and a vice chair, one of whom must be a woman. For both the Democratic and Republican parties, this committee of 64 members is formed at the party's state convention. On that occasion, delegates from each senatorial district choose two members from their district and place their names before the convention. At the same time, the chair and vice chair are chosen at large from convention delegates.

The state executive committee of each party must canvass statewide primary returns and certify the nomination of party candidates. In addition, it arranges for and conducts the state conventions, raises campaign money for party candidates, seeks to promote party unity and strength, and maintains relations with the party's national committee.

The Quest for Political Democracy

Throughout the 1970s and 1980s, Texas experienced intensive population growth resulting from both native births and in-migration from other states. Certain characteristics of this population growth have propelled the state into a major partisan realignment process.

Republicans and Democrats

From the end of Reconstruction in 1874 to 1952, the Texas GOP struggled to stay alive. In the U.S. Senate, for example, Texas Republicans had no representation until 1961, when John Tower, running against an inept Democratic campaigner, won a seat vacated by Vice President-elect Lyndon Johnson. During that period of over 80 years, Texas Republicans served only 14 full terms in the U.S. House of Representatives. In the Texas Legislature, Republican representation steadily declined after Reconstruction. From 1903 to 1927, Republicans held no more than one seat in any session of the Senate and no more than two seats in the House. No Republicans served in either chamber from 1927 to 1951.

New life for the Texas GOP emerged, beginning in the 1950s, with phenomenal successes in presidential elections. From 1952 through 1988, Texas Republicans carried the Lone Star State in six of ten presidential elections, thus confirming a 1956 observation by V. O. Key, Jr., about voting habits in Southern states:

> Indigenous to the South is a strange political schizophrenic, the Presidential Republican. He votes in Democratic primaries to have a voice in state and local matters, but when the Presidential election rolls around, he casts a ballot for the Republican presidential nominee. Locally he is a Democrat; nationally, a Republican.[2]

Democratic Factionalism Widespread Texas Republican victories in 1988 were but the latest product in a long series of developments that tended to weaken the dominant position of the Texas Democratic party and allow the Texas Republican party to fill the void. In the post–World War II era, the Texas GOP was able to capitalize on a bitter division within the Texas Democratic party over the New Deal–Fair Deal administrations of Presidents Franklin D. Roosevelt and Harry S. Truman. The dominant conservative element among Texas Democrats developed a strategy that distinguished between the conservative state Democratic party and the liberal New Deal–Fair Deal party on the national level. This tended to create a gulf between the two hostile factions of the state party that threatened its very foundation, a factional strife that has continued with lessening force into the present. Conducive also to Republican expansion have been the socioeconomic tensions stimulated by Texas's transition from an agrarian society to an urbanized and industrialized social order. Industrialization and urbanization in turn caused the influx of young professional people from Republican states.

Republican Inroads Stimulated by deep-seated partisan and cultural changes, Republican growth has been altering the face of Texas politics. This was especially evident in the 1970s and 1980s, which saw remarkable growth in the number of Texans identifying with the Republican party. In 1952, only 6 percent of Texans admitted they were Republicans, while 66 percent reported they were Democrats. By 1985, however, Texas Democratic and Republican identifiers were equal in number.

Three groups—young voters, migrants from other states, and party switchers—are the major participants in this development. In 1990, the most Republican age group among Texas voters was the youngest—those from ages 18 to 29. No less than 40 percent of these voters said they were Republicans. This group also had the smallest percentage of nonvoters. The largest percentage of Texas's population growth during the 1970s and 1980s was due to in-migration from other states, especially from the Midwest. These new Texans are predominantly Republican. They are significantly influencing both Texas parties, but the Republican party rather than the Democratic party has been the principal beneficiary. In a series of surveys conducted between 1983 and 1987, the Texas Poll found that 16 percent of Democrats switched to the Republican party and another 16 percent became Independents. Only 10 percent of Republicans became Democrats and 11 percent became Independents. This switching habit—primarily by conservative, middle- and upper-class Texans and by Southern white Democrats—has been in effect quite consistently for over two decades. Thus the percentage of defections has been greater among conservative Democrats than among liberal Democrats or Republicans generally.

A Question of Party Realignment

Until 1978, the governorship and all statewide offices remained in the hands of conservative-to-moderate Democrats. In that year, Republican Bill Clements shocked Texas Democrats by winning the governorship while his party gained two congressional seats and five positions in the state Legislature. Two years later, the Reagan-Bush ticket swept the state while Texas Republicans added substantially to their party's membership and to their strength in the state Legis- lature. Organizing behind Mark White, Democrats were able to form a unified coalition in 1982 to retake the governorship from Clements. In this election, Demo- crats retained the offices of lieutenant governor and all five of the other statewide elective offices (attorney general, land commissioner, agriculture commissioner, comptroller, and treasurer).

In November 1984, the Reagan-Bush Republican ticket again carried Texas, this time taking 64 percent of the total vote. In that year, Republicans added 15 seats in the 150-member Texas House (up from 37 to 52); one new member—the only woman—in the 31-member Texas Senate (up from five to six); and four seats in the 27-member delegation to the U.S. House (up from six to ten). At the same time, they retained John Tower's seat in the U.S. Senate as newly turned Republican Phil Gramm scored an impressive 59 percent victory over Democrat Lloyd Doggett. Contrary to the pattern of past Texas elections, the state's huge voter turnout in 1984 benefited Republicans more than Democrats. While Republican candidates were materially aided by the personal popularity of President Reagan, Democrats were discouraged by polls that consistently forecast a Republican landslide nation- ally and in Texas. As the record GOP victory of 1984 spread across the state, Democrats were turned out of legislative, executive, and judicial offices.

Even rural areas—with 28 percent of the state's voting strength and solidly Democratic in the past—gave strong support to Republican candidates in the presidential and U.S. senatorial races. For the first time since Reconstruction, Republican congressional districts blanketed broad sections of the state, and many Texans were convinced that *party realignment* (a shift in majority party status from Democratic to Republican) was near at hand in the Lone Star State. The fact that

Republicans defeated many conservative Democrats as well as liberal Democrats indicated that general elections rather than Democratic party primaries had become the real election in Texas and that two-party politics had gained a solid base in the state.

Texas elections in 1986 re-emphasized the long-term trend in the state's voting practices. Even though the Texas GOP failed to achieve majority status in that year, Republicans did hold on to substantial gains made in congressional and state legislative seats two years earlier. The GOP retained the four congressional seats gained in 1984, giving the party a total of ten U.S. representatives in a 27-member Texas delegation. In the Texas Legislature, Republicans held on to over a dozen House seats gained in 1984 and added another in 1986, giving them a total of 56 in a 150-seat House.

Switching Primaries   In 1986, significant numbers of former conservative Democrats may have voted in Republican primaries, which attracted 250,000 more voters than in 1982. Many of those who voted in the Republican primaries were rural and small-town residents, heretofore the backbone of Democratic dominance. Coupled with a record 1986 Republican primary turnout, the GOP fielded twice as many candidates for state and local offices as in 1984; but as Anglo conservatives abandoned the Democratic primaries, Mexican Americans and blacks filled part of the void. In 1986, Mexican Americans were the strongest faction within the Texas Democratic party; and in that year, the Texas Republican party was larger and more rural than it had been four years earlier. In contrast, the Democratic party was smaller, less rural, and more Hispanic-dominated than it was in 1982.

Dealignment?   Following the return of Bill Clements to the governorship in the 1986 election, Republicans continued to claim that this 1986 contest was further evidence of party realignment. Increased competition statewide at the expense of the Democrats meant to Republicans that the Texas GOP was well on its way to replacing the Democrats as the state's majority party. Yet a closer analysis fails to confirm this conclusion. Instead, there seems to be a stronger *dealignment* rather than realignment of parties in Texas. Rather than voters becoming more Republican and less Democrat, a stronger trend seems to be toward independence of party affiliation. Voters are more candidate oriented. This is not a recent trend. It began decades ago and is still on the rise. Perhaps party labels are still meaningful for a majority of Texas voters, but candidates with appealing issues and skillful campaigning can win regardless of party labels.

Assessment of Gains and Losses   Though losing the governorship for the second time since Reconstruction, Texas Democrats won all other statewide offices in 1986. Lieutenant Governor Bill Hobby won his fifth term over Republican David Davidson, while Treasurer Ann Richards, Comptroller Bob Bullock, Agriculture Commissioner Jim Hightower, and Land Commissioner Garry Mauro retained their offices with comfortable leads over Republican opponents. In addition, Democrat John Sharp easily defeated Republican Milton Fox for an open seat on the Texas

Railroad Commission. In the judicial races, incumbent Texas Supreme Court Justice Raul Gonzalez (appointed by Governor White) was elected to a six-year term in that judicial post and became the first Hispanic candidate to win a statewide office. The son of immigrant parents, Gonzalez defeated his Republican opponent, Waco attorney John Bates, who billed himself as a probusiness candidate.

Before the end of 1987, however, a series of events eroded much of the party's earlier optimism. First, Lieutenant Governor Bill Hobby announced his withdrawal from electoral politics. Though not entirely unexpected by many with whom he served, the announcement by the 15-year veteran president of the Texas Senate produced shock waves among party leaders. A few days later, San Antonio Mayor Henry Cisneros announced his intent to withdraw from further political activity. Cisneros's announcement dashed Democratic hopes of electing Texas's first Hispanic governor, one who later might become a Democratic candidate for president. In addition, many Texas Democrats considered the popular mayor as their party's hope of retaking the U.S. Senate seat held by Republican Phil Gramm. Shortly after these disturbing announcements by Hobby and Cisneros, Democrat Mack Wallace resigned from the Texas Railroad Commission and Governor Clements promptly named Republican Kent Hance of Lubbock to fill the vacancy. Though Hobby and Cisneros were removed as the Democrats' most favored candidates for governor or other high office, the party could still look to such stalwarts as Attorney General Jim Mattox, Comptroller Bob Bullock, and Treasurer Ann Richards (who was chosen to deliver the keynote address at the July 1988 Democratic National Convention in Atlanta).

With 54 percent of the Texas popular vote cast for the Bush-Quayle ticket in the 1988 presidential election, the GOP swept the Lone Star State for the third time in the 1980s and for the sixth time in the last ten presidential elections. In the 1988 election, however, Republicans added only two seats in the Texas Senate and one in the Texas House and lost two seats in the U.S. House of Representatives. Special elections and party switches in 1989 gave Republicans additional Texas House seats, making a total of 60 out of 150 seats. In a special congressional election in 1989, Texas Democrats retained the seat in the U.S. House vacated by former Speaker Jim Wright of Fort Worth. The GOP had hoped to do better than that as an important step toward controlling congressional and state legislative districting in the 1991 session of the Texas Legislature. Thus the party would have to make huge gains in the 1990 election in order to control both houses of the Legislature and then control the all-important drawing of new district boundary lines. More impressive, perhaps, for the first time since Reconstruction, a Republican was elected Chief Justice of the Texas Supreme Court, and two other Republican candidates were chosen by voters to sit on that tribunal. While Texas's senior U.S. senator, Lloyd Bentsen, Jr., won a fourth term in the Senate, he was unable to carry his home state as Democratic presidential nominee Michael Dukakis's running mate.

As Texas enters the last decade of the twentieth century, the transition to a two-party state seems near at hand. In 1990, the Texas Republican party had a higher proportion than the Democratic party of college-educated members, newcomers, Anglos, metropolitan residents, high-income recipients, and those under thirty years of age. Texas Democrats add up to a disproportionate number of minorities, older residents, native Texans, lower-income earners, and those with less formal education.

In the 1990s, a continued influx of migrants from other states will benefit Republicans disproportionately, but growth in the minority population will benefit the Democrats. Young new voters may not continue indefinitely their current allegiance to the Republican party, nor are Democrats assured of holding on to their strong support of elderly voters. It is yet too early to determine how lasting will be the new allegiance of Texas voters toward the Republican party. Texas is no longer a bastion of rural, conservative-minded folk. Today the Lone Star State contains a wide variety of organized special interest groups. Liberal-progressive Democrats hold most of the statewide elective offices. In short, though Republicans have reached near parity with Democrats in Texas, neither party has the least assurance that it will forge ahead and stay ahead of the other party.

Women in Texas Politics

Selection of Geraldine Ferraro as the vice-presidential nominee on the 1984 Democratic party presidential ticket symbolized dramatically the advances made by women in politics across the nation. In increasing numbers, women are occupying positions once considered reserved for males. More women are becoming doctors, lawyers, professors, stockbrokers, architects, engineers, pilots, ministers, and politicians. In all these fields, however, women are still denied room at the top. In Texas, though women outnumber men in the total population and as voters, few women are elected to public office. For example, in the history of the state, only three women have been elected to statewide office. In 1918, Annie Webb Blanton was elected state superintendent of public instruction, and Miriam Amanda "Ma" Ferguson was twice elected to a two-year term as governor of Texas. However, Ferguson's election in 1924 and in 1932 ("Two governors for the price of one") resulted from the influence of her former-governor husband, James E. "Pa" Ferguson. As expected, he served as the unofficial governor during her tenures. In 1982, Ann Richards was elected state treasurer and became the third woman to hold an elective statewide office in Texas. By 1990, women were serving as mayor in the state's five largest cities: Houston, Dallas, San Antonio, El Paso, and Austin. In the 71st Texas Legislature (1989–1990), three women served in the Senate and 16 in the House of Representatives.

Fewer women than men run for elective public office. The reasons are many, chief of which is the difficulty in raising money to pay campaign expenses. Most potential male donors are reluctant to give money to women candidates, perhaps because they think women candidates cannot win. Nor may women candidates expect large contributions from their female supporters, who do not control the large sums of money that men do. Conscious of this, many women are discouraged from running for elective office.

There are other reasons, too. Even in this age of freedom, women are more burdened with responsibilities of family and home than are men. Customary parental obligations, together with age-old prejudices, deny to women their rightful place in the democratic process of government. Yet customs, habits, and attitudes do not remain static; new opportunities for women in public service are expanding accordingly. Like Annie Webb Blanton of Denton, women must not despair. In 1922, after running unsuccessfully for Congress, she said, "Everything that helps to wear away age-old prejudices contributes toward the advancement of women and humanity."[3] (See Reading 4.1.)

Ethnic Politics

Ethnic politics relates directly to over 35 percent of the total population of Texas, the combined totals of the state's blacks and Mexican Americans. This percentage represents sufficient voting strength to count significantly in Texas elections generally and to affect the outcome of many local contests in areas where ethnic minority strength is concentrated.

Blacks in Texas Politics Black Texans, with a voting-age population of over a million (10 percent of the state's voting-age population), have tended to identify with the Democratic party. Nearly 57 percent of blacks say they are Democrats, compared with 33 percent who are independents and 5 percent who are Republicans. Blacks tend to remain with the Democratic party regardless of income status. No less than 56 percent of both low-income and high-income blacks say they are Democrats.

In 1966, Curtis Graves and Barbara Jordan became the first blacks to serve in the Texas Legislature since 1898. From 1970, blacks have substantially increased their membership in the Texas Legislature; and two blacks (first Barbara Jordan and later Mickey Leland) have been elected to the U.S. House of Representatives. In the 1970s, a total of 174 blacks were elected to Texas public offices. Increasing election of blacks continued in the 1980s with 228 chosen by Texas voters in 1984.

In 1986, two black senators and ten black representatives (nine Democrats and one Republican) were elected to the Texas Legislature as blacks continued their strong support of the Democratic party. Thirteen black representatives were elected in 1988 to serve in the 71st Texas Legislature. In Potter County, where Amarillo is located, four black candidates won Democratic nominations in 1986 for the offices of county judge, county commissioner, justice of the peace, and judge of a county court-at-law, respectively; none faced a Republican opponent in the November general election. One of these, Elisha Demerson, thus became Texas's first black county judge.

Hispanics in Texas Politics Texas has the second largest Hispanic population in the nation. The term *Hispanic* is a broad one that includes all peoples in Texas with a Spanish surname. They or their ancestors came to Texas from Mexico, Puerto Rico, Central America, or South America. Perhaps 90 percent of all Texas Hispanics are of Mexican lineage. Most are American citizens with the right to vote and hold public office. It is essential, therefore, that this distinction be clarified. Nearly all those Hispanics that participate directly or indirectly in Texas politics are Mexican Americans. With 1,693 Hispanics holding elective public offices in 1989, Texas led the nation in the number of Hispanic holders of public office. New Mexico and California followed Texas with 640 and 580, respectively. At the start of 1987, there were 25 Mexican Americans serving in the Texas Legislature, four in the U.S. House of Representatives, and 451 in various local offices. In 1989, a total of 19 Mexican Americans were serving as representatives in the 71st Texas Legislature, and six Mexican Americans were serving in the Senate.

Until the early 1980s, voter turnout among Mexican Americans was always low compared with that of the state's total registered voters. In 1978, the low Hispanic voter turnout helped Republican Bill Clements to win the governorship; but the high turnout of Hispanic voters four years later contributed largely to Clements's defeat. In 1986, leaders of both political parties noted the continuing growth of Texas's Mexican-American voting strength. With approximately 1 million of the state's 7.9 million registered voters being Mexican Americans, there was increased party competition to attract Hispanic voters. Among registered voters of that year, one in four Hispanics voted in party primaries compared with one in five for non-Hispanics. In addition, a new and more effective party leadership began to take shape in 1987 and 1988 in counties with large Mexican-American populations. With ten new county judges installed in those counties in 1987, a corps of younger Democrats began to reach out to register more Hispanics. In 1987, the San Antonio–based Southwest Voter Registration and Education Project (SVREP) conducted 60 registration drives in Texas.

Voter participation as a percentage of the Mexican-American population is reduced because a large proportion of their population is under voting age and because many Mexicans and other Hispanics have not obtained U.S. citizenship. In general elections, the Mexican-American turnout rate lags behind the state average, but in Democratic primaries it has exceeded the state average since 1980. In 1988, Michael Dukakis won the Texas Democratic presidential primary with the strong support of Mexican-American voters.

On issues related to religion, abortion, and school prayer, Mexican Americans are more conservative than Anglos, but on civil rights issues they are much more liberal. Mexican-American voters are strongly motivated by economic issues, especially unemployment and inflation. These interests continue to draw them toward the Democratic party. Republicans, however, are making some progress with upwardly mobile, urban Mexican Americans. Those Mexican Americans who are moving up on the social and economic scale tend increasingly to vote Republican.

Some Election Issues: Campaigns and Money

Perhaps in America elections occupy the attention of people more frequently than in any other country, even though the percentage of voter turnout is often discouragingly low. Elections in the states are conducted to fill national, state, county,

Campaigning in West Texas, Tom Green County, 1988. (Courtesy *The San Angelo Standard-Times.*)

city, and district offices. Where so many campaigns are conducted and elections administered, voters are besieged every year by candidates asking for their support at the polls. It is through this election process, however, that people have the opportunity to influence public policies by expressing their candidate preferences when they vote.

Campaigns are no longer limited to speeches by candidates on a courthouse lawn or from the rear platform of a campaign train. Today, prospective voters are more likely to be harried by a barrage of campaign publicity involving television and radio, newspapers, billboards, yard signs, and bumper stickers. Moreover, they probably will encounter door-to-door canvassers, receive questionnaires and candidate leaflets in the mail, be asked to answer telephone inquiries from professional pollsters or locally hired telephone bank callers, and be solicited for donations to pay for campaign expenses. Only a minority of Texans and other Americans are vitally interested in politics; and among those who are interested, there is growing impatience with today's style of political campaigning. Upon retirement in 1986 from long service in the U.S. Senate, Thomas Eagleton of Missouri observed: "The whole nature of the political campaign has degenerated into a war of meaningless little TV spots and meaningless little newspaper articles about the periphery of the campaign, but never the substance."[4] He added that more and more voters are measuring politicians by their stands on a single issue rather than by their abilities to serve in public office. In Texas, during the 1984 race for a seat in the U.S. Senate, Democratic party candidate Kent Hance (later turned Republican) won a first-place position on the primary ballot based on a single issue, that of opposition to granting amnesty to illegal aliens. Two years later, Congress enacted an immigration law that provided amnesty for illegal aliens. Texas Governor Bill Clements twice won the governorship with campaigns based largely on the single issue of no new taxes; then in 1987 he reluctantly supported the largest tax increase in Texas history.

Popular complaints against election campaigns center on three major faults: they are too long; candidates are too prone to engage in personal attacks against each other while neglecting the important responsibility of informing voters on major issues; and campaigns are too expensive.

Financing Campaigns

In 1846, when campaigning in Illinois for a seat in Congress, Abraham Lincoln reported spending a total of 75 cents—for a barrel of cider. In 1982, when campaigning in Texas, Governor Bill Clements spent over $13 million. In 1986, Republican Clements and his Democratic opponent Mark White spent a total of $26 million in another gubernatorial contest. The difference between the spending amounts of Lincoln in 1846 and those of Clements and White in 1986 illustrates the immense changes that have transpired in political campaigning over the past 140 years.

The candidates who campaigned for governor of Texas spent a total of $15 million in 1978, $28 million in 1982, and $34 million in 1986. Political analysts predict a 1990 gubernatorial campaign extravaganza of $40 million to $50 million. A $45 million expenditure in 1990 would be a 200 percent increase over the $15 million spent in 1978. Yet the inflation rate for that 12-year period is estimated to be only 77 percent. With such climbing costs of campaigning for any statewide, district, and even some local offices in Texas, it seems that only a select few citizens can afford to run for public office.

The Need for Money No one denies that money is necessary to run a political campaign. In this age of mass communication, use of expensive media (especially television) is the most important method for getting voter attention. Certainly, a candidate for statewide office in Texas cannot win without communicating with a large percentage of the state's voting population. Nevertheless, if a candidate were to restrict *campaign expenditures* simply to the cost of mailing one postcard to every Texan 18 years of age or older, postage alone would cost over $2 million.

Many daily tasks of campaigning in Texas are still conducted largely by volunteer workers—persons who do door-to-door canvassing, distribute campaign literature, and put up yard signs. But the services of highly paid specialists in campaign management and *public opinion polling* are needed in today's electoral contests.

So huge sums of money must be raised in order to pay for media advertising and to hire professionals who can plan, organize, and direct a campaign. Candidates for statewide office, for example, can no longer rely entirely on volunteers to operate phone banks. For greater assurance of victory, they must hire hundreds of telephone callers. In the face of the increasing *professionalization of political campaigning,* it is unlikely that candidates for most statewide offices in Texas, especially those for governor and U.S. senator, could win without the aid of a staff of highly paid specialists in political campaigning and without the services of a public-opinion polling agency.

Polls are essential but expensive. They tell candidates where to focus their media, what issues to emphasize, and which strengths and weaknesses have been identified. Each Texas poll may cost a candidate from $5,000 to $25,000, depending on the size of the sampling and the number of questions asked. Favorable polls help a candidate in fund raising. Outdoor billboard advertising is another expensive medium that is essential to election campaigning. Five billboards on freeways of major Texas cities will cost from $5,000 to $8,000 per month. A one-day, full-page ad in a major newspaper in Texas will cost up to $10,000. For a 30-second prime-time announcement on a television station in the Dallas–Fort Worth area, a candidate may pay up to $24,000 based on 1988 rates.

Importance of Electronic Media With over 10 million potential voters to be reached in 254 counties, Texas is by necessity a media state for political campaigners. To visit personally every county during a primary campaign, a candidate would need to go into four counties per day, five days a week, from the filing date in January to the March primary date. Such extensive travel would leave little time for money raising and other demands made on candidates. So Texas campaigners must rely more heavily on television and radio exposure than candidates in most other states. With massive amounts of coverage by these media forms, a well-financed candidate sometimes can surge ahead in the final weeks of a close campaign. This has been done in Texas more than once since the advent of television in the 1950s. In 1990, no less than 60 percent of a Texas candidate's statewide campaign budget was spent for television and radio advertising.

In the gubernatorial general election of 1978, multimillionaire businessman William Clements, a Republican who had never held a state office, defeated John Hill, a Democrat with name recognition in public office extending back more than a decade. Clements depended heavily on massive television coverage applied strategically in the final days of the campaign. Four years later, Democrat Mark White successfully employed the same media strategy against Clements. It seems clear, therefore, that major statewide elections in Texas can be influenced heavily, if not won, with sufficient television exposure.

Giving and Spending

In this country, elections have long been influenced by money donated in large sums by relatively small numbers of people. As the need for money increased, the search for "fat cats" (big givers) widened accordingly. Large single contributions by wealthy donors are no longer uncommon.

Campaigning for Governor The bulk of contributions to Governor Clements's general election campaign chests of 1978 and 1982 came from his own pocket and from wealthy Republicans and conservative Democrats. In the 1982 campaign, Clements raised $3.5 million with a $1,000-a-plate dinner at which wealthy guests added donations above the minimum price of attendance. Clements reported spending a total of $13.3 million in losing the governorship to Mark White. Together, Clements and White reported spending $23 million in the 1982 gubernatorial campaign.

In a report on his 1986 election campaign, Governor Clements listed the names of and the amounts given by 32 major donors. Of these, 28 gave $5,000 each, three gave $10,000 each, and one contributed $15,000. Nine *political action committees (PACs) contributed a total of $67,200. Nineteen of the 32 donors were wealthy individuals from Dallas and Houston. Though these gifts represent only a fraction of the total raised by Clements, the reports provide a glimpse of campaign fund raising by candidates for a major office in Texas. During the first half of 1987, Governor Clements raised $290,000 to help retire his $3.6 million campaign debt.

Nearly 20 percent of White's 1986 donations came from people he appointed to government boards and commissions. The average amount donated by appointees to the ten most sought-after agencies was $9,477. Each of those appointed to the State Highway and Public Transportation Commission and the Securities Board contributed to White's campaign chest. Highway Commission member Roy Bass of Fort Worth gave $35,000, while the Bass family gave a total of $90,000 that included $35,000 by the Bass family's own PAC.

Campaigning for Congress In anticipation of his 1988 re-election campaign, Texas's U.S. Senator Lloyd Bentsen, Jr., had by mid-1987 already raised over $5 million. The leader among his colleagues seeking re-election in 1988,* most of Bentsen's contributions arrived after he became chair of the powerful Senate Finance Committee in January 1987. Though unopposed in the primary, in the first six months of 1987 Bentsen raised four times as much as the next highest fundraiser in the U.S. Senate. Among Bentsen's contributions were $54,000 from former members of his defunct "chairman's council," composed of individuals who paid $10,000 each to attend monthly breakfasts with him. In response to public criticism, he disbanded the group and ultimately refunded $94,500 of the money contributed to the council. Commenting in 1988, U.S. Senator David Boren, D-Oklahoma, said the average cost of running a successful race for the U.S. Senate had increased 500 percent in ten years to about $3 million. Republicans, however,

---

*In 1988 Senator Bentsen's name appeared on the Texas general election ballot as the Democratic party candidate for re-election to the U.S. Senate and for vice president of the United States. This dual candidacy was permissible under a Texas law enacted to permit Lyndon Johnson's name to appear on the 1960 Texas general election ballot as a candidate for re-election to the U.S. Senate and for vice president. With the law still in effect in 1988, Bentsen chose to repeat what Johnson had done 28 years earlier.

refused to negotiate with Democrats over spending limits, holding that such restrictions would doom their party to minority status in states where Democrats have an edge in voter registration.

Contributions by PACs   A political action committee is a legal device used by corporations, labor unions, and other organizations to raise large sums of money to be channeled into political campaigns. Federal law permits a PAC to give five times as much money to a particular candidate as may an individual. A PAC may give a candidate up to $5,000 for each primary, runoff, and general election; an individual may give only $1,000 in each of these instances. In 1987 and 1988, some $1.2 billion overall was spent on campaigns for congressional and presidential elections. Of that total, PACs accounted for about 28 percent.

In 1984 congressional campaigns, Texas Senator Phil Gramm was the leading recipient of PAC contributions; he collected over $1.3 million. This Texas Republican ranked fourth in total contributions received from all sources by U.S. Senate candidates in all the states. Gramm's total was nearly $10 million. Therefore, contrary to the belief of many Texans, most candidates for major political offices in this state must look to the more affluent business community for funds rather than to organized labor. In 1985 the U.S. Supreme Court ruled that campaign contributions by PACs are forms of speech protected by the U.S. Constitution and cannot, therefore, be limited by law. This ruling opened the way for well-funded PACs to exert an unbalancing influence in favor of particular candidates. Said Common Cause President Fred Wertheimer in 1985: "This system has lost all resemblance to the democratic ideal that any qualified citizen could run for a seat in the United States Senate." Application of this sentiment is not limited to those seeking a U.S. Senate seat. Increasingly, it is becoming applicable to those seeking any elective office.

Another troublesome question relating to campaign finance concerns wealthy candidates who are able to "buy" public office with their own money. Many critics hold that huge contributions by wealthy candidates to their own campaigns make the race unequal. Some rich candidates subsidize their campaigns by both their own contributions and personal loans. Then, after their election, they solicit donations to help repay the loans. Thus, people are asked to give money not to a candidate but to a public official. Giving money to the winner, who in turn uses it to pay off personal loans, seems to be closer to political payola than to campaign contributions.

Government Regulation of Campaigns

In the mid-1970s, both federal and Texas state laws were enacted to regulate various aspects of election campaigns. The Federal Election Campaign Act of 1974 applies only to election campaigns for president, vice president, and members of Congress. Though no limit is placed on the amount of money that may be contributed to candidates' campaigns, certain restrictions are imposed on expenditures, especially those related to campaign advertising via radio and television. In order that the public may be made aware of amounts and sources involved in campaign financing, the 1974 law requires candidates to make periodic reports of both contributions and expenditures. A bipartisan Federal Elections Commission administers the law.

Regulation in Texas Texas law governing election campaigns requires that every candidate for nomination and election to any state, district, county, or municipal office, along with every political committee (any two or more persons whose purpose is to accept political contributions and make political expenditures) in such elections, designate a *campaign treasurer* before accepting campaign contributions or making campaign expenditures. Campaign contributions may be made by any person; there is no limit as to amount. Direct contributions by both labor unions and corporations from their respective treasuries, however, are prohibited.[5] Candidates and political committees may not accept more than an aggregate of $100 in cash from a contributor. With some exceptions, neither candidates nor political committees may knowingly accept political contributions totaling more than $500 from an out-of-state political committee. Neither candidate, officeholder, nor political committee may convert contributions to personal use. From 30 days before the start of a regular session of the Texas Legislature to the end of the session, a person may not make a political contribution to, nor may a political contribution be accepted by, (1) a member of the Legislature, (2) a statewide officeholder, or (3) a political committee. This restriction does not apply to special sessions of the Legislature. Candidates may not retain unexpended contributions for more than six years after the date of final report of contributions. At the end of six years, unexpended contributions must be remitted to one or more legally designated persons or institutions. Campaign spending is prohibited except by candidates, the treasurer or assistant treasurer appointed by the candidate, or by treasurers of political committees. One exception to this regulation is that an individual, acting alone, may make one or more direct campaign expenditures not in excess of $100.

Candidates and treasurers of campaign committees are required to file sworn statements listing all contributions received and expenditures made during designated reporting periods plus the name and address of each donor of amounts in excess of $50. Any candidate or campaign treasurer who fails to file this report is liable to each opposing candidate for double the amount of the unreported contributions or expenditures and to the state for triple that amount. Candidates who knowingly allow their campaign treasurers to violate any part of the law forfeit the right to have their names placed on the primary or general election ballot. All reports are open to public inspection for two years following the election.

Generally, all candidates and political committees involved in a political campaign for state and local office are required to file three reports in the form of sworn statements as follows: the first no later than 30 days before the election; the second seven days prior to the election; and the third no later than 30 days following the election. A final report must be filed by candidates, officeholders, and political committees by January 15 each year noting any campaign contributions and expenditures not previously reported.

A Question of Public Funding   Americans have a constitutional right under the freedom of speech clause to contribute to candidates of their choice. The U.S. Supreme Court has ruled that campaign contributions may be limited, but independent expenditures in support of a specific candidate cannot be denied. Nor may candidates, continued the court in *Buckley* v. *Valeo* (1976), be prohibited from spending their own money. In the face of these guaranteed rights of persons to contribute to candidates, political parties are in turn weakened. When PACs can collectively contribute a million dollars to a candidate for a statewide office, the candidate no longer needs to remain obligated to a party. Public funding of elections by state governments could, on the other hand, either strengthen or weaken political parties. If state funds were to go directly to candidates, parties would hardly benefit; but if money were given to parties, they in turn could parcel it out to candidates and thereby strengthen party loyalty.

It is interesting to speculate on how candidates and voters would respond to or be affected by public financing of Texas elections. First, challengers would be placed on a more equal financial footing with incumbents. Private financing favors incumbents in raising campaign money. Legislators are well aware of this, and they will surrender their favored position only on strong public demand. Second, public funding would run counter to Texas history; the Lone Star State has never experienced that practice. Besides, many Texans believe that public financing of elections would be in gross violation of freedom of the ballot. It would open the way, they believe, for an individual's tax money to be used to finance a candidate the taxpayer opposes. Others oppose public funding on grounds that adoption of the plan would be a dangerous departure from the private enterprise system.

These and other objections to public funding of elections indicate that for the foreseeable future Texas will continue to allow wealthy individuals and powerful corporate interests to buy political favors from government under the guise of making campaign contributions.

Notes

1. Other U.S. Supreme Court cases involving the Texas white primary are *Nixon* v. *Herndon* (1927), *Nixon* v. *Condon* (1932), and *Grovey* v. *Townsend* (1935).
2. V. O. Key, Jr., *American State Politics: An Introduction* (New York: Knopf, 1956), quoted by James R. Soukup, Clifton McCleskey, and Harry Holloway, *Party and Factional Division in Texas* (Austin: University of Texas Press, 1964), p. 23.
3. Amy Johnson, "The Woman Shortage," *The Texas Observer*, September 25, 1987, p. 4.
4. From *The San Angelo Standard-Times*, November 3, 1986.
5. According to a ruling by the Texas secretary of state, the ban on campaign contributions by corporations and labor unions to aid or defeat a candidate in a primary or general election does not apply to referendum measures on the ballot.

Key Terms and Concepts

universal suffrage	precinct convention
white primary	county convention
poll tax	district convention
voter registration	state convention
county voting registrar	presidential preference primary
voter turnout	"Super Tuesday"
direct primary	permanent party organization
first primary	precinct chair
run-off primary	county executive committee
blanket primary	county chair
open primary	district executive committee
closed primary	state executive committee
crossover voting	party realignment
filing fee	dealignment
nominating petition	campaign expenditures
general election	public opinion polling
special election	professionalization of political
voting precinct	campaigning
county election board	political action committee (PAC)
temporary party organization	campaign treasurer

Selected Readings

4.1 The Gender Barrier Is Coming Down

Sam Attlesey

In 1990, an unprecedented number of Texas women ran for public office, including the governorship and other statewide offices. When state treasurer Ann Richards announced her candidacy for governor in 1989, she became the first serious woman candidate for that office since 1972. In that year, Frances "Sissy" Farenthold finished second in the Democratic primary contest, receiving more votes than incumbents Governor Preston Smith and Lieutenant Governor Ben Barnes. In the Democratic run-off primary that followed, Farenthold was defeated by Uvalde rancher Dolph Briscoe, who went on to become governor. In this reading, several prominent political analysts comment on the attitude of Texas voters toward women candidates for public office.

When Miriam "Ma" Ferguson became Texas' first female governor in 1924, she portrayed herself as a loyal wife who was trying to vindicate her husband, former Gov. Jim "Pa" Ferguson, who had been impeached. Her motto was "two governors for the price of one." It was hardly a victory for women's rights, most historians say. But as the 1990 political season unfolds, an unprecedented number of women are running on their own qualifications for the governor's office and at least two other statewide offices.

Although announced Democratic gubernatorial candidate Ann Richards will draw most of the attention, at least a half-dozen other women contenders are pondering serious campaigns for attorney general and treasurer. The large number of female candidates seeking major state offices is a "natural evolution" of women in politics, and Texas voters are now willing to elect a woman as governor and to other high offices, according to historians and political consultants.

"It's high time, it's long overdue and Texas is ready," said Frances "Sissy" Farenthold, who was the last serious woman gubernatorial candidate, in 1972. "It's political maturity, a natural outgrowth of more women's involvement in politics. Now a woman can get elected to anything," said consultant George Christian. "Women have held lower offices now for some time, and this has allowed them to build credibility in the election process. And the natural result of that is to try and move up," said Kay Bailey Hutchison, a Republican who has said that she will seek the state treasurer's office. "Given the evidence of the number of women mayors in urban areas, women clearly do not frighten the Texas electorate, and those urban areas can elect a governor," said Texas historian T. R. Fehrenbach.

From the *Dallas Morning News*, June 12, 1989, p. 4A. Sam Attlesey is a political writer for the *Dallas Morning News*. Reprinted by permission.

"Women are finally deciding the best way to be represented is for them to run for these offices," said Marilyn Rickman, chair of the Texas Women's Political Caucus. "And with Ms. Richards' being the first one to have achieved a statewide election since years back, it is less intimidating for women to run for high office," said Ms. Rickman. "They've seen that Ann did it and they say, 'If Ann did it, gosh, I can do it.' "

Ms. Richards broke the modern-day gender barrier in Texas in 1982 when she was elected state treasurer, becoming the first woman elected to a statewide public office in 50 years. She established another first with her re-election in 1986, becoming the first woman in the state to be elected to consecutive terms to a statewide office. And now Ms. Richards is off and running for the state's top office, having announced formally Saturday [June 10, 1989], and she is "giving even greater legitimacy to female candidacies," said Mr. Christian, a veteran Texas political watcher.

Analysts and historians agree the state is ready to elect a woman, but they are still uncertain whether Ms. Richards is the right candidate. "The jury is still out, but in this particular year, she is probably the strongest woman candidate that could come forward," said Mr. Christian. "I think there is no problem for Richards being elected because she is a woman," said Mr. Fehrenbach. "She has demonstrated she is competent, but the question becomes, 'Can she raise the money?' "

"Ann Richards has an image as a good ol' girl. She doesn't threaten women and she doesn't threaten men. But Sissy Farenthold did," said the historian, referring to Ms. Farenthold's 1972 race. Ms. Farenthold acknowledged that she ran as an "insurgent" and that her liberal philosophy hurt her as much as the fact she was a woman. "It could have been my politics more than my gender," said Ms. Farenthold, who was a reform-minded state representative when she ran for governor. In 1972, she finished second in the Democratic primary, garnering more votes than the incumbent governor, Preston Smith, and the incumbent lieutenant governor, Ben Barnes. But in a runoff, Ms. Farenthold was defeated by Uvalde rancher Dolph Briscoe. She challenged Mr. Briscoe again in 1974 but was defeated by a more than 2-to-1 ratio. Texas governors were elected to two-year terms before the mid-1970s, when the term was changed to four years.

Mr. Christian, a press secretary to President Lyndon Johnson, said Ms. Farenthold's second-place finish for the Democratic nomination in 1972 was an impressive gain for women's rights in the state. "That was no small potatoes," he said. And he agreed with other analysts that she was defeated because she was a liberal and Mr. Briscoe was a conservative. Their sexes made little difference, he said. And Mr. Christian agreed with GOP consultant Karl Rove that had longtime Republican activist Anne Armstrong run for governor in 1972, she would have won. "If Anne Armstrong had run for governor in 1972, she would have become the first Republican governor in the state in 100 years," said Mr. Rove, adding that the unprecedented number of women seeking statewide office in 1990 is "the natural evolution of women working their way up the political ladder."

That evolution has seen the number of women holding elective office steadily increase in Texas. For example, in 1971, women made up only about 1 percent of the 181-member Legislature. Today, women hold 10 percent of the legislative seats. In 1981, there were only two female mayors in urban cities in Texas. Today, women serve as mayors in such cities as Dallas, Houston, San Antonio, El Paso, Corpus Christi and Garland. "Once women begin to be elected to local offices, they present models to other women and make it look like victory is possible. They make it easier for others to run because people forget it (gender) is an issue," said Diane Sheridan, president of the Texas League of Women Voters. "I just think part of it is that people are becoming accustomed to it," said Ms. Farenthold, a Houston lawyer. She said that the 1990 races "could be a watershed election. The very fact that so many women are running and getting that experience is a real change."

Mrs. Hutchison, who became the first Republican woman elected to the Texas House in 1972, conceded that there may be some lingering sexism in Texas, although she said she has not yet encountered any in her race for treasurer. "I think it has changed dramatically, and I would love to say there are no more barriers, but we haven't tested it enough," said Mrs. Hutchison, a Dallas lawyer. Added consultant Mr. Christian: "Sure, there is a redneck vote that says, 'I'm not going to vote for women.' If that hadn't been there, more women would have been elected, more Hispanics would have been elected and blacks would have been elected."

But Mr. Christian and University of Houston political scientist Richard Murray said that the loss of votes candidates might suffer because they are women will likely be equally offset by gains in the upcoming statewide races. "You'll lose some voters because you are a woman and you will gain some. It's no great advantage or disadvantage," said Mr. Murray, predicting that women will account for 51 percent of the vote in 1990. "It's a trade-off," said Mr. Fehrenbach.

However, the political consultants said that women who run for office in Texas as "feminists" are taking a risk. "Feminism does touch off some Roman candles in people. Voters don't want someone who is nothing more than a man in a dress. They want a man to be manly and a woman to be womanly," said Mr. Christian. "And Ann (Richards) knows that. She is running as a grandmother."

Mr. Murray said that Ms. Richards will have to deal with the feminist issue "quite deftly. A misstep on that front would be fatal." Ms. Richards, who has long been active in the women's movement, will attempt to run a "balanced campaign" that is aimed at representing all Texans. She said she does not know whether her gender will hurt her. "Who knows. They said when I ran for treasurer that, well, a woman couldn't run and I got more votes than anyone else who was running that year. We've elected women as mayors of major cities of Texas now," she said. "And I hope we're reaching that time where gender is really not a factor."

Chapter 5

The Politics of Interest Groups

"Thaddeus & Weez" © 1989 Charles Fincher

*D*uring the spring of 1989 a throng of citizens numbering some 15,000 marched on the state capitol in Austin demanding greater recognition and protection for the rights of homosexuals in Texas. What did those persons hope to achieve by this demonstration? By engaging in a form of political activity—by involving themselves in politics—they were attempting to influence a public policy decision by the Texas Legislature.

Politics involves activities accompanying nomination and election of persons to public office; however, it encompasses much more. Politics is perhaps best understood as the process for affecting public policy decisions that involve the safety and unity of a group, achievement of group goals, and distribution of things valued by group members. These can include financial security, health and welfare, education, protection of person and property, and adequate transportation facilities. Governments make and enforce these public policy decisions.

In the governing of human society, politics is involved in most of what takes place in Texas and elsewhere. People are constantly trying to influence those who make and apply society's rules or policies. One important approach is through group action.

Politics, then, involves the interaction of persons, acting either as individuals or as members of groups organized to achieve common goals. Experience has demonstrated that individuals who form groups for political action are usually more effective in achieving their objectives than are persons acting alone.

Interest Groups in the Political Process

In attempting to influence the making of political decisions or the selection of men and women who will make them, people usually turn either to political parties (examined in Chapter 4) or to interest groups, the subject of this chapter.

What Is an Interest Group?

A political *interest group* (sometimes referred to as a pressure group) is an organization with members sharing common views and objectives and actively supporting programs designed to influence government officials and their policies. Some examples of interest groups in action include efforts by the Texas Farm Bureau and other agricultural groups to effectively nullify Agriculture Commissioner Jim Hightower's authority to regulate use of pesticides, attempts by the Texas Citizen Action group to bring about reform of the insurance industry in Texas, and a campaign by some reform groups to limit the number of bingo hall licenses issued.

When the focus is on the tactics or techniques employed by interest groups to accomplish objectives, other current examples can be seen. Such activities include the National Rifle Association mobilizing its members, their families, and their friends to pressure state legislators to enact legislation legalizing the carrying of handguns; a group of concerned property owners in Dallas, Houston, and other

Texas cities employing a media blitz to block the building of prison units in their neighborhoods; and an alliance of consumer groups urging passage of legislation limiting telephone and electricity rates.

Interest Groups and Political Parties

Interest groups and political parties are different organizations, although both attempt to influence policy decisions by government officials. Political parties try to gain control of governments by nominating candidates for public office and being responsible for their policies and conduct, contesting and winning elections, recruiting leaders to fill party offices, formulating policies to resolve current issues, and serving as intermediaries between citizens—especially voting citizens—and officers of government. The principal purpose of all party activity is to gain control of government and its powers in order to achieve party goals. An interest group seeks to influence government officials to decide issues to the advantage of the group or to implement policies and enforce regulations in ways preferred by the group.

One neglected aspect of interest group activity is *minority representation*. In Texas, blacks and Mexican Americans are outnumbered in most parts of the state. Organized ethnic groups, such as the National Association for the Advancement of Colored People (NAACP) and the League of United Latin-American Citizens (LULAC), often provide their people with opportunities to have minority needs recognized; political party activities may not produce such results.

Economic groups (American Federation of Labor–Congress of Industrial Organizations, Texas Farmers Union, and Texas Bankers Association) and social groups (Texas Congress of Parents and Teachers and Baptist Christian Life Commission) also serve as vehicles by which policy preferences are made known to governments by groups that represent minorities. Because they represent interests that are not geographically defined in American society, interest groups supplement the formal system of territorial (geographic) representation. They provide an internal system of *functional representation*. That is, interest groups offer a form of representation and protection for such functional groups as businesspeople, laborers, farmers, Catholics, Mexican Americans, teachers, college students, and the like. These are people who have similar interests but who may not constitute a majority in any territorial unit—city, county, legislative district, or state.

Interest Groups in American Politics

Over the years the number and variety of interest groups in the United States have increased steadily. Although many citizens are not affiliated with any, others are members of several. One American in every three is affiliated with at least one interest group.

In *NAACP* v. *Alabama* (1958), the U.S. Supreme Court recognized the *right of association* and thereby greatly facilitated the development of interest groups. Since that time, the right of individuals to organize into groups for political, economic, religious, and social purposes has been upheld throughout the country.

Aside from a political and legal culture that fosters and encourages the free association of individuals with organized groups, there are other factors prompting group formation and participation in American politics: (1) a decentralized structure of government, (2) the absence of a unified and responsible party system, and (3) the low ideological content of American politics.

Decentralization of National and State Governments   Nowhere in the American system is the power to govern centralized or concentrated. *Decentralized government* is achieved in two principal ways. First, the choice of a federal system produces a division of power between a national government and 50 state governments. In turn, state governments share their power with a wide variety of local governments—counties, cities, and special districts. Within each level of government thus created, power is separated into three branches or departments—legislative, executive, and judicial. This separation is especially apparent at the national and state levels.

Decentralized structural arrangements enhance the ability of interest groups to influence the activities of the various governments. Each structure permits a group to fight its battles at different levels of government and within different branches at each level.

Dispersal of power within branches or departments of government further enhances an interest group's chance of success. The more governmental power is divided, the more vulnerable is the public administrator who is entrusted with the task of using power. Such vulnerability occurs because administrators are isolated and can count on little support from other officers of government or from citizens who are often unaware that their public officials are under interest group pressure.

Texas officials are especially susceptible to interest group activity because of the public's long tradition of withholding power from its government. Few state constitutions can equal that of Texas in its devotion to the principle of restricting the exercise of power by public officials.

Decentralized and Irresponsible Party System   Another result of decentralized government is a *decentralized party system*. The absence of unified and responsible party organizations further magnifies opportunities for effective interest group action. Policymakers, state and local, are particularly affected by the absence of cohesive, tightly organized political party organizations. A cohesive party can provide policymakers with strength to resist compelling pressures brought to bear by dedicated, highly organized interest groups. Texas legislators are likely to be impressed, therefore, by any reasonably convincing demonstration of an organized demand, although they may lack any real insight into the weight or influence of the interest group.

Legislators favoring gun control laws, for example, quite frequently find that their efforts to enact such legislation are met with massive organized opposition by the National Rifle Association and its allies. In Texas, the beer lobby can mount impressive campaigns of propaganda and intimidation to head off any legislation that would impede the manufacture and sale of their beverage.

De-emphasized Ideologies   The Texas Democratic party has liberal and conservative factions, and the Texas Republican party has presidential and regular factions. Nevertheless, *ideologies* (that is, well-developed systems of political, social, and economic beliefs) are not strong factors in Texas politics. (For a discussion of party factionalism, see pages 88–90.) Most Texas voters do not consistently act in accordance with commitments to ideological programs. Thus, the appeals of interest groups fall on more receptive ears than would be the case if citizens and their political leaders were highly dedicated to ideological objectives.

Organization of Interest Groups

An interest group is generally defined as an organized number of persons who seek to influence governmental decisions. An interest group provides its members with information, holds conventions, and otherwise tries to "educate" them. Such a definition implies that some sort of organization, usually a formal one, is a vital part of American interest groups. Moreover, it implies that any organization becomes an interest group when it decides to influence government decisions.

Membership in Interest Groups

Interest group membership, by and large, is made up of individuals from professional and managerial occupations who are homeowners with high levels of income and formal education, and who enjoy a high standard of living. In other words, a lawyer or accountant is more likely to be active in one or more interest groups than a waitress or grocery clerk.

Leadership in Interest Groups

An organization of any size is almost invariably composed of an active minority and a passive majority. As a result, decisions are regularly made by a minority of members. That minority may range from a small elite of elected officers to a larger minority composed of delegates representing the whole membership.

Factors influencing group leadership include (1) the financial structure of the group (those who contribute most heavily usually have greater weight in group decisions), (2) the time-consuming nature of leadership duties (only a few individuals can afford to spend the time without compensation), and (3) the personality traits of leaders (some individuals have greater leadership qualities than others).

Classification of Interest Groups

Because of the great variety of interest groups at national, state, and local levels of government in the United States, they may be classified in distinctive ways. They may be centralized or decentralized; or viewed from another perspective, they may be categorized according to the level or branch of government to which they direct their attention. Some groups exert their influence at all levels of government and on legislative, executive (including administrative), and judicial agencies. Still other groups try to popularize their views with the general public and can best be classified according to the subject matter in which they are interested. Many groups do not fit readily into any category, and still others fit into more than one. Thus, the classifications that follow are necessarily arbitrary and certainly not exhaustive. They stress the fact that interest groups are involved in most, if not all, decisions at all levels of Texas government.

Still another type of political activity quite similar to that carried on by interest groups is the "lobbying" endeavors engaged in by a single company or corporation for its own self-interest. (Reading 5.1 provides an example of one such activity aimed at the 71st Legislature.)

Economic Groups

Some interest groups exist to promote the economic self-interest of their members. A recent study concludes:

> People will commit their resources to a group in the hopes that they will receive an economic return on their investment. Groups may function to advance the economic interests of a broad class of individuals or institutions, or they may act more narrowly, to protect an individual entity.[1]

This initial analysis will concentrate on the first category of *economic groups,* those falling within a broad class. A later examination of lobbying and lobbyists will concentrate on the narrower second category. The Texas Association of Businesses and the Mid-Continent Oil and Gas Association are examples of the broader type of interest group known as umbrella organizations. Individual corporations, such as Texas Gulf Sulphur Company and Texas Instruments, are examples of the narrower type. There is considerable overlap between the two types.

Business American businesspeople have long understood that they have common interests that can be promoted by collective action. They were likely among the first to organize interest groups that would press for favorable decisions and actions from national, state, and local governments. Traditionally, business organizations have pursued lower taxes, fewer price and quality controls, and minimum concessions to organized labor. At the state level, *business organizations* most often take the form of *trade associations* (power groups that act on behalf of an industry). Some of the many Texas trade associations are the Texas Association of Businesses, Texas Bankers Association, and Texas Oil Marketers Association.

Labor A contemporary four-state study indicates that labor organizations are regarded as among the most active of interest groups, almost as active as business-related groups. *Labor groups* have sought, among other goals, government intervention to regulate wages and hours and to reduce unemployment.

Texans are especially sensitive to the potential political power of labor groups. Only two such groups, however, are commonly identified as significant in Texas government: the Texas unions affiliated with the AFL-CIO and the Texas Oil and Chemical Workers Union. It is doubtful that organized labor's influence really lives up to its image, because union membership is relatively small (some 500,000 members, or less than 10 percent of the work force) and very few elected or appointed officeholders in Texas come from union ranks.

Professional Groups

Closely related to the economic types of interest groups are those dedicated to furthering the interest of a profession or occupation. *Professional groups* are especially concerned with such matters as standards of admission to the profession or occupation and licensing of practitioners. Examples of Texas professional and occupational associations are the Texas Trial Lawyers Association, Texas Classroom Teachers Association, and Texas Society of Certified Public Accountants.

Ethnic Groups

Leaders of *ethnic groups* have long recognized that only through effective organizations can they hope to achieve most of their cherished goals (for example, elimination of racial discrimination in employment, ethnic group representation in state legislatures, city councils, school boards, and other public policymaking agencies of government). Ethnic group organizations, however, have not exhibited great stability; most of them have not been able to maintain over time enough members, resources, and member dedication to survive. Among black organizations in Texas, for example, only the NAACP has endured to achieve some notable results for members of the black community.

In Texas, Hispanic groups are more numerous than those composed of blacks. In recent years, four such organizations have achieved some modest gains for their people, but competition among them has sometimes weakened their impact. The Texas "big four" are: (1) the League of United Latin-American Citizens (LULAC), (2) Mexican-American Democrats (MAD), (3) the Mexican-American Legal Defense and Education Fund (MALDEF), and (4) the Political Association of Spanish-Speaking Organizations (PASSO).

Public Interest Groups

A growing number of interest groups claim to represent the public interest rather than narrower private interests. Environmental, consumer, political participation, civil rights, peace, and church groups are often identified as *public interest groups*.

Public interest organizations have wide-ranging goals. Common Cause of Texas, for example, has focused its attention primarily on governmental and institutional reform, including open-meeting laws, public financing of political campaigns, lobby registration, and financial disclosure laws. The League of Women Voters, on the other hand, has directed its attention to public political education; and the

Women's Political Caucus has promoted equal rights for women and greater participation by them in political activities. The Texas Gay Task Force was organized to promote equal rights and opportunities for homosexuals. The Christian Life Commission (a Baptist agency) has dealt with many social concerns, such as child care and aging, but has gained more public attention for its opposition to pari-mutuel gambling. The Organization for the Reform of Marijuana Laws has lobbied to reduce or abolish penalties for possession and use of marijuana.

Public Officer and Employee Groups

Officers and employees of state and local governments have found that through organizations they can obtain better working conditions, higher wages, greater group insurance benefits, and more satisfactory retirement systems. Organization has also enabled *public officer and employee groups* to resist efforts to reduce significantly the size of state and local government bureaucracies. County judge and justice of the peace associations, for example, have been instrumental in blocking reform of justice courts and county courts in Texas.

At the state level, the most important group is probably the Texas Public Employees Association (TPEA). Groups on the local level include campus organizations of the Texas State Teachers Association (TSTA), the Texas Association of College Teachers (TACT), and the Texas Junior College Teachers Association (TJCTA), as well as municipal government groups such as the Texas Municipal League, the City Management Association, and the City Attorneys Association.

Texas Power Groups

Contemporary Texas legislators readily identify the types of interest groups they consider most powerful: business-oriented trade associations (oil and gas, railroads, chemicals, and other manufacturers), professional associations (doctors, lawyers, and teachers), and organized labor groups. Specifically, they often single out lawyers, teachers, brewers, truckers, oil and gas producers, doctors, automobile dealers, bankers, realtors, and nursing home administrators as wielding more than average amounts of influence. Each of these groups maintains a strong linkage with state legislators (whose policymaking vitally affects group interests) and with bureaucrats (whose regulatory activities vitally affect group operations).

Interest Group Activities and Techniques

Interest groups are involved in all types and areas of political activity, much of which overlaps that of political parties. Group leaders and lobbyists participate in recruiting officers of government, shaping consensus and conflict, building support within and for a political system, and actually making many governmental decisions.

Group Activities

On occasion, the power to make public policy decisions for regulating a section of the economy or a profession is delegated by government to an interest group. For example, the State Bar of Texas is an administrative agency of the judicial branch. Practicing attorneys are automatically members and must conform to its rules and pay dues to the bar. In effect, the state has delegated to the State Bar the authority to regulate the legal profession.

When interest groups urge their members or others to become involved in activities designed to influence agents of government, they are recruiting people into the political system. Local property-taxpayers associations frequently supply candidates for both public school and municipal offices, and realtor organizations gain a distinct advantage when their members are appointed to local planning and zoning commissions.

When interest groups serve as an outlet for discussion of questions of public interest, they are helping to develop conflict or consensus. Conflict is the usual product simply because each group is bent on pursuing its own limited ends; this, in turn, leads to clashes with other groups seeking their own ends. In a local school district, for example, an organization of parents and teachers seeking higher pay for teachers and a better physical plant for the school system often clashes with a local taxpayers association demanding a reduced tax burden for property owners.

Finally, because governments need, indeed must have, support for their policies, interest groups seek to build that support—mostly, of course, for those policies that are in harmony with the goals of the group. For example, the Texas Good Roads and Transportation Association will support strongly any policy leading to the construction of new highways.

Techniques of Interest Groups

Interest group techniques are as varied as the imagination of their leaders.[2] For convenience in analyzing them, techniques may be put into four categories: (1) lobbying, (2) electioneering, (3) campaign financing by political action committees, and (4) bribery and related practices.

Lobbying Perhaps the oldest and certainly the best-known interest group tactic is *lobbying*, carried on nowadays by many full-time and part-time professional practitioners known as lobbyists. Most often associated with legislatures and the lawmaking process, lobbying is defined as a communication by an agent acting on behalf of an interest group, directed at a government decision maker with the hope of influencing the decision-making process.

The first task of the lobbyist, then, is to gain access to legislators, their staffs, and other government officials. Once access is achieved and the lobbyist has obtained the desired attention, a variety of techniques may be employed to make the government official responsive to the group's demands, preferences, and expectations. (See Reading 5.1 for a case study on lobbying in the 71st Legislature.)

One of the principal *techniques of lobbyists* is personal communication with legislators and other public policymakers. The immediate goal of established

Members of the Texas House of Representatives in conference with professional lobbyists outside the House chamber. (Courtesy Joe Ericson.)

lobbyists, who are often former members of the Texas Legislature, is to inform the legislators of their group's position on an issue. Bill Clayton, an energetic and powerful speaker from 1977 to 1983, became a lobbyist immediately after vacating that office. To be most effective in using this technique, lobbyists must select the proper target (for example, a key legislative committee chair, regulatory agency administrator, county commissioner, or city zoning board member), choose the most advantageous time and place, and determine how best to phrase their arguments.

Recent studies of the techniques of successful lobbyists reveal that many of them are coming to rely more and more on computers, calculators, radios, pagers, and cellular telephones. They are also utilizing such political campaign techniques as direct mailings, television and newspaper advertisements, and grassroots committees. The purpose of this activity is to generate information favorable to their cause and to spread it widely among legislators, other policymakers, and the general public.

To do their job well, successful lobbyists should (1) indicate clearly whom they represent, (2) define their interest, (3) make clear what they want to do and why, (4) answer questions readily, and (5) provide enough information for politicians to make judgments. The successful ones also make friends of as many legislators as possible, especially influential legislative leaders, and get to know their interests and needs. Thus, professional lobbyists carefully study members of the Texas House and Senate to learn as much as they can about them.

A second important lobbying technique involves providing favors for legislators and other government decision makers. (See Reading 5.2 for an extreme example.) Some common favors include daily or weekly luncheon and dinner gatherings; free liquor, wine, or beer; tickets for movie houses, transportation facilities, or college and university sporting events; and miscellaneous gifts. (See the cartoon that begins this chapter.) The point is to make a friend of the decision maker, to create an atmosphere of personal admiration and trust, even to create a sense of obligation.

Yet another influential lobbying technique is creating an image of broad public support for the group's goals—support that the group can mobilize readily when the situation demands. Thus, professional lobbyists rarely ask outright for a favorable vote. Instead, they rely heavily on a grassroots network. The Texas State Teachers Association (TSTA) and the National Rifle Association (NRA) are extremely effective at bringing out grassroots pressure. (Further discussion of lobbying and its relation to the legislative process are presented on pp. 160–161.)

Electioneering   Participating in the process of nominating and electing persons to public office, commonly called electioneering, is an ordinary practice among interest groups. If a candidate who favors a group's goals can be elected, the group has some realistic expectation that its interests will be recognized and protected once the candidate takes office. Because of the danger of antagonizing party factions, however, interest groups participate less openly in the nominating process.

Interest group participation in the election process takes a variety of forms. Publishing the political records of the incumbent candidates is one of the simplest and most common forms of interest group participation.

Providing favored candidates with group membership information and mailing lists is a valuable contribution that helps candidates solicit money and votes. Groups may also allow candidates to speak at their meetings, thus giving them opportunities for direct contact with voters and possible media coverage.

A third type of group participation in electioneering involves getting out the vote—the favorable vote. Typically, this entails informational mailings and telephone calls directed to members, transporting of voters to the polls, and door-to-door canvassing.

Campaign Financing by Political Action Committees   Because political campaigns are becoming more expensive with each election, contributions from interest group members constitute an important form of participation. Although money, goods, and services continue to be supplied by individual group members, there is a growing tendency for financial assistance to come from *political action committees* (PACs). Texas statutes prohibit political contributions by corporations and labor unions. These and other groups, however, may form PACs composed of their members and then delegate to the committees the task of raising funds or obtaining goods and services for office seekers. A committee may also provide support for political campaigns in which the group's vital interests are at stake, such as a campaign to promote a constitutional amendment to raise the legal maximum interest rate on home and mortgage loans. With some 1,700 PACs reported in Texas in 1989, PAC activity has continued to increase.

Although PACs bring together persons who are not able to make campaign contributions in the amounts they prefer, that is not the end of their influence. Additionally, individual PACs cooperate to form coalitions or alliances; and, in another sense, they link their activities in electoral politics to other areas of the political process. Two examples of the latter type of activity—that is, *power linkage*—are registering and turning out voters and lobbying in the Texas Legislature.

Perhaps the purest form of linkage between PACs and the state and local governments of Texas is that between their election campaign contributions and the lobbying activities of their related organizations. It is, therefore, a joining of influence in one part of the political process (the campaign) to influence another part (the legislative process). In this way, interest groups are able to exercise far greater influence over the output of the Texas Legislature than their numbers would indicate.

Bribery and Related Practices   At times in the recent past, bribery and blackmail incidents have been notorious in state and local government. There were, for example, some well-publicized scandals in the 1950s involving Texas legislators; and in the 1970s, the Sharpstown Bank scandal, which involved both legislators and executive officers, rocked the state. Each scandal involved charges of bribery and related practices.

More recently, in February 1980, Speaker Bill Clayton was accused by the FBI of accepting a $5,000 bribe to influence the awarding of a state employee insurance contract. The accusations grew out of what came to be known as the Brilab investigation into illegal campaign contributions and other questionable practices. In October, however, a federal district court found Clayton innocent of all Brilab charges; and in January 1981, he was elected to a fourth term as speaker of the Texas House of Representatives. Gross and flagrant illegalities are, however, relatively infrequent because of the risk involved and the effectiveness of laws governing the conduct of public officials. The "Bo" Pilgrim incident in 1989 was, however, a notable exception. (See page 135 for details.)

Interest Group Power and Public Policy

The *political influence of interest groups* is determined by several sets of factors. One set focuses on the particular interest group itself and suggests that a group with a sizable membership, better-than-average financial resources, knowledgeable and dedicated leadership, and a high degree of unity (agreement and commitment to goals among the membership) will almost certainly wield virtually irresistible pressure on agents of government.

Critics of this position, however, insist that other factors external to the groups are also highly relevant. Contemporary research has indicated that there is a strong relationship between certain socioeconomic factors and the power of interest groups. These findings have led some scholars to conclude, for example, that states with high levels of population density, industrialization, per capita wealth, and formal education are likely to have strong political parties and relatively weak interest groups.

Others interested in the relative power of interest groups insist that additional external factors must be taken into account. They point out that the extent to which the aims of the interest group are consistent with broad-based community beliefs greatly increases the probability that the interest group will be successful and will wield considerable power. They also point out that if interest groups are adequately represented in the structure of the government itself, their power will be enhanced materially. For example, black officeholders will wield considerable influence on local housing issues. Finally, if the agents of formal organs of government are given significant power and authority, and if their actions are seen as legitimate by most citizens, interest groups will have much less influence. On the other hand, weak governments will ordinarily mean strong interest groups.

Interest Groups and Public Policy in Texas

Bearing in mind this analysis of the political influence of interest groups, let us consider the role of interest groups in making public policy in Texas. (A public policy is the product of goals, decisions, and processes of government that affect the general public.) As Chapter 1 has shown, Texas is among the most heavily industrialized and urbanized states; thus, it possesses most of the characteristics that tend to produce strong political parties and relatively weak interest groups. The analysis of Texas political parties in Chapter 4, however, fails to confirm this tendency.

Texas has long been included among those states with very strong interest groups and relatively weak political parties. A 1981 study, measuring the strength of interest groups against the strength of political parties in the 50 states, concluded that Texas is one of 14 states with the weakest parties and the strongest interest groups.[3]

Three circumstances may serve to explain why industrial, urban Texas does not fit the expected pattern. First, many Texas interest groups identify with free enterprise, self-reliance, and other elements of the state's culture; thus they are readily accepted. Texans are predisposed to mistrust government and its agents but to trust interest groups and their lobbyists.

Second, the century-long one-party tradition in Texas rendered interparty competition negligible until recent years. The absence of strong parties and meaningful competition between them has made Texas government vulnerable to the pressures of strong interest groups and their lobbyists.

Finally, the Texas Constitution of 1876 and its host of amendments have created state and local governments beset with weak and uncoordinated institutions.

Faced with a government lacking sufficient strength to offer any real opposition, interest groups usually have little trouble obtaining policy decisions favorable to their causes.

Although Texas has long had a reputation of being controlled by interest groups, especially those of the oil and gas industry, there may be, as always, a significant difference between reputation and fact. Texas interest groups' actual control over government probably falls short of their reputation. Nevertheless, interest groups have considerable power and influence in policy areas of their immediate concern. In many cases, a network linking lobbyists, regulatory agency officials (bureaucrats), and friendly legislators zealously guards and protects group interests.

Interest Group Power Linkage

A triangular relationship frequently links interest group, bureaucracy, and legislature.[4] (See Figure 5.1.) Together they can function as a team to gain special treatment for each member from the political system. Some specific examples will help illustrate the ways in which the linkage works to the advantage of team members.

The interest group assists bureaucrats by providing testimony favorable to their proposals when they are under investigation by legislative committees and by lobbying before legislative committees and influential legislators to obtain additional funds for agency operations. From the bureaucrats the legislative committee expects to receive in return assistance in writing agency programs and regulations, staff personnel for agency advisory committees and noncareer positions, and informal vetoes over agency decisions that they did not approve.

Interest groups support the legislative committees by providing campaign contributions for committee members, honoraria (money) for their speeches given at group meetings, and advice and assistance from group lobbyists who are often experts on the subject under consideration. From committees, interest groups expect to achieve formal and informal access to bureaucrats and to obtain budgetary support for programs that benefit the group.

FIGURE 5.1   Interest Group Power Linkage

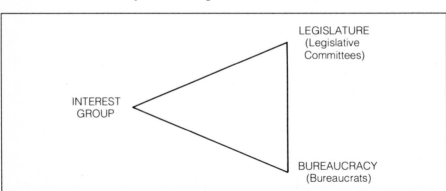

Finally, bureaucrats reward committee members with special treatment of the "folks back home," special consideration for the interest group allied with the committee, and advice concerning the distribution of the goods, patronage, and government contracts at the disposal of the committee. The committee, in return, often develops and acts favorably on legislation giving the bureaucracy more discretion, authority, and money. Also the committee is frequently able to help the bureaucracy acquire better physical facilities and more personnel.

Hazardous Waste Disposal Policies and Interest Group Activity

The problem of hazardous waste disposal affords an excellent example of the importance of organization and of interest group activity created and mobilized at the grassroots level and statewide in Texas. Hazardous waste is defined as any by-product that poses a substantial present or potential threat to plants, animals, and humans because it is harmful to their health and welfare. These problems of disposal of both radioactive and nonradioactive waste raise distinct but related policy issues that directly affect communities across the state.

Disposal of Radioactive Waste

Since 1980, agencies of Texas government have sought a suitable burial ground for a growing accumulation of low-level radioactive waste. (Radioactive waste is the by-product of the military and civilian use of nuclear energy.) Low-level radioactive waste consists of materials that remain toxic (i.e., dangerous) for 200 to 300 years; high-level radioactive waste may remain toxic for thousands of years. Moreover, on the national level, use of atomic materials dating back to World War II has created the need for high-level waste depositories.

Low-Level Radioactive Waste Disposal Nuclear waste is generated in Texas by approximately 1,500 licensed users of radioactive materials. Included are hospitals, medical schools, industries, and research laboratories. As a result, in 1981 the Texas Legislature created an agency to select a site for a permanent nuclear waste burial ground. The Texas Low-Level Radioactive Waste Disposal Authority immediately began searching for a 200-acre burial site for the 4 million cubic feet of nuclear waste that would be generated in the state by the year 2000. The process of selecting a site and preparing it to receive nuclear waste was estimated to take two to four years. By 1984, the selection process pointed to 21 counties in three sections of the state: Southwest Texas, the Panhandle–High Plains, and the Trans-Pecos region. Yet Texans in all of these areas quickly demonstrated reluctance to having their land become a nuclear dumping ground for the entire state.

For example, in each of the High Plains counties considered for a dump site, opposition by local residents was based on fear of a "cancerous health hazard" resulting from contamination of their water supply. A Borden County citizens group in far West Texas raised money for a court battle, and a Mitchell County group calling themselves Citizens Against Radioactive Exposure (CARE) sent a 3,000-signature protest petition to the governor.

When McMullen County in Southwest Texas was announced as a possible site, a storm of local citizen protest arose. Local officials pointed out that the proposed site was only 12 miles above the Choke Canyon Reservoir that provides water for more than half a million people, including the residents of Corpus Christi. As a result, the 69th Legislature prohibited location of any disposal site within 20 miles upstream or updrainage from such a reservoir. It also delayed the selection of any site until after July 6, 1987. The Legislature further specified that studies for site selection should consider "alternative management techniques," such as above-ground isolation facilities, waste processing and reduction, and waste recycling. Following the McMullen citizens' protest, the Legislature ordered the Waste Disposal Authority to consider a site on state-owned land. (Texas owns more than 18 million acres of land in 172 of its 254 counties.) Thus, in 1986, three potential locations were selected on public lands in Hudspeth and Culberson counties in far West Texas, and the next year a Hudspeth County site was chosen. Contracts were let for three disposal technologies, including above-ground waste isolation, enhanced below-ground disposal, and earth-mounded concrete bunkers. Operation of a Texas disposal authority is scheduled to begin in late 1991.

Legislation enacted in 1987 allows affected local governments to receive not less than 10 percent of the dump's gross annual receipts as impact assistance for adverse effects such as a decline in property values. Another part of the fees would be deposited in a fund for use in shutting down and sealing the dump when it is closed. The statute also mandates a citizens advisory committee to oversee waste disposal operations.

Low-level radioactive waste material remains toxic for hundreds of years; thus citizens living in and near proposed disposal zones fear that eventual seepage will pose a threat to water supplies, agriculture, and the food supply. Because geologists cannot cite past experience with nuclear waste burial, they are not in agreement as to the dangers of contamination; consequently, citizens in affected areas organize and bring pressure to bear to prevent disposal in their communities.

In late 1987 West Texans in the vicinity of Hudspeth County resorted to legal actions in the Texas courts to block location of a low-level radioactive waste dump near Fort Hancock. In February 1988, this case was dismissed; thus those citizens were not successful in preventing the selection of this site.

High-Level Radioactive Waste Disposal   While Texas authorities were searching for a burial site for the state's accumulated low-level nuclear waste, the U.S. Department of Energy (DOE) was seeking a suitable location for burial of high-level radioactive waste. This material consists primarily of spent (used) nuclear reactor fuel rods, the liquid waste resulting from reprocessing these fuel rods, and scrap materials left after manufacturing nuclear weapons.

Deaf Smith County, located in the Texas Panhandle and only 35 miles from Amarillo, was designated by DOE in 1986 as one of three areas in the United States to undergo "site characterization" in the nation's search for an underground high-level nuclear waste disposal location. Site characterization in Deaf Smith

County involved sinking two large mine shafts through the Ogallala Aquifer and excavating vast quantities of salt. Farmers and ranchers feared that the West Texas wind would blow this salt in a saline snowstorm across the region and ruin the land. Such testing, they believed, might irreparably damage the region's land and water, even if another site would finally be selected as the burial place. Almost immediately, however, DOE launched a multiyear site characterization study before recommending any location.

Meanwhile, state officials, including Agriculture Commissioner Jim Hightower, and concerned Panhandle farmers united in opposition to the Deaf Smith County site. Declaring that they did not want "a nuclear dump in their backyard," they organized to protect their land and their families. (See Figure 5.2 for a graphic expression of their opposition.) Forming a protest organization called People Opposed to Wasted Energy Repository (POWER), local farmers and ranchers mounted a series of protests that radically changed the mood of the normally quiet community of hard-working people. Three of the largest businesses in Hereford, the county seat of Deaf Smith County, threatened to move their firms out of the county if the dump should be located there. The three businesses were producers of food for human consumption.

Thereafter, in June 1986, U.S. Senator Lloyd Bentsen, Jr. (D-Texas) gained passage in Congress of a bill requiring federal agencies to comply with state safeguards against contamination of water wells. Senator Bentsen said the bill would allow Texas to protect the Ogallala Aquifer from contamination by anyone.

In December 1987, Deaf Smith County residents were elated to learn that their lengthy campaign to prevent high-level radioactive waste from being stored underground in their community had been successful. Senator Bentsen and U.S. Representative Jack Fields announced that Yucca Mountain, Nevada, was the primary site and that Deaf Smith County was totally eliminated as a prospective site.

Disposal of Nonradioactive Hazardous Waste

Emerging in Texas as a major public policy issue is the disposal of nonradioactive hazardous waste generated largely by the state's petrochemical industry. One of the largest generators of hazardous waste among the states, Texas needs to revise its existing regulatory policy and to develop new measures to cope with this

FIGURE 5.2 Bumper Sticker Opposing Proposed Location of High-Level Nuclear Waste Repository

mounting problem. Decisions must be made on controlling the generation of hazardous waste, on where and how to dispose of it, and on cleaning up damage resulting from past failures to police the disposal methods. All three branches of government—legislative, executive, and judicial—are involved in these policy issues. In addition, both private citizens and businesses that generate hazardous waste must work cooperatively with governing bodies to overcome this threat to the natural environment and to human life.

A Major Policy Issue   Deciding what to do with the "chemical garbage" generated primarily by Texas's chemical industry has become one of the state's major public policy issues. Texas chemical plants are among the nation's leading producers of residues that are toxic, corrosive, ignitable, or chemically reactive. In some instances, generated waste contains all of these types of harmful residues. Of course, Texas is not the only state that is producing such hazardous waste. The problem is national in scope, but it is especially troublesome in Texas because of the state's many refineries and chemical plants. Ranking second among the states in generating hazardous waste, Texas produces an estimated 23 million tons annually. This amounts to approximately 3,000 pounds per year for each resident, double the per capita national average.

The huge output of nonradioactive hazardous waste is a by-product of today's mass production of plastics, detergents, synthetic fibers, pesticides, drugs, paints, solvents, and preservatives. All these chemical products make life easier and more enjoyable. Many chemical products that were unknown a quarter century ago are today considered necessities, but we may not be paying the full price for today's "better living through chemistry." Future generations may have to pay a higher price in the form of death, disease, and destruction of the environment because of improper waste disposal.

Unfortunately, almost all hazardous waste produced in Texas and other states is buried in the ground. About 70 percent of the volume produced in Texas is pumped into injection wells; most of the remainder goes into other land-based facilities. Technology is available for destroying this waste material or rendering it harmless, but burying it is cheaper. The greatest threat involved in land-based disposal is contamination of ground water and the resulting harm to human life. Texas must make several policy decisions if hazardous waste disposal is to be regulated effectively. These decisions concern adequacy of enforcement procedures, cleanup of abandoned land-disposal sites, selection of future sites, and a search for alternatives to land-based disposal.

Adequacy of Enforcement   Texas administers its own hazardous waste regulation, subject to oversight by the federal Environmental Protection Agency (EPA). The state's program is administered primarily by the Texas Water Commission (TWC), but some jurisdiction has been assigned to the Texas Department of Health.

To cover the cost of regulation by these two departments, and to pay for monitoring the impact of hazardous waste activity on fish and wildlife, the 69th Legislature in 1985 established the Hazardous Waste Generation and Facility Fees Fund. Designated for this fund are annual fees ranging from $50 to $5,000, collected by TWC and the Department of Health from generators of hazardous waste.

The key to effective enforcement of any government regulation is provision of adequate resources to investigate irregularities. In testimony before the Texas House of Representatives, staff members of TWC have indicated that the agency is understaffed and is too closely tied to the Texas Chemical Council, a lobby organization of the Texas chemical industry. According to this testimony, funding for enforcement is the first item cut from the budget. An administrator admitted that TWC has always been close to the chemical industry, which helps TWC get enacted legislation that it favors.

One weakness in enforcement procedures lies in the transportation of waste material. An investigative reporter from television station WFAA-TV in Dallas testified before a Texas Senate committee that regulations governing transportation of waste are grossly violated by haulers. He reported that drivers of waste-hauling trucks discharge their loads in open fields or in city sewers. Although TWC is responsible for registering generators of hazardous waste, the reporter testified that fewer than one-fourth of the plating firms in Dallas and Fort Worth are registered. Nevertheless, these businesses generate hazardous wastes composed of heavy metals, cyanides, and other toxic waste substances. TWC can threaten unregistered firms with enforcement actions, but the agency is lenient in practice. Fines are not high, and few cases are referred to the attorney general's office for prosecution.

Site Cleanup Scores of uncontrolled dump sites, many abandoned by their owners, are identified in Texas as possible threats to the environment. Once an abandoned and inactive waste site is recognized, TWC applies for federal cleanup funds from the EPA. Lengthy delays and conflicts over funding usually follow. Before long-term action begins, however, the EPA can undertake emergency action to contain waste discharges. Also, state money from the Hazardous Waste Disposal Fee Fund may be used by TWC for remedial action. Money for this fund comes from annual fees ranging from $250 to $20,000 paid by facilities that store or dispose of hazardous waste.

A sample site cleanup operation occurred at the Motco dump near Texas City in Galveston County. Wastes stored at the site included resins, tars, soot, styrene, polyethylene, waste oil, pitch, heavy oils, organic hydrocarbons, vinyl chloride catalyst, copper chloride, mercury, mercuric chloride, and lead. From 1959 to 1968 the site was used for disposal of waste generated by the area's petrochemical plants. Its most recent owner, Motco, Inc., of Minnesota, abandoned the site when it filed for bankruptcy in 1974. The site requires various forms of construction to keep surface-water runoff from carrying toxic chemicals off-site. Another operation, the Sikes Pits, was described by a TWC administrator as follows: "The Sikes Pits site is grotesque—25 acres of purple goo 10 to 12 feet thick, with surface runoff discharging directly into the San Jacinto River."[5] The cleanup project was delayed for months because of difficulties in relocating the Sikes family, whose members resided in the waste disposal area. Meantime, the contaminated area continued to expand and pollute ground and surface water.

Selection of Disposal Sites Selecting a disposal site for hazardous waste is bound to provoke controversy and public resistance. Thus, a decision concerning where to put a new facility requires critical policy choices for state officials. For example, should the state intervene to break an impasse between waste managers and the public? Should the state set statutory requirements for site selection? Should the state take over the building and operation of waste-management facilities rather than contract for this work? The Legislature partially answered these questions with a law that requires TWC and the Department of Health to adopt rules governing the choice of new sites. These rules must define characteristics that render a site unsuitable for such facilities. In all cases, site selection must minimize the risk of water contamination.

Alternatives to Land Disposal   According to scientific authority, no buried container filled with hazardous waste is permanently leakproof. Studies conducted at Texas A&M University indicate that no liner can stand up to the range of chemicals now disposed of by landfill. Chemical companies, however, support continued use of landfills because that is the most economical method available to their industry.

Hazardous waste can be managed either by disposal or by treatment. Disposal is a form of containment of wastes through use of landfills, surface impoundments, and underground injection wells. Treatment by chemical, biological, or physical processes reduces the hazard level by either separating waste into component parts, thus reducing volume and hazardousness, or completely destroying the waste. A 1982 report to the Legislature from the Lyndon B. Johnson School of Public Affairs indicates that almost all hazardous waste materials are recyclable and many are recoverable. This report emphasizes, however, that there is generally insufficient pressure to encourage recycling as long as the disposal industry remains largely private enterprise and disposal methods remain cheaper than the cost of resource re-use.

Hazardous Waste: A Continuing Problem?

Coping with the disposal of hazardous waste will undoubtedly continue to produce major policy issues in the Lone Star State for the next decade. The Texas Legislature and the U.S. Congress will continue to encounter difficulty in finding policy solutions acceptable to concerned citizens in local communities. Those citizens will most likely continue to organize and to exert pressure to prevent "dumping" in their areas.

Pinpointing Political Power

It has never been easy to assess the distribution of political power and influence in American government, and this distribution in Texas is especially complex. There is no simple top-down or bottom-up arrangement; rather, political decisions, especially policy decisions, are made by a wide variety of persons and groups. As the example of hazardous waste demonstrates, some of these decision makers participate in local organizations, others in statewide groups, and still others in nationwide clusters. Which persons or groups have the greatest influence quite often depends on the issue or issues involved.

The influence of any interest group cannot, however, be fairly calculated by looking at the distribution of only one political asset, whether it is money, status, knowledge, organization, or sheer numbers.[6] Because of these facts of political life, we may safely conclude that organized interest groups in Texas put the unorganized citizenry at great disadvantage when public policy issues are at stake.

Notes

1. Norman J. Ornstein and Shirley Elder, *Interest Groups, Lobbying and Policy-making* (Washington, D.C.: Congressional Quarterly Press, 1978), p. 31.
2. Thomas R. Dye, *Politics in States and Communities,* 4th ed. (Englewood Cliffs, N.J.: Prentice-Hall, 1981), pp. 91–92.
3. Sarah M. Morehouse, *State Politics, Parties and Policy* (New York: Holt, Rinehart and Winston, 1981), p. 117.
4. Kenneth J. Meier, *Politics and the Bureaucracy* (North Scituate, Mass.: Duxbury, 1979), p. 180.
5. Rick Pilts, *Hazardous Waste: Gross National By-product,* House Study Group Special Report No. 100 (Austin: Texas House of Representatives, February 24, 1984), p. 41.
6. Frank J. Sorauf, "Political Action Committees in American Politics," in *What Price PACs?* edited by M. J. Rossant (New York: Twentieth Century Fund, 1984), pp. 94–95.

Key Terms and Concepts

politics	professional group
interest group	ethnic group
minority representation	public interest group
functional representation	public officer and employee group
right of association	interest group technique
decentralized government	lobbying
decentralized party system	techniques of lobbyists
ideology	political action committee (PAC)
economic group	power linkage
business organization	political influence of interest
trade association	groups
labor group	

Selected Readings

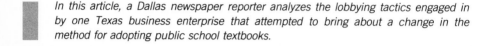

5.1 A Case of Textbook Lobbying

Wayne Slater

In this article, a Dallas newspaper reporter analyzes the lobbying tactics engaged in by one Texas business enterprise that attempted to bring about a change in the method for adopting public school textbooks.

Even for billionaire Robert Bass, this wasn't peanuts. Any company picked to supply a textbook for Texas schoolchildren stands to make hundreds of millions of dollars, and Mr. Bass wanted his company—Merrill Publishing Co.—to be chosen for the new elementary science book.

"It's big bucks," acknowledged Texas Education Commissioner William Kirby. "They really want to get in on the Texas market because it is such a big market." But when Mr. Bass, the reclusive Fort Worth billionaire and a scion of the wealthy Bass family, discovered last year that his company's science textbook wouldn't be ready in time for the bidding process, he faced two options—don't compete or change the rules. He chose the latter.

Lobbying Begins with Campaign Contributions

In recent months, Mr. Bass has mounted an elaborate, high-dollar lobbying campaign aimed at delaying adoption of the text for the 1991–1992 school year. The effort, although in many ways typical of the frenetic wheeling and dealing that accompanies legislative sessions, has nevertheless angered some lawmakers and startled even veteran lobbyists familiar with hardball politics in the Texas Capitol. "You see a lot of self-interest legislation around here," said one knowledgeable lobbyist, "but this one is really blatant."

Last week, Rep. Bill Hammond, R-Dallas, sought to scuttle legislation that Merrill sought by publicly complaining that the effort was designed to "protect one publisher's profits from the mistakes of its own bad planning." But by then the Bass lobbying campaign was several months old and gaining momentum. It began last year when Mr. Bass made campaign contributions to key legislators who might consider his effort to delay adoption of the science text for 1991–1992, according to interviews and public records. In February, Merrill executives asked the State Board of Education

From the *Dallas Morning News,* May 11, 1989. Wayne Slater is a member of the Austin Bureau of the *Morning News.* Reprinted by permission.

to alter its plans to adopt both the math and science textbooks at the same time, in November 1990.

A Six-Year Adoption Schedule

State public school textbooks are changed every six years on a staggered basis. Publishers seeking to win contracts for the science and math textbooks for the 1991–1992 school year must submit samples to the Board of Education by April 1990. Final board approval is scheduled in November 1990.

In prepared testimony, Kenneth French, a Merrill regional sales manager based in Carrollton, said delaying the adoption of one of the books would be good for schoolchildren because it would ensure that publishers focus maximum attention on preparing a single book of the highest quality. Although all publishers have known since 1984 that both texts would be adopted this year, Mr. French acknowledged in testimony that Merrill's elementary science book wouldn't be ready.

Lobbyist "Buddy" Jones Fails But Tries Again

Behind the scenes, Mr. Bass' chief lobbyist in Austin, Neal T. "Buddy" Jones, set up meetings and telephone calls with most members of the Board of Education. "Several days prior to the actual vote on that particular proposition, we began in earnest making an effort to take our position to the state board," said Mr. Jones, a former aide to House Speaker Gib Lewis and widely considered one of the most skilled lobbyists in Austin. The meetings, telephone calls and public presentation failed, however. The board rejected Merrill's request, and Mr. Jones moved his campaign to the Legislature. The goal: pass legislation that would force the Board of Education to consider only one basic elementary textbook, either science or math, at a time.

Rather than getting a separate bill introduced, Mr. Jones prepared an amendment to an existing bill sponsored by Mr. Hammond dealing with textbook selection committees. Mr. Hammond's bill was before the House Governmental Affairs Committee, chaired by Rep. Bruce Gibson, D-Cleburne, a close friend and one-time officemate of Mr. Jones when both served in the Legislature. Seven of the nine committee members received campaign contributions from Mr. Bass in late 1988, according to reports filed with the secretary of state's office, including all three members of a subcommittee: Mr. Gibson ($750); Rep. Al Granoff, D-Dallas ($500); and Rep. Lena Guerrero, D-Austin ($500). On the Senate side, all but one member of the Education Committee—Sen. Eddie Bernice Johnson, D-Dallas—received contributions ranging from $500 to $2,500 just before the session, according to reports filed in January 1989.

On April 24, after a long day in the House, the subcommittee met about 8 P.M. at Mr. Granoff's desk on the House floor. The amendment, given in advance to Mr.

Gibson by Mr. Jones, was adopted unanimously. All three subcommittee members defended their vote, saying the proposal is good policy. "The fact that it was promoted by Merrill, which is a Bass Texas-type company, didn't make it offensive to me," said Mr. Granoff. "But the reality is that I agree with the concept that each of the five subject matter areas should have its own year." Ms. Guerrero agreed, saying math and science should be adopted in separate years. "I don't think Granoff and I meant to carry water for anybody," she said.

Results of a "Shotgun Session" of the Governmental Affairs Committee

A week later, on May 1, the Governmental Affairs Committee gathered around Mr. Gibson's desk in what is called a "shotgun session," a procedure often used near the end of legislative sessions to move bills quickly. The bill, with the Merrill amendment attached, was approved on a 6–1 vote and sent to the full House for consideration. Meanwhile, Mr. Jones recruited two of the Capitol's top lobbyists, Rusty Kelly and Nub Donaldson. Over lunches and dinners at the richly appointed private clubs of Austin, sometimes in quick conversations in the marble hallways outside the chambers, the trio began recruiting support from House and Senate members. Further, Mr. Bass telephoned Mr. Lewis, D-Fort Worth, personally seeking support for the bill. "He [Mr. Lewis] has a great deal of respect for Robert," said the speaker's chief of staff, Mike Milsap. "And frankly, he sees some merit in his position. But that issue will be decided by the members of the House."

Alarmed, Mr. Hammond, the bill's original sponsor, decided the best way to scuttle the effort was to call a news conference. A week ago, he complained publicly that the proposal would hurt schoolchildren by delaying the adoption of either the math or science text, cost taxpayers money and burden teachers. Mr. Jones was unavailable to respond to the charges because he was helping host the Gib Lewis golf tournament benefitting the American Cancer Society at an Austin club. "To me, it was embarrassing as a member of the Legislature to see this kind of thing float through," Mr. Hammond said this week.

A Damage Control Packet

In response to Mr. Hammond's news conference, the Bass lobbying team last Friday hired Bill Miller of MEM & Associates, Inc., an Austin political consultant, for damage control. By Monday morning, legislators had a six-page packet of information, complete with executive summary, prepared by MEM and designed to shift the focus of the debate. The packet made two points: The proposal is good for teachers and schoolchildren, and the real enemy is "the entrenched bureaucracy at the Texas Education Agency" that won't change its established textbook adoption cycle and delay selection of either the science or math text. The packet outraged Mr. Kirby.

"That's a typical propaganda technique," he said. "If you really don't have a good argument, then pick somebody else out to serve as the scapegoat." Meanwhile, several major publishers opposing the delay mustered lobbying teams of their own. Scott Foresman, Inc., hired the high-powered lobby team of Don Adams and Angelo Zottarelli, who have close ties with Lt. Gov. Bill Hobby. Further, Simon & Schuster fielded lobbyists from a law firm whose principals include former U.S. Rep. Tom Loeffler, although Mr. Loeffler is not involved in the lobbying.

A David and Goliath Affair?

Sitting at midweek in the Senate chamber, Mr. Jones acknowledged that the lobbying campaign had reached an intense level, both sides buttonholing lawmakers, counting votes and distributing memos with charges and countercharges. For his part, Mr. Jones depicted the battle as a David and Goliath affair. "Us being David against the Goliath of the publishing world, the four or five major, big mega-publishers," he said. Merrill, he said, was just seeking to clarify state law on how many basic texts should be considered in a single year, a message he has been delivering to legislators.*

5.2 Legislator Defends Free Perks

Mike Ward

In this article, an Austin reporter reveals a defense of "free riding" and other freebies enjoyed by Representatives Ron Lewis and Bill Carter, along with other members of the Texas Legislature. It shows that the "free rides" are provided at the expense of lobbyists and the groups they represent.

An East Texas lawmaker, whose cross-country traveling at lobbyists' expense has drawn criticism, defended the trips Thursday, saying such freebies are "one of the things about this job that's fun." But two veteran colleagues who do not accept perks disagreed, warning that the practice is so widespread in the Legislature that it encourages influence-peddling.

The developments came after one Texas law enforcement group . . . called for a Travis County grand jury investigation of a December ski trip, paid for by a rival group, which they claim influenced the veto of a bill. Prosecutors have not decided whether to investigate. The December trip was partly sponsored by the Texas State Troopers Association, which later opposed a bill that would have required police

From the *Austin American-Statesman,* June 30, 1989. Mike Ward is a member of the *American-Statesman* Capitol Staff. Reprinted by permission.

*Editors' note: The Jones amendment was not adopted and thus the Bass and Merrill Publishing Co. lobbying effort failed.

groups to publicly disclose where they spend money raised through phone-solicitation campaigns.

Trips Called Legal

Rep. Ron Lewis, one of three lawmakers who took the Utah ski trip, said the practice by Texas lawmakers of accepting free out-of-state trips is legal and not unusual. "I don't know of anybody in this chamber who hasn't taken a golfing outing, who hasn't taken a hunting trip, something," said Lewis, a Mauriceville Democrat, and member of the powerful House Appropriations and Calendars committees.

"We get $600 a month for this job. If you take away my golfings, if you take away my outings, my hunting trips, then what's fun about this job anymore? We don't get paid any money so that's one of the things about this job that's fun. . . . As far as influence-peddling or buying support with all this, that's the most ridiculous thing in the world. Nobody's buying influence from me."

Making the ski trip in addition to Lewis were House Appropriations Committee Chairman Jim Rudd, D-Brownfield; Ways and Means Committee Chairman James Hury, D-Galveston; Mike Toomey, now the governor's chief of staff; and Cliff Johnson, the governor's legislative liaison. Toomey and Johnson are former House members.

Lewis said it was one of three lobbyist-paid trips he has taken in recent months, including an Acapulco vacation earlier this month paid for by the troopers' association. "It was a friendly rest trip—a vacation. I don't feel bad about it," he said. In April, he traveled to Washington at the expense of the Department of Public Safety Officers Association with seven other House members. The association's executive director, Lane Denton, said the trip cost about $4,000.

The Washington Trip

Rep. Bill Carter, R-Fort Worth, said the entourage included himself, Lewis, and Reps. Bill Blackwood, Dick Swift, Bill Arnold, Jim Tallas, Sam Johnson, and Frank Madla. In three days, Carter said, the group toured the FBI academy in Quantico, Virginia, the FBI headquarters, and the White House. They also met with several Texas congressmen and Virginia troopers, and did some sightseeing. The lawmakers who went are members of the House Public Safety and Appropriations committees. At the time, they were considering bills to bolster training for Texas law enforcement officials and fund an automated fingerprint system, which the association supported. "I don't think anybody voted any differently because we got a free trip," Carter said.

Lewis said he accepted the trips from the Texas State Troopers Association because he has been a longtime friend of the association's lobbyist, Mario Martinez. He said the ski trip cost him $2,000 because he hurt his foot on the first day. In addition to the trips, he said, Martinez furnished meals to the Appropriations Committee. He said one reason the troopers' association spent more than $35,000 on legislative entertainment this year was that so many lawmakers were seeking perks. "Mario can't tell a member of the Appropriations Committee no when [a member] says, 'Hey, would you bring us something to eat. We're working late tonight,' " Lewis said. "Everybody, everybody asks Mario to help them. Because he's a great guy, because he buys committee dinners."

Some Don't Accept Perks

Lewis and Carter said dozens of other House members and committees were treated to trips and perks, and they see no problem with the practice. Criticism of the freebies, Lewis said, "is so ridiculous, I think it's funny." But Reps. Doyle Willis, D-Fort Worth, and Bill Hollowell, D-Grand Saline, disagreed. Both said they do not accept such perks, and are a small minority with such a policy in the Legislature.

"This whole business of trips and free this and free that is getting way out of hand. It's just wrong," said Willis, who has been a member of the Legislature since 1947. "I don't know how people can tell you, with a straight face, that they aren't influenced by free trips. These special interests wouldn't be spending all this money up here unless they were buying something, now would they?"

During January and February, Willis said, lobbyists reportedly spent an average of $1,500 per lawmaker. With 181 legislators, the two-month total would be more than $271,000. "Does that influence people? Why, of course, it does," said Hollowell, who has served since 1957. Legislators "develop a rapport with these people they take trips with to New York, Europe, wherever. It gives [lobbyists] an entree to people in the Legislature to talk to them about their business, buys them some time, if nothing else."

Need for Change Cited

Hollowell and Willis said the present system needs to be changed. Hollowell said that "if legislative pay were raised, and the junkets and freebies were prohibited, Texas would be better off."

"I think all this affects bills, what passes, everything," Willis said. "We'd be better off if the House and Senate met someplace with a fence around it to keep all these lobbyists out."

Chapter 6

The Legislature

Poultryman Bo Pilgrim's CHICKEN RANCH

Jimmy Margulies Houston Post reprinted by permission

*R*eform of the Texas workers' compensation law had been given a high priority before the 71st Legislature began its regular session in January 1989. Nearly everyone agreed that something was wrong with a system that featured high insurance rates for employers and low payments to injured workers. Because the regular session ended in May without producing "workers' comp" legislation, Governor Clements called a special session in June. When the business-influenced House produced a bill that encountered strong opposition in the trial-lawyer-influenced Senate, East Texas chicken magnate Bo Pilgrim buttonholed nine un-committed senators in their offices and on the Senate floor. After explaining why a business-friendly bill should be enacted, Pilgrim slipped each of these senators some of his propaganda along with a "campaign contribution" in the form of a $10,000 check that was signed but had the space for the payee's name left blank. Senator John Montford reported later that he refused to accept his check, and Senator Hugh Parmer promptly returned his check and called the matter to the attention of Lieutenant Governor Bill Hobby and Travis County District Attorney Ronnie Earle. Subsequently, Texas cartoonists ridiculed the affair (see the cartoon that begins this chapter); Austin journalist Molly Ivins reported that Parmer was called "Senator Snitch" by other senators who wanted to keep Pilgrim's money but feared unfavorable publicity; and the special session ended in July without passage of a workers' compensation bill.

A Preliminary View

Of course, enacting a law is not the only way to get things done in Austin, but passing bills and adopting resolutions are the principal means whereby members of the Texas Legislature participate in making public policy. Usually, lawmaking is a slow, frustrating, and often disappointing process. But most citizens are im-patient with delays, even if their policy objectives are achieved; and usually they are dissatisfied with the inevitable compromises that must be made.

Looking down at the House or Senate floor from gallery seats, visitors are likely to be appalled by the shouting, pushing, prank playing, and even sleeping that all too frequently can be observed in the chambers of the Texas Legislature. Debate seldom reflects a high level of statesmanship, and legislative conduct is sometimes best described as bizarre—especially during the hours that mark the end of a session. (And there was one memorable occasion when a stripper performed in the House lobby to celebrate the birthday of a representative.)

Regardless of the behavior of some Texas lawmakers, all of them must dem-onstrate sufficient political ability to compete successfully in primary and general election campaigns. And to function effectively in office, senators and representa-tives must establish satisfactory relationships with fellow legislators, executive officials (especially the governor), lobbyists, bureaucrats at various levels, and others.

Some Texans learn firsthand about the legislative process when they go to Austin and watch their legislators on the House and Senate floors or in committee

The Austin AIDS Coalition to Unleash Power (ACT UP) responds to Senator Carl Parker's joking about AIDS. (Senate Media Services.)

meetings. Other concerned citizens may even talk to legislators and legislative staff personnel, or they may communicate their comments and questions by mail. And in the course of every legislative session there are groups of like-minded activists who seek to send strong messages to legislators by organizing public demonstrations in the vicinity of the Capitol. During the regular session of the 71st Legislature in 1989, for example, Senator Carl Parker's joking about killing homosexuals with AIDS caused Austin's AIDS Coalition to Unleash Power (ACT UP) to stage a highly publicized demonstration in front of the Capitol. (Enactment of AIDS legislation by the 71st Legislature is described in Reading 6.1.)

Regardless of how much they know about the Texas Legislature, most Texans 18 years of age or older are eligible to become registered voters and to participate in the primaries and elections whereby state senators and representatives are nominated and elected. Popular election of lawmakers is the essence of representative government.

Legislative Framework

In all their state constitutions, Texans have entrusted enactment of bills and adoption of resolutions to popularly elected legislators. As in a majority of the states, the lawmaking branch of Texas government is officially termed the Legislature.

Nebraska has a *unicameral,* or single-house, legislature; but Texas and 48 other states have *bicameral,* or two-chamber, lawmaking bodies.

Composition

The smaller chamber of each bicameral legislature is the *Senate.* In Texas and in 40 other states, the larger chamber is called the *House of Representatives.* The remaining states use the terms assembly, house of delegates, or general assembly. Texas has 150 members in its House of Representatives and 31 members in its Senate.

Election and Terms of Office

Texas legislators are elected by qualified voters residing in representative and senatorial districts. Terms of office for members of both houses begin in January of odd-numbered years. Representatives serve for a term of two years; senators are elected for four years. After statewide senatorial redistricting in the first odd-numbered year of each decade (for example, 1991), all Senate terms expire and a new Senate is elected in the general election of the following year (for example, November 1992). Then senators draw lots to determine who will serve for four years and who will serve for two years. Thereafter, one-half (that is, 15 or 16) of the senators are elected in even-numbered years. If a legislator dies, resigns, or is expelled from office, the vacancy is filled by special election. A legislator may be expelled by a two-thirds majority vote of the membership of the legislator's chamber.

Sessions

When the 71st Legislature convened in Austin on the second Tuesday in January 1989, its members knew (or should have known) that their session would end on or before May 29 of that year. This certainty is spelled out in the Texas Constitution, which provides for a *regular session* of not more than 140 calendar days in each odd-numbered year. (In practice, regular sessions always run for the full 140 days allowed.) A *special session* lasting no longer than 30 days may be called by the governor at any time, but during a special session the Legislature may consider only those matters placed before it by the governor. Such limits indicate a deep-seated popular distrust of legislators and a fear of change. Governor Bill Clements expressed his sentiments with the statement that "all kinds of bad things can happen when the Legislature is in session."

Districting

Because population distribution changes constantly, it is logical to redraw the boundaries of legislative districts periodically to ensure equitable representation for the people. But *redistricting* can be politically painful to a legislator. It may take away territory that has provided strong voter support for a particular lawmaker; it may add to a legislator's district an area that produces little support and much opposition; or it may include in a new district the residences of two or more representatives or senators, only one of whom can be elected.

Framers of the Texas Constitution of 1876 stipulated that "the Legislature shall, at its first session after the publication of each United States decennial census, apportion the State into Senatorial and Representative districts." Nevertheless, in the decades that followed, the Legislature sometimes failed to redivide the state's population and map new districts for legislators. Thus some districts became heavily populated and greatly underrepresented; and others experienced population decline or slow growth, resulting in overrepresentation.

In 1948 the inequities of legislative districting in Texas finally led to adoption of a state constitutional amendment designed to pressure the Legislature to remedy this situation. Under the amendment, failure of the Legislature to redistrict during the first regular session following a decennial census brings into operation the *Legislative Redistricting Board.* This board consists of the following five ex officio (that is, holding another office) members: lieutenant governor, speaker of the House of Representatives, attorney general, comptroller of public accounts, and commissioner of the General Land Office. The board must meet within 90 days after the legislative session and carry out the necessary redistricting within another 60 days.

Although new legislative districts were drawn after the federal censuses of 1950 and 1960, the Texas Constitution's apportionment formulas for the House and Senate discriminated against heavily populated urban counties. These formulas were not changed until after the U.S. Supreme Court held in *Reynolds* v. *Sims* (1964) that "the seats in both houses of a bicameral state legislature must be apportioned on a population basis." This "one-man, one-vote" principle was applied first in Texas by a federal district court in *Kilgarlin* v. *Martin* (1965). Over the next 20 years, every redistricting measure enacted by the Texas Legislature resulted in complaints about *gerrymandering* (that is, drawing district boundaries in ways that unfairly benefit a group or a political party); and many court battles were fought before district boundaries were established. Similar litigation can be expected following legislative redistricting by the 72nd Legislature (or by the Legislative Redistricting Board) in 1991.

Senatorial Districts Members of the Texas Senate have always represented *single-member districts*—that is, the voters of each district elect one senator. Many of the 31 senatorial districts cover entire counties, but 8 of them are wholly or partially composed of territory within Harris County (where Houston is located).

Until the 73rd Legislature convenes in January 1993, every Texas senator will continue to represent an area that contained approximately 458,980 inhabitants when the federal decennial census was taken in 1980. This ideal population for a senatorial district was obtained by dividing Texas's population in 1980—a total of 14,228,282—by 31, the total number of Senate seats. Assuming that the number of senators will not be increased by constitutional amendment, projected higher population figures for the decennial census of 1990 should result in an ideal senatorial district population of around 600,000 for the 73rd Legislature.

Representative Districts   Until 1971, a Texas county with two or more seats in the House used *multimember districts* to elect representatives at large. Thus, a voter in such a county could vote in more than one House race. In 1971, however, single-member districts were established in Harris, Dallas, and Bexar counties; and in 1975 the single-member districting system was extended to all other counties electing more than one representative. Nevertheless, there were complaints that the new district lines in some counties had been drawn to favor conservative Anglo Democrats and to minimize election opportunities for blacks, Mexican Americans, Republicans, and liberal Democrats. Subsequently, some of these district boundaries were changed by federal court order, but the requirement for single-member districts had been established. Election results have demonstrated that single-member districts do reduce campaign costs and increase the probability that various Texas minorities will win House seats.

On the basis of the 1980 census figures, the ideal population for each Texas representative district was computed to be 94,856 (the total population of Texas divided by 150). Because the state's population increased greatly between 1980 and 1990, the ideal population for each representative taking office in 1993 should be about 120,000 (assuming that the number of representatives is not increased by constitutional amendment).

Compensation

Many states pay legislators ridiculously low salaries (for example, an average of $300 per year in Rhode Island and $100 per year in New Hampshire), but lawmakers in New York receive annual salaries of $57,500. Texas legislators' salaries and per diem allowances can be changed only by constitutional amendment, and the state's voters have been reluctant to approve increases. A 1975 amendment to the Texas Constitution increased annual salaries from $4,800 to $7,200 for senators, representatives, the speaker of the House, and the president of the Senate (the lieutenant governor). That amendment also increased their per diem allowance from $12 to $30 a day for the first 120 days of a regular session and for every day of a special session.

The most recent effort to obtain a legislative pay raise came in 1989, when the 71st Legislature proposed a constitutional amendment linking annual salaries for senators and representatives to the annual salary appropriated for the governor, which was $93,432 for fiscal years 1990 and 1991. Each legislator would receive a salary amounting to one-fourth ($23,358) the amount paid to the governor, and the speaker of the House and the president of the Senate would get one-half ($46,716) the governor's salary. Another proposed amendment set the per diem allowance at the maximum amount allowed for federal income tax purposes as a deduction for a legislator's living expenses, which was $81 in 1989. Both proposals were rejected by Texas voters in November 1989.

At the beginning of a session, each house authorizes contingency expense allowances for its members. For example, in 1989 the House resolved that during the 71st regular session every representative's operating account would be credited with $7,000 per month while the Legislature remained in session and with $6,000 per month when it was not in session. Representatives use money in this account to cover the cost of postage, office operations, and staff salaries. In 1989 no representative's employee could receive a salary of more than $2,250 per month. The Senate of the 71st Legislature restricted each senator to a total of not more than $15,500 per month for secretarial and other office staff but did not impose a staff salary limit.

Under the terms of the State Employees Retirement Act of 1975, legislators contribute 8 percent of their salary to a retirement fund. Retirement pay for senators and representatives amounts to 2 percent of a district judge's salary for each year served. At current salary levels, a 55-year-old legislator can retire at about $46,000 per year after completing 30 years of legislative service. Very few legislators, however, remain in office for even half that length of time.

Membership

Membership in the Texas Legislature is limited by state constitutional qualifications concerning citizenship, voter status, state residence, district residence, and age. Despite these restrictions, millions of Texans have all the prescribed legal qualifications. As is true of other state legislatures and the U.S. Congress, however, biographical characteristics of members of recent Texas legislatures suggest that opportunities for election to either of the two legislative chambers are restricted.

Qualifications of Members

The Texas Constitution specifies that House and Senate members must be citizens of the United States, qualified Texas voters, and residents of the districts they represent for one year immediately preceding the general election. Qualifications differ between the houses, however, in matters of state residence and age. Thus, a House candidate must have resided in Texas for two years before election, whereas a Senate candidate must have five years of state residence. To be eligible for House membership, a person must be at least 21 years of age; to serve in the Senate, a person must be at least 26.

Characteristics of Members

The typical Texas legislator is an Anglo, Protestant, male Democrat between 35 and 50 years of age who was born in Texas, practices law, and has served one or more previous terms of office. Such characteristics do not guarantee any predetermined reaction to issues and events, but it is probable that legislators are influenced by their experience and environment, which therefore have policy consequences. Thus, a study of the Legislature must give some attention to the biographical characteristics of legislators.

Ethnic and Gender Classification   Anglo males continue to dominate the Texas Legislature, but their number has declined slightly over the last two decades. At the beginning of the 62nd Legislature (1971), only one woman was listed on the legislative rolls (Senator Barbara Jordan), but by 1989 the number of women in the 71st Legislature had increased to 19: three senators and 16 representatives. Nevertheless, because about 51 percent of the inhabitants of Texas are women, their representation in the Legislature continues to be disproportionately low.

Ethnic minorities, however, made proportionately greater gains in the 1970s and 1980s. Former Representative Craig Washington, a black from Houston, first was elected to represent a Harris County senatorial district in 1982. He was joined by Eddie Bernice Johnson, a black senator from Dallas, in 1987. Thirteen black representatives were elected in 1988 to serve in the 71st Legislature (1989–1990), and 19 Mexican-American representatives were elected in the same year. A total of six Mexican Americans were serving in the Senate at the beginning of the 71st Legislature. Both blacks and Mexican Americans have been underrepresented in the Texas Legislature, but from 1971 to 1989 black representation increased seven-fold and the number of Mexican-American legislators more than doubled.

Political Party Affiliation In the elections of 1960, no Republicans won seats in the 57th Legislature (1961–1962); but in 1980, 20 years later, the Republican party elected 7 senators and 36 representatives to the 67th Legislature (1981–1982). Not only were more Republicans elected in 1980 than ever before, but two Democratic representatives switched to the Republican party during the regular session of 1981 and one Democratic senator became a Republican in August of that year. As in several other states, there were fewer Republican victories in Texas in 1982; and Republican representation in the 68th Legislature (1983–1984) declined slightly to 5 senators and 35 representatives. As a result of the 1984 elections, however, Republican representation in the Senate of the 69th Legislature (1985–1986) increased to 6, and the number of Republican representatives in the House jumped to 52 at the beginning of that session.

With the election of Governor Bill Clements in 1986, the number of Republican senators remained the same, but Republican representation in the House increased to 56 in the 70th Legislature (1987–1988). In 1988, when GOP presidential candidate George Bush carried the state, 57 Republicans won House seats and 8 won Senate seats. Before the 71st Legislature's regular session ended in May 1989, Republican victories in two special elections had increased the number of Republican representatives to 59. Later, Rep. Rick Perry switched parties, increasing the Republican total in the House to 60.

Summarizing the political history of the Texas Legislature between 1961 and 1989, one notes that the political lineup in the House shifted from a total of 150 Democrats and no Republicans to 90 Democrats and 60 Republicans; during the same period, the political lineup in the Senate changed from 31 Democrats and no Republicans to 23 Democrats and 8 Republicans.

Black and Mexican-American legislators have been Democrats, except for one black (Ron Givens from Lubbock) who served for two terms in the House. Like most black and Mexican-American legislators, Republicans have tended to reside in metropolitan areas. But whereas black and Mexican-American lawmakers have usually been elected by central-city residents, Republican senators and representatives have received their strongest support from suburban voters.

Age Because of the age qualifications set by the Texas Constitution (26 years for senators as opposed to 21 years for representatives), the age level in the Senate tends to be slightly higher than in the House. Senators are rarely under 30 years of age. On the other hand, there were three representatives in their 20s at the beginning of the 71st Legislature in 1989.

Occupation Traditionally, Texas legislators have included many attorneys, several farmers and ranchers, a few skilled laborers (but no unskilled workers), and persons engaged in various businesses—primarily real estate, insurance, and construction. Although most legislators are identified with only one occupation, others claim two or more occupational interests, and several are business executives who serve on boards of directors of various firms. Such a large number of occupational backgrounds provides a broad range of expertise in dealing with diverse public problems. In recent legislatures, one-third of the representatives and one-half of the senators have been law school graduates. Thus, members of the legal profession have a powerful influence.

Although there may be some logic behind selecting lawyers to make laws, this hardly explains the disproportionate number of attorneys in the Texas Legislature, especially when one considers that the drafting of bills and resolutions is chiefly a technical matter handled by the bill-drafting experts who staff the Legislative Council or are employed as lobbyists. Perhaps the reason is that lawyers are often more available as candidates than persons in other occupational groups. Even an unsuccessful political campaign gives an attorney publicity that may attract clients. If the attorney is successful in a bid for election, one or more partners may take over much of the legal work, leaving the lawyer-legislator with time to concentrate on legislative duties. In return, business and government contacts made during the course of legislative service may profit the law firm.

It is generally known that some lawyer-legislators receive retainer fees that are paid by corporations and other special interests, with the understanding that legal services will be performed if needed. In some cases, these retainer payments are intended to influence legislation rather than to guarantee the availability of legal counsel. Also noteworthy is the fact that lawyer-legislators exercise a decisive influence in amending and revising the penal code and the code of criminal procedure under which all lawyers practice.

Clients hoping to delay trial may seek the services of lawyer-legislators because these attorneys are entitled to obtain a continuance (that is, a postponement) of any case set for trial during a period extending from 30 days before to 30 days after a legislative session. Because of some blatant abuse, a law was enacted that allows a judge to deny the privilege of continuance when a lawmaker has been hired to assist other lawyers in handling a case within ten days of the trial or of any proceeding involving it. This rule does not apply to a new suit or to a suit that a lawyer-legislator is handling alone.

Education In government, as in business, most positions of leadership call for college credentials. Thus, it is not surprising to find that nearly all members of recent Texas legislatures attended one or more institutions of higher education and that most could claim at least one degree. Of course, any group with many lawyers will certainly include a high percentage of college and university graduates.

Religious Affiliation Although the Texas Constitution contains a detailed requirement for the separation of church and state, religion may play a critical role in the formulation of public policy. Therefore, a legislator's denominational ties and the doctrines of the lawmaker's church must be taken into consideration by political analysts. This is especially important when one is considering legislation involving abortion, birth control, gambling, sale of alcoholic beverages, state aid to parochial schools, Sabbath observance, and other matters of vital importance to some religious groups but of indifference to others. In the 71st Legislature, Baptists and Catholics each constituted about one-fourth of the total membership.

Legislative Experience Except for special circumstances, such as those that arise after redistricting, the percentage of first-term representatives in each legislative session is usually less than 20 percent. Following the redistricting of 1981 and elections of 1982, for example, this turnover rate rose to 30 percent in the House. In the Senate, where the turnover rate ranged from 9 to 13 percent between 1974 and 1981, it rose to 39 percent following redistricting in 1981 and elections in 1982. As a result of elections in 1988, the turnover rate for the 71st Legislature was 17 percent in the House and 16 percent in the Senate.

Once elected, senators tend to remain in the Senate longer than representatives usually serve in the House. To some extent, the higher rate of turnover in the House is influenced by the fact that representatives occasionally pass up opportunities for nomination and re-election in order to make a bid for a Senate seat or some other more desirable office.

Powers and Immunities

Although bound by restrictions not found in many state constitutions, the Legislature is the dominant branch of Texas government and the chief agent in making public policy. Through control of government spending, for example, lawmakers cause state agencies and personnel, and to some extent even units of local government, to be dependent on them. In addition to their constitutional powers, legislators enjoy certain immunities designed to allow them to function freely.

Nonlegislative Powers

Although the principal powers of the Texas Legislature are exercised by enacting civil and criminal statutes, the House and Senate have other important powers that relate only indirectly to the lawmaking function.

Constitutional Amendment Power Both state legislative chambers are involved in proposing amendments to the Texas Constitution. A proposal is officially made when approved by a two-thirds majority of the total membership of each house.

Control over Administration   Most appointments made by the governor must be submitted to the Senate for *advice and consent* by two-thirds of the senators present. Thus one chamber of the Legislature is in a position to influence the selection of many important officials. (See page 170 for a discussion of senatorial courtesy.) Further legislative control over administrative matters is exercised through enactment of laws establishing, and in some cases abolishing, various state agencies. The Legislature also defines the responsibilities of these agencies and imposes restrictions through appropriations of money for their operations and through general oversight of their activities.

One form of administrative supervision involves requiring state agencies to make periodic and special reports to the Legislature. The state auditor, who provides information concerning irregular or inefficient use of funds by administrative agencies, is appointed by the *Legislative Audit Committee.* This six-member body is composed of the speaker of the House of Representatives, chairs of the House Appropriations and Ways and Means Committees, the lieutenant governor, and chairs of the Senate Finance and State Affairs Committees. The *Legislative Budget Board,* the lawmakers' own budgeting agency, helps the Legislature evaluate government operations for the purpose of determining how large the appropriation should be for each department, board, and commission. (See page 246 for further information concerning this board.)

Another important instrument of control over state administration is the Legislature's *Sunset Advisory Commission.* It makes recommendations concerning the continuation of nearly all state agencies. (See page 193 for details concerning the organization and function of this commission.)

Investigative Power   In order to obtain information on problems requiring remedial legislation, the Legislature may subpoena witnesses, administer oaths, and compel the submission of records and documents. Such action may be taken jointly by the two houses as a body, by one house, or by a committee. Legislative investigations that have led to some reforms include probes of higher education in South Texas, rural health care delivery, and the insurance industry.

Impeachment Power   The House of Representatives has the power to impeach district court judges and judges of higher appellate courts, although this power is rarely used. Also, the House may impeach executive officers, such as the governor, treasurer, attorney general, and commissioner of the General Land Office. *Impeachment* involves bringing charges by a simple majority vote; it resembles the indictment process of a grand jury. Following impeachment, the Senate renders judgment after a proceeding resembling a court trial. Conviction requires a two-thirds majority vote of the Senate membership. Thus, District Judge O. P. Carrillo was impeached by the House in August 1975 and was convicted by the Senate in January 1976. The only punishment that may be imposed is removal from office and disqualification from holding any other public office under the Texas Constitution. But if a crime has been committed, the deposed official also may be prosecuted like any other person before a state or federal court having jurisdiction over the offense.

President George Bush addresses a joint session of the 71st Legislature, with representatives and senators assembled in the House chamber. Lieutenant Governor Bill Hobby is seated on the far left and Speaker Gib Lewis is seated on the far right. In the background is the battle flag that flew over General Sam Houston's men at San Jacinto in 1836. (Senate Media Services.)

Legislative Powers

Using language reminiscent of George Orwell's *Animal Farm,* we can say that whereas all powers exercised by the Texas Legislature are in a sense legislative, some are more legislative than others. Thus, the more typical exercise of legislative power involves making public policy by passing bills and adopting resolutions. Each bill or resolution is designated by a number, which indicates the order of introduction during a session, and each legislative proposal is identified by a distinctive abbreviation, which indicates the chamber of origin.[1]

Simple Resolution   Abbreviated as H.R. (House Resolution) if originating in the House and S.R. (Senate Resolution) if originating in the Senate, a *simple resolution* involves action by one house only and is not sent to the governor. Adoption requires a simple majority vote. Matters dealt with by simple resolution include an invitation extended to a nonmember to address the chamber, rules of the House and the Senate, and procedures for House and Senate operation.

Simple resolutions couched in humorous and satirical language are traditionally passed on the occasion of a legislator's birthday and at other times. Although some people believe that such resolutions waste time, others contend that this buffoonery is helpful in relieving tensions and cooling passions produced by sharp debate and tiresome haggling over more important policy matters.

Concurrent Resolution   After adoption by a simple majority vote in both houses, a *concurrent resolution* (H.C.R. or S.C.R.) is sent to the governor, who (as in the case of a bill) may sign it, allow it to pass without signature, or veto it. Typical examples are a resolution requesting action by the U.S. Congress or information from a state agency, establishing a joint study committee composed of senators and representatives, or granting permission to sue the state. An exception is the concurrent resolution to adjourn at the end of a legislative session; this measure does not require approval by the governor.

Joint Resolution   Adoption of a *joint resolution* (H.J.R. or S.J.R.) requires approval of both houses, but the governor's signature is not necessary. Proposed amendments to the Texas Constitution are examples of joint resolutions requiring a two-thirds majority vote of each house. To date, all proposed amendments to the U.S. Constitution initiated by Congress, with the exception of the Twenty-first Amendment, have been submitted to state legislatures for ratification. The Texas Legislature ratifies such amendments with a joint resolution adopted by a simple majority of each house.

Bill   Before enactment, a proposed law or statute is known as a *bill* (H.B. or S.B.). For purposes of classification, bills are divided into three categories: special, general, and local. A *special bill* makes an exception to general laws for the benefit of a specific individual, class, or corporation. Of greater importance are *general bills,* which apply to all people or property in all parts of Texas. To become law, a bill must pass by a simple majority vote in both the House and the Senate, but a two-thirds majority vote of the total membership of each house is required to pass an emergency measure that will take effect as soon as the governor signs it.

A *local bill* affects a single unit of local government (for example, a city, county, or precinct). Such bills are usually passed without opposition if sponsored by all legislators from affected districts. Constitutional limitations on the subjects of local bills have led to the practice of enacting *bracket bills*, or local bills disguised as general bills. A bracket bill usually applies to a city or other unit of government that is the only one in Texas falling within the specified population bracket. For example, a bill referring to "cities with population between 149,000 and 149,300" would have covered only Amarillo, according to the 1980 decennial census. In some instances, Texas courts have ruled that such measures are unconstitutional; but House Rule 8, section 10, states that a bill may provide for a population maximum or minimum that "bears a reasonable relation" to the bill's purpose.

Immunities

In addition to their constitutional powers, state senators and representatives enjoy legislative immunities conferred by the Texas Constitution. First, they may not be sued for slander or otherwise held accountable for any statements made in a speech or debate during the course of a legislative proceeding. Of course, this protection does not extend to remarks made under other circumstances. Second, they may not be arrested while attending a legislative session, or while traveling to and from the Legislature's meeting place for the purpose of attending, unless charged with "treason, felony, or breach of the peace."

Organization and Procedure

Merely bringing 181 men and women together in the Capitol does not ensure the making of laws or any other governmental activity. If several people are to engage in official business, there must be organized effort guided by established rules.

Formal Organization

The basic organization of the Texas Legislature is prescribed by the state Constitution. Other organizational matters are dealt with in greater detail by statutes and resolutions and by House and Senate rules. Important organizational activities involve the election of House and Senate officers and the establishment of committees.

President of the Senate: The Lieutenant Governor   Chosen by the people of Texas in a statewide election for a four-year term, the lieutenant governor is first in line of succession in the event of the death, resignation, or removal of the governor; but the most important function of the lieutenant governor is serving as *president of the Senate*. This legislative position as the Senate's presiding officer is assigned by the Texas Constitution, even though the lieutenant governor is not a member of the Legislature. The arrangement is not unique, however; in approximately two-thirds of the states, the lieutenant governor presides over the upper house. Furthermore, in approximately half of the states the lieutenant governor appoints members of Senate standing committees to which bills and resolutions are sent after being introduced.

In Texas, the lieutenant governor's power to name committee members has been curtailed to some extent since 1973 (see below), but all committee chairs are still appointed by the lieutenant governor. Other powers exercised by the president of the Senate include recognizing senators who wish to speak or to make a motion (for example, a motion to take up a bill out of order of calendar listing), voting to break a tie, serving on the Legislative Council (a research arm of the Legislature) and the Legislative Budget Board, and determining the committee to which a bill is sent.

Given these powers (most of which have been granted by the Legislature rather than by the Constitution) and the tradition of leadership by the lieutenant governor of Texas, it is not surprising that the office has been recognized as the most powerful in the state. William P. Hobby, Jr., set a record for tenure in that office. Following his initial election for a two-year term in 1972, he was re-elected for four successive four-year terms before announcing that he would not seek re-election in 1990.

At the beginning of each session, the Senate elects the president pro tempore, who presides when the lieutenant governor is absent or disabled. At the end of a session, a new president pro tempore is named to serve during the interim period. Usually the office is passed around among senators on the basis of seniority.

Speaker of the House The presiding officer of the House of Representatives is the *speaker,* a representative who is elected to the office by the House membership for a two-year term. Like the lieutenant governor in the Senate, the speaker controls House proceedings through appointment of committee chairs and committee members, recognition of representatives who wish to speak, assignment of bills and resolutions to standing committees, and membership on the Legislative Council and the Legislative Budget Board.

House rules authorize the speaker to name another representative to preside over the chamber temporarily. Also, the speaker may name a member of the House to serve as permanent speaker pro tempore for as long as the speaker desires. If appointed, a speaker pro tempore performs all duties of the speaker when this officer is absent.

Because of the importance of the office, selection of the speaker (especially a first-term speaker) involves intense political activity. Lobbyists representing special interest groups make every effort to ensure the selection of a sympathetic speaker, and aspirants to the position begin to line up support several months or even two or more years before the beginning of a speaker's race. This is a unique political contest. Campaigning is conducted on a personal and often unpublicized basis, because the voting is limited to House members. The outcome of the election, however, greatly influences the work of the chamber in regular and special sessions and the roles of individual representatives. Those who figure prominently in organizing support for a winning candidate expect to obtain important committee assignments and chairs or vice chairs, and they hope to become members of the *speaker's team* that controls most House activities.

By law, a candidate for the office of speaker must report to the secretary of state all loans and contributions of money, services, and other items of value received on behalf of the campaign. Also to be reported are the names and addresses of lenders and contributors and of persons to whom payment in excess of $10 is made. Corporations and labor unions are prohibited from lending or giving money or any other item of value, either directly or indirectly, to aid or to defeat a candidate for the speakership. Ordinary campaign expenses in a race for the speakership involve presession visits to representatives in their districts and numerous long-distance telephone calls.

Under the terms of the legislative bribery law enacted in 1973, it is a felony offense for anyone (including a candidate for the speakership) to attempt to influence a member of the House or a candidate for the House by promising particular committee or subcommittee assignments or appointment to a chair or vice chair of a committee or subcommittee. Also prohibited are attempts to influence the election of a speaker by promises or threats pertaining to any legislation or appropriation, employment of any person, or economic benefit to any person.

But because promises, threats, and rewards are essential tools of leadership, these devices are still used covertly and with discretion.

Long before a speakership election, a person aspiring to that office will attempt to induce House members to sign cards pledging their support. Once elected, a speaker usually finds it easier to obtain similar pledges of support for re-election at the beginning of future regular sessions. Gib Lewis, a conservative Democrat from Fort Worth, tied Billy Clayton's record for tenure as speaker by serving for four terms after his initial election in 1983. And in 1989 Lewis announced his intention to retain the speakership in 1991, even though his legislative career has been marred by instances of illegal and unethical conduct. In 1989, for example, it was reported that he had stocked two of his ranches with deer obtained from the Texas Parks and Wildlife Department in violation of that agency's regulations.

Committee System   Presiding officers interpret the rules of their respective chambers, and they determine the *committees* to which bills will be referred. (See Table 6.1.) In addition, and of special importance, is their power to appoint members of committees as well as to designate committee chairs and vice chairs. Until 1973, presiding officers appointed all members of standing committees, and there was no seniority system in either chamber. Consequently, from one regular legislative session to another, the turnover of committee membership was high.

House rules provide for a limited seniority system. There are 30 *substantive committees* for which half of the membership (exclusive of the chair and vice chair) is based on seniority, that is, years of cumulative service as a member of the House. When a regular session begins, each representative in order of seniority designates three desired committees, listed in order of preference. A representative is entitled to become a member of the committee of highest preference on which there is a vacant seniority position. Other committee members are appointed by the speaker. Seniority does not apply to membership on the Appropriations Committee (the most important substantive committee) and the six *procedural committees:* Calendars, General Investigating, House Administration, Local and Consent Calendars, Redistricting, and Rules and Resolutions.

Chairs and vice chairs of committees may be removed by the speaker at any time. To ensure that the efforts of the representatives are not divided among too many committees, membership is limited to not more than two substantive committees. The chairs of the powerful Appropriations Committee and State Affairs Committee may not serve concurrently on another substantive committee.

Substantive committees are responsible for participating in the budget hearing process and for sending recommendations to the Appropriations Committee for funding state agencies and institutions under their jurisdictions. For example, the Agriculture and Livestock Committee makes budget recommendations for the Texas Department of Agriculture. Twenty-one of the substantive committees have a subcommittee on budget and oversight with a chair and a vice chair appointed by the speaker. The 21 chairs of subcommittees on budget and oversight, together with a committee chair and vice chair appointed by the speaker, make up the membership of the important Appropriations Committee.

TABLE 6.1 Committees (and Number of Members), 71st Texas Legislature (1989–1990)

Thirty-six House Committees	Eleven Senate Committees
Agriculture and Livestock (9)	*Administration (11)
Appropriations (23)	Criminal Justice (7)
Business and Commerce (9)	Economic Development (11)
†Calendars (9)	Education (11)
Corrections (9)	Finance (13)
County Affairs (11)	Health and Human Resources (9)
Criminal Jurisprudence (9)	Intergovernmental Relations (11)
Cultural and Historical Resources (9)	Jurisprudence (7)
Elections (9)	Natural Resources (11)
Energy (9)	*Nominations (7)
Environmental Affairs (9)	State Affairs (13)
Financial Institutions (9)	
†General Investigating (5)	
Government Organization (9)	
Higher Education (9)	
†House Administration (9)	
Human Services (9)	
Insurance (9)	
Judicial Affairs (9)	
Judiciary (9)	
Labor and Employment Relations (9)	
Liquor Regulation (9)	
†Local and Consent Calendars (9)	
Natural Resources (9)	
Public Education (9)	
Public Health (9)	
Public Safety (9)	
†Redistricting (9)	
Retirement and Aging (9)	
†Rules and Resolutions (9)	
Science and Technology (9)	
State Affairs (13)	
State, Federal and International Relations (9)	
Transportation (9)	
Urban Affairs (11)	
Ways and Means (13)	

*Two Senate committees are designated as special committees; the other nine are designated as standing committees.
†Six House committees are designated as procedural committees; the other 30 are designated as substantive committees.

Senate rules provide for nine *standing committees* and two *special committees.* Chairs and vice chairs of all these committees are appointed by the lieutenant governor, as noted above. Power of appointment extends also to the membership of all Senate standing committees, with the exception that at least four members of each committee with more than ten members must be senators who were members of the committee during the previous legislative session. A senator serves on not more than three standing committees and is restricted to holding no more than one standing committee chair.

Because House and Senate committees play an important role in the fate or fortune of any bill, the selection of committee personnel goes far toward determining the amount and type of legislative output during a session. Some committees (for example, the House Committee on Ways and Means, which has jurisdiction over taxation) are generally considered to be more important than others (for example, the House Committee on Cultural and Historical Resources, which is concerned with legislation promoting tourism and preserving Texas's monuments and shrines). Consequently, committee assignments and distribution of chairs and vice chairs are significant keys to understanding the power structure of each chamber.

The Legislative Reorganization Act of 1961 calls for each standing committee to "make a continuing study of matters under its jurisdiction" with a view to formulating and introducing legislative programs. The act also envisions committee work continuing in the interim between sessions. Since the 63rd regular session, permanent staff personnel have been available to assist legislators with interim work; however, tasks that might be performed by standing committees are often given to interim study committees. Members of these study committees have been appointed by presiding officers and sometimes by the governor. In many instances, membership has included private citizens as well as senators and representatives. Some interim committees have concluded their work in one or two meetings; others have required several days of labor by members and staff personnel.

House Research Organization   Governed by an independently elected, bipartisan steering committee of 15 representatives serving for staggered four-year terms, the *House Research Organization* (HRO) produces special reports on a wide variety of policy issues, such as judicial selection, high-speed trains, and driving while intoxicated. During each legislative session the HRO staff also publishes its *Daily Floor Report*, which analyzes important bills by providing an objective summary of their contents and arguments for and against each bill.

To preserve the HRO's independence from the House leadership, the House guarantees that the funding level negotiated biannually by the HRO steering committee and the House Administration Committee will not be reduced. At the beginning of each regular session, the steering committee selects its new members, with all regions, parties, and factions represented; and the House membership must approve the new steering committee members by a two-thirds vote. All representatives receive HRO publications; and senators, members of the Capitol press corps, law firms, libraries, businesses, and others can subscribe to these publications.

Caucuses

With the House and Senate firmly controlled for several years by Speaker Gib Lewis and Lieutenant Governor Bill Hobby, caucuses of like-minded members had limited impact on the Texas Legislature. Each of these presiding officers sought to absorb potential opponents within his team and to discourage legislative organizations based on partisan, philosophical, or ethnic interests. Nevertheless, caucus organizations have been increasing in importance.

Party Caucuses The *House Democratic Caucus* was organized in 1981 with 37 members; however, then-Speaker, then-Democrat Bill Clayton did not join, nor did many other conservative Democrats. State Democratic Chair Bob Slagle attempted to work closely with House Democrats during the 1981 redistricting fights. Despite Slagle's efforts, a large number of Democratic representatives supported Speaker Clayton, who teamed with House Republicans to push a redistricting plan favorable to Republicans and conservative Democrats.

By 1983, the House Democratic Caucus had grown to include 94 representatives. But it was the return of Republican Bill Clements to the governor's office in 1987, along with the election of 56 Republican representatives and 6 Republican senators, that brought new life to Democratic caucuses in both chambers. Ralph Wallace headed the House Democratic Caucus in the 70th Legislature. In the Senate, the Democratic Caucus was chaired by Hugh Parmer, who directed Democratic attacks on the Clements budget and led a "truth squad" that followed the governor to various cities in order to counter his campaign against a tax hike required to fund essential state services. Wallace continued to chair the House Democratic Caucus in the 71st Legislature, while John Montford chaired the Senate Democratic Caucus.

For many years, Republicans in both the House and Senate tended to oppose attempts to create formal GOP caucuses in those chambers. They feared that calling attention to partisan differences could cause Republican legislators, as members of the minority party, to lose influential committee positions and memberships on the leadership teams of Speaker Lewis and Lieutenant Governor Hobby. Some Republican legislators did meet informally for breakfast once a week during legislative sessions, but neither formal Republican leadership nor any organization based on GOP affiliation emerged.

During the special session on budget and taxes in 1987, partisan divisions in the Texas Legislature were more openly displayed than at any other time since the redistricting battles of 1981. Finally, the *House Republican Caucus* was organized at the beginning of the 71st regular session in 1989. Under the leadership of Chair Tom Craddick (Midland) and Vice Chair Ashley Smith (Houston), the new Republican organization took policy positions on important legislation (for example, workers' compensation and prison reform measures).

Texas Conservative Coalition Organized in 1985, the *Texas Conservative Coalition* is composed of both Republicans and conservative Democrats. This organization owes its creation to the increased number of Republican legislators elected in the 1980s and to dissatisfaction with the education reforms and tax increases enacted during a special session in 1984. It was chaired initially by conservative Democratic Representative Tom Waldrop, later by Republican Representative Gerald Geisweidt, and then by conservative Democratic Representative L. B. Kubiak. Until the House Republican Caucus was established in 1989, the Conservative Coalition

Attorney General Jim Mattox addresses a meeting of the Legislative Black Caucus in the House chamber during the regular session of the 71st Legislature. (Senate Media Services.)

functioned as a near equivalent to an organized opposition to Speaker Lewis on issues such as state spending, taxation, and health care for poor people. Staff personnel working for coalition leaders produce brief research reports expressing conservative viewpoints on public policy issues.

Ethnic Caucuses   Composed of black senators and representatives, the *Legislative Black Caucus* has concentrated on issues such as protecting Prairie View A&M University and Texas Southern University from budget cuts. In 1987 this caucus ran afoul of Speaker Lewis when it supported Senator Craig Washington's amendment to a Lewis-backed bill creating the Texas Department of Commerce. The amendment would have required a limited state purchasing preference for minority-owned firms. When Lewis refused to accept the amendment, Washington accused him of racism. Later, the Legislative Black Caucus joined Republicans and voted against the 1987 tax increases, claiming that they were regressive and that the state budget had failed to fund adequately various social services. Representative Larry Evans (D-Houston) chaired the Legislative Black Caucus in the 71st Legislature.

The *Mexican American Legislative Caucus* has successfully pushed legislation placing farmworkers under state workers' compensation, unemployment compensation, and minimum wage protection. Also, it has played a major role in establishing an indigent health care program for Texas and in fighting budget cuts affecting social services. Because several of the more prominent Mexican-

American representatives have been on the speaker's team, the Mexican American Legislative Caucus has tended to avoid open confrontation with Speaker Lewis. Chaired by Representative Juan Hinojosa (D-McAllen) in the 71st Legislature, the caucus joined other Mexican-American organizations in supporting legal complaints alleging discrimination against South Texas in state funding for colleges and universities in that region. This pressure contributed to legislative action that merged Pan American University into the University of Texas system and Laredo State, Texas A&I, and Corpus Christi State universities into the Texas A&M University system.

Procedure: A Bill Becomes a Law

The Texas Constitution calls for regular sessions to be divided into three periods for distinct purposes. The first 30 days are reserved for introduction of bills and resolutions, action on emergency appropriations, and confirmation or rejection of recess appointments made by the governor between sessions. The second 30 days are meant to be devoted to consideration of bills and resolutions by committees. The remainder of the session, which amounts to 80 days because regular sessions always run the full 140 days allowed, is designated for floor debate and voting on bills and resolutions.

Throughout the session, action may be taken at any time on emergency matters submitted by the governor. Because the Texas Constitution also allows either house to determine by a four-fifths majority vote its own order of business, it has been customary for both the House and the Senate to permit unlimited consideration of bills during the first 60 days. (In 1981, however, a motion to modify the schedule called for by the state Constitution was defeated in the House.) The Texas Constitution specifies that all revenue bills must originate in the House; other kinds of legislation may originate in either chamber.

Although the full process of turning a bill into a law is not without its complexities, certain basic steps are clearly outlined. In the following paragraphs, these steps are traced from introduction to action by the governor. (Location of step numbers in Figure 6.1 will help the reader to visualize the bill's progress.) For our purposes, we will describe the path of a bill that originates in the House.[2] (For a case study of the enactment of a bill dealing with the AIDS problem, see Reading 6.1.)

1. *Introduction*   Any House member may introduce a bill by filing 12 copies (14 copies of a water district bill) with the *chief clerk,* who is employed to supervise legislative administration in the House. Prefiling of bills is allowed as early as the first Monday following the November general election before a regular session begins in January, or 30 days before the start of a special session.

2. *First reading and referral to committee*   After receiving a bill, the chief clerk assigns it a number in order of submission and turns the bill over to the reading clerk for the *first reading.* The reading clerk reads aloud the *caption,* which is a brief summary of the contents, and gives the bill to the speaker. The speaker then assigns the bill to an appropriate standing committee.

FIGURE 6.1   Routes Followed by Bills from Texas Legislature to Governor

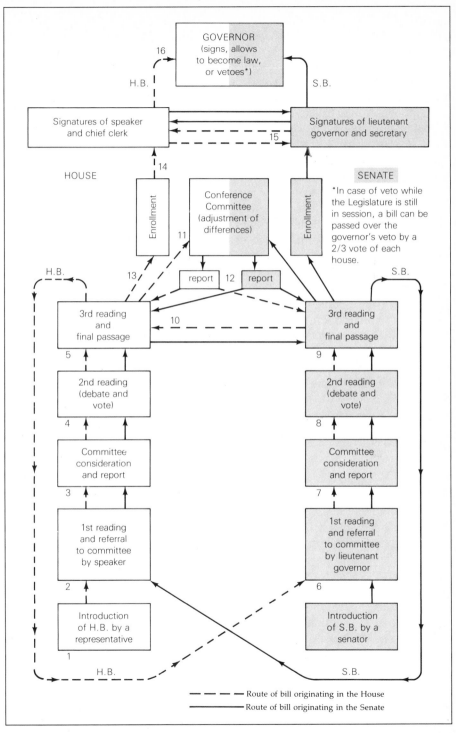

Source: Prepared with the assistance of Dr. Beryl E. Pettus, Sam Houston State University.

3. *Committee consideration and report* Before any committee action, the committee staff prepares a *bill analysis* that summarizes important provisions of the bill, and the staff of the Legislative Budget Board prepares a *fiscal note* projecting costs of implementing the proposed legislation. As a courtesy to the sponsoring representative, most bills receive a committee hearing at which interested persons have an opportunity to express their views. After the hearing, a bill may be sent to a subcommittee as a delaying tactic, or for the purpose of changing it with amendments, or to kill it. If a majority of the committee members decide that a bill should be passed, perhaps with amendments, a favorable report is filed with the committee coordinator. In 1989 a House subcommittee approved Representative Al Edwards's bill that would have authorized amputation of a drug dealer's fingers, but the bill died in committee.

Because there is insufficient time for debating every favorably reported bill on the House floor, the ordering and selecting of bills for floor action is entrusted to two calendars committees. The Local and Consent Calendars Committee assigns its bills to the Local Calendar or the Consent Calendar, and the Calendar Committee is responsible for placing other bills on one of the following four bill calendars: Emergency, Major State, Constitutional, and General State.

A constitutional rule requires that a bill cannot be brought to the floor for debate and vote unless it is reported out of committee at least three days before the end of a session. Except in the case of a general appropriations measure, a printed copy of a bill must be placed in the newspaper mailbox of each House member 24 hours before it is considered on the floor. For a general appropriations bill, according to House rules, delivery must be made to "the newspaper mailbox of each member at least 168 hours during a Regular Session and at least 72 hours during a Special Session before such a bill can be considered by the House."

4. *Second reading* The *second reading* is usually limited to the caption only. Debate follows, and ordinarily speakers are limited to not more than 10 minutes each, unless extra time is granted by a simple majority vote. The author of a bill, or the committee member reporting on behalf of the committee, is given the privilege of beginning and ending floor debate with a speech of not over 20 minutes. After discussion ends and any amendments are added, a vote is taken on *engrossment* (preparation of an officially prescribed copy). In the House, a record vote usually involves using an electronic system that records and tallies votes as each representative presses a desk button. Approval of an engrossment motion requires a simple majority vote. In the event that a bill contains an *emergency clause* (and almost without exception, bills are drafted with this clause included), a motion may be made to suspend the rules by a four-fifths majority vote and to give the bill an immediate third reading. Thus, although seldom done in the House, an exception can be made to the constitutional rule that all bills must be read on three separate days.

5. *Third reading* After the *third reading* takes place, a simple majority vote is required to pass the bill. Amendments may still be added at this stage, but such action requires a two-thirds majority vote. Following the addition of an amendment, a new printing is made, checked over by the engrossing and enrolling clerk, and stamped "Engrossed."

6. *First reading (Senate)* After passing on the third reading in the House, the chief clerk adds a statement certifying passage and transmits the bill to the Senate (where the original House number is retained). In the Senate, the House bill's caption is read by the reading clerk; then the lieutenant governor assigns the bill to committee. It is also common practice for identical or companion bills to be introduced in both houses at the same time, thus speeding the legislative process. A senator's sponsorship of a House bill is necessary if it is to be given serious consideration.

7. *Senate committee consideration and report* Senate procedure differs some-what from House procedure. If a majority of committee members want a bill to pass, it is given a favorable report. Then the bill's sponsor in the Senate indicates a desire for floor debate by filing a notice so that the measure will be placed on the Intent Calendar. But Senate rules establish a *regular order of business,* which is a listing of bills according to the order in which they are reported favorably out of committee. This is also the order in which those bills are supposed to be debated on the Senate floor. At the beginning of each session, however, a bill on which floor action is not intended is "parked" at the head of the list and left there. As a result, all bills on the Intent Calendar must be taken up outside of the regular order of business; such action requires a two-thirds majority vote (21 of the 31 senators).

8. *Second reading (Senate)* As with second readings in the House, the Senate at this stage debates the bill, considers proposed amendments, and routinely puts the measure to a voice vote. Each senator's vote is registered as the roll is called by the *secretary of the Senate,* who is employed to supervise legislative administration in that chamber. Although a two-thirds majority vote has previously been obtained in order to bring the bill to the second reading stage, one cannot assume that the measure will receive the simple majority vote required for passage. A senator may vote to allow a bill to be taken up for a second reading and then vote against it after debate. Although Senate rules allow debate to be limited by a simple majority vote, custom permits a senator to speak as long as physical endurance permits, which on one occasion in 1977 amounted to 43 hours. Such *filibustering* is most effective if undertaken during the final days of a session.

9. *Third reading (Senate)* If passed on second reading, a bill can have its third reading immediately, assuming that rules have been suspended (as is routinely done) by the required four-fifths majority vote.

10. *Return to the House* After passage by the Senate, a House bill is returned to the chief clerk and then sent to the engrossing and enrolling clerk. The latter has the responsibility for supervising the preparation of a perfect copy of the bill and for its delivery to the speaker. When an amendment has been added in the Senate, the change must be voted on in the House. If the House is not prepared to accept the amended bill, the ordinary procedure is to request a conference. Otherwise, the bill will die unless one of the chambers reverses its position.

11. *Conference committee* When the two houses agree to send the bill to conference, each presiding officer appoints five members to serve on the *conference*

committee. Attempts will be made to adjust differences and produce a compromise version acceptable to both houses. At least three Senate members and three House members must reach a common agreement before the committee can recommend a course of action to the two houses. The author of the House bill serves as conference committee chair.

12. *Conference committee report* The conference committee's recommended settlement of questions at issue must be fully accepted or rejected by each house. Amendments may not be added without special permission authorized by a majority vote of each house. But both houses may agree to return the report to the committee or, by request of the House, the Senate may accept a proposal for a new conference.

13. *Enrollment* When a conference report has been accepted by both houses, the bill is sent to the enrolling clerk of the House for the preparation of a perfect copy.

14. *Signatures of the chief clerk and speaker* When the enrolled conference committee report is received in the House, the reading clerk of the House reads the bill by caption only. It is then signed by the chief clerk, who certifies the vote by which it passed, and by the speaker.

15. *Signatures of the secretary of the Senate and the lieutenant governor* Next the engrossing and enrolling clerk of the House takes the bill to the Senate, where it is read by caption only. With certification of the vote by which it passed, the bill is signed by the lieutenant governor and by the secretary of the Senate.

16. *Action by the governor* While the Legislature remains in session, the governor has three options: sign the bill; allow it to remain unsigned for ten days, not including Sundays, after which time it becomes law without the chief executive's signature; or, within the ten-day period, veto the measure by returning it to the House unsigned with a message giving a reason for the veto. A vote of "two-thirds of the membership present" in the first house that considers a vetoed bill (in this case, the House of Representatives) and a vote of "two-thirds of the members" in the second house (in this case, the Senate) are required to override the governor's veto.[3] Because most important legislation, including appropriation bills, is passed during the last week of a session, the governor's postadjournment veto is of special importance because it cannot be overridden. Individual items in an appropriations bill can be vetoed without rejecting the remainder of the bill.

After a session ends, the governor has 20 days, counting Sundays, in which to veto all legislation considered undesirable and to file the rejected measures with the secretary of state. A bill not vetoed by the governor automatically becomes law at the end of the 20-day period.* Ordinarily, acts of the Legislature do not take effect until 90 days after adjournment, or even later if specified in the bill. Exceptions to this rule include general appropriation acts and emergency

---

*During a regular session and for a month thereafter, information concerning bills and resolutions may be obtained by calling the Legislative Reference Library's toll-free number, 800-252-9693. At other times (and at all times for callers in the Austin area), the library's number is 512-463-1252. Located on the second floor of the Capitol, this library is open to the public. Its books, periodicals, government documents, and newspaper clippings provide an abundance of information for persons engaged in research concerning the Texas Legislature.

measures that take effect earlier. The latter must be identified by an emergency statement in the text or preamble and must pass each house by a two-thirds majority vote of the total membership.

Influences in the Legislative Environment

In theory, elected legislators are influenced mostly, if not exclusively, by their constituents. In practice, however, many legislators' actions bear little relationship to the needs or interests of the "folks back home." Unfortunately, many citizens are uninterested in most governmental affairs and have no opinions about how the Legislature should act in making public policy. Others may have opinions but are inarticulate or unable to communicate with their legislators. Therefore, lawmakers are likely to yield not only to the influence of presiding officers in the House and Senate but also to the influence of other powerful figures seeking to win their voluntary support or to force their cooperation: the governor, judges, the comptroller of public accounts, the attorney general, and lobbyists.

The Governor's Influence

We have already noted the roles of legislative leaders and the governor's veto power. It is also important to point out that the ever-present threat of executive veto plays an equally important part in legislative behavior. Even though a bill might prove to be popular with many senators and representatives, knowledge that the governor will oppose the measure is often sufficient to discourage its introduction, to bury it in a committee, to keep it on a calendar, or to table it or defeat it on the floor.

Legislators may support a bill that is backed by the governor even though it is considered injurious to the interests of constituents. After all, voters in a legislator's district may never learn of the matter. Even if they do, they probably live far from Austin and election time could be many months ahead. Meanwhile, the governor is close at hand and may offer some tangible rewards for cooperation: reciprocal support for a legislator's own bills, an appointment to some state office for a job-seeking friend, or merely the promise of future favors.

There is nothing illegal about such actions, but they do suggest a contradiction between the representative ideal and the reality of executive influence. Yet the governor is also a representative—the representative of all the people of Texas. Each chief executive is elected on a platform of promises and feels a compulsion to promote certain policies. Thus legislators must be influenced to ensure the success of the governor's plans for taxing, spending, building, and educating, among others. And if there is any doubt as to what the governor wants, gubernatorial policies will be outlined in messages from time to time. Extensive popular acceptance of the chief executive's ideas will make opposition difficult, even though the people in a legislator's district may be adversely affected.

Influence of the Courts, the Attorney General, and the Comptroller of Public Accounts

An act that may be politically expedient and even popular with constituents may be unconstitutional. Thus, in their lawmaking, all legislators are influenced by what courts have done or may do about possible legislative action. Usually senators and representatives wish neither to spend time nor to invest political capital in legislative efforts that will be struck down by judicial decisions or by opinions of the attorney general. Therefore, while a bill is being considered, the committee chair may turn to the attorney general for an opinion regarding its constitutionality; sometimes, however, this is merely a delaying tactic or a device to justify killing a bill in committee. By estimating how much revenue can be expected under current and projected revenue laws, the comptroller exercises great influence, because the Legislature must keep state spending within the limits of anticipated revenue. (See pages 182 and 245 for further information concerning the role of this executive official.)

Influence of Lobbyists

Opinions vary concerning the influence of lobbyists on legislative behavior and public policy. In many minds, *lobbying* carries with it an image of corruption. Others see lobbyists as performing a useful role by supplying information and serving as links with organized groups of constituents. But it is a nagging fact that special interests spend large amounts of money in efforts designed to induce legislative action that otherwise would not be taken on a legislator's own initiative or in response to requests by constituents. (Lobbying as an interest group tactic was discussed in Chapter 5.)

A Texas statute prohibits campaign contributions to lawmakers during a regular legislative session, but state senators and representatives are subjected to intensive lobbying activities throughout the year—especially when they convene in Austin for regular and special sessions. For example, on July 13, 1989, the *Austin American-Statesman* revealed that lobbyists had reported spending $1.86 million on meals, gifts, and trips for legislators during the regular session running from January through May of that year. This amounted to an average of over $10,000 for each state senator and representative.

Passed in 1973 and amended in 1975, 1981, 1983, and 1987, a weak lobby registration law declares that democratic government requires the fullest opportunity for the people to communicate with legislators and state agencies. Also, the statute requires disclosure of the identity, expenditures, and certain activities of lobbyists. It calls for registration with the secretary of state by anyone who both receives and spends $200 or more in a calendar quarter for "communicating directly with one or more members of the legislative or executive branch to influence legislation or administrative action." Excluded from this reporting requirement are a lobbyist's personal expenditures for travel, food, lodging, and membership dues. Also required to register are persons who lobby as only part of their regular employment.

A lobby registration includes the full name and address of the lobbyist, the lobbyist's normal occupation and business address, the name and address of every person who has hired or retained the lobbyist and on whose behalf lobbying has been conducted, and a list of matters about which lobbying has been undertaken. When lobbying is done for a group other than a corporation, the lobbyist must give the number of group members, provide the name of each person who determines group policy relating to the influencing of legislative or administrative action, and describe the methods by which the lobbyist develops and makes decisions about policy positions.

Supplemental lobby registration and activities reports must be filed monthly for a legislative session and quarterly thereafter. These reports must include total expenditures by a lobbyist (or by others on behalf of a lobbyist) for mass media advertising and for gifts, awards, loans, and entertainment. Also required is a listing of specific categories of subjects that have been lobbied during the period covered by the report. For the benefit of persons who are uncertain concerning any requirements of the lobby registration law, a 1983 amendment provides that an advisory opinion "based on a real or hypothetical situation" may be obtained from the secretary of state and may be used as a defense in a judicial proceeding arising under the statute.

Since enactment of the lobby registration law of 1973, there have been no court actions against lobbyists charged with violating it. This record over a period of nearly 20 years suggests one of two explanations: either the activities of thousands of lobbyists have been reported as required by the statute or enforcement of the law has been ineffective. All indications point toward the latter explanation.

Without doubt, much of the money and effort expended for public relations and other programs of business, labor, agricultural, and professional groups is designed to have a direct influence on the nomination and election of legislators as well as on their conduct after they reach the Capitol. But lobbyists and political action committees contribute directly to the campaign funds that cover legislators' election expenses and to the officeholder accounts that are used to pay for a wide range of Austin living expenses (in some cases, cars, planes, and homes) and political activities. Based on a study of senators and representatives who chaired the 47 committees of the 70th Legislature in 1988, the *Austin American-Statesman* reported that they collected a total of nearly $4.7 million (an average of about $100,000 for each chair) and that 63 percent was contributed by lobbyists and political action committees. Of special interest is the fact that 31 of these legislators were neither engaged in a contested election race nor planning to run for another office. In view of this economic influence, some observers insist that the so-called *Third House,* composed of well-financed lobbyists, plays a more important role in passing, weakening, or defeating critical bills and resolutions than do the popularly elected senators and representatives who sit in the two houses established by the Texas Constitution.

Prospects for Legislative Reform

In its much-publicized comparative study of state legislatures in 1971, the Citizens Conference on State Legislatures ranked the Texas Legislature 38th in terms of legislative capabilities.[4] Later, in a study prepared for the Texas Constitutional Convention of 1974, the Citizens Conference made the following summary assessment and recommendations:

> Burdened by restrictions from another century, the [Texas] Legislature has been unable fully to rise to the challenges of the present age. Instead of a strong legislature performing its intended tasks of representation, problem resolution and oversight of state administration, the present Legislature is a weakened body constrained by limited biennial sessions, by its inability to review vetoed bills after adjournment or to call itself into special sessions. These limitations together with constitutionally prescribed salaries, a senate presided over by an executive branch official, and a multitude of constitutional legislation that restricts the Legislator's power to act effectively should be among the targets for revisions to articles.[5]

Proposition 1 of the proposed constitutional revision package of 1975 was designed to remedy some of the weaknesses listed above, but it was rejected overwhelmingly by the state's voters. In 1989, Texas voters rejected a proposed constitutional amendment linking legislators' salaries and salaries for the speaker and the lieutenant governor to the governor's salary. There is no indication that Texans are ready to overhaul the structure of their Legislature or to increase its powers. Nevertheless, the publicized misdeeds of some legislators have resulted in repeated demands that higher ethical standards for lawmakers should be established and enforced.

In response to these demands, a special committee on ethical conduct was established by the House of Representatives during the 68th regular session. Composed of the five members of the House General Investigating Committee and four other representatives, the Committee on Ethics was given jurisdiction over all matters pertaining to the conduct of House members. Subsequently, some citizens were disappointed but probably not surprised when the committee's first action in July 1983 was to vote unanimously not to pursue an investigation of Speaker Gib Lewis's failure to report his financial ties with alcoholic beverage distributors and with horse-race lobbyist C. Dean Cobb. Such reports are required under an ethics law that Lewis voted for in 1973, when the Legislature responded to the notorious Sharpstown State Bank scandal that resulted in Speaker Gus Mutscher's conviction for conspiracy to accept a bribe. Committee members decided that Lewis had been punished sufficiently when in May 1983 he was fined $800 after pleading no contest to the charge of incomplete financial disclosure.[6] With the beginning of the 69th legislative session in 1985, the House Ethics Committee ceased to exist.

Instances of legislative misconduct and corruption create distrust of lawmakers, but most Texans strongly support the principle of representative government. Nevertheless, if this system of government is to endure, its weaknesses must be identified and reforms must be made. Currently, however, prospects for meaningful change are uncertain. For example, there has been strong opposition to proposals for annual sessions of the Legislature, which would permit more effective handling of the state's multibillion-dollar budget problems as well as other critical issues.

Of course, critics of the Texas Legislature should realize that the role of the lawmaker is a difficult one. In Texas, it is made more difficult by a mismatch between a nineteenth-century constitution (much amended, to be sure) and the problems of one of the biggest, most rapidly developing states in the Union. In the absence of significant constitutional amendments in the future, or complete constitutional revision, the most likely reform of the Texas legislative system will result from development of a genuinely competitive two-party system. Continued increases in the numbers of Republican senators and representatives could be expected to produce more party voting on policy issues, strong partisan caucus organizations, and formal legislative leadership that would reflect party strength and political ideology.

During more than a century of one-party politics and a "no-party" Legislature,[7] Texans have allowed the Austin lobby, rather than popularly elected legislators, to become the center of the policymaking process. If the Texas Legislature is the "people's branch" of state government, it should be strong but also responsive to public opinion at the ballot box. Nevertheless, as long as political action committees and special interest lobbyists play decisive roles in financing election campaigns and setting the legislative agenda, Texas lawmakers are not likely to respond to the state's critical problems with the most enlightened and effective public policies. Too many of the Lone Star State's senators and representatives appear to be comfortable with the lobbyists' cynical definition of an honest legislator: One who stays bought!

Notes

1. Each regular session brings forth an avalanche of bills and resolutions. During the regular session of the 71st Legislature (January 10 to May 29, 1989), 3,210 bills were introduced in the House and 1,859 were introduced in the Senate. Only 719 of the former and 599 of the latter passed both houses and were sent to Governor Clements, who vetoed 54 bills and 1 concurrent resolution. See Texas Legislative Council, *Summary of Enactments: 71st Legislature, Regular, First, and Second Called Sessions* (Austin: 1990), p. 1.

2. For more detailed descriptions of the lawmaking process, see Thomas M. Spencer, *The Legislative Process: Texas Style* (Pasadena, Tex.: San Jacinto College Press, 1981); and House Research Organization, *The House Rules, 71st Session: How a Bill Becomes a Law*, Special Research Report No. 148 (Austin: February 6, 1989). This HRO publication is updated for each regular legislative session.

3. As explained by one authority, this difference in the two-thirds majorities required by Article IV, Section 14, represents "a mysterious error in the present

constitution." See George D. Braden, *Citizens Guide to the Proposed New Texas Constitution* (Austin: Sterling Swift, 1975), p. 15.

4. John Burns, *The Sometime Governments: A Critical Study of the 50 American Legislatures* (New York: Bantam Books, 1971), p. 49.
5. *The Impact of the Texas Constitution on the Legislature* (Houston: Institute for Urban Studies, University of Houston, 1973), p. 55.
6. A concise account of this case is found in Thomas L. Whatley, "Gib Comes Clean," *Texas Government Newsletter,* June 6, 1983, p. 1.
7. For an excellent study of the development of the House Democratic Caucus, see Robert Harmel and Keith E. Hamm, "Development of a Party Role in a No-party Legislature," *Western Political Quarterly* 39 (March 1986): 72–92.

Key Terms and Concepts

unicameral	speaker's team
bicameral	committee
Senate	substantive committee
House of Representatives	procedural committee
regular session	standing committee
special session	special committee
redistricting	House Research Organization
Legislative Redistricting Board	House Democratic Caucus
Reynolds v. *Sims*	House Republican Caucus
Kilgarlin v. *Martin*	Texas Conservative Coalition
gerrymandering	Legislative Black Caucus
single-member district	Mexican American Legislative
multimember district	Caucus
advice and consent	chief clerk
Legislative Audit Committee	first reading
Legislative Budget Board	caption
Sunset Advisory Commission	bill analysis
impeachment	fiscal note
simple resolution	second reading
concurrent resolution	engrossment
joint resolution	emergency clause
bill	third reading
special bill	regular order of business
general bill	secretary of the Senate
local bill	filibustering
bracket bill	conference committee
president of the Senate	lobbying
speaker	Third House

Selected Readings

6.1 AIDS: A Big Issue in the 71st Legislature

Kaye Northcott

Federal expenditures for AIDS prevention, education, and research amounted to about $2.2 billion in 1989 and were expected to be double that amount by 1993. State and local governments also joined in the battle against AIDS. This reading describes the politics involved in passing AIDS legislation in the 71st regular session of the Texas Legislature.

From gay rights activists' parading 15,000 strong to the steps of the Capitol to the passage of a comprehensive bill during the final eight minutes of the session, the AIDS issue brought more drama to the Texas Legislature than any other topic. During the 140-day legislative session, AIDS became as much a political issue as a health issue, said Rep. Mike McKinney, one of the sponsors of the bill and the only physician in the 181-member Legislature.

House and Senate Difference

The Senate bill dealt mainly with the health aspect of the epidemic. But even though acquired immune deficiency syndrome is spreading rapidly among heterosexuals, many in the House seemed fixated on the fact that the 4,000 Texas deaths attributed to AIDS have been primarily homosexual men, prostitutes or drug abusers who shared dirty needles.

Many in the House did not want to cast any recorded votes on the AIDS problem. Fifty-four removed their names from a resolution passed in memory of AIDS victims. And the lower house turned down two resolutions—one suggesting state college health centers stock condoms and the other recommending the institutions develop materials on how to safeguard against the virus that leads to AIDS and is transmitted by the exchange of body fluids. The actions infuriated Rep. Debra Danburg of Houston, who asked the members, "How many of our students have to die before some elected officials are able to overcome their homophobic attitudes on AIDS?"

Interest Group Tactics

Members who opposed the resolutions said they didn't want it to appear that state colleges condoned homosexuality or promiscuity. Some of those same members

From the *Fort Worth Star-Telegram*, June 3, 1989. Kaye Northcott is political editor of the *Fort Worth Star-Telegram's* Austin Bureau. Reprinted by permission.

were hissed at during the final days of the session by a group called Austin AIDS Coalition to Unleash Power [ACT UP]. Members dressed in black tights and wore skeleton masks to dramatize the growing death toll from AIDS. But the tactics of the group were not representative of those of the 15,000 people who marched up Congress Avenue on April 30 in support of fair treatment of gay men and lesbians. Some observers said that the large number of marchers, many of whom stayed over to lobby their legislators, helped persuade the Legislature to prohibit work-place discrimination against people with the human immunodeficiency virus.

Conference Committee Conflict and Compromise

The AIDS bill passed a major hurdle when both houses of the Legislature approved $18.4 million for AIDS education, prevention, and treatment. But on Monday [May 29, 1989], the final day of the legislative session, there was still no AIDS bill saying how the money should be spent. House-Senate conference committee members appointed to produce a compromise met for the first and only time Monday morning. In the audience was the Rev. Chris Steele, who as head of the Legislative Task Force on AIDS had worked for two years to formulate a comprehensive AIDS policy for Texas. The Episcopal minister said she was appalled by the politicization of the issue and the vilification of those suffering from the disease. Also present was Glen Maxey, a former Senate aide who had revealed his own homosexuality to lead the Lesbian/Gay Rights Lobby of Texas. Maxey did not hold out much hope for a compromise and commented that he was glad that if no bill passed, the Department of Health could still fashion its own AIDS program with the $18.4 million already appropriated. Sen. Chet Brooks, the Senate's chief negotiator, was more upbeat. And House bill sponsors McKinney and Rep. Nancy McDonald, a registered nurse, seemed to have patched up their differences with Reps. Brad Wright and Billy Clemons, who had virtually hijacked the bill and persuaded the House to take a punitive approach to the disease. That was contrary to the wishes of the AIDS panel, which concluded that any state policy that frightens people away from early testing could contribute to the spread of AIDS.

Because the human immunodeficiency virus can lie dormant in the system for many years, people can transmit it unknowingly. The AIDS panel said that because medical science has not discovered a cure for the fatal disease, education and testing are the major defenses against its spread. The House and Senate bills had both conceded this point when they agreed to make test results confidential, Maxey said. And the House made a major concession when it agreed that the bill should prohibit discrimination against AIDS victims in the work place.

Maxey insisted there was still a problem with the House's emphasis on homosexual acts being crimes. The conference committee agreed to put statements in all state materials targeted for adolescents that a homosexual lifestyle is unacceptable to the general public and that homosexuality is a criminal offense; that abstinence is the best protection against the virus before marriage; and that marital faithfulness is the best protection after marriage. The Senate also gave in to the House demands to deny state AIDS grants to support community organizations that "advocate or promote conduct contrary to state criminal law," thereby eliminating gay support groups. Maxey said the prohibition was unfair because most of the existing community services offered to AIDS victims other than hospital care are provided by such support groups. In addition, the committee agreed that even though HIV test results must be confidential, the Department of Public Health may trace and contact those who have had sex with the person tested.

Conference Committee Work Completed

The meeting broke up after covering only about half the bill. Sen. Bob McFarland, R-Arlington, and McKinney were assigned to work out disagreements in the latter half of the bill, dealing with testing of certain criminal suspects for AIDS and segregation of those with the virus. The 10 members of the conference committee returned to their respective chambers with marked-up copies of the 76-page bill. "We really thought several times that we had consensus," said Brooks. "But every time we had to do the paper work and circulate the changes, because of the workload and the pressure of time we had difficulty getting the wording that would be acceptable to both houses."

Maxey predicted that if the committee had not signed off on the bill by 5 P.M. it would have died. Brooks didn't lose hope until 10 P.M., when the House's two-hour rule took effect. On the last day of the session, copies of a bill must be provided for study two hours before a vote is taken. And a vote had to be taken before midnight, the end of the session. Time apparently had run out. "Then the House conferees came back with one more version," Brooks said. "Mostly they wanted minor changes. Someone had left two pages out of the bill. One was on contact tracing." Brooks added the errant pages. "At that point the bill sprang back to life," he said.

Dramatic Ending

Soon most of the conference committee members were huddled in a group on the Senate floor. When the TV crews started homing in on them, they decamped to the Senate Members Lounge where reporters couldn't follow. Brooks said they raced through the 76 pages, making sure all the compromises were included. Everything was in place. They had a deal.

As Brooks and his staff set to work making the six copies of the bill necessary for floor action, House members met with Speaker Gib Lewis and asked him to suspend the two-hour rule. He agreed.

The House passed the bill at approximately 11:20 P.M. McKinney was beaming as he walked into the Senate. First he whispered the news to Sen. Eddie Bernice Johnson, D-Dallas, then to Brooks. There were handshakes and congratulations all around. The Senate approved the bill at 11:52 P.M., and Lt. Gov. Bill Hobby said it was the most dramatic ending to a session he had seen during his 16 years in office. The next day, Maxey said: "The gay community can't live with this bill because of the onerous anti-gay thrust, but many people will die without it."

Chapter 7

The Executive

Jimmy Margulies Houston Post reprinted by permission

*N*owhere in Texas politics is there a more intense struggle for power than in a gubernatorial election that never lacks for candidates. (See the cartoon that opens this chapter.) As discussed in Chapter 4, candidates spend millions of dollars in seeking an office described by scholars as *"primis inter pares"* (first among equals). What follows is a discussion of Texas's numerous executive offices, beginning with that of the governor.

Overview of the Governorship

Restricted gubernatorial power is established in Article IV of the Texas Constitution. Texas's executive branch is an organizational maze of bureaucracies, most of them neither controlled nor directed by the governor. (See Figure 7.1.) Examination of the many departments, agencies, boards, and commissions leads to an irrefutable conclusion: the governor lacks constitutional powers to implement public policy in such major fields as education, energy, business regulation, and welfare. In fact, state programs affecting the largest groups of people are the products of a fragmented process of initiatives from the governor, pressures from interest groups, decisions from elected and appointed administrators, and most important, spending directives from state legislators jealously guarding their power over the public purse.

Certainly, the governor of Texas enjoys much prestige. Furthermore, the Texas Constitution declares that the governor "shall be the *chief executive officer* of the State"; but this is a deceptive description of an official who must share power with other elected and appointed executive officials. The state Constitution also provides for election of a lieutenant governor, attorney general, comptroller of public accounts, treasurer, and commissioner of the General Land Office; the secretary of state, however, is appointed by the governor. According to statute, the commissioner of agriculture and the three members of the Railroad Commission are all popularly elected. As the result of a 1987 referendum, a 15-member State Board of Education is elected by the people. Also in the executive branch are members of about 200 appointive boards and commissions that have been established by the Legislature to perform various functions.

Constitutionally, the Texas governor is "weak" in terms of formal authority. Shared executive power ties every chief executive's hands in trying to manage a bulky bureaucracy. Influence and high visibility are two magnets that draw gubernatorial aspirants every four years. Winners retain for life the title "Governor," and they enjoy the status and prestige found in no other Texas political office.

Since 1978, when Republican Bill Clements was elected to his first term as governor, competition for Texas's biggest political prize has been a genuine two-party struggle. Before that time, factional conflicts, largely stemming from conservative versus liberal interests within the Democratic party, were the principal political battlegrounds. Beginning in 1978, however, races for the governorship have pitted Democrats against Republicans in multimillion-dollar campaigns.

FIGURE 7.1 The Texas Executive Structure

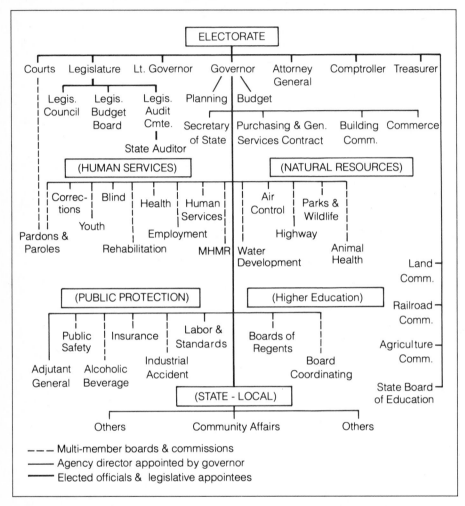

Source: *To Make Texas State Government Modern, Visible, Responsive* (Austin: Texas Research League, February 1975), p. 5; updated and printed by permission.

Thus, many perplexed voters have wondered, "If this office is so 'weak,' why would Bill Clements and Mark White spend $46 million (combined) in 1982 and 1986 to become governor?" A partial answer is that constitutionally, the governorship is "weak," but politically it is a very "strong" office. Because of rising campaign costs, some cynics have described the governorship as the "best office money can buy."

After Clements and White slugged it out in two bitterly fought gubernatorial contests in 1982 (won by White) and 1986 (won by Clements), Texas's economy spiraled downward; and most Texans expected more leadership from both governors than the Constitution of 1876 would allow. At the beginning of his second term, businessman Clements was touting good management as the one important solution to fiscal problems, but his abrasive manner and foot-in-the-mouth statements ruffled many Texans and caused consternation among close associates. In the meantime, an apprehensive public was taking a more critical view of a system that could produce heavy-spending gubernatorial candidates but could not cope with a fiscal crisis that threatened to close public schools and paralyze state government.

As Clements began his second term in 1987, a highly publicized play-for-pay football scandal at Southern Methodist University severely damaged his credibility and leadership. A 48-page report prepared by a three-member panel of Methodist bishops revealed that while serving as chairman of SMU's board of governors, Clements had authorized payments to football players from a $400,000 slush fund financed by wealthy boosters of the university's athletic program. The governor did not deny wrongdoing and confirmed that the payments had been made. While managing to conceal the scandal during his 1986 gubernatorial race, Clements's admission of involvement in authorizing illegal payments to student athletes se-verely tainted his second term. Referring to SMU's mascot, press accounts labeled the scandal "Ponygate," a Texas version of corruption like "Watergate" and "Iran-gate" at the national level.

Qualifications and Term of Office

There are three constitutional qualifications for the office of governor: a mini-mum age of 30, U.S. citizenship, and Texas residence for five years immediately preceding the gubernatorial election. Originally, the term of office was two years; but since 1974, Texas governors have been elected for four years with no limitation on the number of terms they may serve. Forty-six other states provide for four-year terms. Only New Hampshire, Rhode Island, and Vermont retain the two-year term.

Election and Compensation

Superimposed on constitutional prerequisites are numerous extralegal restraints that historically have produced a common mold for successful gubernatorial as-pirants in Texas. From Richard Coke's election in 1873 until 1978, all winning candidates were Democrats, usually conservative or moderate. In 1978, Bill Clem-ents broke the mold by becoming Texas's first Republican governor since the administration of E. J. Davis (1870–1874). As a successful, conservative business-man, Clements resembled most of his Democratic predecessors in the governor's chair. But his Republicanism and the fact that he previously had neither sought nor held a state government office represented dramatic departures from tradi-tional gubernatorial practice.

As the result of a 1954 constitutional amendment, the Legislature sets the gov-ernor's salary. For fiscal years 1990 and 1991 it was set at $93,432 per year.

The Texas Constitution forbids the governor and other executive officers to hold any other civil or corporate office, and they may receive neither compensation nor the promise of compensation for other employment while in office. Fringe benefits for the governor include allowances for staffing and maintaining the governor's mansion; also, the governor uses a state-owned limousine and a state-leased airplane.

Succession

Article IV of the Texas Constitution and a statute spell out the line of succession should a governor die, resign, be removed from office, refuse to take office, or be unable to fill the office. Constitutionally, the order of succession is headed by the lieutenant governor; next in line is the president pro tempore of the Senate. After these two officials, the Legislature has designated the following line of succession: speaker of the House, attorney general, and chief justices of the 14 courts of appeal in ascending numerical order beginning with the chief justice for the First Court of Appeals District.

Unlike the Twenty-fifth Amendment to the U.S. Constitution, the Texas Constitution does not stipulate who is to conduct the duties of the office of governor in case of physical or mental disability of the incumbent. The lieutenant governor is acting governor while the governor is absent from the state. By custom, Texas governors and lieutenant governors arrange their schedules so that on at least one occasion both are conveniently out of state at the same time. In such circumstances, the president pro tempore of the Senate has the honor of becoming acting governor until the governor or lieutenant governor returns.

Removal from Office

Impeachment and conviction constitute the only legal process of forcing a Texas governor from office before the end of a term. The state Constitution empowers the House of Representatives to initiate impeachment proceedings during regular or special sessions of the Legislature. Each article of impeachment (similar to a grand jury's indictment) must be approved by a majority vote of the House. One or more impeachment articles passed by the House must be approved by a two-thirds majority vote of the Senate membership in order to remove the governor. When a governor or lieutenant governor is tried, the chief justice of the Texas Supreme Court presides over the Senate. The penalty for conviction on an impeachment charge is removal from office and disqualification from holding any other appointive or elective public office in the state, but such conviction does not bar the person from holding a federal office. Following removal, a former governor may be tried and convicted in a criminal proceeding or a judgment may be rendered in a civil action.

Although all Texas constitutions have provided for impeachment of the governor, only Governor James Ferguson has been impeached and removed. Ferguson's troubles stemmed from a personal feud with the University of Texas. He tried to dictate policy to the university's Board of Regents, including the firing of professors.

Interestingly, although impeachment charges related to the SMU scandal were not brought against Governor Clements, the possibility of such action was raised during the second special session of the 70th Legislature. Had the legislators removed Clements, Lieutenant Governor Bill Hobby, Jr., would have followed in his father's footsteps. Lieutenant Governor William P. Hobby, Sr., was acting governor during the impeachment of Ferguson in 1917 and then succeeded "Farmer Jim" when he was removed from office.

Grounds for removing governors or other officials in the executive branch are not stipulated in Texas's Constitution. Rather, impeachment proceedings are highly charged political affairs with legal overtones. Ironically, both Clements's and Ferguson's problems emanated from their involvement with the politics of higher education.

Staff

Although the governor's hands are often tied when dealing with the state bureaucracy, the chief executive's personal staff functions directly under gubernatorial supervision. A governor's success in dealing with interest groups, the Legislature, and the general public depends largely on staff input and support.

The *Governor's Office* administers many programs that stem from the governor's priorities and personal interests, from federal grants, and from special-interest needs. Beginning in the 1960s and continuing into the late 1980s, the governor's staff mushroomed from a mere 68 full-time and 12 part-time employees under Governor John Connally to over 200 employees under Governor Bill Clements in his second term (1987–1991). The principal cause of the increase in staff personnel in the Governor's Office during recent years has been the expansion in the number of federally funded programs requiring gubernatorial coordination. Failure to provide proper direction for federal programs can cause problems that might jeopardize a governor's political future.

In the past decade, two developments have significantly affected the Governor's Office. First, there has been a nationwide trend to personalize the office so that every interested citizen may have access to the governor or a staff member. Both the first administration of Governor Clements and White's administration emphasized accessibility through weekly press conferences and a monthly television program called "The Governor's Report." Another trend is the increasing importance of intergovernmental relations involving cities, councils of governments, interstate councils, federal agencies, and international affairs, particularly matters involving Mexico. The governor appoints and may remove officials charged with planning and coordinating the responsibilities of the Governor's Office.

To what extent informal relations among the governor's appointed assistants and unofficial advisers influence gubernatorial decisions is open to speculation. Staff appointments do not require Senate confirmation. Appointed aides are responsible only to the governor. They assist in carrying out formal and informal powers bestowed on the governor by the Texas Constitution, statutes, custom, and practice.

Powers of the Governor

Inaugurated on the third Tuesday in January of every fourth year (always the odd-numbered year before a presidential election), the governor of Texas takes an oath "to cause the laws to be faithfully executed." Herein lies the general constitutional responsibility of the office; however, few formal powers are given the governor to carry out this mandate. Whatever success the governor may achieve stems less from constitutional or statutory power than from the chief executive's ability to rally public opinion behind gubernatorial programs and to balance the ever-present demands of lobbyists. Because of their distinctive nature, powers of the governor may be classified as executive, legislative, judicial, and informal.

Executive Powers

Constitutional and statutory weaknesses of the Texas governorship are apparent on examination of formal powers. Despite legal barriers, however, some governors have transcended such restrictions by using their political skills.

Appointive Power It is a fundamental principle of management (whether in government, business, or education) that the power to appoint is a necessary executive function. *Appointive power* is the most significant tool given to the governor of Texas. Statutes creating administrative agencies make possible the appointment of a governor's friends and political supporters (especially those who have made major financial contributions in an election campaign) to policymaking positions on some 200 boards and commissions. Department heads appointed by the governor include the adjutant general, commissioner of labor statistics, director of the Department of Community Affairs, and director of the Office of State-Federal Relations. Members of the governor's personal staff are also appointed.

Because most governors of Texas have served at least four years, they have had the opportunity to appoint hundreds of persons to such powerful boards and commissions as the Board of Human Services, the Highway and Public Transportation Commission, and boards of regents for four multicampus university systems and ten regional state universities. However, the governor's appointive power is not without limitations. First, the constitutional requirement of senatorial confirmation of appointments by a two-thirds majority vote, combined with the political necessity of *senatorial courtesy,* sometimes blocks an appointment. Senatorial courtesy involves consultation with the senator from a prospective appointee's district in an attempt to gain support for confirmation. The governor may try to circumvent the Senate by making *recess appointments*—those made while the Senate is not in session. But the Constitution requires that all recess appointments be submitted to the Senate for confirmation within ten days after it convenes for a regular or special session. Failure of the Senate to confirm a gubernatorial recess appointment prevents the governor from reappointing that person to the same position.

A second limitation results from the fact that most state boards and commissions are composed of members who serve for six years with overlapping terms of office. Thus, a new governor must work with carry-overs from previous administrations; such persons may not be particularly supportive of the new administration.

A third limitation on the governor's appointive power is the fact that some important state agencies are composed of elected rather than appointed members. The three members of the Railroad Commission are elected statewide, and the 15 members of the State Board of Education are elected from single-member districts drawn by the Legislature. The governor has no direct control over these agencies.

The governor's appointive power also extends to filling vacancies involving heads of the executive departments, members of the Railroad Commission, and judges within the state (with the exception of those for county courts, municipal courts, and justice of the peace courts). Also, if a U.S. senator from Texas dies or resigns before the expiration of a term, the vacancy is filled by a gubernatorial appointee. Officials appointed to fill vacancies serve until the following general election. If a vacancy occurs in the Texas Legislature or in the Texas delegation to the U.S. House of Representatives, the governor must call a special election to fill the position.

During a four-year term, a Texas governor appoints about 4,000 persons to oversee various state agencies. These are the men and women who really direct state government. Other than receiving travel money for official meetings, most board-commission members are unpaid state policymakers. They approve budgets, establish personnel practices, and determine policy directions for their agencies. Almost without exception, appointees are tied politically to the governor, usually with campaign donations. (See Table 7.1.)

Until recently, one recurring problem faced by newly elected governors has been that of having to live with *midnight appointments* made by outgoing governors during the last few months of a term. In 1987, this matter became the subject of a constitutional amendment whereby an outgoing governor, who has either been defeated for or did not seek re-election, is barred from making appointments to boards and commissions during a period extending from November 1 to January 20, when a new governor takes the oath of office.

Removal Power   In creating numerous boards and commissions, the Legislature has given the governor extensive appointive power but no independent removal power. Lack of effective *removal power* greatly limits gubernatorial control over the state bureaucracy. Although members of the governor's staff and some statutory officials (for example, the director of the Department of Community Affairs) may be removed directly by the governor, they represent only a small percentage of the state's administrative officials. Elected department heads and their subordinates are not subject to the governor's removal power. The governor may informally pressure a board member to resign or accept another appointment, but this is not as effective as the power of direct removal. Under a constitutional amendment adopted in 1980, however, governors may remove their appointees with consent of two-thirds of the state senators present. This change still falls short of independent removal power.

TABLE 7.1 Major Appointments by Governor Bill Clements, January–April 1987

Board or Commission	Appointee	Contribution
A&M University Board of Regents	Douglas R. DeCluitt, Waco	$ 6,000
	William A. McKenzie, Dallas	5,500
	Wayne A. Showers, McAllen	0
Board of Corrections	Jerry H. Hodge, Amarillo	3,000
	F. L. "Steve" Stephens, San Angelo	2,500
	Charles T. Terrell, Dallas	2,000
Economic Development Commission	Edward O. Vetter, Dallas	7,000
Highway and Public Transportation Commission	Robert H. Dedman, Dallas	25,000
Optometry Board	Clinton M. DeWolfe, Houston	6,000
Pharmacy Board	Jerry D. Pyle, Arlington	5,000
Turnpike Authority	Clive Runnells, Houston	30,000
University of Texas Board of Regents	Sam E. Barshop, San Antonio	15,000
	W. A. "Tex" Moncrief, Jr., Fort Worth	25,000
	Louis A. Beecherl, Jr., Dallas	21,000

Source: Dallas Morning News, April 27, 1987, p. H-2.

Impeachment by the House of Representatives, with conviction by the Senate, is one of three constitutional methods of removing state officials. Although rarely used, two other legal processes exist. First, *legislative address* to the governor requires a two-thirds majority vote in each legislative chamber to remove a district or appellate court judge or justice. Second, *quo warranto proceedings* are initiated by the Texas attorney general and involve the trial of a state official who, if found guilty of some official misconduct, may be removed from office. The governor thus has no independent removal power over state officials, except those who serve as gubernatorial staff members.

Military Power The governor of Texas is commander-in-chief of the state's military forces, which include both air and ground units, except when the president of the United States calls the Texas National Guard into federal service. Acting under gubernatorial direction, the state adjutant general may mobilize the Texas National Guard to enforce state law, repel invasion, curb insurrection and riot, and maintain order in times of natural disasters such as tornadoes and floods. The governor may declare *martial law* (temporary rule by the Texas National Guard and suspension of civil authority) if deemed necessary because of civil disorder, such as a riot that cannot be handled by local authorities.

Law Enforcement Power Some control over state law enforcement accrues to the governor through power to appoint, with Senate approval, the three members of the Public Safety Commission. The commission-appointed director of public safety oversees a staff of nearly 5,000 employees in the Department of Public

Safety. Included among the department's responsibilities are highway traffic supervision, driver licensing, motor vehicle inspection, and narcotics and other criminal law enforcement in cooperation with local and federal agencies. If circumstances demand swift but limited police action, the governor is empowered to assume command of the Texas Rangers, a branch of the Department of Public Safety composed of fewer than 100 highly trained law enforcement personnel. In Texas, law enforcement is primarily a local responsibility rather than a state function.

Budgetary Power   Gubernatorial *budgetary power* is subordinated in part to the Legislature's prerogative of controlling the state's purse strings. Furthermore, a duality exists in preparing the Texas state budget. By statutory requirement, the governor and the Legislative Budget Board submit separate budgets for consideration by the Legislature. Interestingly, Governor Bill Clements accepted the board's recommendations in 1989 and did not submit an executive budget. Traditionally, both houses are inclined to accept the board's spending proposals.

Acting alone, the governor is prevented from impounding (freezing) funds appropriated by the Legislature, transferring funds from one state agency to another, and increasing or decreasing an appropriation. In the final analysis, the governor's only constitutional control over state spending lies in the power to veto an entire appropriations bill or to veto individual budget items.

Recognizing that the governor's hand needed strengthening in managing the budget, the Legislature has relinquished some of its budgetary control. (See pages 246 and 247 for the budget execution power granted in 1987.) After declaring a fiscal emergency, the governor may recommend the following changes in state agency funding if the Legislature is not in session: budget cuts up to a maximum of 10 percent and budget increases of as much as 5 percent. Final approval of any budgetary increase or reduction must be given by the ten-member Legislative Budget Board. With the exception of public education funding, all departmental budgets are subject to this law.

Legislative Powers

Perhaps the most stringent test of a Texas governor's capacity for leadership involves handling of legislative matters. The governor's *legislative power* is exercised through three major functions authorized by the Texas Constitution: delivering messages to the Legislature, vetoing legislation, and calling special sessions of the Legislature. But success of a legislative program depends heavily on a governor's ability to use informal persuasion with influential lobbyists, legislative leaders, the press, and, occasionally, the general public.

Message Power   The Texas Constitution requires the governor to deliver a State of the State message at the beginning of each regular session of the Legislature. On occasion, special messages may be presented either in person or in writing. By custom, the governor delivers a farewell message at the conclusion of a term of office. Successful use of the *message power* in promoting a harmonious relationship between the governor and the Legislature depends to a large degree on such variables as timing of special messages relative to volatile issues, support of the governor's program by chairs of powerful legislative committees, and personal popularity of the governor.

Veto Power   The most direct legislative tool of the governor is the power to veto legislation. This is done by returning a bill unsigned, with written reasons for not signing, to the house in which it originated. The Legislature can override the governor's veto by a two-thirds majority vote of the membership of each house, but this has seldom occurred. *Veto power* takes several forms. For example, the governor may veto an entire bill, or may veto any item in an appropriation bill while permitting enactment of the remainder. Governor Clements cut $11 million from the 1990–1991 budget in this way. Hence, the *item veto power* places the governor in a powerful bargaining position with individual legislators in the delicate game of pork-barrel politics. That is, the governor may strike a bargain with a senator or representative whereby, in exchange for the chief executive's promise not to deny funding for a lawmaker's pet project, the legislator agrees to support a bill favored by the governor. Thus, the strong veto power given to the governor by the Texas Constitution provides a formidable weapon for dealing with uncooperative legislators.

Both the governor of Texas and the president of the United States have the prerogative of neither signing nor vetoing a bill within ten days (Sundays excepted) after its passage, thus allowing the measure to become law without executive signature. But if the president "pockets" a bill that is passed within ten weekdays before congressional adjournment, such failure to act kills the measure. Although not possessing pocket-veto power, the governor of Texas may exercise a *post-adjournment veto* of pending legislation within 20 days after a session has ended.

Of the 1,318 bills passed in the regular session of the 71st Legislature (1989), Governor Clements vetoed 55,[1] thereby running his total to 179 in his two terms in office. In wielding this formidable power, Clements assured himself of the nickname "Veto Bill." He now holds the record for the most bills vetoed by any Texas governor, surpassing the previous record of 117 set by Governor Dan Moody (1927–1931).

Calling Special Sessions   Included among the governor's powers is the authority to call special sessions of the Legislature. No constitutional limitation is placed on the number of special sessions that may be called, but a *special session* is limited to 30 days. During a special session, however, the Legislature may consider only those matters that the governor specifies in the call or subsequently presents to the Legislature. Effective use of this power depends to a large extent on a governor's timing and rapport with legislative leaders.

Judicial Powers

Although possessing few formal judicial powers, the governor of Texas may fill vacancies on many courts and perform acts of clemency to lighten the sentences given to some convicted criminals. (Judicial and penal affairs are covered in more detail in Chapter 8.)

Appointment and Removal of Judges and Justices   Nearly two-thirds of Texas's district and appellate court judges and justices first serve after gubernatorial appointment to fill a vacancy caused by death, resignation, or removal. As authorized by Article XV, Section 8, of the Texas Constitution, the governor may remove judges and justices of these courts "on address of two-thirds of each house of the Legislature for willful neglect of duty, incompetency, habitual drunkenness, oppression in office, or other reasonable cause which shall not be sufficient ground for impeachment."

Acts of Executive Clemency   In November 1983, Texas voters approved a constitutional amendment making the Board of Pardons and Paroles a statutory body composed of six gubernatorial appointees. *Parole* involves release from prison before completion of a sentence and is conditioned on good behavior. It is granted by the board without action by the governor, but the governor may perform various acts of *executive clemency* that set aside or reduce a sentence for a felony conviction. For example, a *full pardon* or a *conditional pardon* may be conferred by the governor on recommendation of the board. Restoration of all civil rights, including the right to vote, is conferred by a full pardon but not by a conditional pardon. Acting independently, the governor may revoke a conditional pardon and grant one 30-day *reprieve* in a death sentence case. A reprieve temporarily suspends execution of the penalty imposed by a court. Aside from the single reprieve that the governor may grant independently in a capital punishment case, the chief executive may grant others only on recommendations of the board. If recommended by the Board of Pardons and Paroles, a governor also may reduce a penalty through *commutation of sentence* and may remit fines and forfeitures.

Informal Powers

Any description of the Governor's Office would be incomplete without noting executive involvement in ceremonial functions. In the eyes of most Texans, the impressive office in the eastern wing of the Capitol holds center stage. Its occupant is a symbol of the government of Texas. Within the limits of time and priorities, every governor attempts to play the role of *chief of state* by participating in dedications, banquets, parades, and other public events. The breadth and depth of this role cannot be fully measured, but its significance should not be underestimated in determining the effectiveness of a governor.

The Plural Executive

Further attributes of the weak-executive structure are found in the various elective offices established under Article IV of the Texas Constitution. Although millions of Texans cannot readily identify them, the attorney general, comptroller of public accounts, treasurer, land commissioner, and agriculture commissioner oversee large departments with multimillion-dollar budgets. Their salaries are set by the Legislature—in 1990, $74,698 each for the five elected department heads. Along with the governor, lieutenant governor, and appointed secretary of state, these state officials are referred to collectively as the *plural executive.* This structural arrangement contributes significantly to the state's long ballot because these executive officials, except the secretary of state, are popularly elected to four-year terms with no limitation on their re-election. There is no restriction on the number of terms a secretary of state may serve, although new governors usually appoint their own secretary of state. Each of the elected department heads is largely independent of gubernatorial control; however, the governor makes appointments to fill vacancies in these offices. Unlike department heads in the federal government, those in Texas do not form a cabinet to advise the governor.

Lieutenant Governor

Considered by some political observers to be the most powerful official in Texas government, the lieutenant governor functions more in the legislative area than in the executive branch. The state Constitution makes the lieutenant governor president of the Senate; and under Senate rules, this office allows significant influence over lawmaking. In the event of the governor's death, resignation, or removal from office, the lieutenant governor becomes governor. A 1984 amendment to the Texas Constitution requires the Texas Senate to convene within 30 days whenever a vacancy occurs in the lieutenant governor's office; that body then elects a state senator to fill the office until the next general election. The elected senator would wear two hats: lieutenant governor and state senator. The annual salary for the office of lieutenant governor is only $7,200, the same as that paid to members of the Legislature.

The office of lieutenant governor has grown in importance primarily because of its influence on legislation. Lieutenant Governor William Hobby's role in state affairs (1973–1991) took on added significance in the 1980s as the Legislature grappled with financial problems. Long a friend of higher education, the lieutenant governor locked horns with Governor Clements on spending levels for public colleges and universities. Speculations concerning gubernatorial aspirations were put to rest late in July 1987 when Hobby announced that he would not seek re-election or any political office in 1990. His 18-year tenure as lieutenant governor set a record for that office.

Attorney General

Aside from the governor and lieutenant governor, the most powerful constitutional executive in Texas is the attorney general, who, to qualify for the office, must be licensed to practice law in Texas. Serving as the state's lawyer, this officer gives advisory opinions to state and local authorities and represents the state in civil litigation. Overseeing a staff of over 1,000, the attorney general influences public policy in many areas. One example is enforcement of the consumer protection law. Also, with increasing frequency, legislators have turned to the attorney general for advice concerning the constitutionality of pending bills. The governor, heads of state agencies, and local government officers also request the attorney general's opinions on the scope of their jurisdiction and on vaguely worded laws. Although neither judges nor other officials are bound by these opinions, such rulings are considered authoritative if not overruled by a court.

It is not uncommon for a Texas attorney general, one of the most visible state officeholders, to aspire to the governorship. First elected in 1978, former Attorney General Mark White did not seek a second term, choosing instead to challenge Clements for the governorship. White's successor, Democrat Jim Mattox, threw his hat into the gubernatorial election ring in 1989.

Commissioner of the General Land Office

Since its creation under the Constitution of the Republic of Texas (1836), the General Land Office has grown in responsibility and importance. The commissioner exercises broad powers that include awarding oil, gas, and sulfur exploration leases for land owned by the state; serving as chairman of the Veterans Land Board; and sitting as an *ex officio* (i.e., having another office) member of other boards responsible for handling public lands. After his first election in 1982, Commissioner Garry Mauro completely reorganized the General Land Office.

Commissioner of Agriculture

With over 500 employees, the Texas Department of Agriculture (TDA) has become a controversial state agency. It is headed by an elected commissioner whose salary is set by the Legislature. In 1989 the TDA survived an attempt to "sunset" (i.e., eliminate) it. (See page 193 for details on the sunset process.) In order to extend the life of the department and to avoid a veto by Governor Clements, the Legislature stripped the TDA of its pesticide regulatory powers by creating a nine-member ex officio pesticide board chaired by the agriculture commissioner. Clements had wanted the agriculture commissioner to be appointed by the governor, but the office remains elective. Nevertheless, the governor axed $2.5 million from the department's budget for fiscal years 1990 and 1991. The department has responsibility for enforcing agricultural laws and providing service programs for Texas farmers, ranchers, and consumers. Enforcement powers of the department include inspection to determine the accuracy of commercial scales, pumps, and meters.

By law, the commissioner of agriculture is supposed to be a "practicing farmer," but this criterion is vague enough to allow anyone who owns a piece of agricultural land to qualify. The political reality of winning the office stems principally from name identification with the state's voters. A former editor of the *Texas Observer,*

Texas Agriculture Commissioner Jim Hightower addresses a political rally at Stephenville. (Texas Department of Agriculture.)

Jim Hightower swept to electoral victories in 1982 and 1986. Hightower's identity grew as he stumped the state, lambasting Republicans Clements and Reagan for their ineffectiveness in dealing with Texas farm and ranch issues. (See Reading 7.1 on the struggle within the 71st Legislature to preserve the TDA and Hightower's job.)

Comptroller of Public Accounts

One of the most powerful elected officers in Texas government is the comptroller, the state's chief accounting officer and tax collector. Before an appropriations bill is passed by the Legislature, the comptroller must certify that revenue is expected to be available to cover all proposed expenditures. Otherwise, an appropriation must be approved by a four-fifths vote of the membership of each house. The required certification of anticipated revenue is prompted by the state constitutional mandate for pay-as-you-go financing of government operations.

Upon taking office in 1973, Bob Bullock completely reorganized the department. Included among his innovations is a toll-free telephone number (1-800-252-5555) for persons who have questions about state taxes. Supervising a staff of 1,300 employees, Bullock made headlines with dire projections of state budgetary deficits before new tax legislation was enacted in 1987. In 1988, he announced his candidacy for the office of lieutenant governor, an office he hoped to win in 1990.

Treasurer

Functions of the state treasurer are principally to receive state revenues and administer deposits of state funds in Texas banks approved by a three-member State Depository Board. This board is composed of the treasurer, a banking commissioner, and a third person appointed by the governor.

Contrary to popular assumption, the office of state treasurer is more than just a record-keeping position. Opportunities to wield political patronage stem from the treasurer's ex officio membership on the State Banking Board. Because all state-regulated banks must be chartered by the board, the treasurer is in a position to favor political supporters by influencing charters.

Not since Governor Miriam "Ma" Ferguson's two administrations (1925–1927 and 1933–1935) had Texas elected a woman to a statewide executive office. In the Democratic electoral sweep of 1982, however, Ann Richards won the state treasurer's post following public service as a Travis County commissioner. Reelected in 1986, she, like Bullock, received unprecedented publicity for dealing with the state's fiscal crisis. In June 1989 she announced her candidacy for governor in the crowded field of 1990 gubernatorial aspirants.

Secretary of State

As mentioned above, the only constitutional executive officer appointed by the governor is the secretary of state. To be effective, this appointment must be confirmed by the Senate. Since 1975, the secretary of state has served a four-year term with no limitation on the number of reappointments.

Receiving a salary of $66,000, the secretary of state is the chief election officer of Texas. Principal duties include the following: administering state election laws, certifying election returns, receiving personal financial statements from state officials, registering lobbyists, granting charters to some Texas corporations, and processing extradition agreements for the governor.

Obviously, the Legislature has given the secretary of state a myriad of functions that might more properly be given to other department heads or to independent boards and commissions. Possible conflicts of interest in the administration of election laws and campaign finance laws are heightened by close relations between the secretary of state and the governor. For example, Governor Clements appointed George Bayoud, Jr., formerly chief of staff in the Office of the Governor, to the secretary of state position in 1989, when Jack Rains resigned to run for the governorship.

The Bureaucracy and Public Policies

"Who is in charge here?" muses a concerned Texan in pondering issues that face the Lone Star State. Further reflection raises more questions: "Why can't the governor and Legislature cooperate?" "Why won't someone get 'a handle' on the bureaucracy?" "Who is responsible for regulating Texas's businesses?" Answers to these and related queries may not be forthcoming until one probes Texas's *bureaucratic system,* which features many boards and commissions. Also, one must be aware of the formidable interlocking of special interests that influence gubernatorial appointments, legislative appropriations, and departmental operations.

Personnel

Bureaucracies start and end with people. State government is the biggest employer in the Texas economy. Texas has neither a central personnel office nor a merit selection system for most state jobs. Each of the 216 agencies and departments determines its own employee policies, excluding salary and benefits that are set by the Legislature.

Headquartered in office buildings throughout Austin, state employees are the backbone of the Capital City's economy, but most members of the Texas bureaucracy work in departmental field offices scattered throughout the Lone Star State. Excluding college and university personnel, the state employs over 100,000 full-time people, 28 percent of whom work in Austin. Their numbers swell in proportion to new programs and policies authorized by the Legislature. Examples of bureaucratic proliferation can be seen in each of five major policy activities requiring state funding: educating, serving, regulating, licensing, and promoting.

Public Education Policy Issues

No single topic has occupied the Texas public agenda more than education reform. In January 1983, then U.S. Secretary of Education Terrell Bell shocked Texas's educational community with a report indicating that the state's public school system, with 3 million students enrolled, ranked well below the national average in standardized test scores (Scholastic Aptitude Test), pupil-teacher ratios, and teacher salaries. Furthermore, Bell's report placed Texas 42nd among the states in percentage of students who finish high school and next to last in the portion of per capita income spent on public education.

Education Reform in Texas Governor Mark White responded quickly to Bell's report by appointing a 21-member Select Committee on Public Education to study the problem and recommend reform measures to the Legislature. Subsequently, in a June 1984 special session, the Texas Legislature hastily enacted an education reform law that included most of the basic recommendations of the reform committee.

Texas's comprehensive education reform law of 1984 affected students, teachers, and administrators. The powers, functions, and selection process of the State Board of Education were altered to implement new educational policies. Teachers were given salary increases and a career ladder salary supplement plan, but they are required to be tested for competency in basic skills. For students to be eligible for promotion to the next higher grade or to participate in extracurricular activities, including athletics, a grade of 70 for each course was mandated by the law. Basic skills tests were required of students during elementary and high school. In addition, students were required by law to pass a minimum competency test before receiving a high school diploma.

Aftermath of Reform   In 1986, a basic literacy test was given to teachers in the midst of outcries by those who claimed that the requirement was degrading to their profession and in violation of their constitutional rights. When 98 percent of the teachers passed the test, resentment gradually subsided, but not before some teachers sued the state for breach of contract. The 1984 reform law allowed cancellation of teacher contracts for failure to pass the literacy test. In February 1987, the Texas Supreme Court ruled in favor of the state. When the 71st Legislative Session ended in 1989, Texas's five-year-old school reform law had, with few exceptions, withstood legislative assault. The 71st Legislature strengthened evaluation standards for the teacher career ladder and ruled that school districts cannot retain teachers who fail to meet state requirements.

Responsibility for providing free elementary and secondary schools and low-cost institutions of higher education is essentially a state function. About 45 percent of Texas's state budget is committed to education. Under pressure from lawsuits filed by plaintiffs in poor school districts, the 71st Legislature authorized spending $450 million to narrow the funding gap between rich and poor school districts. That outlay is misleading, however, when Texas's per-pupil spending, teacher salaries, and university research dollars consistently lag far behind the levels of many other states. Furthermore, the Texas Supreme Court in *Edgewood ISD* v. *Kirby* (1989) ordered the Legislature to devise an "immediate" and "long overdue" remedy by May 1, 1990, to reduce funding-per-student disparities among rich and poor school districts.

The *Texas Education Agency* has emerged as one of the state's most powerful departments. The chief administrator of the TEA is the commissioner of education, who is appointed to a four-year term by the 15-member elected State Board of Education representing districts drawn by the Legislature. Since 1985, William N. Kirby has held the position of commissioner, which is budgeted for a salary of $114,305 per year.

Higher Education

Texas's public college and university system is highly decentralized. Since 1965, an 18-member *Higher Education Coordinating Board* has tried to unify higher education policy, but with little success. Appointed to six-year terms by the governor, board members establish planning and development policies that affect institutions of higher learning in Texas—including some aspects of education at private institutions such as Baylor, SMU, and TCU. The chief administrator is the board-appointed commissioner of higher education.

Reform   In February 1987, the Select Committee on Higher Education, created by the 69th Texas Legislature in 1985, released its comprehensive study. Chaired by lawyer Larry Temple, the 23-member body included the governor, lieutenant governor, speaker of the House, 6 state legislators, 1 state judge, and 12 businesspersons.

Public higher education in Texas, the committee learned, is a massive enterprise with 37 universities, 49 community colleges, 4 technical institutes, and 8 medical and health-related institutions. The public higher-education system costs almost $4.5 billion annually to operate. Out of economic necessity, reported the committee, a better way must be found to manage the entire enterprise more effectively and efficiently. To spur government action, LULAC and other Mexican-American groups led successful legal and lobbying efforts to focus attention on lack of higher education opportunities in South Texas. The 71st Legislature responded by establishing a law school at Texas A&I University in Kingsville, merging Texas A&I, Laredo State, Corpus Christi State, and West Texas State* into the Texas A&M system, and increasing support for the two units of Pan American University at Edinburg and Brownsville by merging them into the University of Texas system. In a special session, lawmakers added first- and second-year classes to the University of Texas at Dallas.

Perhaps the most significant response to reform pressures is the Texas Academic Skills Program (TASP), administered by the Higher Education Coordinating Board. Designed to measure deficiencies in reading, writing, and mathematics, the program became effective September 1, 1989. All entering college freshmen must pass basic skills tests before taking credit courses. Enrollment in remedial classes is required for those students who score less than 70 on one or more of the three examinations. A "grandfather" clause waived students who passed at least one 3-credit-hour course (or its equivalent) prior to September 1, 1989. Students at institutions such as Baylor and SMU are exempt from TASP requirements, except for those seeking admission to teacher education programs at private and church-supported colleges.

Human Services

Issues affecting persons suffering from poverty, illness, and joblessness are never glamorous topics for public discussion. Add to that list the needs of blind, deaf, crippled, addicted (drugs and/or alcohol), and incarcerated persons. (See pages 223–225 for information on Texas's prison system.) Wards of the state are virtually powerless, because there are no strong lobbies to represent welfare recipients, hospital patients, and prison inmates.

Public Assistance Coupled with the Lone Star State's revenue problems is the poverty faced by many of its people. According to a report released in late 1984 by the State Senate Interim Committee on Hunger and Nutrition, the number of Texans living at, or below, the poverty line had increased substantially since the 1980 census. In 1980, 14.7 percent of the state's population (over 2 million people)

---

*These institutions will retain their separate names.

lived below the poverty level. By 1987, the percentage had climbed to 18.3, or over 3 million Texans. In 1988, four of the six poorest metropolitan areas in the United States were in Mexican border regions of Texas. A 1986 survey conducted by Harvard University's School of Public Health identified 29 hunger counties in Texas, the largest number for any state among 150 such counties across the nation. A hunger county was one in which 20 percent or more of the residents lived below the poverty level. Many of these new-poor Texans were facing a hunger crisis for the first time in their lives. Thousands were without health insurance. These Texans were newly poor because of a depressed condition that began in the mid-1980s; for them, it reflected a reversal of the trend of upward mobility that Texans had been pursuing since 1933.

As the 1980s drew to a close, millions of federal dollars available as state matching funds for temporary relief of Texas's needy poor remained untaken while life for the poor in Texas worsened. Texas's average monthly Aid to Families with Dependent Children (AFDC) payment per person was $56.49, or 46th among the states. Only Louisiana, Tennessee, Alabama, and Mississippi had lower payments. The Texas payment was less than half of the national average. In per capita Medicaid expenditures, Texas ranked 45th, with expenditures of slightly more than half of the national average.

Texas is no longer a rural society. Its economy, its entire social order, is as complex as that of any other highly urbanized state. Yet Texans continue to be among the lowest-taxed citizens of any state. (See Chapter 9 for more detail on how Texans are taxed.)

Responsibility for addressing these sobering statistics has been assigned to the *Texas Department of Human Services* (TDHS). Headed by a three-member board appointed by the governor, it administers over 20 programs, including AFDC, food stamps, Medicaid services, child protective services, and medical services to the aged and disabled, in addition to licensing day-care centers. Federal aid to AFDC, food stamps, and Medicaid continued to decrease (less than 1 percent of the federal budget in 1988) as the Reagan and Bush administrations forced states to assume more responsibility for welfare funding.

Another interesting fact is that of the estimated 1,090,000 Texas children living in poverty, only 275,000 receive AFDC benefits. Texas law restricts eligibility for cash assistance payments to single persons whose assets are less than $1,000, excluding a home and a car valued at less than $1,500. Thus, thousands of newly unemployed persons are barred from public relief because of accumulated assets that exceed the state's eligibility minimum. Given Texas's swelling unemployment ranks, one wonders whether such a miserly approach can long endure as public policy.

Two major changes by the 71st Legislature affecting state welfare programs include increasing the monthly income eligibility cap for nursing-home care to the federal Medicaid limit of $1,104; increasing eligibility limits for medical assistance to pregnant women and infants up to age 1, to not less than 130 percent of federal poverty guidelines; increasing state medical assistance for children age 6 or younger to 100 percent of the federal poverty levels set by the U.S. Census

Bureau in 1990 and 1991 (poverty levels differ according to family size); and allowing the state to provide more benefits for long-term health care.

Aging Another aspect of Texas's fast-growing population is the increasing proportion of older citizens. By 1980, those Texans 60 years of age and older represented 14 percent of the state's population. Nationwide, 15 percent of the population falls in that category. In 1965, the Texas Legislature created the Governor's Committee on Aging, which in 1981 became the *Texas Department on Aging*. Its basic responsibility is to develop and strengthen public and private services for Texas's elderly population. A growing minority with increasing political clout, the elderly are active as a pressure group before the Texas Legislature.

Health

Nearly 5,000 employees work for the *Texas Department of Health* (TDH). Policies are formulated by the Board of Health, whose 18 members are appointed by the governor to overlapping six-year terms. Since January 1980, Dr. Robert Bernstein has served as Commissioner of Health, a board-appointed post responsible for administering TDH. Diversity is assured in the board's make-up by the 1977 law creating the current Health Department. Gubernatorial appointees must include six licensed physicians, two hospital administrators, a dentist, a registered nurse, a veterinarian, a pharmacist, a nursing home administrator, an optometrist, a civil engineer, and two public members.

Service agencies are housed in 11 bureaus with functions that range from pro-viding personal health services to licensing over 500 hospitals, administering the federally funded Medicare program, and evaluating health maintenance organiza-tions (HMOs) for certification by the State Board of Insurance. Health issues, such as the Acquired Immune Deficiency Syndrome (AIDS), have received increasing attention from the Legislature and public alike. The 71st Legislature increased AIDS funding from $3.4 million to $18.4 million. This figure represents 40 cents per capita, far below the national average of 65 cents.

Promotion of rural health care received a boost in 1989, when the 71st Legisla-ture created the Outstanding Rural Scholar Recognition Program. Jointly adminis-tered by a student loan fund (through the state treasurer), an advisory committee (the Higher Education Coordinating Board), and rural communities, incorporated or unincorporated, outside a metropolitan area, it provides students aspiring to medical professions an incentive to return to the rural communities where adequate health care is sorely lacking. Upon completion of health-care degrees, graduates must practice in the sponsoring communities in which they finished high school.

Mental Health and Mental Retardation

Today, a record number of Texans require treatment for mental disorders. Nearly 200,000 victims of some form of behavior dysfunction or retardation are served by the *Texas Department of Mental Health and Mental Retardation* (MHMR). A nine-

State Treasurer Ann Richards (left) testifies before the Senate Health
and Human Services Commitee with Senator Steve Carriker (D-Roby)
(seated right) on rural health care legislation. (Senate Media Services.)

member board, appointed by the governor, selects a commissioner who administers a department with 30,000 employees in state and community MHMR centers.
Organizationally, a network of 8 state psychiatric hospitals, 13 state schools for
people with mental retardation, 5 state centers, a center for emotionally disturbed
youth, a research institute, a recreational rehabilitation center, and 31 community
centers provides a wide range of professional services. MHMR is particularly vulnerable to lawsuits because of the intensely personal care required in treating
mentally ill and retarded persons.

Employment

One of the oldest and largest state agencies is the *Texas Employment Commission*
(TEC), created by the Legislature in 1936 and employing nearly 4,000 persons.
Unlike the previously discussed departments, TEC is governed by three full-time,
salaried commissioners. Each is appointed by the governor to a six-year term.
The chair must represent the general public, one commissioner represents work-
ers, and the third commissioner represents employers.

With certain exceptions (for example, religious groups), employers of four or
more persons must pay a payroll tax. TEC collects the tax and makes weekly
payments to unemployed workers who are covered by the law. The commission
helps employers recruit workers and helps unemployed persons find work. It also
administers federal programs, such as the Manpower Development and Training
Act, that are designed to assist in preparing the unemployed for new jobs.

Major Areas of State Economic Regulation

Historically, Texas policymakers (particularly members of the Legislature) have
taken a hands-off approach to business. Thus, laissez-faire economics gave way

to monopolistic practices—most notably among railroads in the nineteenth century. Today, however, one finds a complex group of state regulatory agencies. Consumers, environmentalists, and small business leaders have championed governmental involvement in attempts to improve Texas's business climate and its quality of life.

Oil and Natural Gas   The state's oldest and most powerful regulatory body is the *Texas Railroad Commission,* which was created in 1891. Originally designed to regulate intrastate railroads, the Railroad Commission is important today principally because of its authority to regulate the petroleum and natural gas industries. Federal court decisions in 1984 stripped the Railroad Commission of its power to regulate intrastate railroads, which are regulated by the federal Interstate Commerce Commission. Thus, today more than ever before, the term *Railroad Commission* is very much a misnomer for an agency with major impact on the state's energy policy. Cozy relationships among oil interests, both major oil producers and independents, are recognized political facts in Texas. It is no accident that oil producers have preferred to retain the term *railroad* in the name of their regulatory body; the misnomer tends to obscure, for the voting public, the commission's oil connections. Elected statewide to six-year overlapping terms, each of the three members of the Railroad Commission receives an annual salary of $74,698.

In addition to regulating oil and natural gas industries by granting permits to drill, setting maximum allowable rates of production, and inspecting wells for safety and water intrusion, the Railroad Commission exercises other responsibilities imposed by the Legislature. Included among its regulatory duties is licensing for all intrastate motor vehicle transportation. Rate-setting for intrastate bus lines remains an exclusive duty of the commission, but the Legislature has modified trucking regulation. Beginning in 1987, intrastate truck companies are free to set their own rates within 15 percent of a base imposed by the commission. Free-market proponents have hailed the new law as a stimulus to Texas's economy. Other duties of the Railroad Commission include adjudicating gas-rate cases between municipalities and gas companies, enforcing controls on strip mines, regulating the injection and disposal of waste water from oil field operations, and approving gas rates for unincorporated areas.

Much controversy swirls around the Railroad Commission's scope of responsibility. Environmental groups, as an example, complain that regulation of surface mining for coal, lignite, uranium, iron ore, and gravel is a function that should be assigned to a separate agency.

Public Utilities   From the perspective of the general public, the Texas Legislature took a progressive step when it created the three-member *Public Utility Commission* (PUC) in 1975. Following an intense legislative struggle between consumer advocates and utility companies, the 64th Legislature established a system whereby consumers' utility rates are subject to state regulation. PUC was given original jurisdiction over rates and services for telephone utilities statewide, for electric utilities in unincorporated areas, and for radio-telephone rates statewide. The commission does not regulate municipally owned utilities or political subdivisions such as municipal utility districts or public utility districts. These utilities are regulated at the local level. Appellate jurisdiction, however, is given to PUC over municipal decisions involving privately owned utilities.

Members of the commission are appointed by the governor to six-year overlapping terms, subject to Senate confirmation. Following a heated struggle between the 71st Legislature and the governor, the Texas Senate confirmed Clements's nominees, Marta Greytok and William Cassin, who joined Jo Campbell, a Mark White appointee. Receiving an annual salary of $71,400, each of the three PUC commissioners is a full-time state employee. Cassin's term expired August 31, 1989, and he was replaced by Paul Meek.

Numerous public policy issues will have to be addressed by the PUC in the future. Heading the list is regulation of controversial nuclear energy projects, such as the South Texas Nuclear Project (STNP), which involves the cities of Houston, San Antonio, Corpus Christi, and Austin.

Water   Bureaucratic reorganization is symptomatic of Texas's board-commission system. Water regulation and development are two public policy areas that have undergone significant restructuring since 1985. In that year the 69th Legislature abolished the Texas Department of Water Resources (TDWR). Out of this dissolution came two separate agencies: one for water regulation and the other for planning and administering a statewide water plan.

The larger of Texas's two water agencies is the *Texas Water Commission* (TWC). Three full-time commissioners are appointed by the governor to six-year overlapping terms, subject to Senate confirmation. Commissioners are paid $71,400 annually. The TWC is responsible for issuing permits, carrying out enforcement operations, and developing plans for programs involving surface water and water rights, flood control improvement, hazardous solid waste, water quality, and weather modification. Other duties of the TWC include supervision of water districts, determination of suitability of certain federal projects, regulation of dam construction and maintenance, and administration of the water rates program. Decisions by the commission can be appealed to the Texas Supreme Court.

Planning for Texas's future water needs is the responsibility of the *Texas Water Development Board* (TWDB). Composed of six members appointed by the governor to six-year overlapping terms, the TWDB administers the state's water development fund. Voter-approved water bonds are sold for the purpose of obtaining money that the board loans to municipalities and other political entities for water conservation and wastewater treatment projects. Preparing and updating a statewide water plan that maximizes usage of Texas's 3,700 streams and tributaries are other duties of the board.

Other Important Areas of State Economic Regulation

Although state economic regulation extends into many areas, the following six fields of business are regulated by a state board or commission: finance, insurance, alcoholic beverages, amusement machines, securities, and air transportation.

Members of the regulatory bodies are gubernatorial appointees and serve for six-year overlapping terms after Senate confirmation. Only the three members of the Insurance Board are paid, full-time officials.

Certification in Trades and Professions

Have you ever wondered who licenses your physician, dentist, lawyer, teacher, nurse, barber, plumber, or water well digger? Some 52 Texas boards and commissions administer admission standards and license renewal requirements for practicing many trades and professions in Texas.

Gubernatorial influence on the *licensing boards* is pervasive because virtually all the board members are appointed by the governor. Exceptions are teachers, who are certified according to standards set by the elected State Board of Education, and lawyers, who must pass examinations administered by the Texas Board of Law Examiners.

Promotion of Commerce and Economic Development

In 1987, the *Texas Department of Commerce* was added to the Lone Star State's bureaucracy. Composed of six members appointed by the governor (with Senate concurrence) to six-year terms, the department's governing board represents different geographic regions of the state. A chair is selected by the governor from the board members.

Responding to pressures for worldwide expansion of Texas's businesses, state lawmakers specified that the Department of Commerce is responsible for attracting and locating new businesses in Texas, stimulating expansion of international markets for Texas products, and developing small and minority business ownership throughout the state. Within the department, the Texas Economic Development Corporation (TEDC) is charged with directing Texas's world trade and developing domestic business. Board members serve as ex officio corporation directors. Revenue bonds, whose principal and interest are retired by the activity financed, may be issued by the corporation, but only with consent of the TEDC Review Board. This board is composed of the governor (chair), lieutenant governor, speaker of the House of Representatives, state treasurer, and comptroller of public accounts. As a nonprofit organization with tax-exempt status, the corporation deposits its net earnings in Texas's general revenue fund, after bonds and other expenses are paid.

Conservation of Wildlife and Plant Resources

Somewhat lost in what may appear as an obsession with promoting business is Texas's effort to preserve the state's wildlife and plant resources. From 1919, when the Legislature provided funding for six game wardens, to 1963, when the present *Texas Parks and Wildlife Department* was created, state budgetary support for public parks and wildlife conservation was weak. Most alarming is the fact that, among the 50 states, Texas ranks near the bottom regarding state-owned park land (12 acres per 1,000 population).

A nine-member commission, gubernatorially appointed with Senate confirmation to six-year terms, oversees protection of state-owned wildlife and plant resources; state parks maintenance and acquisition; regulation and conservation of game; management of state-owned fisheries; enforcement of state law by game wardens; and administrative services (e.g., issuing boat permits and fishing and hunting licenses).[2] Although environmental concerns have been given a low priority by the Legislature, urbanization and population growth may force Texas's policymakers to re-evaluate spending directives, because no one disputes the proposition that outdoor recreation space and preservation of the natural habitat are important elements in providing a higher quality of life for all Texans.

Coping with the Problem of Bureaucratic Proliferation

Growth of the state bureaucracy has continued unabated. Little or no control has been imposed by the governor or the Legislature, but any significant reform or reorganization of the executive branch must be approached as a shared responsibility of the executive and legislative branches. To promote more effective management of the state bureaucracy, in 1977 the 65th Legislature created the *Sunset Advisory Commission.* Now a permanent arm of the Legislature, this ten-member commission studies each state agency that is directly funded by an appropriations act. Such studies are conducted on a rotating basis according to a 12-year schedule. Upon completion of a study, the commission makes a recommendation as to whether the agency should be continued, abolished, or merged with another state agency. Final authority over whether to accept or reject the commission's recommendations lies with the Legislature.

It is axiomatic in bureaucratic politics that, once in operation, an agency develops legislative ties making abolition virtually impossible. Since 1983, over 80 departments have been reviewed by the Legislature, following Sunset Commission recommendations. As of 1990, however, only 24 small or inactive boards had been "sunsetted," that is, abolished.

Conclusion

Continuation of Texas's decentralized, weak-executive model of government seems inevitable. Structural reform of Article IV in the present state Constitution is certainly not a remedy for all of Texas's governmental ills. But as this chapter indicates, the state's weak-executive structure features popular control through a few elected officials and many boards and commissions composed largely of appointed members. Whether the state should continue to operate in this manner will remain an ongoing topic of debate.

Notes

1. See House Research Organization, *Vetoes of Legislation: 71st Legislature,* Special Legislature Report No. 150 (Austin: Texas House of Representatives, July 25, 1989).
2. Texas Parks and Wildlife Department, *Six-Year Plan, 1986–1991* (Austin, 1986), pp. 4, 7.

Key Terms and Concepts

chief executive	chief of state
Governor's Office	plural executive
appointive power	ex officio
senatorial courtesy	bureaucratic system
recess appointment	Texas Education Agency
midnight appointment	Higher Education Coordinating Board
removal power	
legislative address	Texas Department of Human Services
quo warranto proceeding	
martial law	Texas Department on Aging
budgetary power	Texas Department of Health
legislative power	Texas Department of Mental Health and Mental Retardation
message power	
veto power	Texas Employment Commission
item veto power	Texas Railroad Commission
postadjournment veto	Public Utility Commission
special session	Texas Water Commission
parole	Texas Water Development Board
executive clemency	licensing board
full pardon	Texas Department of Commerce
conditional pardon	Texas Parks and Wildlife Department
reprieve	
commutation of sentence	Sunset Advisory Commission

Selected Readings

7.1 Agriculture Commissioner Hightower: The Popular Populist

Curtis Wilkie

As a colorful Texas politician, Agriculture Commissioner Jim Hightower has been the focus of national media attention. Here is an in-depth chronicle of his career.

It was not Jim Hightower's fault that the 1988 Democratic campaign was bereft of passion and humor. If the Texas agriculture commissioner, who describes himself as a "kick-ass populist," had been in charge, the general election would have been turned into a class struggle with George Bush as a foil. In a speech at the Democratic National Convention in July, Hightower warned that Bush was a "toothache of a man" who would continue the policies of the Reagan administration, leading the nation "from Tweedledum to Tweedledumber." The patrician Bush, he said, "is a man who was born on third base and thinks he hit a triple."

Hightower provoked so much laughter from the partisan audience that Senator Edward M. Kennedy, who had addressed the convention a few minutes earlier, said afterward that he was relieved he did not follow Hightower on stage. Other than the Reverend Jesse Jackson, there may be no figure in the Democratic Party who is as fervent, provocative, outrageous—and funny—as Hightower.

A Democrat Linked to the Left

Unlike most prominent Democrats, Hightower does not mind being linked to the left. He is one of the purest populists in America, and when he talks about the plight of the common man, he does not use ambiguous language. When he challenged conventional politics in Texas and endorsed Jackson last March [1988]—a decision that seemed to jeopardize Hightower's future in his home state—he said he was compelled to take sides. "There's nothing in the middle of the road but yellow stripes and dead armadillos," Hightower said.

He is best known for his invective. During the course of the campaign, Hightower said of Bush: "If ignorance ever gets up to $40 a barrel, I want the drilling rights to that man's head." He also observed that Dan Quayle "is a genetic throwback to the time when a man's tongue was heavier than his brain."

From *The Boston Globe Magazine*, January 29, 1989. Curtis Wilkie is a staff writer for the *Globe*. Reprinted by permission.

James J. Kilpatrick, the old segregationist editor from Virginia, denounced Hightower as an "idiot" on the TV show "Inside Washington," claiming that the perform-
ances by Hightower and Kennedy at the convention forced Bush to wage his negative
campaign last fall. Back home, Texas Republicans dismiss Hightower as a dangerous
demagogue.

He is theatrical. Wiry and rail-thin, he looks smaller than his actual height—5 feet
8 inches—because he is usually dwarfed by the ten-gallon hats he wears and waves
for emphasis. His voice has the twang of the Southwest, and he uses it, like a
homespun comedian, for effect. He is a 46-year-old bantam rooster who enjoys a
good fight. Hightower loved it when he heard that Bush had called him "that crazy
little guy from Texas."

He announced that he was abandoning his plans to challenge U.S. Senator Phil
Gramm, a conservative Republican, in 1990. Instead, Hightower said, he will seek
re-election as agriculture commissioner in 1990 and will begin working to re-energize
the Democratic Party by rallying the blocs of voters who have supported him: blacks,
poor whites, Mexican-Americans, disaffected "Reagan Democrats," and the "Yellow
Dog Democrats"—those who would vote for a yellow dog before they would vote for
a Republican. "That's what Jesse Jackson did so well that just about everybody
misunderstood," Hightower says. "He tapped anger, but he also tapped the aspirations of everyday Americans. That's what brought tears to the eyes of people who
came out to hear him speak. . . ."

Hightower has a penchant to goad and insult his rivals, and his speeches are full
of populist rhetoric. He inveighs against corporate greed and Big Business while
championing consumer and environmental issues. As each Hightower *bon mot* is
repeated on the political circuit, his reputation grows. The demand for him to make
public appearances around the country is becoming so great, he says, that he is
considering a booking agent.

Hightower is convinced that if Democratic candidates push the class issues en-
thusiastically, instead of relying on bland sloganeering, they can appeal to millions
of alienated voters. "The Democratic Party's constituency," he says, "is a populist
constituency that believes that the Big Boys have way too much power that's been
bestowed on them by government. The government has allowed them to wield this
power, pretty much at will, against people like them. The Democratic Party has got
to do two things: recognize that this is their constituency and pursue them with a
passion that's hotter than high school love."

Learning Class Values

Jim Hightower was born and grew up in the northeast Texas town of Denison, in
hard-scrabble country along the Red River, across the Oklahoma state line. The land
is poor, but the area is rich in politics, producing two modern speakers of the House,
Sam Rayburn and Carl Albert, as well as Wright Patman, a populist Texas con-
gressman who challenged Big Business for decades. Hightower's parents still have
a small business, literally a mom and pop operation, the Main Street Newsstand in

Denison, and it was there, Hightower says, that he learned his class values and developed his gift for talk.

He was the first member of his family to go to college, North Texas State (now named University of North Texas), and he graduated in 1965 with a degree in government. "I was Joe College, I did the whole deal," he says of the period when he was out of character for a "kick-ass populist." He was president of the student body and belonged to a fraternity. "I was active in the civil rights movement," he adds defensively when recalling his college days, "which my fraternity brothers thought was kind of dumb. I remember going to Dallas to see Peter, Paul, and Mary, and I thought I had died and gone to heaven. 'Blowing in the Wind' was the center of my universe. Sometimes I travel with them now, but I still get chills when I hear them singing 'Blowing in the Wind.' " He was also influenced by Mark Twain—"his iconoclastic style, his attitude, his language and storytelling ability."

Hightower helped pay for college by working at the local Chamber of Commerce in Denton, the home of North Texas State, and he nurtured his sympathies for small business. "That chamber spent a lot of resources trying to lure business to Denton. I came to believe it's best to have homegrown enterprise. Why give away a railroad spur to bring business in?"

Losing a Race for the Railroad Commission

Hightower chose to run in 1980 for a seat on the Texas Railroad Commission, or, as he called it, the Railroading Commission. The powerful agency regulates oil and gas production. Hightower called its members "well-fed dogs" who were beholden to the energy and transportation industries they were supposed to be regulating. He presented himself as the "candidate of all Texans who don't own an oil well. . . ."

Hightower lost his race for the Railroad Commission, but he captured 48 percent of the vote and made a name for himself. In conservative Texas, not all of the publicity was favorable. The Establishment branded him a "left-wing, radical liberal" and a troublemaker. He took a temporary job as head of the Texas Consumer Association, preparing to run for the position of agriculture commissioner two years later.

A Controversial Lifestyle

Throughout Hightower's political career he has been dogged by questions about his lifestyle. Like his ideology, he refuses to change it, and his living arrangements have not proved to be an insurmountable problem. He was married in college and divorced after seven years. Since 1972 he has been living with Susan DeMarco, an economist and public-policy analyst. They share a house in Austin as well as political views and are co-authors of two books, *Hard Tomatoes, Hard Times* and *Eat Your Heart Out.* After Hightower was elected agriculture commissioner, he made DeMarco one of his chief deputies. Though she served without pay, they were criticized for the arrangement, and she left the office at the end of his first term. "We're not married, so we weren't violating any (nepotism) laws," he says.

Otherwise they are private about the relationship. Hightower calls her "DeMarco," just as he encourages his employees to call him by his last name rather than "Commissioner." "My opponents have tried to use it against me, and it doesn't work," he says. "If DeMarco and I tried to flaunt our relationship, we'd have a problem, but we don't. Some people get riled up about it, but that's the way we choose to be. We don't have any children and we're not getting married. . . ."

When *60 Minutes* did a profile on Hightower in 1987, Harry Reasoner asked him why he and DeMarco didn't get married. With an impish grin, Hightower replied, "I've asked her, but she won't have me."

Unseating Reagan Brown

His opponent in the primary in 1982 was the incumbent, Reagan Brown, an old Tory Democrat who attacked Hightower for his lack of experience on the farm while his followers whispered about Hightower's relationship with DeMarco. In an attempt to divert attention from Hightower's challenge, Brown held a press conference to discuss the threat of fire ants. He escorted reporters a couple of blocks from the Department of Agriculture to the lawn of the State Capitol, where he pointed out an infestation of fire-ant hills. To emphasize his point, Brown stirred up a nest of the insects and was bitten so many times he had to seek medical treatment. Hightower pounced on the fiasco. "My opponent accuses me of not knowing enough about agriculture," he said. "At least I know enough not to stick my hand in a mound of fire ants."

Brown sealed his own doom with another unfortunate appearance late in the campaign. Before a predominantly black audience, he praised the educator Booker T. Washington as "the great black nigger." A television camera was there, and the event was widely publicized.

Putting Government Into Service

Hightower won, and the Department of Agriculture has not been the same since. In the department's reception room, there are copies of *The Texas Observer* and *Mother Jones* instead of *U.S. News & World Report*. Taking over a bureaucratic empire with 575 employees and a budget of $17 million, he turned it into a force for small farmers, consumers, and environmentalists. He hired allies from his days as an activist in Washington, and after he was criticized for having more interest in reform than in agriculture, he appointed Mike Moeller, a Texas family farmer, as his deputy commissioner.

Hightower initiated a program to develop a network of farmers' markets in Texas. The markets, which are located in more than 70 cities, are designed to give the producers direct access to consumers, thus bypassing wholesalers. He encouraged farmers to diversify their crops. Instead of relying on the old staples of cotton, corn, and cattle, some farmers are now growing blueberries. The department is trying to find markets for the crop. Hightower says he has reached an agreement with Kroger so that the supermarket chain will buy the Texas-grown product directly from the farmers. Hightower says there is potential in other crops that are exotic to Texas. Some rice farmers are using their marshland for crawfish, a Southern delicacy, and others are raising game and making wine. "We're talking about changing an economy," he says. "We're not saying: Get out of cotton. We are saying: Don't just depend on cotton."

He is constantly promoting Texas wine, and in his office a wooden wine rack is full of bottles of local vintage. He traveled to Israel to stimulate agricultural cooperation between Texas and Israel. While he was there, he presented the prime minister with a bottle of Texas wine. "Hightower is the only agriculture commissioner in America who has a foreign policy," says his friend Ray Mabus, the progressive governor of Mississippi.

During his travels Hightower has cultivated political enemies just as carefully as he wants farmers to cultivate experimental crops. When he thought he would be running against Gramm, Hightower referred to him as the "senator from Pluto." At Texas's Democratic convention last year, he recalled how some people felt that Gramm was his own worst enemy. "Not while I'm alive, he's not," Hightower informed the crowd, as though a man is made by the enemies he makes rather than the company he keeps. Hightower is also proud of the "terrible" relationship he has had with the U.S. Department of Agriculture under the Republican administrations.

Early in his first term he angered chemical interests and big farmers by establishing rules to protect farm workers from pesticides. In 1985 the Texas Chemical Council and the Texas Farm Bureau, two conservative groups, lobbied for legislation that would have turned the job of agriculture commissioner from an elective position to one that is appointed by the governor. Hightower defeated the initiative, then won re-election in 1986 with 60 percent of the vote.

John C. White's Assessment

John C. White, a veteran Texas politician who was agriculture commissioner for 26 years before joining the Carter administration and serving as Democratic national chairman, says Hightower has carried out "an aggressive consumer and environmental program which has made him some strong opponents. Agribusiness is alienated." White was one of those who felt that Hightower's chances against Gramm were slim; that he was better suited to exercise his "kick-ass" populism as agriculture commissioner. "It's a great political office in Texas," says White. "If you have political idiosyncrasies, you can get away with them. He can say something wild, and people will slap their leg and say, 'Ain't Jim something?' If you tried to do that crap in any other office, you'd be in trouble."

Chapter 8

Law, Courts, and Justice

Jimmy Margulies Houston Post reprinted by permission

*D*uring the presidential election campaign of 1988, Texas Governor Bill Clements and other Republicans reminded voters that convicted murderer Willie Horton had committed outrageous crimes while on furlough from the Massachusetts prison system. They declared that because Massachusetts Governor Michael Dukakis was soft on criminals, Americans should vote for Republican presidential candidate George Bush in the November election. Much to Governor Clements's embarrassment, however, he later discovered that convicted murderers had also been given furloughs from the Texas Department of Corrections under a policy that had been approved by him. The controversy over prison furloughs, which is the subject of the cartoon that opens this chapter, is only one of many justice-related issues confronted by the state's public policymakers in recent years. As will be explained in this chapter, laws, courts, judges, lawyers, and institutions of correction and criminal rehabilitation are intimately involved in the practice of Texas politics—especially when judges and prosecutors are popularly elected.

An Introduction to Texas's Justice System and Its Problems

The most significant connection between politics and justice in the Lone Star State results from constitutional requirements that judicial officials—from justices of the peace to members of the Supreme Court of Texas and the Court of Criminal Appeals—must be popularly elected. This means campaigning for nomination in a party primary, running as a Democratic or Republican candidate in a general election, and soliciting financial contributions from lawyers and others who have an interest in judicial politics. Many Texas judges are initially appointed to fill a vacancy caused by a judge's death or retirement before the end of a term of office, but such appointments are usually affected by political affiliation.

Although Texas's judges are involved in the policymaking process, they attract less public attention than the state's legislative and executive officials. Occasionally, however, a court ruling provokes heated public controversy. Such was the result of the Texas Supreme Court's decision in *Spring Branch Independent School District* v. *Stamos* (1985). In this case, the state's highest court of civil jurisdiction upheld the constitutionality of House Bill 72's "no-pass, no-play" provision requiring public school students to maintain a 70 percent average in all classes to be eligible for extracurricular activities such as football.

With over 2,800 judges and justices, and almost that many courts, Texas has one of the largest judicial systems in the country. Counting traffic violations handled by lower courts, millions of cases are disposed of each year. Some of these cases result from disputes over money and property; thousands of others concern crimes that lead to jail and prison sentences for the convicted perpetrators. Sooner or later, most Texans become involved in cases affecting life or property. Also, as voters, they elect judges, prosecuting attorneys, sheriffs, and constables; and when called to serve as jurors, they participate directly in the judicial process.

Consequently, every Texan should ask, "Do we have adequate laws and legal procedures, honest judges, diligent prosecutors, competent defense attorneys, efficient courts, modern correctional institutions, and effective rehabilitation programs that promote public safety and ensure justice for all persons?"

Although informed observers differ in their opinions concerning the administration of justice in Texas, there are indications that improvement is needed. For example, the forced resignation of Texas Supreme Court Justice Don Yarbrough in 1977 and his subsequent trials and imprisonments called attention to the need for selecting honest judges.

With regard to criminal investigations, tactics of prosecuting attorneys, and judicial procedures, two Texas cases have received nationwide publicity. One of these cases involved Lenell Geter, a young black engineer without a prior criminal record, who was indicted, convicted, and imprisoned for life for an armed robbery that he did not commit. After confinement for 19 months, Geter was released in 1984, primarily because "60 Minutes," a CBS television program, attracted national attention to his plight.

A more recent case involved Randall Dale Adams, an innocent man who was sentenced to death after his conviction for murdering a Dallas police officer. On one occasion, Adams was within hours of being executed when he was saved from lethal injection by action of the U.S. Supreme Court. After a dozen years in prison, Adams's conviction was thrown out by the Texas Court of Criminal Appeals in response to public indignation aroused by "Thin Blue Line," a documentary film that exposed this gross miscarriage of justice. Although the court ordered a new trial, the Dallas County district attorney's office opted to drop the case in 1989, and Adams returned to his home in Ohio.

Throughout the 1980s, a rising tide of drug-related crimes and increased overcrowding of Texas's prisons and jails produced a near breakdown of the criminal justice system. Charges of mismanagement and mistreatment of inmates in the state's prisons resulted in several years of federal court intervention designed to modernize Texas's correction policies and to ensure minimum standards of health and safety for all inmates. At the same time, prison overcrowding produced stepped-up release schedules. This situation prompted complaints from citizens who contended that unrehabilitated criminals were being put on the street in order to make room for an incoming flood of newly convicted persons. Meanwhile, expenditures for prison and jail construction soared in years when the state was confronted with fiscal crises and voters' opposition to higher taxes.

State Law in Texas

Courts of the State of Texas hear cases involving *civil law* (for example, a suit involving a business contract) and cases involving *criminal law* (for example, prosecution of a thief). Thus a court has civil and/or criminal *jurisdiction*, a term that refers to a court's authority to hear cases. Some courts have *original jurisdiction* only. These tribunals are limited to trying cases being heard for the first time. Other courts are restricted to hearing appeals from lower courts and thus have only *appellate jurisdiction*. Still other courts exercise both original and appellate jurisdiction.

Regardless of their jurisdiction, Texas courts are responsible for interpreting and applying state law. This responsibility is established in statutes enacted by the Legislature, in the Texas Constitution, and in the body of judge-made *common law* that is based on custom and tradition dating back to the days of medieval England.

Code Revision

Newly enacted laws passed in each legislative session are compiled by the Office of the Secretary of State and published under the title *General and Special Laws of the State of Texas*. For easier reference, these laws are arranged by subject matter and are codified in *West's Texas Statutes and Codes, Vernon's Annotated Texas Civil Statutes,* and *Vernon's Texas Codes Annotated. A legal code* is a systematically arranged and comprehensive collection of laws.

In addition to piecemeal changes resulting from routine legislation, pressure occasionally mounts for the extensive revision of an entire code. Thus in 1965, after years of much pressure from judges, lawyers, and the public, the Texas Legislature for the first time in over a century revised the *Code of Criminal Procedure* (a body of laws that prescribe how criminal cases are to be handled). At the same time, a committee of the State Bar of Texas (a professional organization for lawyers) began work on a revision of the state's century-old *Penal Code,* a collection of laws defining crimes and prescribing punishments. Finally, a revision of that code was enacted by the 63rd Legislature in 1973.

Criminal Law

Texas has a well-organized body of criminal law. Among its most distinctive features are a system of graded penalties for noncapital offenses and a two-step procedure for establishing whether a capital felony has been committed and, if so, whether a death sentence should be ordered.

Graded Penalties   There are three degrees of *felonies* for which penitentiary sentences and fines may be imposed in cases involving the most serious noncapital crimes. Also, there are three classes of *misdemeanors* for which jail sentences and/or fines are outlined in cases involving lesser offenses. (See Table 8.1.) Repeated felony conviction may result in punishment for the next higher degree of felony, and a third felony conviction allows a sentence ranging from imprisonment for 25 to 99 years or life. For repeated misdemeanor convictions, punishment is allowed for the next higher class of misdemeanor.

Capital Punishment   The Penal Code bill passed by the 63rd Legislature in 1973 did not provide for capital punishment for any crime, but murder is classified as a first-degree felony carrying possible penalties of from 5 to 99 years or life

TABLE 8.1 Noncapital Offenses, Penalties for First Offenders, and Courts Having Original Jurisdiction

Selected Offenses	Category of Offense	Maximum Fine	Period of Confinement	Court with Original Jurisdiction
Aggravated sexual assault, aggravated robbery, causing serious bodily injury by tampering with food or drugs, murder, burglary of a habitation	1st degree felony	$10,000	5–99 years or life	District Court
Theft of property valued at $20,000 or more, sexual assault, robbery, sale or possession of armor-piercing ammunition, arson, tampering with food or drugs, damage or destruction of a place of worship if the loss is $20,000 or more	2nd degree felony	$10,000	2–20 years	District Court
Theft of property valued at $750 or more but less than $20,000, bigamy, conduct causing suicide, carrying a deadly weapon while confined to jail or prison, unauthorized recruitment of an athlete by offering anything of benefit to influence enrollment and participation in intercollegiate athletics, threat to commit a felony as a means of coercing a voter or public employee, damage or destruction of a place of worship if the loss is less than $20,000	3rd degree felony	$10,000	2–10 years	District Court
Theft of property valued at $200 or more but less than $750, possession of a hoax bomb, false alarm or report, breach of computer security if loss or damage is $200 or more but less than $750, operation of a	Class A misdemeanor	$2,000	1 year maximum	County/County Court at Law

Selected Offenses	Category of Offense	Maximum Fine	Period of Confinement	Court with Original Jurisdiction
boat while intoxicated, solicitation or acceptance of illegal recruitment for enrollment and participation in intercollegiate athletics, burning or destroying the Texas or U.S. flag, unlicensed practice of medicine, unauthorized release of results of a required AIDS test, failure of an athletic agent to register with the secretary of state before contacting an athlete, requiring a female child to work topless				
Theft of property valued at $20 or more but less than $200, prostitution, indecent exposure, knowing communication of a venereal disease, telephone harassment, unauthorized TV interception, evading arrest, owning or keeping a vicious dog that is unrestrained and not covered by $100,000 in liability insurance, encouraging or engaging in hazing	Class B misdemeanor	$1,000	180 days maximum	County/County Court at Law
Theft of property valued under $20, gambling, attending a dog fight, public intoxication, shooting on a public road, drinking an alcoholic beverage while driving in a public place, manufacturing or distributing false driver's licenses or identification certificates unless marked "not a government document"	Class C misdemeanor	$200	None	Justice of the Peace/ Municipal Court

Source: Vernon's Texas Codes Annotated.

imprisonment. Later, however, the 63rd Legislature enacted a *capital felony law* that covers (with subsequent amendments) the following six crimes:

▪ Murdering a peace officer or firefighter who is acting in the lawful discharge of an official duty and who the person knows is a peace officer or firefighter
▪ Intentionally committing a murder in the course of committing or attempting to commit kidnapping, burglary, robbery, aggravated sexual assault, or arson
▪ Committing a murder for pay or the promise of pay or employing another to commit a murder for pay or the promise of pay
▪ Committing a murder while escaping or attempting to escape from a penal institution
▪ While incarcerated in a penal institution, murdering another who is employed in the operation of the penal institution
▪ Murdering two or more persons (serial murders) during the same criminal transaction or during different transactions pursuant to the same scheme or course of action

This law specifies also that after a jury has found a defendant guilty of a capital offense, it must answer the following questions:

1. Was the conduct of the defendant that caused the death of the deceased deliberate and with the reasonable expectation that the death of the deceased or another would result?
2. Is there a probability that the defendant will commit criminal acts of violence that would constitute a continuing threat to society?
3. If raised by the evidence, was the conduct of the defendant in killing the deceased unreasonable in response to the provocation, if any, by the deceased?

Until 1989, when the U.S. Supreme Court (by a vote of 5 to 4) overruled the capital murder conviction of mentally retarded John Paul Penry, unanimous jury answers of yes to each of the three questions above made the death sentence mandatory. (A single answer of no to any question results in a life sentence with eligibility for parole within 15 years.) While stating in *Penry* v. *Lynaugh* that the "cruel and unusual punishment" provision of the U.S. Constitution does not bar states from executing mentally retarded persons, Justice Sandra Day O'Conner asserted that Penry had been deprived of due process because the jury was not allowed to consider his mental retardation and history of child abuse as mitigating factors. (On the same day, the U.S. Supreme Court ruled in another 5–4 decision that murderers 16 and 17 years of age at the time of a killing may be given the death sentence under state laws. Texas law authorizes the execution of murderers 17 years of age or older.)

For nearly a century, death by hanging was the means of capital punishment in Texas. Between 1924 and 1964, a total of 361 persons were put to death in "Old Sparky," the state's electric chair. Because of federal court rulings, there were no executions in Texas during the following 18 years; in December 1982, however, Charlie Brooks became the first condemned murderer to receive an intravenous lethal injection. By mid-1989, 30 additional murderers had been put to death, and

Texas had more prisoners awaiting execution (over 300, including 4 women) than any other state.

Courts, Judges, and Lawyers

Article V of the Texas Constitution is titled "Judicial Department." This article declares that state judicial power "shall be vested in one Supreme Court, in one Court of Criminal Appeals, in Courts of Appeals, in District Courts, in County Courts, in Commissioners Courts, in Courts of Justices of the Peace and in such other courts as may be provided by law." Each county does have a commissioners court, composed of four elected commissioners and presided over by the county judge. This court, however, is an administrative and quasi-legislative body (as explained on page 54). Not included among the courts listed in Article V are the municipal courts in cities, towns, and villages; but municipal courts play an important role in the administration of justice in Texas.[1]

Admittedly, the Texas judicial system is complex. (See Figure 8.1.) Nevertheless, gaining an understanding of the basic organization and jurisdiction of the state's courts is not impossible, especially if they are approached in a logical manner. In our approach, we examine minor trial courts first, county-level trial courts next, then the district-level trial courts, and finally the appellate courts. Judges and their courts are discussed together. A separate section is devoted to lawyers.

Minor Trial Courts

At the base of the Texas judicial structure are the municipal courts and the justice of the peace courts. The latter also function as small claims courts. These three types of minor trial courts handle great volumes of litigation, but their jurisdictions are limited to such matters as civil suits for limited amounts of money or criminal cases involving the least serious class of misdemeanors. Both municipal judges and justices of the peace serve as *magistrates* of the state. In this capacity, they issue warrants for search and arrest of suspects and conduct hearings to determine whether a person charged with a criminal act shall be jailed pending indictment in a felony case.

Municipal Courts   The judicial bodies of over 850 incorporated cities, towns, and villages in Texas are termed *municipal courts*. Because most of their cases involve violations of motor vehicle traffic regulations, municipal courts are often called traffic courts. Traditionally, many "speed-trap" towns (for example, Patton Village near Houston) have raised significant amounts of revenue from traffic fines collected by municipal courts. Since 1989, however, municipalities with fewer than 5,000 residents may collect not more than 30 percent of their revenue from traffic fines. Except for a fee of $1 that is retained by the city, any fine over that amount must be forwarded to the state treasurer for deposit in the general revenue fund. In 1989 the Legislature enacted another law that prohibits any unit of government

FIGURE 8.1 The Court Structure of Texas

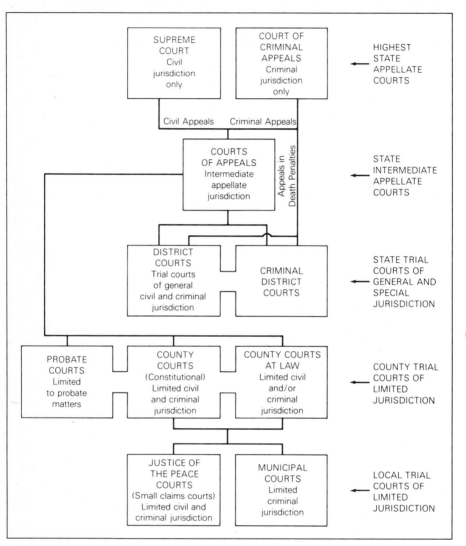

Source: Texas Judicial Council.

or state agency from establishing a system that pressures a peace officer to issue a predetermined or specified number of traffic tickets.

The mayor of a general-law city functions as municipal judge unless the city council provides for the election or appointment of someone else to hold this office. Usually the municipal court judge of a home-rule city is named by the council. Large cities may have one or more full-time judges, but most municipal judges serve in a part-time capacity and hold court for a short period each day or on certain designated days of the week.

Municipal courts have neither civil nor appellate jurisdiction. Their original and exclusive criminal jurisdiction extends to all violations of city ordinances, and they have concurrent criminal jurisdiction with justice of the peace courts over Class C misdemeanors committed within city limits. Since 1987, municipal court judges have been authorized to impose maximum fines of $2,000 in cases involving violation of some municipal ordinances (for example, regulations governing fire safety and public health). The maximum fine for violations of other city ordinances and state criminal laws is $500. In about 1 percent of municipal court cases, appeals are taken to a county court or a county court at law. If a city does not have a municipal court of record, an appealed case is given a *trial de novo* (a completely new trial) at the county level. Over the years, the Legislature authorized some of the state's larger cities to have municipal courts of record with court reporters to record testimony. Since 1987, all incorporated cities have been authorized to establish such courts, but most medium-size and small municipalities have opted not to do so because of the expense.

Justice of the Peace Courts   Often called the JP, a *justice of the peace* is elected for a term of four years by voters residing in a precinct created by the county commissioners court. In 1989 there were over 920 justices of the peace in Texas, most of whom served on a part-time basis. Annual salaries are set by county commissioners courts and range from $1 to over $60,000.

The Texas Constitution authorizes justice of the peace precincts according to the following three categories of total county population:

1.   30,000 or more inhabitants, 4 to 8 precincts
2.   18,000 to 29,999 inhabitants, 2 to 5 precincts
3.   17,999 or fewer inhabitants, 1 to 4 precincts

Ordinarily, a precinct elects only one justice of the peace, but in a county with a population of less than 150,000, a precinct that contains an entire city of 18,000 or more inhabitants elects two. Precincts in counties with populations of 150,000 or more are allowed to have more than one justice of the peace per precinct.

Neither previous legal training nor experience is required by law for the position, but a few justices of the peace (usually found in large cities) are lawyers and may retain a private legal practice while serving in that judicial office. Within a year after election, a justice of the peace who is not a lawyer is required by law to complete a 40-hour course concerning performance of the duties of that office. Thereafter, 20 hours of instruction are supposed to be received annually. These training programs are administered by the Justice Training Center at Southwest Texas State University in San Marcos. Some justices of the peace have not fulfilled training requirements because there is no penalty for noncompliance.

Duties of justices of the peace in urban areas often constitute a full-time job, whereas in rural precincts very few cases are tried. Justice of the peace courts have both criminal and civil jurisdiction. In all cases, their jurisdiction is original. In criminal matters, these local courts try Class C misdemeanors, but any conviction may be appealed to the county court or a county court at law for a new trial.

Exclusive civil jurisdiction of JP courts extends to cases in which the amount in controversy is $200 or less, not including interest. Concurrent civil jurisdiction is shared with county courts and district courts if the amount in controversy exceeds $200 but is not more than $2,500. Appeals from a JP court are taken to the county level, where cases are tried de novo. If judgment is for $20 or less, the JP court is the state court of last resort and its decision is final, but there is the remote possibility of appeal to the U.S. Supreme Court if a federal constitutional question is involved. This is also true of the decisions of other Texas tribunals that are courts of last resort for certain types of cases.

In addition to performing judicial duties, a justice of the peace serves as an ex officio notary public and, as do other Texas judges, may perform marriages. Also, a JP functions as a coroner when the county commissioners court has not named a county medical examiner. Thus, although few justices of the peace can claim significant medical training, most of them are required to determine by inquest the cause of death when someone dies without the presence of witnesses or when death takes place under circumstances suggesting the possibility of foul play. If a JP determines that an autopsy is needed, the county health officer is requested to perform it, or the services of a duly licensed, practicing physician with training in pathology will be procured.

A constable, a peace officer with full law enforcement authority, is elected for a four-year term in each JP precinct. Most constables, however, leave law enforcement and crime detection to local police and the county sheriff's department. The principal function of constables is to serve subpoenas and other processes issued by justices of the peace. In a precinct with a large population, the constable is usually assisted by one or more deputy constables.

Small Claims Courts A justice of the peace also functions as judge of a *small claims court,* which is the Texas version of "The People's Court" featuring TV's Judge Joseph A. Wopner. Anyone wishing to collect unpaid wages or salary not exceeding $2,500, or to collect a bill amounting to not more than $2,500, may bring a case before a small claims court. Because these proceedings are informal, the assistance of a lawyer is not required. When the amount in controversy exceeds $20, the losing party may appeal to a county-level court.[2]

County-Level Trial Courts

Every Texas county has a constitutional county court, and some have one or more additional county-level courts. All are courts of record, and each is presided over by a single judge, who is elected on a countywide basis for a term of four years. Any judge at the county level may be removed by order of a review tribunal if recommended by the State Commission on Judicial Conduct. A vacancy on a county-level court is filled by action of the county commissioners court. Salaries vary widely and are set by the commissioners court of each county.

Constitutional County Courts Under the Texas Constitution, each of the state's counties has a county judge who is supposed to be "well informed in the law of the State." Until 1983, this provision simply meant that these judges had to have the political skills necessary to be nominated and elected. In that year, the Legislature enacted a law requiring that county judges performing judicial functions—along with judges of county courts at law, district courts, and appellate courts—take Supreme Court–approved courses in court administration, procedure, and evidence. Only one-fourth of Texas's constitutional county court judges are licensed attorneys.

Most of the 254 *constitutional county courts* have original and appellate jurisdiction as well as civil and criminal jurisdiction, but in some instances the Legislature has established statutory county courts to exercise such jurisdiction. Generally, original civil jurisdiction of a constitutional county court covers cases involving between $200 and $2,500. Original criminal jurisdiction includes all Class A and Class B misdemeanors. When a county court's sentence specifies confinement of a convicted person, this sentence is served in a county jail, a regional jail, or another local correctional facility.

Appellate criminal jurisdiction extends to cases originating in JP courts and municipal courts. A constitutional county court's appellate jurisdiction is final with regard to criminal cases involving fines of $100 or less. For cases in which greater fines are imposed, appeal may be taken to a court of appeals. Civil cases are heard on appeal from JP courts when the amount in controversy is greater than $20. Jurisdiction is final with regard to those cases in which the amount in controversy does not exceed $100.

County Courts at Law   In counties with large populations, the burden of presiding over the county commissioners court and handling many administrative responsibilities has left the judges of constitutional county courts with little or no time to try civil, criminal, and probate cases. Thus, the Legislature has authorized over 180 statutory courts that are most commonly titled *county courts at law.* Statutory court judges, who must be licensed attorneys, relieve constitutional county court judges of some or all courtroom duties in over 70 counties. Nacogdoches County, for example, has only one county court at law; but Harris County has 18: four designated as civil courts and 14 as criminal courts. The criminal jurisdiction of county courts at law is limited to misdemeanors. Civil jurisdiction varies, but in some counties it extends to controversies involving a maximum of $100,000.

Probate Courts   In designating constitutional county courts as *probate courts,* the Texas Probate Code empowers county judges to probate wills of persons who have died and to appoint guardians of minors and incompetents (that is, persons lacking mental capacity to make a contract or to engage in business transactions). In some heavily populated counties, the Legislature has established one or more county-level probate courts that hear probate cases only. Thus Bexar County has two, Dallas County has three, and Harris County has four.

District-Level Trial Courts

The principal trial courts of Texas are the state's nearly 400 district-level courts. Most of them are designated simply as district courts, but a few are called criminal district courts. Each district-level court has jurisdiction over one or more counties, but a heavily populated county may have several district courts with countywide jurisdiction. More confusing is the fact that some multicounty districts overlap, so a single county may be included in different combinations of nearby counties to form two or more districts.

Judges are elected on a districtwide basis for a term of four years. Annual state salaries paid to judges of district-level courts were set by the 71st legislature at $76,309 for fiscal years 1990 and 1991 (5 percent less than the salary for a justice of a court of appeals). Supplemental pay from a county or counties within a district may not exceed $10,325. Thus, total salary and supplemental pay for a district-level judge must be at least $2,000 less than the salary of a Supreme Court justice.

Qualifications for judges of a district-level court include U.S. citizenship, residence in the district for two years immediately before election or appointment, and a license to practice law in Texas. As a guarantee of practical legal experience, a district-level judge must have been a practicing lawyer or a judge, or both, for at least four years prior to election. A vacant judgeship (resulting from death, resignation, retirement, or removal) is filled by gubernatorial appointment, with the advice and consent of the Senate. Similarly, when the Legislature creates a new district-level court, its first judge is usually appointed by the governor. Thus, as in the case of Texas judges in other state courts, over half of the judges in district-level courts initially reach the bench as a result of appointment. Then, running as incumbents, they retain their positions by winning subsequent elections. Like justices of the state's appellate courts, they may be removed from office through impeachment by the House of Representatives and conviction by the Senate or through action by a review tribunal on recommendation of the State Commission on Judicial Conduct.

District Courts Most judges of Texas's *district courts* are authorized to try both criminal and civil cases, although a statute creating a court may specify that the court shall give preference to one or the other. All criminal jurisdiction is original; and except within those counties in which the Legislature has transferred jurisdiction over misdemeanor cases from county to district courts, it is limited to misdemeanors involving misconduct by government officials and to felonies. But a district court may punish a person convicted of a third-degree felony with a sentence for a Class A misdemeanor, if the judge determines that this action would best serve the ends of justice. Criminal actions have accounted for nearly onefourth of the cases filed in district courts in recent years. Most types of stolen property must be valued at $750 or more to constitute a felony. Appeal following a capital felony conviction is taken directly to the Court of Criminal Appeals. Other criminal convictions are appealed to a court of appeals.

District courts hear civil cases involving divorce, land titles, contested elections, and slander or defamation; and they have original civil jurisdiction in controversies involving $200 or more. Thus, concurrent jurisdiction with lower courts begins at this level; and above the maximum "dollar-amount" jurisdiction of those courts, district courts exercise exclusive civil jurisdiction. Appeals for civil cases go to a court of appeals.

Criminal District Courts Five courts in Dallas County and four in Tarrant County have been designated as *criminal district courts*. Nevertheless, only three of these courts are limited to criminal, district-level jurisdiction. The Criminal District Court of Jefferson County (the state's tenth court with criminal designation) is authorized to hear criminal cases *and* cases involving divorce, dependent and neglected children, adoption, and civil habeas corpus proceedings. More confusing, however, is the fact that three courts designated as district courts have been instructed by the Legislature to hear criminal cases only, and 45 have been instructed "to give preference" to criminal cases. Such a hodgepodge of jurisdictions is but one indication that reorganization and simplification of the Texas judicial system are needed.

Appellate Courts

The Lone Star State's appellate courts consist of 14 courts of appeals, the Court of Criminal Appeals, and the Supreme Court of Texas. Each of these courts has more than one judge or justice, and all members are popularly elected for terms of six years. Terms are staggered so that one-third of the members are elected or re-elected every two years. This arrangement helps to ensure that at any given time each appellate court will have two or more judges with prior experience on that court. Judges must be at least 35 years of age, and they must have had ten years of experience as a practicing lawyer or ten years of combined experience as a practicing lawyer and judge of a court of record. Vacancies on these courts resulting from death, resignation, or removal from office are filled by gubernatorial appointment (with the advice and consent of the Senate) until the next general election. Judicial decisions are reached by majority vote of appellate court membership; juries are not used. The Supreme Court of Texas and the Court of Criminal Appeals are authorized to answer questions about Texas law that are asked by federal appellate courts (for example, the U.S. Supreme Court).

Courts of Appeals The Legislature has divided Texas into 14 courts of appeals districts and has established a *court of appeals* in every district. Each of these courts is composed of a chief justice and from two justices (Beaumont, Tyler, and Waco) to 12 justices (Dallas). A court of appeals justice receives a state salary that is 10 percent less than the salary of a Supreme Court justice. In fiscal years 1990 and 1991, this amounted to $80,325. Chief justices receive an extra $500 per year. Counties within each court of appeals district are authorized by law to provide supplemental compensation, but the combined salary and supplement for a court of appeals justice must be at least $1,000 less than the salary received by a justice of the Supreme Court.

Courts of appeals hear civil cases and criminal cases (but not cases involving capital punishment) appealed from district courts and county courts. Final jurisdiction includes cases involving divorce, slander, boundary disputes, and elections held for purposes other than choosing government officials (for example, bond elections). Courts with more than three members may hear appeals in panels of no fewer than three justices, as do the three-member courts. A majority vote of a panel of justices is required for a decision.

Court of Criminal Appeals   Texas's highest tribunal with criminal jurisdiction is the *Court of Criminal Appeals.* This nine-judge court hears noncapital criminal cases on appeal from the 14 courts of appeals. Capital punishment cases are appealed directly to it from district courts. Because the Supreme Court of Texas has no criminal jurisdiction, judgments of the Court of Criminal Appeals are final.

Members of this court, including one who serves as presiding judge, are popularly elected on a statewide basis for six-year terms. From its creation in 1891 until December 1988, when Governor Clements appointed Republican David A. Berchelmann to fill a vacancy on the court, Democrats held all Court of Criminal Appeals judgeships. Special legislation and an across-the-board pay raise of 5 percent for state officials and employees set the annual salaries of judges of the Court of Criminal Appeals and justices of the Supreme Court of Texas at $89,250 for fiscal years 1990 and 1991. Both the presiding judge of the former and the chief justice of the latter receive $2,625 more. Supplemental pay from counties is not authorized.

Supreme Court   Officially titled the *Supreme Court of Texas,* the state's highest court with civil jurisdiction is composed of nine members elected on a statewide basis: one chief justice and eight justices. At the beginning of 1989 the court's membership was composed of six Democrats and three Republicans. Lacking criminal jurisdiction, this high court is supreme only in cases involving civil law. Because it has very limited original jurisdiction (for example, issuing writs), nearly all the court's work involves hearing appeals under the following conditions:

- When there has been a disagreement among members of a court of appeals on a material question of law
- When a court of appeals renders a decision that conflicts with a decision of the Supreme Court or of another court of appeals
- When an act of the Legislature has been held unconstitutional
- When state revenue is involved
- When the Railroad Commission is a party
- When it appears that an error of substantive law affecting the judgment has been made by a court of appeals, except when the Legislature has conferred final jurisdiction on those courts

Much of the Supreme Court's work involves handling applications for a writ of error, which can be requested by a party who alleges that a court of appeals has erred on a question of law. If as many as three justices favor issuing the writ, the case is docketed as a regular cause and is scheduled for argument in open court.

In addition to hearing motions and applications and to deciding cases, the Supreme Court performs other important functions. It is responsible for making rules of civil procedure, which become law unless rejected by the Legislature. Also, the Supreme Court is empowered to transfer cases for the purpose of equalizing the dockets of courts of appeals. The chief justice has authority to temporarily assign district judges outside their administrative judicial districts and to assign retired appellate justices (with their consent) to temporary duty on courts of appeals. Early

The Supreme Court of Texas, June 1989. Front row, left to right: Justice Franklin S. Spears (Dem.), Chief Justice Thomas R. Phillips (Rep.), and Justice C. L. Ray (Dem.); back row, left to right: Justices Nathan L. Hecht (Rep.), Eugene A. Cook (Rep.), Raul A. Gonzalez (Dem.), Oscar H. Mauzy (Dem.), Jack Hightower (Dem.), and Lloyd Doggett (Dem.). (1989 © Thomas P. Murray.)

in each regular session of the Texas Legislature, the chief justice delivers a "State of the Judiciary" address to a joint meeting of senators and representatives.

Lawyers

The Supreme Court has a role in the training and licensing of lawyers, some of whom become judges and prosecuting attorneys. It is authorized to approve Texas schools of law, which enroll about 7,000 students at nine universities, although accreditation is largely in the hands of the American Bar Association.[3] But the Supreme Court appoints the eight-member Board of Law Examiners, which passes on the qualifications of persons seeking to become licensed attorneys in Texas and certifies the names of successful applicants to the court.

In order to practice, a licensed attorney must obtain membership in the *State Bar of Texas* and pay dues for its support. Although the State Bar is well known for its high-pressure lobbying activities, it promotes high standards of ethical conduct for Texas lawyers and conducts an extensive program of continuing legal education. To maintain their active status, practicing attorneys must complete at least 15 hours of continuing education each year.

As an administrative agency of the state, the Texas Bar is empowered to discipline, suspend, and disbar attorneys. Investigations and hearings involving professional misconduct by attorneys are conducted by local grievance committees composed of lawyers and persons outside the legal profession. In 1989, over 51,000 active lawyers were licensed to practice in Texas.[4] This means that one Texan out of every 350 is a lawyer. Incomes vary greatly for lawyers in private practice, but the median income for Texas lawyers in 1986 was about $60,500.

The state salary paid to a district attorney is the same as that paid to a district judge, if the district attorney is prohibited from engaging in private legal practice. If there is no prohibition, the state salary of the district attorney is 80 percent of a district judge's salary. A maximum of $10,325 is placed on total supplemental pay by a county or counties within a district. Salaries of county attorneys vary greatly because they are set by the commissioners court of each county.

Juries

The jury system enables citizens to participate directly in the administration of justice. Texas has two types of juries: grand juries and trial juries. The Bill of Rights of the state Constitution guarantees that persons shall not be charged with a felony except by grand jury indictment. Also, it guarantees that everyone charged with either a felony or a misdemeanor has the right to trial by jury. A jury trial is required in civil cases if requested by one or both parties in a suit.

The Grand Jury

A *grand jury* is composed of 12 citizens who are selected from a list of 15 to 20 county residents. They must have the qualifications of trial jurors, and their pay is the same as that of trial jurors. (See "Compensation of Jurors," below.) A *jury commission*, composed of three to five citizens from different parts of the county, is appointed by the district judge (or judges when a county has two or more district courts). This commission prepares the list of prospective grand jurors. Then the judge examines those persons listed, selects 12 for grand jury service, and appoints one of them as *foreman* (either male or female) to preside during jury sessions. The life of a grand jury extends over the length of a district court's term, which varies from three to six months. During this period, the grand jurors are empowered to inquire into all criminal actions, but most of their time is devoted to felony matters.

Sessions of the grand jury are secret. Jurors and witnesses are sworn to keep secret all they hear in grand jury sessions. Although a grand jury may function independently, in actuality a grand jury depends heavily on information and recommendations provided by the district attorney. If after investigation and deliberation (often lasting only a few minutes) at least nine grand jurors decide there is sufficient evidence to warrant a trial, an *indictment* is prepared with the aid of the prosecuting attorney. It is a written statement accusing some person or persons of a particular crime (for example, burglary of a home). An indictment is referred to as a *true bill;* failure to indict constitutes a *no bill.*

For misdemeanor prosecutions, grand jury indictments are not required. Any creditable person may file a *complaint,* which is a sworn statement asserting that there is good reason to believe that a certain individual has committed a particular offense. On the basis of this complaint, the district or county attorney may prepare an *information.* It is a document that formally charges the accused with a misdemeanor offense (for example, evading arrest).

The Trial Jury

Although most Texans never serve on a grand jury, they can expect to be summoned from time to time for duty on a *trial jury* (petit jury). Qualifications for *jurors* are not high, and many thousands of jury trials are held in the Lone Star State every year.

Qualifications of Jurors   All persons who are citizens of the United States and of the state of Texas are eligible for jury duty if they are 18 years of age or older, of sound mind, able to read and write, and not convicted felons or under indictment or other legal accusation of theft or of any felony. They have a legal responsibility to serve when called, unless exempted or excused.

Exempted from jury duty are persons 65 years of age or older, persons who have legal custody of a child or children under the age of ten, and full-time college and secondary school students. Nevertheless, judges retain the prerogative of excusing others from jury duty in special circumstances. A person who is legally exempt from jury duty may avoid reporting to the court as summoned by filing a signed statement with the court clerk at any time before the day on which appearance is scheduled.

Selection of Jurors   Prospective jurors (known officially as *veniremen,* regardless of sex) are chosen for county and district court service by random selection from voter registration lists and, if authorized by the county commissioners court and a majority of the district judges in a county where the most populous city extends into another county, lists of persons holding a driver's license. A trial jury is composed of 6 to 12 persons—6 in a justice of the peace court and county court, and 12 in a district court.

In a capital murder case, a special venire, or panel composed of hundreds of persons, may be called and examined before a district court jury of 12 is ultimately selected. Veniremen who indicate that they cannot be fair and impartial are excused from serving on a jury. Attorneys are allowed to challenge prospective jurors either by *peremptory challenge* (up to 15 per side, without having to explain the reason for excluding the veniremen) or by *challenge for cause* (an unlimited number). A challenge for cause is evaluated by the judge, who must decide whether the cause is sufficient.

Only ten peremptory challenges are allowed per side in noncapital felony cases and five or fewer in misdemeanor cases. In any criminal case, however, if a judge decides that a prosecutor has used peremptory challenges to exclude veniremen because of their race, the defendant is allowed to have a new panel of prospective jurors. In a district court, the trial jury is made up of the first 12 veniremen who are neither excused by the district judge nor challenged peremptorily by the parties in the case. For lower courts, the first 6 veniremen accepted form a jury.

In a civil case, attorneys for the parties are permitted to examine the jury panel to ascertain whether any of the prospective jurors should be disqualified because of partiality, prejudice, or kinship. Such persons are excused by the judge for cause, without limitation on the number. Attorneys for each party are allowed to exclude by peremptory challenge six persons in a district court and three at the county court level. From those remaining, the trial jury is chosen.

If for some reason a juror cannot finish the trial of either a civil or a criminal case, an alternate juror may be used as a replacement. When jurors are impaneled, a district judge may direct the selection of four alternates and a county judge may require the selection of two alternates.

Compensation of Jurors   Daily pay for veniremen and jurors varies from county to county. In 1975, the Legislature authorized each county commissioners court to set payment at an amount not to exceed $30 per day, but many counties still pay veniremen only $6 per day and pay jurors $10 for each day of jury service. Employers are prohibited by law from discharging permanent employees because they have been summoned as veniremen or selected as jurors.

Judicial Procedures

Not only do most citizens have the experience of being summoned as veniremen for possible jury service at least once in a lifetime, but on one or more occasions many Texas residents (both citizens and aliens) appear in court as litigants or witnesses. As a *litigant,* for example, a person becomes a party to a civil case arising from damages growing out of an automobile accident or from domestic relations involving divorce or child custody. A person becomes a party in a criminal case, for example, when accused of robbery or homicide. As a *witness,* a person may be summoned to testify in any type of case brought before the trial courts of Texas. In still another capacity, a citizen may be elected to the office of county judge or justice of the peace. For these reasons, Texans should understand what happens in the courtrooms of the state.

Civil Trial Procedure

The Supreme Court of Texas makes rules of civil procedure for all courts with civil jurisdiction, but these rules cannot conflict with any general law enacted by the Legislature. Furthermore, the Supreme Court's rules of civil procedure can be disapproved by the state's lawmakers. With the help of the State Bar of Texas and other interested persons, the Supreme Court has promulgated the *Rules of Civil*

Procedure, which, together with amendments, constitute the procedures followed in all civil actions in the state's courts.

Pretrial Actions   Included among topics dealt with in civil cases are property rights, domestic relations, personal injuries, workers' compensation, collective bargaining, deceptive trade practices, truth in lending, and environmental protection. These cases normally begin when the injured party, who is known as the *plaintiff,* files a *petition*. It is a written document containing the plaintiff's grievance against the *defendant* and the remedy that is sought. The petition is filed with the clerk of the court in which the action is contemplated, whereupon the clerk issues a *citation*. The citation is served upon (delivered to) the defendant, directing that person to answer to charges. If the defendant wants to contest the suit, a written *answer* to the plaintiff's charges must be filed. The answer explains why the plaintiff is not entitled to the remedy sought.

Before the judge sets the trial date (which might be many months or even years after the petition is filed), all interested parties should have had an opportunity to file their petitions, answers, or other pleas with the court. These written instruments constitute the *pleadings* in the case and form the basis of the trial.

Either party has the option of having a jury determine the facts. If a jury is not demanded, the trial judge determines both facts and the law. When a jury determines the facts after receiving instructions from the judge, then the judge's only duty is to apply the law to those predetermined facts.

Trial of a Civil Case   As the trial begins, brief opening statements are made by the lawyers. The plaintiff's case is then presented. The defendant has the opportunity to contest the relevance or admissibility of all evidence introduced by the plaintiff and to cross-examine the plaintiff's witnesses. After the plaintiff's case has been presented, it is the defendant's turn. Evidence presented on behalf of the defendant may be challenged by the plaintiff. The judge is the final authority as to what evidence may be introduced by all parties, though objections to the judge's rulings may be used as grounds for appeal.

After all parties have finished their presentations, the judge writes a *charge to the jury*, submits it to the parties for their approval, makes necessary changes suggested by them, and then reads it to the jury. In the charge, the judge instructs the jury on rules for deliberation and defines various terms. After the charge is read, the attorneys present their arguments to the jury, whereupon the jury retires to deliberate. To reach a decision, at least ten jurors must agree in a district court and five must agree in a county court. If agreement cannot be reached by the required number of jurors, the foreman reports a *hung jury*. Then, if requested by one party to the suit, a new trial will be scheduled; otherwise, the case will be dismissed.

A court decision is known as a *verdict*. On the basis of the verdict, the judge prepares a written opinion, known as the *judgment* (or decree of the court). Either party may then file a motion for a new trial based on the reason or reasons it is believed that the trial has not been fair. If the judge agrees, a new trial will be ordered; if not, the case may be appealed to a higher court. In each appeal, a complete written record of the trial is sent to the appellate court.

Appeal of a Civil Case   In a court of appeals or in the Supreme Court, a case is heard by the justices without the assistance of a jury. The appellate court proceeds on the basis of the record sent up from the lower court. After the appeal has been heard in open court, the judges take the case to conference. There they discuss it among themselves and arrive at a decision by a majority vote. The usual route of appeals is from a county or district court to a court of appeals and then in some instances to the Supreme Court of Texas.

Criminal Trial Procedure

Rules of criminal trial procedure are made by the Legislature. The Texas Code of Criminal Procedure remained virtually unchanged from its adoption in the early days of statehood until revised in 1965 and substantially amended in 1967. In large measure, these changes were designed to bring Texas procedures into line with the U.S. Supreme Court's rulings regarding confessions, arrests, searches, and seizures. Other changes resulted from pressure by the State Bar of Texas.

Pretrial Actions   Probably millions of illegal acts are committed daily in Texas. For example, many people drive while intoxicated. After an arrest has been made, but before questioning, a suspect must be informed of the right to remain silent, of the possibility that any statement may be used as evidence by the state, and of the right to consult with *counsel* (that is, with an attorney, more commonly called a lawyer). Then a suspect must be taken "without unnecessary delay" before a magistrate (a justice of the peace or municipal court judge), who in turn must reveal the offense or offenses charged and must provide information concerning legal rights. Included are the rights to remain silent, to have an examining trial, and to have an attorney present during any questioning by law enforcement officers or prosecuting attorneys. Indigent persons (people too poor to hire a lawyer) must be provided with the services of an attorney in any felony or misdemeanor case in which conviction may result in a prison or jail sentence. Accused persons must be informed by the magistrate that they are not required to make any statement and that, if they do, it may be used against them in a subsequent trial. Since 1989, however, recorded statements made during questioning at the time of arrest may be used as evidence even though the accused was not aware that an electronic recording was being made.

Under Texas law, the right to trial by jury is guaranteed in all criminal cases, even those involving charges of the most minor misdemeanors. Except in a capital felony, however, the defendant may waive jury trial regardless of the plea—guilty, not guilty, or *nolo contendere* (no contest). To expedite procedures, the prosecuting attorney and the defense attorney may engage in *plea bargaining,* whereby the accused pleads guilty in return for the promise that the prosecution will seek a lighter sentence or will recommend probation. Usually, the judge will accept the plea bargain. If the defendant waives a trial by jury and is found guilty by the judge, the judge also determines the punishment to be imposed.

Trial of a Criminal Case After the trial jury has been selected, the indictment or information is read by the prosecuting attorney. The jury is thus informed of the basic allegations of the state's case, and the defendant enters a plea.

The state begins by calling its witnesses and introducing any other evidence supporting the information or the indictment. The defense may challenge the truth or relevance of the evidence presented and is allowed to cross-examine all witnesses and challenge all evidence. Next, the defense presents its case, calling witnesses and submitting evidence that is subject to attack by the prosecution.

After all evidence and testimony have been presented, the judge charges the jury, explaining the law applicable to the case. Both prosecuting and defense attorneys must also be given an opportunity to address final arguments to the jury before it retires to reach a verdict.

Verdict and Sentence Juries in district and county courts may determine only questions of fact, but juries of justice of the peace and municipal courts decide questions of both fact and the law. A unanimous decision is required for the jury to reach a verdict of guilty or innocent. If the jurors are hopelessly split and the result is a hung jury, the judge declares a mistrial, discharges the jurors, and if requested by the prosecuting attorney, orders a new trial with another jury.

When the jury brings a verdict before the court, the judge may choose to disregard it and order a new trial on the grounds that the jury has failed to arrive at a verdict that achieves substantial justice. In a jury trial, the sentence may be fixed by the jury if the convicted person so requests; otherwise, the judge determines the sentence. In either event, a separate hearing on the penalty is held, at which time the person's prior criminal and/or juvenile record, general reputation, and other relevant factors are introduced.

Appeal of a Criminal Case A convicted defendant has the right to appeal. If an appeal is made, the court clerk forwards the attorneys' briefs and the trial record to the appropriate court of appeals. All capital punishment cases and a limited number of other criminal cases are taken to the Court of Criminal Appeals; but the U.S. Supreme Court has ruled that the state does not have to provide legal counsel for indigent Death Row inmates appealing to a federal court (for example, to the U.S. Supreme Court). Because Texas lawyers have failed to meet this human need for unpaid (*pro bono*) counsel, the American Bar Resource Center has been forced to seek volunteers from among the lawyers of other states.[5]

Until 1987, Texas was the only state where a prosecutor (district attorney or county attorney) had no right of appeal. In that year, however, Texas voters approved a constitutional amendment allowing the Legislature to authorize a limited right of appeal by the prosecutor. Implementing legislation permits a prosecutor to appeal the following court actions:

- Dismissal of an indictment, information, or complaint (or dismissal of any portion of one)
- Delay or modification of a judgment
- Granting of a new trial
- Approval of a claim of former jeopardy (e.g., a former trial for the same offense)
- Suppression of evidence of substantial importance
- Sentencing that is alleged to be illegal

An appeal must be filed by the state within 15 days of the trial. During the course of a trial, the prosecution has the right to a stay of proceedings until a court of appeals acts on an appeal.

Correction and Rehabilitation Policies

Institutions of correction (for example, prisons and jails) are designed to punish lawbreakers, deter others from committing similar crimes, and isolate criminals from society, thus protecting the life and property of persons who might otherwise become the victims of criminals. Another important function is that of rehabilitating lawbreakers so that they may be able to make positive contributions to society. This difficult task is undertaken with varying degrees of success in prisons and jails and through community-based probation and parole systems.

The Texas Department of Criminal Justice

Under terms of the Criminal Justice Reform Bill (H.B. 2335) passed by the Legislature and signed by the governor in 1989, the principal criminal justice agencies of the state are organized within the new *Texas Department of Criminal Justice* (TDCJ). This department is headed by a nonsalaried board composed of nine members appointed by the governor (with the advice and consent of the Senate) for overlapping six-year terms. The governor selects one member to chair the board. Dual headquarters for the board are maintained in Austin and Huntsville. The board employs a full-time executive director, who hires the directors of the department's three divisions. Each division director is responsible for hiring division personnel.

The *Community Justice Division* establishes minimum standards for programs (for example, adult probation programs), facilities, and services provided by units of local government; and it certifies those programs for state funding. This division and the board are assisted by the Judiciary Advisory Council, composed of 12 nonsalaried members: 6 appointed by the chief justice of the Supreme Court of Texas and 6 appointed by the presiding judge of the Court of Criminal Appeals. The *Institutional Division* is responsible for the operation and management of the state prison system, which comprises over 30 prison units located largely in East Texas. The *Board of Pardons and Paroles Division* determines which prisoners are to be released from prison and placed on parole, sets conditions of parole and mandatory supervision, and makes decisions concerning revocation of parole and mandatory supervision.

To oversee and review the implementation of legislative criminal justice policy, including fiscal policy, the *Legislative Criminal Justice Board* has been established as an agency of the Legislature. This board is composed of the lieutenant governor or a senator designated by him or her; the speaker of the House or a representative designated by the speaker; chairs of two House committees (Corrections and Appropriations); chairs of two Senate committees (Criminal Justice and Finance); two representatives appointed by the speaker; and two senators appointed by the lieutenant governor. The board is chaired by the lieutenant governor and the speaker for alternate two-year periods.

Institutions of Correction

Adults who are confined after felony convictions usually serve sentences in the state prison system. Those who are confined on misdemeanor convictions serve sentences in a county jail or another type of community corrections facility. Generally, young people between the ages of 10 and 17 are treated as delinquent children when they commit acts that would be classified as felonies or misdemeanors if committed by adults. Sometimes, however, a juvenile court judge will certify a youth for trial as an adult—for example, in a case involving murder of or serious injury to a person—if the delinquent was 15 years of age or older at the time of the alleged felony. Although most juvenile offenders are not confined, some are institutionalized in units administered by the Texas Youth Commission or in facilities established by county governments.

Prison System Huntsville is the location of the headquarters of the Texas Department of Criminal Justice's Institutional Division, which is the administrative successor to the former Texas Department of Corrections (TDC) that was abolished on September 1, 1989. During the nine years before it was replaced by the Institutional Division, TDC was the subject of much controversy and litigation.[6]

In *Ruiz* v. *Estelle* (1980), U.S. District Court Judge William Wayne Justice condemned TDC's overcrowded, understaffed, substandard facilities. Although parts of Judge Justice's order (for example, one prisoner per cell) were overruled by a higher federal court in 1982, his principal findings were upheld. Then, in May 1985, Judge Justice announced that TDC lawyers and attorneys representing prison inmates had agreed on ways to end overcrowding and to improve prison life.

Made public on July 15, 1985, when the inmate population exceeded 37,000 in 26 prison units, the agreement called for reducing the number of persons in those units to 32,500 by September 1989. All new units were to have a maximum capacity of 2,250, and 200-inmate dormitories were to be constructed for work-camp operations involving low-risk prisoners. Other terms of the agreement provided for contact (touching) visits for some inmates, improved shower and toilet facilities, more frequent changes to clean clothing, expansion of dining room and kitchen facilities, and single cells for disruptive persons and those most vulnerable to abuse by other inmates.

These changes—together with new leadership for TDC and an appropriation of nearly $1 billion for the 1986–1987 biennium—represented important steps toward modernizing Texas's prison system. Such action was long overdue, as indicated by the killing of 52 inmates in 1984–1985 and the stabbing of hundreds during those years. In 1986 the number of murders in TDC units was reduced to three, but Judge Justice chafed at what he believed to be a deliberate delay by TDC administrators in implementing his orders. On January 5, 1987, the federal judge caught the attention of TDC—and the 70th Legislature—when he threatened to fine the state $24 million a month until his directives were obeyed. Despite the fact that the state was about $1 billion in the red at that time, the lawmakers quickly appropriated $20 million to satisfy Judge Justice's immediate demands.

In an attempt to deal with overcrowding, the 70th Legislature authorized TDC to raise $250 million for prison construction by issuing bonds (approved by Texas voters in 1987) that would provide 12,500 new beds by the end of 1989. Two thousand beds were to be made available through private construction and management of 500-bed, low-security facilities to be operated at a cost of at least 10 percent less than would be needed to operate comparable state facilities. But even as a privately financed lease-purchase project provided new beds for another 2,250 inmates at the Michael Unit near Palestine, Governor Clements reported that the Criminal Justice Policy Council had projected "an unrelenting growth in the inmate population," a growth that could raise the total inmate population to nearly 56,000 prisoners by 1991. Later estimates of future prison needs were even higher.

While the Legislature met for its 71st regular session during the first five months in 1989, the prison population rose to more than 40,000 (43 percent black, 35 percent Anglo, and 22 percent Hispanic), including over 1,600 women in the Gatesville and Mountain View units. Each prisoner cost the state over $46 per day, or about $17,000 per year. At the same time, most county jails throughout Texas were jammed to overcapacity because much of their cell space was occupied by more than 10,000 convicted felons (including about 1,100 women) awaiting transfer to units of TDC. With admissions surpassing 3,000 per month, TDC could keep the inmate population under the 95-percent-of-capacity ceiling required by the state's Prison Management Act only by periodically refusing to accept new prisoners and by speeding the release of nonviolent offenders through grants of unearned, good-time (good behavior) credits ranging from 30 to 180 days.

Some counties sued the state in an attempt to recover funds spent to incarcerate convicted felons that TDC refused to accept because of overcrowding in its units. At the same time, Governor Clements called on the Legislature to propose a constitutional amendment authorizing the selling of bonds to finance another construction program providing prison facilities for an additional 10,000 to 11,000 prisoners. In May 1989, after more than four months of prolonged skirmishing involving legislators, county officials, and the governor, the 71st Legislature passed its sweeping criminal justice reform package. In addition to a $400 million bond proposal, the reform measure merged existing prison, parole, and probation agencies into the new Department of Criminal Justice; authorized use of rural hospital facilities for treatment of persons with alcohol and drug abuse problems; and provided for state funding to support county-operated facilities, including work-release centers, boot camps, restitution centers, and drug treatment units. Texas voters approved the bond proposal in November 1989.

Jails All but about a dozen Texas counties maintained a jail in 1989. Operated under the direction of the sheriff, these institutions were established originally for the purpose of detaining persons awaiting trial, if not released on bail, and for holding persons serving sentences for misdemeanor offenses. Jail facilities vary in quality and have not usually had rehabilitation programs. Conditions in big urban jails have been especially poor because of overcrowding caused by increasing numbers of convicted felons for whom cell space has not been available in state prison units. Texas's Commission on Jail Standards is responsible for establishing minimum jail standards, requiring an annual report from each county sheriff, reviewing reports, and arranging for inspection of jails. In case of failure to comply with commission rules, a jail may be closed or the commission, represented by the attorney general, may take court action against the county.

Juvenile Facilities Responsibility for supervising the care and rehabilitation of juveniles (10 to 17 years of age) is vested in the *Texas Youth Commission*. This body is composed of six members appointed for six-year terms by the governor with Senate approval. The commission appoints an executive director, who implements its policies for operating a residential treatment center at Corsicana for emotionally disturbed youths, a classification and reception center in Brownwood, and training centers for delinquents in Pyote, Giddings, Gainesville, Crockett, and Brownwood. Several halfway houses and state homes for dependent and neglected children are operated by the commission, and many private child-care facilities accept custody of wards of the state on a contractual basis.

Community-Based Programs

Although Texas prisons, jails, and juvenile units are usually successful in isolating lawbreakers, these institutions have left much to be desired in the area of rehabilitation. Confinement is expensive for the taxpayers and often produces embittered criminals rather than rehabilitated, law-abiding citizens. Thus, the criminal justice reform measure enacted in 1989 places a new emphasis on community-based supervision and rehabilitation.

Adult Probation In cases involving adult first offenders who are convicted of misdemeanors and lesser felonies, jail and prison sentences are commonly probated, that is, the convicted person is not confined if the terms of *probation* are fulfilled. As required by the Criminal Justice Act of 1989, the district judge or judges trying criminal cases in a district must establish a *community supervision and corrections department* and hire personnel to conduct presentence investigations and risk assessments, supervise and rehabilitate probationers, enforce probation rules, and staff corrections facilities. Judges of county courts at law that try criminal cases may participate in the management of the department.

A county commissioners court may establish a county correctional center under the operational direction of the sheriff. In consultation with the director of the community supervision and corrections department, the sheriff may provide work programs and counseling for persons serving sentences in the jail or persons being confined for violation of probation. In order to qualify for state funding, a county correctional center must meet standards developed by the Justice Assistance Division and the Commission on Jail Standards.

As a prerequisite to creation of a county correctional center, a community justice council must be established to provide policy guidance and direction for development of criminal justice plans and community corrections facilities and programs. Established by the district judge or judges, a council should consist of the following persons or others designated by them:

- a sheriff
- a county commissioner or county judge
- a city council member from the most populous municipality
- no more than two legislators
- the presiding judge for a judicial district
- a judge of a county court at law exercising criminal jurisdiction
- a county attorney with criminal jurisdiction
- a district attorney or criminal district attorney
- an elected member of a board of trustees of an independent school district

The community justice council appoints a community justice task force to develop a community justice plan. This task force may be composed of any number of members but should include several officials involved in providing parole, probation, education, mental health, law enforcement, and other social services. A county served by a community supervision and corrections department is required to provide physical facilities, equipment, and utilities for that department.

Juvenile Probation　After a juvenile court has conducted an adjudication hearing and has determined that a "child between the ages of 10 and 17 years" has engaged in delinquent conduct, a disposition hearing is conducted to determine if rehabilitation of the child or protection of the public is necessary. If committed to a facility administered by the Texas Youth Commission, a person may be detained until the age of 21. As an alternative to commitment to a facility administered by the Texas Youth Commission, a delinquent child may be placed on probation and remain under the care of the juvenile court until completion of the period of probation. Terms of probation may specify that the child is to be placed in a foster home or agency rather than remain in the custody of parents or other relatives. The governor appoints the nine-member Texas Juvenile Probation Commission (three district court judges and six other citizens) to maintain uniform probation administration standards throughout the state.

Parole　An inmate of the Texas prison system is eligible to apply for release on *parole* after having served one-fourth of a sentence or 15 years, whichever is the lesser (minus "good time" or time off for good behavior), but a person convicted of aggravated robbery or other violent crime must serve a minimum of two calendar years before becoming eligible for parole. Application is made to the Board of Pardons and Paroles of the Texas Department of Criminal Justice. The board is composed of 18 full-time, salaried members appointed by the governor (with the advice and consent of the Senate) to serve for six-year terms. A parole panel of three board members reviews applications and recommends granting or denying parole for persons imprisoned or in jail. A panel also conducts hearings to determine whether parole or release to mandatory supervision should be revoked. In addition to requiring that a parolee report periodically to a parole officer, the board may specify that the parolee submit to drug testing and/or electronic monitoring. Before release, arrangements must be made for the parolee's employment or maintenance and care.

A parolee's status is similar to that of a probationer. Thus, a parolee must report regularly to a parole officer, must pay a monthly parole supervision fee of $10, must refrain from all illegal conduct, and must fulfill other conditions imposed by the board—such as making reparation or restitution to a victim of the parolee's crime. Otherwise parole may be revoked and the parolee confined to serve out the full sentence. By late 1989, more than 60,000 persons were on parole or had been released under mandatory supervision. Over 10 percent of these parolees were classified as "absconders" because they had ceased reporting to parole officers and had disappeared.

Problems and Reforms: Implications for Public Policy

As we have seen, in 1973 the 63rd Legislature took positive action on a draft proposal by the State Bar Committee on Revision of the Texas Penal Code. There has also been continuing reform of the Rules of Civil Procedure since 1941, and the Texas Code of Criminal Procedure underwent a thorough revision in 1965 and was substantially amended two years later. Throughout the 1980s, the state's criminal justice system experienced a series of crises resulting from an increase in violent crimes and stiffer sentences for criminals. The Legislature responded (often slowly) with increased appropriations for correctional institutions and facilities, changes in probation and parole systems, new punishment and sentencing alternatives, and expanded programs for the rehabilitation of offenders. Ongoing efforts to deal with other policy areas are described below.

Rights of Crime Victims

Traditionally, Texas law has given more attention to the correction and rehabilitation of criminals than to the rights of crime victims. With enactment of the *Crime Victims Compensation Act of 1979,* however, the Texas Legislature took an important step to aid persons who have lost wages and incurred expenses (for example, medical and legal costs) as a result of injuries suffered at the hands of adult criminals or (since 1989) juveniles. Administered by the Texas Industrial Accident Board, this compensation program is financed through payments made by persons convicted of felonies and misdemeanors, including traffic violations. (See Reading 8.1.)

In the 1980s the Legislature enacted more statutes to benefit crime victims; and in 1989 it proposed H.J.R. 19, a constitutional amendment incorporating the following guarantees throughout the criminal justice process: "the right to be treated with fairness and respect for the victim's dignity and privacy" and "the right to be reasonably protected from the accused." Also, on the request of a crime victim, H.J.R. 19 specifies that the victim has the following additional rights related to the crime:

- To be notified of court proceedings
- To be present at all public court proceedings, unless a judge decides that testimony by the victim might be materially affected
- To confer with a representative of the prosecutor's office
- To restitution
- To information concerning conviction, sentencing, imprisonment, and release of the accused criminal

This proposed amendment was approved by Texas voters in November 1989.

Coping with Crowded Dockets

Few people would dispute the adage "Justice delayed is justice denied." Yet one of the most common problems facing American courts is that of dockets crowded with pending cases. This results in long delays before new cases can be heard. In an effort to minimize this problem, the district courts of Texas have been grouped into nine administrative judicial regions. For each region, the governor names one district judge as presiding judge. The presiding judge is responsible for calling a council of the region's district judges and judges of county courts at law at least once a year for the purpose of receiving reports on the status of court dockets.

The long-term solution to the problem of overloaded dockets is legislative action to establish additional courts. In the short term, however, the problem may be alleviated by using the services of retired judges or by temporarily transferring judges with relatively light dockets to districts in which large numbers of cases are awaiting trial.

As approved by the voters in November 1985, a constitutional amendment established the 13-member *Judicial Districts Board* to make a continuous study of districting for state district courts. In addition to the chief justice of the Supreme Court, who chairs the board, other members are the presiding judge of the Court of Criminal Appeals, the presiding judges of the nine administrative judicial regions, the president of the Texas Judicial Council, and one attorney appointed by the governor. Should the Legislature fail to provide for statewide judicial reapportionment following a federal decennial census (such as that held in 1990), the

Judicial Districts Board would prepare a reapportionment plan during the third year after the census (e.g., 1993). The plan would then have to be approved by the Texas House of Representatives and Senate. If the Judicial Districts Board should fail to prepare a plan by August 31, the Legislative Redistricting Board would make the judicial reapportionment within 150 days. It remains to be seen whether the Judicial Districts Board will be able to bring order out of the current chaos of overlapping districts, unequal dockets, and proliferating courts that sometimes owe their existence to political influences rather than to judicial needs.

Disciplining and Removing Judges and Justices

Each year, a few of Texas's judges and justices commit acts that warrant discipline or removal. Traditionally, the most common method of dealing with erring judges was to vote them out of office at the end of a term; but situations involving the most serious judicial misconduct were handled through trial by jury, legislative address, or impeachment. Although all of these methods are still available, the *State Commission on Judicial Conduct* now plays the most important role in disciplining the state's judiciary at all levels. This 11-member commission is composed of one justice of the peace, one judge of a municipal court, one judge of a county court at law, one district court judge, and one justice of a court of appeals—all appointed by the Supreme Court; two attorneys appointed by the board of directors of the State Bar; and four citizens (who must be at least 30 years of age and neither licensed to practice law nor holders of salaried public office or public employment) appointed by the governor.

On its own authority, the State Commission on Judicial Conduct can suspend from office any judge (or justice) who has been indicted by a grand jury for a felony or who has been charged with a misdemeanor involving official misconduct. As a result of a complaint or on the basis of its own investigation, the commission may privately or publicly admonish, warn, or reprimand a judge; in some cases involving incompetence, it may require additional judicial training or education. If the commission decides that stronger action is merited, it may order a formal hearing concerning public censure, removal, or retirement of a judge, or it may request the Supreme Court to appoint a *master* (an active or retired justice or judge) to hear evidence on the matter and then report to the commission.

On the basis of a hearing or a master's report, the commission may issue an order of public censure or may recommend to a *review tribunal* the removal or retirement of the judge. A review tribunal is composed of seven justices of courts of appeals who are drawn by lot by the chief justice of the Supreme Court. The tribunal has 90 days in which to accept or reject the commission's recommendation or to order the public censure, retirement, or removal of the judge. Any appeal must be addressed to the Supreme Court, which selects by lot the members of a court of review composed of three court of appeals justices. Hearings by the court of review are public and its decision is final. (See Reading 8.2 for the case of Judge Jack Hampton.)

Selecting Judges

Late in August 1987, Chief Justice John Hill announced that as of January 1, 1988, he would resign from the Supreme Court of Texas in order to fight for reform of the state's judicial system. Coming halfway through his six-year term, Hill's resignation surprised most Texans. It gave Governor Clements an opportunity to fill the vacancy by appointing Tom Phillips, a Republican district court judge in Houston. Resignations by two other Democrats were followed by gubernatorial appointment of two more Republicans, and the general election of November 1988 featured hard-fought contests involving six Republican candidates and six Democratic candidates. Although one Republican incumbent (Barbara Culver) was defeated, three other Republican candidates won their races and preserved the 6 to 3 partisan lineup of the court.

For some observers, close Supreme Court electoral contests and split-ticket voting suggested that Texas voters had been well informed and discriminating in their support of these judicial candidates. Thus, it was argued that the system of election by popular vote had produced good results. On the other hand, many Texans were in agreement with John Hill's principal criticisms of the state's judiciary: that judges are elected as candidates of political parties, and that the expensive election campaigns of judicial candidates are financed largely with contributions from lawyers who practice in their courts.

Once a solidly Democratic stronghold, Tarrant County is an example of changing judicial politics in Texas. The rising tide of Republican votes that swept most Dallas County judgeships in the 1980s reached the Fort Worth area in November 1988, when nine formerly Democratic judgeships were won by GOP candidates. Fearing a similar fate in 1990, eight of Tarrant County's Democratic judges met with Governor Bill Clements and Republican party officials on July 14, 1989, to announce their defection to the GOP. At the beginning of 1989, the GOP could claim the Supreme Court's chief justice and 2 justices, a judge on the Court of Criminal Appeals, 20 justices on courts of appeals, 92 district judges, 82 county-level judges, and 83 justices of the peace.

Critics of partisan election of judges tend to favor a merit selection model, such as the one used in Missouri and several other states. The *Missouri Plan* features a nominating commission that recommends a panel of names to the governor whenever a judicial vacancy is to be filled. The appointee then serves for a year or so before the voters decide, on the basis of the record of judicial performance, whether to give the new judge a full term or to allow the nominating commission and the governor to make another appointment on a similar trial basis.

At the beginning of the regular session of the 71st Legislature, Governor Clements, Lieutenant Governor Bill Hobby, House Speaker Gib Lewis, and Chief Justice Thomas Phillips all voiced their preference for merit selection of judges. A Texas Plan calling for merit selection of all appellate court judges, as well as for all district court judges in the state's six most populous counties, was widely publicized but received little support from legislators. Neither was there strong legislative interest in an all-single-member-district plan championed by Democratic party chair Bob Slagle, minority lawmakers, and liberal Democrats. According to

Governor Bill Clements welcomes eight of Tarrant County's Democratic judges on July 14, 1989, when they announce that they will run for re-election as Republicans in 1990. Behind Governor Clements are, from left, Holly Deherd, vice chairwoman of the state GOP; Senator Bob McFarland; Judges Howard Fender, Pat Ferchill, Don Leonard, Frank Sullivan, Brian Carper, Bob Burnett, Joe Drago, and Albert White, Jr.; and the chairman of the Tarrant County Republican Party Committee, Steve Hollern. (Courtesy *Fort Worth Star-Telegram* / Sonnel Velazquez.)

Slagle, this plan would "cut the cost of campaigns, reduce the length of the ballot, and put voters closer to their elected judges." As for public opinion on judicial selection, a Texas Poll showed that 69 percent wanted to change the election system, but there was no consensus on an alternative.

Although the regular session of the 71st Legislature did not produce a judicial reform law, Hispanics invoked the Voting Rights Act to challenge at-large systems for electing justices to the six-member court of appeals based in Corpus Christi (*Rangel* v. *Mattox*) and for electing 172 district court judges in nine urban counties (*LULAC* v. *Clements*). Just as single-member legislative districts increased representation of minorities in the Texas House and Senate, it was argued that election of more Hispanic and black judges and justices would result from single-member judicial districting.

On July 28, 1989, U.S. District Judge Felemon Vela of Brownsville noted in *Rangel* v. *Mattox* that only one Mexican-American justice was sitting on the 13th Court of Appeals although it serves 20 South Texas counties where Hispanics comprise 46 percent of the registered voters. Overturning the at-large election system for this court, Judge Vela gave parties to the suit 30 days in which to propose an acceptable method for selecting justices.

On September 25, 1989, Judge Vela ordered single-member elections in 1990 and 1992 for one justice in the Cameron County area and one justice in the Hidalgo County area, respectively. The other four justices for the Corpus Christi–based court of appeals are to be elected from single-member districts in 1994. In the *LULAC* case, on November 8, 1989, U.S. District Court Judge Lucius D. Bunton of Midland condemned at-large election of state district judges in Bexar, Dallas, Ector, Harris, Jefferson, Lubbock, Midland, Tarrant, and Travis counties. He directed the legislature to resolve this problem by January 3, 1990.

Notes

1. For statistics and other information on the Texas judicial system, consult the jointly published annual reports of the Texas Judicial Council and the Office of Court Administration. In addition to compiling and reporting statistics relating to the operations of all courts of the state (including municipal, justice of the peace, and county courts), the Texas Judicial Council makes a continuous study of court operations, receives and considers suggestions for improving the administration of justice, formulates methods for simplifying judicial procedure, and investigates matters of justice referred to it by the Legislature or the Supreme Court. The council is composed of nine appointed members (seven lawyers and two nonlawyers, one of whom must be a journalist) and ten ex officio members, including the chief justice of the Supreme Court of Texas and the presiding judge of the Court of Criminal Appeals.
2. For an easy-to-follow account of small claims court procedure, see *How to Sue in Small Claims Court,* published by the State Bar of Texas (P.O. Box 12487, Austin, TX 78711); see also Ralph Warner, *Everybody's Guide to Small Claims Court,* National 2nd ed. (Berkeley, Calif.: Nolo Press, 1985).
3. Monthly issues of the *Texas Bar Journal* feature reports on legal education in the state's nine law schools: Baylor, Texas Southern, St. Mary's, Southern Methodist, South Texas (in Houston), Texas Tech, Houston, the University of Texas at Austin, and the Reynaldo G. Garza School of Law on the campus of Pan American University.
4. For a listing of legal firms and practicing lawyers in each county, see the *Texas Legal Directory,* published annually by Legal Directories Publishing Corporation, Los Angeles, Calif.
5. For comments by the president of the Texas Bar, see James B. Sales, "Indigent Death Row Inmates—Society's Ultimate Sentence and the Lawyer's Ultimate Obligation," *Texas Bar Journal* 51 (September 1988): 782–783.
6. For a detailed account of developments during this troubled period, see Ben M. Crouch and James W. Marquart, *An Appeal to Justice: Litigated Reform of Texas Prisons* (Austin: University of Texas Press, 1989).

Key Terms and Concepts

civil law	Code of Criminal Procedure
criminal law	Penal Code
jurisdiction	felony
original jurisdiction	misdemeanor
appellate jurisdiction	capital felony law
common law	*Penry* v. *Lynaugh*
legal code	magistrate

municipal court
trial de novo
justice of the peace
small claims court
constitutional county court
county court at law
probate court
district court
criminal district court
court of appeals
Court of Criminal Appeals
Supreme Court of Texas
State Bar of Texas
grand jury
jury commission
foreman
indictment
true bill
no bill
complaint
information
trial jury
juror
venireman
peremptory challenge
challenge for cause
litigant
witness
Rules of Civil Procedure
plaintiff
petition
defendant

citation
answer
pleadings
charge to the jury
hung jury
verdict
judgment
counsel
nolo contendere
plea bargaining
Texas Department of Criminal
  Justice
Community Justice Division
Institutional Division
Board of Pardons and Paroles
  Division
Legislative Criminal Justice Board
Ruiz v. *Estelle*
Texas Youth Commission
probation
community supervision and
  corrections department
parole
Crime Victims Compensation Act
  of 1979
Judicial Districts Board
State Commission on Judicial
  Conduct
master
review tribunal
Missouri Plan

Selected Readings

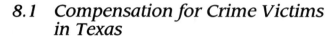

8.1 Compensation for Crime Victims in Texas

John Forshee

Although a violent crime's traumatic impact on a victim cannot be measured with money, the State of Texas has a compensation program that helps many crime victims and their dependents to cope with resulting financial problems. The data in this reading are from annual crime victim compensation reports of the Texas Industrial Accident Board.

More than 80 percent of all people living in the United States today have been or will become victims of violent crime. While most crime victims do not suffer loss of life, homicide has become the second leading cause of death among men 18 to 34 years of age. For many years, victims of crime were almost forgotten, but recently they have received well-deserved attention.

Compensation for victims of crime has had a long history. Some type of restitution was provided for victims of certain crimes in ancient India and in Israel under the Law of Moses. During the early years of American history, a thief might have been ordered to pay the victim three times the value of stolen property. With the rise of the American legal concept that crime is an act against the state, the idea of compensation for victims of crime fell into disrepute, and official concern for the victim declined.

The Crime Victims Compensation Act of 1979

Texas was among the last states to provide compensation to victims of crime. Enacted by the 66th Legislature in 1979, the Crime Victims Compensation Act (CVCA) took effect on January 1, 1980. This law is administered by the Crime Victims Compensation Division of the Texas Industrial Accident Board (IAB). A victim or a victim's dependent is eligible to receive payment of money under terms of CVCA subject to the following provisions:

- The crime must be committed in Texas.
- The victim must suffer personal injury or death and must be a resident of a state or territory of the United States at the time of the crime.
- The crime must be reported to proper authorities within 72 hours.

This article was written especially for *Practicing Texas Politics*. John Forshee is a senior content specialist for the Center for Telecommunications, Dallas County Community College District.

- A claim must be filed within 180 days of the crime unless "good cause" can be shown for allowing an extended period for filing.
- Compensation is not awarded for injury or death resulting from the operation of a motor vehicle, an aircraft, or a water vehicle unless there is an underlying criminal offense.

A victim or dependent may receive payment of up to $150 per week for lost wages as well as compensation for medical care, child care, counseling, vocational rehabilitation, attorney's fees, and funeral and burial expenses.

Funding Crime Victims Compensation

Texas funds its CVCA program by imposing additional court costs on persons convicted of committing felonies and misdemeanors. Anyone found guilty on a felony indictment has $20 added to ordinary court costs. For a Class A or Class B misdemeanor, $15 is added to court costs; $5 is added for a Class C misdemeanor conviction, except for pedestrian and parking violations; and $5 is collected from persons who take defensive driving instruction as part of the penalty for a traffic violation. The philosophy behind CVCA is that those who break the law should fund the compensation program that benefits victims of violent crimes.

During fiscal year (FY) 1987 (September 1986–August 1987), claims paid amounted to $5 million more than revenue collected; in FY 1988 the difference between claims paid and revenue collected dropped to $2.1 million. These deficits were absorbed by dipping into the compensation fund's reserve. To restore a positive cash flow to the fund, the 71st Legislature increased the court cost for a Class C misdemeanor from $3 to $5 and imposed the defensive driving charge.

Claims Under the Crime Victims Compensation Act

Compensation under the terms of CVCA is intended for those who suffer genuine financial hardship as a result of a violent criminal act. Applications for compensation are reviewed by the Crime Victims Compensation Division of the Texas Industrial Accident Board and either referred to the Office of the Attorney General or returned to the applicant for additional information. After the attorney general's office has completed its verification procedure, applications are sent back to the IAB's Crime Victims Compensation Division. An average of 90 days is required to process an application. Claims for lost wages have the highest priority, and a total of $2.65 million was awarded for lost wages in FY 1988. Payments to providers of services take longer to process and account for the larger part of CVCA payments. For example, payments to physicians, hospitals, and attorneys totaled $12.6 million in FY 1988.

In emergency situations, payments can be made quickly. For example, a Dallas man and his two children left their automobile after running out of gas. While walking along an interstate highway, they were struck and killed in a D.W.I. accident. Without sufficient funds to pay for burial of the three bodies, the wife faced the prospect of having them buried by the county in paupers' graves. But her CVCA application was processed as an emergency claim, and money was provided promptly to cover funeral and burial costs. Not all claims are approved, however. Reasons for denial include inability to show evidence of financial stress, failure to report the crime to a law enforcement agency within specified time limits, and late filing of the claim. But the two principal reasons for denial are a finding that the victim's behavior contributed to the injury or that the victim failed to cooperate with a law enforcement agency.

The number of claims filed has increased dramatically, from 1,900 in FY 1985 to 6,777 in FY 1988. A total of $7 million was distributed to 1,257 claimants in FY 1985, and $17.4 million was disbursed to 3,938 claimants in FY 1988. The increase in the number of claims filed is due to an increase in public awareness of Texas's crime victim compensation program. Support groups for victims, law enforcement agencies, physicians, and hospitals have been making greater efforts to inform the public about the program and the rights of individuals under CVCA.

Conclusion

Crime victims have not been forgotten in Texas. Public awareness of CVCA has grown, the number of claims has increased, and the dollar amount of compensation awarded has risen. Claims are handled in a timely fashion, and lawbreakers are forced to fund the program. For victims of violent crimes there is some consolation in receiving compensation that can be used to cover part of their crime-related losses and expenses.

8.2 Judicial Oversight in Texas: The Case of Judge Jack Hampton

Jeffrey E. Key

Usually, little is heard about Texas's Commission on Judicial Conduct. Because of publicity given to the case involving Judge Jack Hampton, however, the work of the commission became a center of interest for many Texans in 1989. This reading presents details of the Hampton case and explains the importance of the commission in the administration of justice in the Lone Star State. Final disposition of the Hampton case was expected in late 1989.

Tucked away in the back corner of the second floor of the Texas County and District Retirement System building in Austin is the small, tidy office of the Commission on

Jeffrey E. Key is a doctoral candidate in the Department of Government of the University of Texas at Austin. He wrote this essay especially for *Practicing Texas Politics*.

Judicial Conduct. A first-time visitor would have difficulty finding the office. There is no sign outside the building and no directory in the foyer indicating the Commission's presence. As illustrated by widespread interest in a case involving State District Court Judge Morris Jackson (Jack) Hampton of Dallas, however, work that goes on there is vitally important to the administration of justice in Texas.

The Commission's Responsibilities and Methods

The Commission on Judicial Conduct is responsible for overseeing the conduct of all of Texas's judges, from local justices of the peace and municipal court judges up to members of the Supreme Court of Texas and the Texas Court of Criminal Appeals. The Commission hears all complaints against judges and investigates them. When a judge is found to have violated the Code of Judicial Conduct, it disciplines the judge according to the severity of the infraction. Punishments range from an admonishment for lesser violations of the Code to removal from office in the most severe cases.

The Commission's business is generally conducted in the strictest possible secrecy. There are two reasons for reviewing cases of possible judicial misconduct out of the public eye. While judges themselves must sometimes be scrutinized in order to preserve the public's faith in the integrity of the courts, judges' work also exposes them to unfounded charges by unhappy litigants. Publicizing each and every complaint and investigation undertaken by the Commission would undercut the same public confidence that requires judicial oversight in the first place. Politics further complicates the Commission's work and encourages a low public profile. Judges at all levels in Texas are elected, so they are subject to the politically motivated allegations of past and future political opponents and to complaints from interest groups opposed to their judicial philosophies.

The case involving Judge Jack Hampton illustrates both the need for judicial oversight and the need for careful handling of such cases.

Bednarski's Sentence

The Commission filed seven formal charges against Judge Hampton on February 23, 1989, after receiving 2,000 complaints from gay rights and civil liberties activists critical of the judge's handling of a murder trial involving an eighteen-year-old defendant convicted of murdering two homosexuals. Despite his reputation for imposing stiff sentences, Judge Hampton gave the defendant, Richard Lee Bednarski, only a thirty-year sentence. Though Dallas's gay community was outraged at this "light" sentence, it was not an issue in the Commission's formal charges against Hampton. Even nationally known civil liberties advocate Alan Dershowitz conceded, "Perhaps the sentence itself was appropriate, considering the fact that the defendant was a first-time offender."

Comments Published in the "Dallas Times-Herald"

While Bednarski's light sentence was insufficient grounds for charging Hampton with misconduct, the judge's public comments justifying the sentence raised questions about his impartiality. Three of the Commission's charges resulted from comments published in the *Dallas Times-Herald* on December 16, 1988. Though doubts have been raised as to whether Hampton had agreed to submit to an "interview," his statements set off a storm of protest when published the next day. In Lori Montgomery's article "Why Judge was Easy on Gay's Killer," comments attributed to Hampton suggested that Bednarski's sentence was based on the victims' history of engaging in public homosexual activities rather than on the defendant's potential threat to society.

According to the *Times-Herald* article, Judge Hampton repeatedly referred to the victims' homosexual conduct as a contributing factor in their deaths. Hampton reportedly said:

> These two guys that got killed wouldn't have been killed if they hadn't been cruising the streets picking up teenage boys. I don't care much for queers cruising the streets picking up teenage boys. I've got a teenage boy. These homosexuals by running around on weekends picking up teenage boys, they're asking for trouble. They really are. . . .
>
> Some murder victims are less innocent in their deaths than others. In those cases a defendant is unlikely to deserve a maximum sentence. I put prostitutes and gays at about the same level. If these boys had picked up two prostitutes and taken them to the woods and killed them, I'd consider that a similar case. And I'd be hard put to give somebody life for killing a prostitute.

Furthermore, Hampton reportedly dismissed the impact his comments might have on his 1990 reelection bid. As if inviting a public confrontation, Hampton said, "Just spell my name right . . . if it makes anyone mad they'll forget it by 1990."

According to the Commission's formal charges, Hampton's remarks violated three provisions of the Code of Judicial Conduct. That Hampton made any comments regarding the case constituted a violation of Canon 3A(8) of the Code which prohibits judges from commenting on "pending or impending proceedings in any court." At the time, Bednarski's motion for a new trial was pending. Hampton's statements violated two additional provisions of the Code of Judicial Conduct. Canon 2A of the Code states, "A judge should respect and comply with the law and should conduct himself or herself at all times in a manner that promotes public confidence in the integrity and impartiality of the judiciary." The Commission's charges stated that Hampton's statements "gave an appearance" that he was not impartial in the Bednarski case and that Hampton "would not be impartial in any case involving a homosexual or prostitute as a victim." Finally, Article V, Section 1-a, paragraph 6A warns against judges engaging in "willful or persistent conduct" that "casts public discredit upon the judiciary or the administration of justice." The Commission charged that Hampton's comments "were so blatantly prejudiced in suggesting that the life of a prostitute or homosexual was of lesser value than that of some other individual" as to discredit the judiciary and the administration of justice.

Remarks Released by the Associated Press

Judge Hampton's problems did not stop with the charges stemming from the *Times-Herald* article. Hampton made similar remarks to an Associated Press reporter in a tape-recorded telephone interview which was released to affiliated radio stations for broadcast. On the tape, Hampton said, "The victims were homosexual. They were out in the homosexual area picking up teenage boys. Had they not been out there trying to spread AIDS around, they'd still be alive today." Referring to complaints about the appropriateness of Bednarski's sentence, Hampton added, "It does not upset me if somebody in the Gay Alliance disagrees with me." This second episode resulted in three additional charges identical to those stemming from the *Times-Herald* quotes.

Involvement of Hampton's Staff

A final charge was lodged against Judge Hampton over his staff's handling of the flood of telephone complaints to court offices following the newspaper and radio reports. Court personnel reportedly referred callers to a Dallas attorney's office and told them to "Have a gay Christmas." This action represented a possible violation of Canon 3A(3) of the Code of Judicial Conduct, which requires that "A judge should be patient, dignified, and courteous to litigants, jurors, witnesses, lawyers, and others with whom he or she deals" and must "require similar conduct of lawyers, and of the staff, court officials, and others subject to the judge's direction and control." Hampton's staff's handling of the calls was deemed "cavalier, disdainful and undignified," and the judge was charged with failure to "require a dignified response" from his staff to the persons who called.

The Supreme Court Appoints a Master

Shortly after formal charges were lodged against Judge Hampton, the Commission asked the Texas Supreme Court to appoint a "master" to hold hearings on the charges. On May 3, 1989, the Supreme Court responded to the Commission's request by appointing former appeals court judge Robert Murray, a San Antonio Democrat, to hear the case against Hampton, a Dallas Republican. The first official hearing, convened by Murray in Dallas on May 11, 1989, marked the beginning of the "discovery" process to gather and review relevant facts pertaining to the charges against the accused judge. At the end of the discovery process, Murray ruled on October 31, 1989, that Hampton should not have commented on a pending case but was not biased and had not discredited the judiciary. The Commision must now decide whether to admonish, censure, or reprimand Judge Hampton, or to seek his removal from the bench. Should the Commission call for Hampton's removal, the petition would be heard by a panel of seven judges selected by the Texas Supreme Court from among the state's fourteen appeals courts.

Judge Hampton's Future

The Commission on Judicial Conduct's careful handling of the case of Judge Jack Hampton reveals the many pressures influencing its work. The emotional issues raised by the case have generated the intense public interest that makes the Commission's task more difficult. Groups seeking Hampton's ouster have initiated a public campaign against him while supporters have rallied to his defense.

According to William Waybourn, president of the Dallas Gay Alliance, "There is an epidemic of violence against gays in this country. If the judge gets away with this, it produces a chilling effect and sends a green light that you can do it and get by with it because there is a judge who says he agrees." Hampton's attorneys best expressed the feelings of his supporters: "The real complaint of those who seek to oust Judge Hampton is that he disapproves of the practice of homosexual sodomy." In contrast to the usual secrecy surrounding judicial investigation, the charges against Hampton were framed and have been investigated more openly to avoid any appearance of a whitewash.

The Hampton case highlights the problems of overseeing elected judges. What is to prevent an elected judge from systematically discriminating against certain segments of society when they are victimized? Those opposed to Hampton claim that his removal would be a watershed for judicial oversight in Texas, indicating that the higher standards represented by the Code of Judicial Conduct will be applied vigorously to all elected judges. If the Commission votes not to remove Hampton, it will indicate that all that is needed for a biased judge to remain in office is an electoral majority. Unless he is removed from the bench, Hampton may seek reelection in 1990. Depending on the relative strength of the groups arrayed against the judge versus the number of his supporters, Hampton may be reelected.

The Hampton case will have at least three important results. First, the Commission's ruling will attract nationwide attention and will fuel debates about gay rights and the wisdom of electing judges. Second, whatever the Commission's findings, one and perhaps both sides will be disappointed. Based on the Commission's record in other highly publicized, politically sensitive cases, a decision to admonish, censure, or reprimand Hampton is the most likely outcome. Finally, regardless of the Commission's ruling, the Hampton case will prompt other Texas judges to exercise greater restraint in their public comments on hotly debated moral and social issues of the day.

Chapter 9

Revenues, Expenditures, and Fiscal Policy

Since the adoption of the present state Constitution in 1876, fiscal policy in Texas has been dominated by the notion of a balanced budget achieved by low tax rates and low to moderate levels of spending. As late as the *fiscal year* 1990 (beginning on September 1, 1989, and ending on August 31, 1990), the state was able to continue with the traditional formula. The only significant departure took place in 1987 when the 70th Legislature enacted the largest state tax increase in U.S. history. Texas, however, continues to limp along with an antiquated tax system too dependent on variables beyond its control, including oil prices. (See the cartoon that begins this chapter.)

Fiscal Crises of the 1980s

When oil prices declined drastically after 1982, Texas experienced a critical depression that threw the state's government into a fiscal emergency. A special session of the Legislature met this crisis by enacting a number of "temporary" taxes and increasing the cost of fees and permits. The price of oil, however, continued to drop in 1984 and 1985, precipitating yet another economic decline and bringing on a second fiscal crisis for the state. Thus, when the 70th Legislature convened in January 1987, the state was facing a budget deficit of more than $1 billion for that fiscal year. As a result, tax increases were enacted to avoid the anticipated deficit. Also included in the new tax legislation was provision for funds needed to finance the 1988–1989 biennial budget.

The Texas Economy in Transition

The fiscal crises of the 1980s were the result of significant changes in the state's economy. The 1984 emergency developed because of a "national recession, the decline in oil prices, adverse weather conditions in the state, and the drop in the value of the Mexican peso."[1] The 1986 downturn was triggered by a further and more dramatic plunge in oil prices together with a sharp decline in construction and real estate sales.

Texans are slowly realizing that the state's economy will need to be restructured and reorganized for the 1990s and beyond. For a half-century the economy has relied heavily on petroleum and natural gas to account for the lion's share of the state's gross product and its tax revenue. Now, however, in the face of fiscal problems brought on by lower oil and gas prices and declining production, the state is increasingly relying on service-producing industries (e.g., transportation, public utilities, finance, insurance, real estate, legal and medical services, retail trade, and government) along with a gradual recovery of manufacturing (especially in high-technology industries, such as those involving computers, electronics, and aerospace) as well as printing and publishing.

In May 1987 the State Comptroller's Office predicted that over the succeeding 20-year period, economic recovery in Texas would be slow but steady and spread over a wider variety of businesses. One year later, the Comptroller's Office forecasted an even more promising future for the Texas economy. Its Economic Analysis Center announced in May 1989 that the Texas economy is on a road to recovery destined to lead the state back to the forefront of the nation's economic growth over the next decade. The center anticipated that the state's gross product would increase 3.5 percent per year. This is a slower rate than Texas experienced from 1970 through 1985 but faster than the projected 2.7 percent for the rest of the nation.[2]

Demands for Services

In the midst of transition in the Texas economy and continuing inflation nation-wide, citizen groups in Texas multiplied their demands for significant expansion of state expenditures for education and highways. Pressures also mounted for increased spending for prisons, welfare benefits, water supply, and state employ-ees' salaries. This predicament contributed materially to the fiscal crisis of the mid-1980s. Since the 1970s, revenue increases had permitted the Texas Legislature to satisfy many such demands without raising taxes; but in 1984 this was no longer possible. Some contributing factors are examined below.

Public School Pressures   Texas's principal policy issue in the 1980s was public education. Not since the Soviet Union's Sputnik awakened the public to the fron-tiers of space had the attention of Texans been so focused on a single issue. After the 68th Legislature adjourned in 1983 without increasing state spending for teachers' salaries, Governor Mark White appointed a distinguished special com-mittee—the Select Committee on Public Education (SCOPE). Its members included legislative leaders, educators, and other concerned citizens. Their mission was to review the entire field of public education in Texas.

Headed by H. Ross Perot, a Dallas businessman who made a fortune in the computer industry, SCOPE labored for several months before producing a package of recommendations calling for fundamental reforms in the state's public schools. One of the more controversial recommendations called for revamping the system of state funding for local schools. Perot's committee was joined by teachers' or-ganizations demanding higher salaries for classroom instructors; but the two groups disagreed on details for recruiting, retaining, and paying teachers.

Increases in public school spending exceeded $12 billion in 1988 and again in 1989. The Texas Supreme Court upheld the decision in the case of *Edgewood* v. *Kirby* in October 1989. This decision necessitated a special legislative session in early 1990, with observers predicting increases exceeding $3 billion a year for 1990–1991. Clearly, increases of this magnitude would require new fiscal policies. (*Fiscal policy* is that branch of public policy dealing with taxes, government spend-ing, public debt, and money management.)

Highway Demands   The rapidly deteriorating conditions of Texas's highway sys-tem produced a second major fiscal policy issue in the mid-1980s. Highways are usually designed to last 20 years; the average Texas highway was 18 years old in 1984.[3] Because of deterioration from excessive use and old age, replacement and repair costs that increased at a rate exceeding the rate of inflation, and new construction needed to accommodate a growing population, highway officials in 1984 projected a cost of more than $60 billion over the next 20 years.[4] They also estimated that more than 40 percent of the existing state highway system would require major repairs from 1984 through 1988. Some $5.6 billion was needed in the 1984–1985 biennium alone, but highway budgeting fell far short of these projections.

Other Stress Points   A federal court decision in 1980 condemned the over-crowded, substandard conditions in units of the Texas Department of Corrections. This decision made prison reform an important policy issue. (See pages 223–225 for details of *Ruiz* v. *Estelle* and its consequences.) Housing a fast-growing prison population while keeping within court guidelines required sharp increases in spending for prisons. Lieutenant Governor Bill Hobby called this problem "a bottomless pit" and indicated that realistic projections of future costs were almost impossible.

Because of inflation, changes in the federal welfare system, and increases in the number of welfare recipients, the $80 million per year ceiling on welfare spending for aid to dependent children and their caretakers, for example, became inadequate. A constitutional amendment adopted in 1982 fixed the ceiling at 1 percent of total state budgets. One percent of total state revenues for the 1982–1983 biennium was about $237 million; but that amount had increased to more than $400 million for the 1987–1988 biennium and $450 million for the 1990–1991 biennium.

The 1990–1991 Budget

Early in 1989 as the 71st Legislature began its regular session, there were pessimistic projections for budget shortfalls of over $500 million. Nevertheless, there was no deficit; and a $47.4 billion spending plan for the 1990 and 1991 fiscal years emerged from the appropriations process without new taxes. In fact, the Texas budget for those years included a $560 million reduction in taxes.

A state budget that reduced taxes and increased some expenditures was possible because of two major factors: (1) an expansion of the state's economy, resulting in new jobs and new industrial growth, and (2) some bookkeeping adjustments that freed funds already on hand. Many observers foresaw, however, that when the 72nd Legislature met in 1991, inflation, pressures for new and increased levels of services, and related factors would necessitate additional tax revenue.

Traditional Fiscal Policies

Traditionally, Texas fiscal policies have been shaped by widespread popular dedication to a set of basic principles. Those principles have reflected hostility to state indebtedness (deficit financing), opposition to taxes, and insistence on very limited spending for most public services.

Budget Policy

Hostility to public debt is demonstrated in constitutional and statutory provisions designed to force the state government to operate on a pay-as-you-go basis, that is, on a *balanced budget*. The Texas Constitution prohibits the state from borrowing money "except to supply casual deficiencies of revenue, repel invasion, suppress insurrection, and to defend the state in war." The comptroller of public accounts must submit to the Legislature in advance of each regular session a sworn statement of cash on hand and revenue anticipated for the coming two years. Appropriation bills enacted at that particular session and any subsequent special sessions are limited to not more than the amount certified unless passed by a four-fifths majority in each house, or unless new revenue sources are provided.

Despite these constitutional provisions, *casual deficits* (that is, unplanned shortages) occur periodically. These deficits usually arise in the *General Revenue Fund* (the fund available to the Legislature for general appropriations). Only one of over 400 funds in the state treasury, it is the critical fund in that maze of accounts. Like a fever thermometer, the General Revenue Fund measures the state's fiscal health. If the fund shows a surplus, fiscal health is good; if it reveals a deficit, fiscal health is poor. Although less than one-half of the state's expenditure comes from the General Revenue Fund, nearly all state spending affects it.

A second factor influencing budget policy is the constitutional mandate that state budgets must be prepared and enacted on a biennial basis. Thus, state agencies and legislators are forced to estimate governmental spending needs more than two years in advance. Texas's comptroller also encounters difficulty in predicting revenue collection that far in advance.

Taxing Policy

Given traditional opposition to taxes, Texans have pressured their state government to maintain a low level of taxation. When additional revenues have been needed, Texans have indicated strongly their preference for *regressive taxes* (that is, for taxes whereby the burden decreases as personal income increases).

Texas lawmakers have developed a strongly regressive tax structure. A general sales tax and selective sales taxes (for example, "sin taxes" on tobacco products and alcoholic beverages) have been especially popular. *Progressive taxes* (that is, those whereby the impact of the tax increases as income rises) have been unpopular. Thus, Texas has neither a personal income tax nor a corporate income tax, although both are authorized by the Texas Constitution.

Spending Policy

Historically, Texans have shown little enthusiasm for state spending. Consequently, public expenditures in Texas have remained relatively low in comparison with those of other state governments. Although Texans have indicated their willingness to spend for highways, roads, and other public improvements, they have demonstrated much less support for welfare programs, prisons, recreational facilities, and similar social services.

Politics of Budgeting and Fiscal Management

The state's *fiscal* (money) *management process* begins with a budget and ends with an audit. Other phases of the process include tax collection, investment of public funds, purchasing, and accounting. Each activity is important if the state is to derive maximum benefits from the money it handles.

Budgeting

A plan of financial operation is usually referred to as a *budget*. In modern state governments, budgets serve a variety of functions, each of which is important in its own right. A budget is a plan for spending; it serves as a statement of the financial condition at the close of one fiscal year and the anticipated condition at the end of the next; it also makes recommendations for the coming fiscal year. Usually two budgets are prepared and presented to the Texas Legislature in each odd-numbered year.

Legislative Budget Board In 1949, the Texas Legislature created the *Legislative Budget Board*, whose director and staff prepare a biennial budget and help draft a general appropriation bill for introduction at each regular session of the Legislature. During the 1970s, attempts were made to put state appropriations on an annual basis; however, each of the proposed constitutional changes was rejected by the voters.

Executive Budget Office Headed by an executive budget officer who works under the direction and supervision of the governor, the *Executive Budget Office* is required by statute to prepare and present a biennial budget to the Legislature within five days after the opening of each regular session. In 1989, however, Governor Bill Clements did not submit a separate executive budget to the 71st Legislature.

Budget Preparation Actual compilation of each budget begins with preparation of forms and instructions by the Legislative Budget Board and the Executive Budget Office. These materials are sent to each spending agency early each even-numbered year. For some six months thereafter, representatives of the budgeting agencies work closely with operating agency personnel in preparing departmental requests. By early fall, departmental estimates are submitted to the two budgeting agencies. These agencies then carefully analyze all requests and hold hearings with representatives of spending departments to clarify details and supply any additional information that may be needed. At the close of the hearings, usually in mid-December, budget agencies compile their estimates of expenditures into the two separately proposed budgets.

Thus, at the beginning of each regular session, legislators are normally confronted with two sets of recommendations for all state expenditures for the succeeding biennium. Since inception of the dual budgeting system, however, the Legislature has shown a marked inclination to prefer the recommendations of its own budget-making agency to those of the Executive Budget Office and the governor.

In most state governments the Governor's Office or an executive agency responsible to the governor supervises *budget execution* (the process by which a central authority in government oversees implementation of a spending plan approved by the legislative body). Incorporation of such a process in Texas state government has been strongly recommended for over a decade.[5]

In 1987, the 70th Legislature enacted a statute providing a measure of budget execution authority. Under this statute, the governor has increased power to adjust agency spending by prohibiting part of its appropriation, transferring money from one agency to another, and suggesting timing for particular expenditures. There are some limits on the governor's authority, such as a maximum 5 percent increase or 10 percent decrease in an agency's appropriation. A proposal by the governor must be published, whereupon the Legislative Budget Board may ratify, reject, or recommend changes. When the board recommends changes in the governor's proposals, the chief executive has a chance to accept or reject the board's suggestions.

In August 1987, Governor Clements and the Legislative Budget Board used this budget execution authority for the first time. They transferred some $50 million to help ease prison and jail overcrowding and upgrade mental health facilities.

Tax Collection

As Texas's *chief tax collector*, the comptroller of public accounts collects more than 90 percent of state taxes—including those on motor fuel sales, oil and gas production, chain store sales, and franchises. A franchise is a special privilege granted by a government, such as a monopoly granted to a public utility company. The Department of Highways and Public Transportation collects motor vehicle registration and certificate of title fees; the Alcoholic Beverages Commission collects liquor taxes and licensing fees; the State Board of Insurance collects insurance taxes and fees; and the Department of Public Safety collects driver's license, motor vehicle inspection, and other such fees.

Investment of Public Funds

Working under relatively restrictive state money management laws, the Texas state treasurer keeps temporary surplus funds deposited so as to gain interest income and to pay claims against the state. Recent federal legislation and improved treasury procedures have made it possible for the state to earn more interest on these funds. Among a wide range of changes made since 1981 are conversion of noninterest-bearing to interest-bearing accounts, establishment of interest-bearing Negotiable Order Withdrawal (NOW) accounts, and improved collection of the state's share of unclaimed property located in Texas. In 1983, the state treasurer was authorized to buy treasury bills from the U.S. Treasury and repurchase agreements from private banks. Thus the state's earnings have climbed. Income from interest and other investments, for example, increased from $100 million in 1981 and $329 million in 1982 to more than $1.17 billion in 1989. Treasury practices have probably been modernized as much as they can be until some current legal restrictions are removed.

Purchasing

Agencies of state government must make purchases through or under supervision of the State Purchasing and General Services Commission. It is directed to place greater emphasis on serving state agencies for which it purchases goods than on controlling what they purchase. The commission's three members are appointed by the governor, with the advice and consent of the Senate, to six-year overlapping terms. As a general rule, competitive bids by two or more suppliers are necessary for all types of purchases from state funds.

Accounting

Handling of the state's money is supervised by the comptroller of public accounts, who is held responsible by statutory provisions for maintaining a double-entry system with such ledgers and accounts as are deemed necessary. Other statutes, however, narrow the comptroller's discretion by creating numerous special funds or accounts. These are really nothing more than separate entries composed of designated revenues that must be used for financing specified activities of the state. They include constitutional trust funds, such as the Permanent School Fund and the Permanent University Fund; retirement and other trust funds, such as the Teacher Retirement and State Employee Retirement funds; constitutionally dedicated funds, such as the State Highway and Available School funds; and over 400 other special funds. Into these funds pour over $19 billion annually, amounting to some 68 percent of the state's expenditures. Because this money is usually earmarked for special purposes, it is not subject to appropriation upon the Legislature's own judgment.

Major accounting tasks of the Comptroller's Office include preparing warrants (checks) used to pay state obligations, acknowledging receipts from various revenue sources of the state, and recording information concerning receipts and expenditures in ledgers and other account books. Contrary to usual business practice, state accounts are set up on a cash rather than an accrual basis. *Cash accounting* means that expenditures are entered when the money is actually paid rather than when the obligation is incurred. This practice permits the state to create obligations in one fiscal year and to carry them over into the next fiscal year before paying. Unfortunately, it complicates the task of fiscal planning by failing to reflect an accurate picture of current finances at any given moment. The comptroller issues annual and quarterly reports that include statements of operation for the various funds of the state treasury. These reports, however, do not constitute a series of balance sheets. They are only financial statements.

Auditing

State accounts are audited under direct supervision of the state auditor, who is appointed to a two-year term by the Legislative Audit Committee with approval by two-thirds of the Senate. The auditor may be removed by the committee at any time without the privilege of a hearing. With the assistance of a sizable staff, the auditor checks financial records and transactions on a random basis after

Data processing center, Texas State Comptroller's Office. (Courtesy Bob Bullock, Comptroller of Public Accounts.)

expenditures have been made. Auditing, therefore, involves reviewing records and accounts of disbursing officers and those of custodians of all state funds.

As a check by the legislative branch of government on the integrity and efficiency of the executive branch, auditing is a necessary part of the fiscal system. The auditor is authorized to require changes in accounting or record keeping by any state agency in order to promote a more uniform system of accounts. Thus, this official has access to all state records, books, accounts, and reports and may demand assistance from state officers and employees.

Another important duty of the auditor is to examine the activities of each state agency in order to evaluate the quality of its services and to determine whether duplication of effort exists. Following each examination, the auditor makes a written report to the head of the agency. This report includes recommendations for correcting deficiencies and suggestions for improvement. Copies of each report are sent to legislators. An annual summary of all auditor's reports is prepared for the Governor's Office.

Politics of Revenue and Debt Management

Through constitutional provisions, statutes, and public pressures, Texans have sought to force the state government to operate on a balanced budget. Despite more than 30 years of such efforts, however, Texas's budget has not always

FIGURE 9.1 Net Texas State Revenue by Source, Fiscal Year 1988, All Funds (millions of dollars)

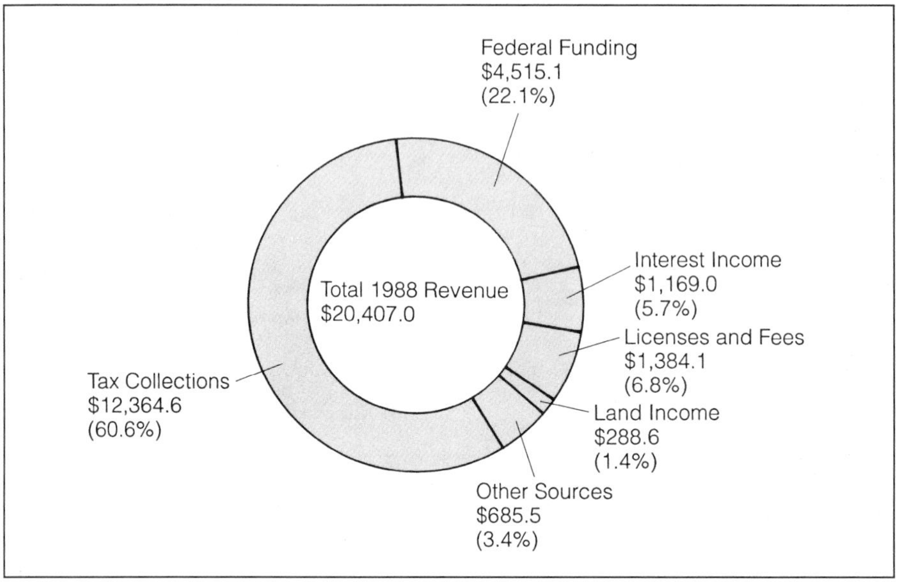

Federal Funding
$4,515.1
(22.1%)

Total 1988 Revenue
$20,407.0

Interest Income
$1,169.0
(5.7%)

Licenses and Fees
$1,384.1
(6.8%)

Tax Collections
$12,364.6
(60.6%)

Land Income
$288.6
(1.4%)

Other Sources
$685.5
(3.4%)

Source: Comptroller of Public Accounts, *Annual Financial Report, State of Texas, 1988* (Austin, 1988), p. 3.

balanced. (Reading 9.1 explores the part played by the State Comptroller's Office in balancing the Texas budget.) Undertaxation, casual deficits, and constitutional amendments authorizing borrowing have combined to produce a persistent state debt. Although the state's total revenue is not derived from taxation, it is clearly the principal source from which funds are derived. (See Figure 9.1.)

The Politics of Taxation

Imposed by governmental authority, a tax is a compulsory contribution for a public purpose rather than the personal benefit of an individual. According to generally accepted standards, each tax levied and the total tax structure should be just and equitable. Of course, there are widely varying notions of what kinds of taxes and what sort of structure can meet these standards.

Current Trends in Texas Taxation   Throughout the 1970s and well into the 1980s, five trends shaped the state's tax pattern. Foremost among the five trends was the sharp increase in revenue from taxes on oil and gas production brought about by frequent increases in oil and gas prices. A second trend was the erratic pattern of growth in revenues from oil and gas. Surges and slowdowns in domestic production of oil and gas resulted in mercurial behavior of revenues from those taxes. Another significant trend was the strong, stable growth of the sales tax as the dominant tax in the Texas system. A fourth key trend has been the steadily receding importance of the state's quantity-based consumption taxes on motor fuels, alcoholic beverages, and tobacco—sometimes referred to as selective sales taxes. A fifth trend could be identified as a series of taxes tied in one way or another to business gross receipts, such as the franchise tax (a tax on the privilege of doing business in the state), the insurance company tax, and a variety of taxes on public utilities.

An analysis of trends in state taxation in the 1980s indicates that in the 1990s there will be no single source of tax revenue likely to replace failing revenue from production taxes on natural gas and oil.[6]

Sales Taxes   By far the most important single source of tax revenue in Texas is sales taxation. Altogether, sales taxes account for almost three-fifths of all state tax revenue. The burden imposed by sales taxes on individual taxpayers varies with their particular patterns of spending. Moreover, the effective rate of taxation declines as personal income rises. For example, a sales tax of 5 percent on an automobile selling for $10,000 amounts to $500, which would be 5 percent of a $10,000-per-year income for a laborer but only 0.5 percent of a $100,000-per-year income for a business executive. As previously noted, the Texas tax system, therefore, tends to be regressive, drawing a greater percentage from the income of individuals in lower income brackets than from those in higher brackets or from businesses and corporations. Whether a regressive tax system is just and equitable depends on the perspective from which it is viewed and on the viewer's notions as to the purpose of taxation.

For almost 30 years the state has levied and collected two kinds of sales taxes: a general sales tax and a number of selective sales taxes. First imposed in 1961, the limited sales, excise, and use tax (commonly referred to as the *general sales tax*) has become the foundation of the Texas tax system. The base of the tax is the sale price of "all tangible personal property" and "the storage, use, or other consumption of tangible personal property purchased, leased, or rented." There are a number of exempted items, including receipts from water, telephone, and telegraph services; sales of goods otherwise taxed (for example, automobiles and motor fuels); food and food products (but not restaurant meals); medical supplies sold by prescription; and animals and supplies used in agricultural production. A close analysis of the general sales tax reveals that the sales tax has become the most widely accepted state tax among Texans.

Since 1931, when the Legislature imposed a sales tax on cigarettes, many items have been singled out for *selective sales taxes.* For convenience of analysis, these items may be grouped into three categories: highway user taxes (e.g., gasoline), "sin" taxes (e.g., liquor), and miscellaneous sales taxes (e.g, hotel and motel room rentals).

Business Taxes   As is the case with sales taxes, Texas imposes both general and selective business taxes. Texas businesses operating in this state pay three *general business taxes*: (1) because businesses are consumers—the sales taxes; (2) because most businesses operate in corporate form—the franchise tax; and (3) because most businesses are also employers—the unemployment compensation payroll tax. Most important of the state's selective business taxes are those on oil and gas production, insurance company gross premiums, and public utilities gross receipts. These business taxes account for more than 35 percent of the state's tax revenue.

Several kinds of supplies, machinery, and equipment purchased by Texas businesses are subject to the general sales tax, although the Legislature has exempted some machinery and equipment purchased by manufacturing industries. Goods purchased by Texas businesses for specific resale, however, have long been exempt from the general sales tax.

Another important general business tax is the *corporate franchise tax,* now some 90 years old. It is a tax imposed on corporations for the privilege of doing business in Texas. The tax is levied on the capital, surplus, and undivided profits of most corporations. Exempt from the franchise tax are banks, insurance companies, nonprofit corporations, and certain transport companies—mainly railroads and oil pipelines. A relatively high tax rate makes the Texas franchise tax the most productive franchise tax in the nation.[7]

Because of federal legislation over 50 years ago, all states now have unemployment compensation systems supported by *payroll taxes.* The payroll tax is levied against a portion of the wages and salaries paid to persons insured against unemployment.

Selective business taxes are those levied on businesses engaged in specific or selected types of commercial activities. Because of a long history of reliance on oil and natural gas taxes, Texas has depended far more than other states on *severance taxes.* Currently, however, they account for about 8.4 percent of all tax collections. A severance tax is an excise tax levied on a natural resource when it is severed (mined, pumped, or gathered) from the earth. Texas severance taxes are based on the quantity produced or on the value of the resource when severed.

The Texas *crude oil production tax* was designed with two objectives in view: to raise substantial revenue, and to assist in the regulation of oil production. In 1987, five state taxes brought in more revenue, and the prospect for a return to high revenue production from the oil tax remains uncertain. This means that Texans in the future should not count on surging oil tax revenues to meet increased spending demands. The *gas gathering tax* produces more revenue than the crude oil tax, but revenues from this tax will grow less rapidly in the future if production continues to decline. Deregulation, however, will likely trigger a short-run increase in production and price.[8]

Texas levies a selective business tax—a *gross receipts tax*—on electric, gas, gas pipeline, telephone, telegraph, and water utilities where privately owned and operated for profit. A *gross premium tax* and an *insurance administration tax* on insurance companies are other forms of selective business taxation. The 70th Legislature in 1987 added a new insurance administration tax, which imposes a 2.5 percent levy on administrative services of insurance companies.

Death Tax For many years, Texas levied a tax on beneficiaries of inheritances—a tax that was graduated according to size of inheritance and degree of relationship between beneficiary and deceased. In 1981, however, the Legislature abolished the basic Texas inheritance tax. Under the terms of new legislation, the state now collects a *death tax* equal to the amount that would go to the federal government if Texas did not levy such a tax.

Tax Burden The record-making 1987 tax package raised taxes in 30 different areas. In conjunction with existing taxes, it was anticipated that changes would produce about $5.7 billion in revenue. Even with the 1984 and 1987 tax increases, however, the State Comptroller's Office places Texas well below the national average in the tax burden imposed on its residents. During the 1987 fiscal year, Texas collected less tax money and spent less general revenue per person than any other state. An analysis prepared by the Comptroller's Office showed that the Lone Star State obtained $1,168 per person in general revenue, 32.4 percent less than the 50-state average of $1,728. The principal reason the Texas tax bill per person is the lowest in the nation is the absence of a state income tax. As a result, a significant part of the tax toll falls on Texas businesses—especially oil companies, insurance corporations, and public utilities. Based on past experience, these burdens on business operations will likely be passed on to consumers.

Nontax Revenues

Although about 60 percent of all Texas state revenue comes from the taxes analyzed above, nontax revenues are also an important source of funds. Almost half of this revenue (some 22 percent of total revenue in 1988) is derived from federal grants, but state business operations and borrowing are also significant sources of revenue.

Federal Grants-in-Aid For more than two decades, federal grants-in-aid contributed more revenue to Texas than any single tax levied by the state. When this trend was reversed in 1982, the principal losers were education, welfare, and health programs. As federal funds declined, Texas and most other states responded by reducing expenditures rather than raising taxes or redirecting expenditures.[9]

Grants-in-aid are defined as gifts of money, goods, or services from one government to another. For several years more than 80 percent of all federal grant money reaching Texas was allocated to three programs: public welfare, public education, and public transportation. Other programs receiving funds were public health, social and rehabilitation services, unemployment compensation, public safety and law enforcement, and environmental protection. (Reading 9.1 examines the relationship between Texas's tax effort and federal grants.) Federal grants to Texas exceeded $4.5 billion in fiscal year 1988.

Traditionally, many Texans have been opposed in principle to federal grants, usually on grounds that grants tend to drain away the rights and powers of the state. Nevertheless, Texas has not been reluctant to take part in programs whereby it would receive large sums of money for projects that have hearty popular approval (for example, the highway construction and maintenance program). Currently, there is not a widespread disposition to refuse federal grants in any area, although many Texans have opposed all of them in principle.

Land Revenues Texas receives a substantial amount of nontax revenue (more than $288 million in the 1988 fiscal year) from land sales, rentals, and royalties. Sales of land, sand, shell, and gravel—combined with rentals on grazing lands, building equipment, and prospecting permits—account for approximately 4 percent of this revenue. The remaining 96 percent is received primarily from oil and natural gas leases and royalties.

Miscellaneous Sources Fees, permits, and income from investments are major miscellaneous nontax sources of revenue for Texas. Fee sources include motor vehicle inspection fees, college tuition fees, other student fees, patient fees at state hospitals, and certificate-of-title fees for motor vehicles. The most significant sources of revenue based on permits are special truck and automobile permits; liquor, wine, and beer permits; and cigarette tax permits. Income from fees and permits currently approximates $680 million per year. By 1991, income from wagers on races—5 percent on horses and 6 percent on greyhounds—is expected to exceed several million dollars per year.

At any given moment, Texas actually has on hand several billions of dollars that are invested in securities or are on deposit in interest-bearing accounts. Trust funds in excess of $14.8 billion constitute the bulk of the money invested by the state (for example, the Texas Teacher Retirement Fund, the State Employee Retirement Fund, the Permanent School Fund, and the Permanent University Fund). The state's investment income from all sources currently accounts for more than $1 billion each year.

The Public Debt

When expenditures exceed income, governments finance budget shortfalls through public borrowing. Such deficit financing is essential to meet short- and long-term crises and to pay for major projects involving large amounts of money. Most state constitutions, however, severely limit the authority of state governments to incur indebtedness.

For more than 30 years, Texans have sought, through constitutional provisions and public pressures, to force the state to operate on a balanced budget. Despite those efforts, five types of state bonds authorized by constitutional amendment accounted for an indebtedness of almost $3 billion by August 31, 1988. Thus, many Texas voters approve both a balanced budget *and* bond amendments that cause the state to borrow funds.

Growth of Bonded Indebtedness The exact amount of bonded debt owed by the state fluctuates daily as new bonds are issued and sold, and as old ones are redeemed and retired. Most of the outstanding bonded debt is in the form of either *self-liquidating revenue bonds,* which are guaranteed from income produced by the activity financed (for example, college student loan funds), or *limited obligation bonds,* which are guaranteed by income from specific taxes or assessments (for example, college building bonds).

As a part of the overall financial plan enacted by the 70th Legislature, on November 3, 1987, Texas voters adopted a number of proposed constitutional amendments authorizing almost $2 billion in additional bonded indebtedness. Voters also approved the creation of two new treasury funds: one from which money could be granted or loaned to encourage economic development in the state, and another to establish an "economic stabilization" fund (popularly called the "rainy day" fund).

Continuing the strategy of asking Texas voters to approve additional bond issues rather than submit to new or increased taxes, the 71st Legislature proposed six amendments for voter consideration in a special election called for November 7, 1989. These proposed changes involved an additional $1.8 billion in bonded debt. Revenue from these bond sales would finance construction of new prison facilities, mental health and mental retardation institutions, youth correctional institutions, and statewide law enforcement facilities, as well as major repairs and renovations of such facilities. Other bond revenue would be earmarked for loans to public school districts for physical facilities, water supply, water quality, flood control, college student loans, and promotion of agricultural, new product, and small business development. Each of these proposed amendments was approved by Texas voters.

Bond Review Since 1987, specific projects to be financed with bond money require legislative approval, and any bonds issued also have to be approved by the Bond Review Board. This five-member board is composed of the governor, the lieutenant governor, the speaker of the House, the state treasurer, and the comptroller of public accounts.

The 1987 bond authorizations increased the total bonded indebtedness authorized by Texas voters to over $4 billion, although not all of that amount was actually borrowed. As a result of actions by voters in the 1989 special election, the state's authorized bonded debt was increased by an additional $1.8 billion.

Politics of Spending

Analysts of a government's fiscal policy have two ways of looking at public expenditures. One way is according to function (that is, the services being purchased: for example, education, highways, welfare, health, and protection of persons and property). (Figure 9.2 illustrates Texas's *functional expenditures* for fiscal year 1988.) The other way is according to the object of the expenditure (goods and services purchased to render the functional services: for example, wages and salaries of public employees, medical assistance to the needy, and supplies and materials).

For more than two decades, functional expenditures have centered on three principal areas: public education, public welfare, and highway construction and maintenance. Similarly, three items have led all objective expenses for most of that period: salaries and wages, medical and other assistance to the needy, and

FIGURE 9.2   Net Texas State Expenditures by Function, Fiscal Year 1988 (millions of dollars)

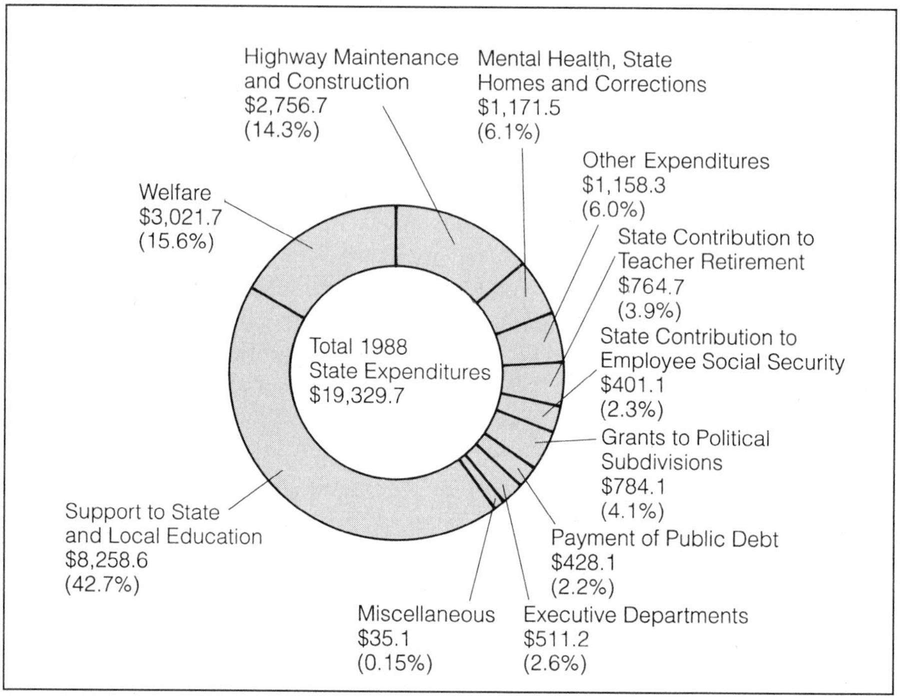

Highway Maintenance and Construction $2,756.7 (14.3%)

Mental Health, State Homes and Corrections $1,171.5 (6.1%)

Other Expenditures $1,158.3 (6.0%)

Welfare $3,021.7 (15.6%)

State Contribution to Teacher Retirement $764.7 (3.9%)

State Contribution to Employee Social Security $401.1 (2.3%)

Total 1988 State Expenditures $19,329.7

Grants to Political Subdivisions $784.1 (4.1%)

Support to State and Local Education $8,258.6 (42.7%)

Payment of Public Debt $428.1 (2.2%)

Miscellaneous $35.1 (0.15%)

Executive Departments $511.2 (2.6%)

Source: Comptroller of Public Accounts, *Annual Financial Report, State of Texas, 1988* (Austin, 1988), p. 11.

grants to public schools. The analysis below concentrates on functional expenditures, but some attention is devoted also to expenditures by object.

Spending to Purchase Services

Three factors are usually identified as significant causes for increased public demand for more and better services. First, a changing social and economic order leads to increased demand for government activity. For example, increased dependence on automobiles requires expensive highways, streets, bridges, and parking facilities; technological advances in communications, heavy industry, and energy spur demands for government regulations; and labor-management conflicts trigger public demand for government intervention. Moreover, accelerating urbanization creates new problems for government and aggravates others, including control of AIDS and other communicable diseases, collection and disposal of waste materials, and supply of water for residential and industrial purposes.

Second, a changing attitude toward the proper role of government also contributes to public demand. Traditionally, the American public expected its governments to provide few if any services. Gradually, however, this attitude has changed to that of expecting government to take positive action to promote the general welfare.

Finally, an expanded concept of democracy affects the demand for public services. For today's Americans, democracy has come to include some degree of economic equality as well as political equality. This has brought about demands for government regulation of wages, prices, and working conditions. In addition, citizens expect government to help them find jobs, provide unemployment compensation for the jobless, and stabilize prices paid to some producers, such as farmers.

Also affecting growth of services are population increases, continuing inflation, and rising unemployment. Texas government has responded to public demands primarily by increasing dollar amounts expended rather than by adding new types of services. (Reading 9.2 demonstrates the relationship between general revenue spending and state services.)

Public Schools: Kindergarten Through High School   Although public education in elementary and secondary schools is a major state function, it is administered largely by locally elected school boards.

Providing a basic education to all school-age children in Texas (more than 3 million in 1989) is the state's most expensive public service. By 1989 this activity accounted for approximately one-half of the state's expenditures (almost $9 billion per year). Projections place the cost between $10 billion and $12 billion by 1991 ($10.8 billion was budgeted for fiscal years 1990 and 1991). This educational system operates, in part, within a legal framework established by state constitutional mandates, court decisions, and legislative and executive policies. Local school officials also have legal authority to make rules and regulations.

The state has usually confined its activity to establishing minimum standards and providing basic levels of financial support. The federal government also began extending aid to public education with the Morrill Land Grant College Act of 1862 and the Smith-Hughes Vocational Education Act of 1917. But not until 1965, with the passage of the Elementary and Secondary Education Act, did the federal government's involvement become a major factor.

Since 1949, state funding policy for public education has been based on three principles that underlie the *Foundation School Program*. First, the state establishes minimum or foundation standards for various areas of public school operations. Second, the cost of the program is funded by a combination of state and local resources channeled to the local districts on an equalized basis. Rich districts, thus, should pay more of the cost from local taxes and receive less state aid, and poor districts should contribute less from local taxes and receive more state aid. Finally, local districts are authorized to enrich their programs by levying a higher local tax than that required to support the minimum program. Through this Foundation School Program, Texas provides financial support for more than 1,000 locally administered public school systems in the state.

By 1984, critics were regularly attacking the Minimum Foundation Program, the Texas Education Agency, and local school systems. Some of the problems that

David Kolasta, Houston Post

(*Authors' note:* As this cartoon suggests, the 71st Legislature in 1989 increased beginning public school teachers' salaries from a minimum of $15,200 to a minimum of $17,000, while submitting to Texas voters on November 7, 1989, a proposed constitutional amendment increasing legislators' salaries from $7,200 to $23,358, one-fourth the governor's salary in 1990–1991. This amendment was not approved.)

received the most attention were shortages of qualified teachers, demands for higher salaries, reductions in federal aid to education, erosion of the foundation program, disparity in state-local funds available to individual school districts, rapidly increasing school-age population, and growing numbers of children whose first language is not English.

In general, the Foundation School Program sets minimum standards for various areas of public school operations. The cost of these three elements—salaries, transportation, and operating expenses—is then shared by local districts and the state. Each school system's local share is based primarily on the market value of taxable property in the school district, because local schools must raise their share primarily through property taxes. Average daily attendance of pupils in the district as well as types of students and local economic conditions are used to determine the state's share, which by 1989 exceeded 90 percent of the amount needed to provide basic educational programs.

Funds to finance the Foundation School Program are allocated to each school system from the *Foundation School Fund.* This fund receives its money from the Available School Fund, the School Taxing Ability Protection Fund, and the General Revenue Fund.

The *Available School Fund* gets money from taxes and from *Permanent School Fund* earnings. After funds are withdrawn to provide free textbooks for public school pupils, the remainder goes into the Foundation School Program. A product of the 1978 Tax Relief Amendment, the *School Taxing Ability Protection Fund* was created to help, on a formula basis, local school districts offset revenue losses resulting from homestead exemptions (i.e., exclusion of a part of the value of residences from taxation) and property tax valuations based on agricultural use. The General Revenue Fund is an all-purpose treasury fund into which approximately one-half of all state money is deposited.

Prior to 1965, the federal government's role in financing public education had been confined to a few modest grant programs. The Elementary and Secondary Education Act of 1965 commits the federal government to a fund allotment system based on poverty criteria, and it promises to deliver to the states 50 percent or more of the cost of educating each eligible student. The Education of All Handicapped Children Act of 1975 requires states to provide a free and appropriate education to all school-age handicapped children. These and other federal grants for education totaled more than $700 million in the 1987 fiscal year, or about 14 percent of the total amount expended by Texas on public education programs.

Public Higher Education: Colleges, Universities, and Technical Institutes   State financing of public community/junior colleges is based on a "contact hour of instruction" rate (that is, hours of contact between instructor and students) approved for vocational/technical and academic courses. To finance their operations, these institutions use local property tax revenues, tuition fees, gifts, and state and federal grants. State aid currently provides over 60 percent of the total cost.

More than 30 state universities and technical institutes obtain basic financing from money appropriated biennially from the General Revenue Fund. They also obtain money from fees other than tuition fees (which are deposited to the General Revenue Fund), auxiliary services income (rent for campus housing and food service fees, for example), grants, gifts, and special building funds. The University of Texas and Texas A&M University systems share revenue from Permanent University Fund investments, with the University of Texas receiving two-thirds of the money and Texas A&M one-third. More than half of this money is used to finance building construction and other permanent improvements.

From 1947 to 1979, other Texas colleges and universities received construction money from a constitutional fund (the College Building Fund) supported by a state property tax. A constitutional amendment abolished the state property tax in 1982, but the Texas electorate approved a constitutional amendment that created from general revenue a special higher education assistance fund for construction and related activities.

In addition to increasing tax revenues at a record-setting rate, the 69th and 70th Legislatures also chose to curtail spending in several areas. One of the major victims of this "budget slashing" was higher education. The 69th Legislature cut spending for higher education by more than $511 million; spending cuts made by the 70th Legislature totaled almost $80 million. At the same time, enrollment in state-supported senior colleges and technical schools increased steadily. The 71st Legislature, however, increased spending for higher education by more than 17 percent.

Public Welfare Historically, responsibility for providing financial assistance to the needy belonged exclusively to state governments. Public welfare services today, however, are a prime example of a state function that is shared with the federal government.

Income maintenance programs to provide support for the nonworking poor were developed by many state governments as early as 1914. In 1935, because of rapidly growing costs, the U.S. Congress came to the aid of the states by passing the Social Security Act. It established two income maintenance programs that have survived: (1) contributory social insurance—unemployment and old-age insurance, and (2) assistance to the needy—aid to the needy, blind, aged, disabled, and dependent children. The second, commonly called welfare, was expanded to include aid to families in which a parent has been lost through death, incapacity, or absence from the home; in some states, aid is extended if a parent is unemployed.

Since 1972, when Congress enacted the Supplementary Security Income Act, the U.S. Social Security Administration has been responsible for direct payments for old-age assistance, aid to the blind, and aid to the permanently and totally disabled. Aid for families with dependent children continues, however, to be each state's responsibility, as is medical assistance to most public aid recipients in all four categories.[10] A clear trend has developed in Texas welfare spending over the past five fiscal years, a trend toward limiting expenditures.

Public Transportation Providing *public transportation services* in the United States is primarily a responsibility of state and local governments, although this function is another example of one that is financed in part by the federal government. While public transportation may involve mass transit systems (e.g., subways and railways), public transportation in Texas has come to mean a system of highways and roads designed for automobiles, trucks, and buses. Thus, state transportation policy in Texas has become highway policy.

Traditionally, transportation policy in Texas has been shaped by a number of popular commitments. First, Texans desire a highway system second to none in convenience and engineering quality. Second, they are convinced that highways should be paid for by persons using them; this idea is summed up in the popular slogan "Pay as you ride." Third, in response to pleas from the state's farmers and ranchers, Texans have committed their state to paving farm-to-market and ranch-to-market roads for most, if not all, of the state's rural dwellers.

Adoption of these transportation priorities produces two important results: Texas policy encourages motor vehicle use to the detriment of other forms of transportation (especially mass transit systems), and it favors construction of new highways and roads over the maintenance of existing ones. In the past, more than

90 percent of all highway expenditures were earmarked for new construction. Today, however, emphasis is often placed on reconstruction and maintenance.

The pay-as-you-ride system of financing roads and highways has led Texas to transfer much of the cost to users. The principal sources of highway funds are motor fuel taxes, motor vehicle registration fees, and the federal Highway Trust Fund. Federal aid to states is dedicated primarily to highway construction; maintenance and operating expenses are exclusively the responsibility of the state. Rural roads, except those designated as farm- and ranch-to-market roads, remain the fiscal responsibility of county governments. Despite low tax rates, Texas has built one of the best highway systems in the nation; but meeting future highway needs will almost surely require more money and thus higher taxes.

Public Health Programs   Virtually all the *public health programs* that Texas provides are administered by two agencies: the Texas Department of Mental Health and Mental Retardation and the Texas Department of Health. During the 1987 fiscal year the health department lost more than $6 million in general revenue, but much of this was offset by increases in federal funding. Appropriations for 1988 and 1989, however, restored state funding to its pre-1987 level. Although the Department of Mental Health and Mental Retardation also lost funding during fiscal 1987, federal grants and reimbursements made up for most of the lost revenue. The 70th Legislature increased appropriations for this department by more than 10 percent, and the 71st Legislature added an additional 26.2 percent.

Public Safety Programs   Historically, responsibility for protecting persons and property and for other *public safety programs* was first delegated to Texas local governments. Today, however, a variety of state agencies share the responsibility. The Department of Public Safety, for example, performs routine highway patrol functions, assists local law enforcement authorities in handling major crimes, and coordinates statewide efforts against lawlessness. For confinement of convicted felons, the Texas Department of Corrections operates a growing number of prison units. The Texas Youth Commission provides for the care, rehabilitation, and re-establishment into society of persons under 18 years of age who have engaged in delinquent conduct. It operates a reception center, five training schools, a treatment center for emotionally disturbed youths, and several halfway houses.

A 1983 study by the Texas Research League demonstrated that the Texas adult and juvenile corrections programs posed serious problems to be resolved by future fiscal policy decisions. The 68th Legislature in 1983 attacked the corrections problems by funding and expanding community corrections programs more than 90 percent. Succeeding legislatures, while continuing to increase appropriations for community corrections programs, have embarked on an extremely expensive construction program. In 1987, for example, the Legislature proposed and voters adopted a constitutional amendment authorizing up to $500 million in general obligation bonds to finance construction of adult and youth correction facilities and mental health and mental retardation facilities. The 71st Legislature in 1989 increased appropriations for criminal justice by 38.5 percent, or more than $500 million. In addition, Texas lawmakers proposed a $400 million general obligation bond issue for construction of new facilities for prisons, youth correctional institutions, statewide law enforcement facilities, and major repairs and renovations of such facilities. Voters on November 7, 1989, approved this proposal.

Spending to Perform Services

Governments invariably spend money to see that public services are performed. Some funds, for example, must be spent to defray day-to-day costs of government operations and to assist political subdivisions with their financial needs.

Aid to Political Subdivisions State and federal *aid to local governments* is concentrated in five major program areas: (1) public safety and law enforcement, (2) general costs of government, (3) natural resources and environmental protection, (4) highways and transportation assistance, and (5) social services. Some 11 percent of the funds allocated come from federal grants. As previously noted, state and federal governments also extend financial aid to school districts. Other political subdivisions, such as hospital and water districts, receive aid from the federal government but not from the state.

Administrative Costs During the 1988 fiscal year, the *cost of general government* at the state level was slightly more than 4 percent of total state expenditures. Spending for this item fell into four categories: (1) executive departments—for example, Governor's Office, Attorney General's Office, Comptroller's Office; (2) business regulatory commissions—for example, Railroad Commission, Public Utility Commission, Air Control Board; (3) legislative department; and (4) judicial department.

Fiscal Forecast

The decade of the 1980s was a period of fiscal adjustment for Texas state government. Officials struggled to maintain public service programs at the same level while trying to respond to demands brought about by a rapidly growing population, inflation, recession, and high interest rates. Factors over which Texas has little control also added to the state's fiscal woes. Changes in federal grant policies sharply reduced available revenues in many areas, notably in higher education. At the same time, voter resistance to big government in the form of more regulation and higher taxes grew stronger, and demands for funds by local governments increased. The Legislature responded by repeatedly raising taxes and proposing additional bonded debt, while administrations adopted strategies leading to better money management, including a more streamlined accounting system. Nevertheless, serious fiscal problems still confront the state.

When the 71st Legislature assembled in January 1989, Comptroller Bob Bullock estimated that the state would have some $45 billion to spend over the 1990–1991 biennium. But by the time the appropriations bill was passed late in May, that spending figure exceeded $47 billion. In his report to the Legislature, Comptroller

Bullock predicted that the Texas economy would continue to grow and state revenues would increase. He predicted that the Texas economy would grow 3.6 percent per year in 1990 and 1991, a little more than 1 percent faster than the national growth rate. Bullock concluded by observing, "As long as the U.S. economy remains healthy and oil prices remain relatively stable in the current range, the Texas economy will continue to prosper.[11]

Fiscal policies for the immediate future are likely to reflect at least four responses to changing economic and political conditions in Texas: (1) tax rates will gradually but steadily increase along the lines laid out by tax legislation enacted in 1984, 1986, and 1987; (2) the state will assume a growing responsibility for programs jointly funded with the federal government; (3) capital construction, maintenance, and renovation will be deferred whenever possible; and (4) public employees will demand increased compensation rates.

Despite encouraging prospects, Texas legislators may be compelled to examine new sources of revenue in the decade of the 1990s. In December 1988, for example, the Third Court of Appeals by a two to one vote reversed a district court ruling in *Edgewood ISD* v. *Kirby* that Texas's public school funding system was unconstitutional. The appellate court's decision was carried to the Texas Supreme Court in 1989. A Supreme Court ruling that the system violated the Texas Constitution required the Legislature to enact legislation aimed at curing the existing inequities in funding between "rich" and "poor" districts. Such legislation required significant increases in appropriations to local school districts and additional tax revenues. Perhaps Texas legislators will give income taxes serious consideration now that sales taxes are no longer deductible from the federal income tax and state expenditures continue to increase.

In 1987 the 70th Legislature created a 13-member Select Committee on Tax Equity composed of key legislators, private citizens, and Comptroller Bob Bullock. Its principal task was to recommend a better way to finance Texas government— including an overhaul of the state's tax system. The committee's report was submitted to the 71st Legislature, but no significant action was taken on the committee's recommendations.

Notes

1. Denise Urs, "Texas Budget Holds Up Through Recession," *Fiscal Notes,* November 1983, p. 9.
2. "Texas Economy Takes New Road," *Fiscal Notes,* May 1987, p. 1; "Record Retail Sales in 1988," *Fiscal Notes,* May 1988, p. 1.
3. Clint Winters, "Texas Highways Run into Age, Finance Problems," *Fiscal Notes,* March 1984, p. 11.
4. Denise Urs, "Funding Texas Highways: A Decision for the Legislature," *Fiscal Notes,* February 1983, p. 7.
5. See "Better Budgeting and Money Management for Texas," *Texas Research League Bulletin,* February 1971, pp. 1–10.

6. For a full analysis of these trends, see Billy Hamilton, "Past Growth Patterns Unlikely to Repeat," *Fiscal Notes,* May 1984, pp. 1–7.

7. "General Business Taxes," *TRL Analysis,* May 1983, pp. 2–3.

8. "Natural Gas Outlook Brightens," *Fiscal Notes,* July 1989, pp. 1–6.

9. Roy Bahl, *Financing State and Local Government in the 1980's* (New York: Oxford University Press, 1984), p. 14.

10. Sarah M. Morehouse, *State Politics, Parties and Policy* (New York: Holt, Rinehart and Winston, 1980), p. 33.

11. "Biennial Revenue Forecast," *Fiscal Notes,* January 1989, p. 4.

Key Terms and Concepts

fiscal year	gas gathering tax
fiscal policy	gross receipts tax
balanced budget	gross premium tax
casual deficit	insurance administration tax
General Revenue Fund	death tax
regressive tax	grant-in-aid
progressive tax	self-liquidating revenue bond
fiscal management process	limited obligation bond
budget	functional expenditure
Legislative Budget Board	Foundation School Program
Executive Budget Office	Foundation School Fund
budget execution	Available School Fund
chief tax collector	Permanent School Fund
cash accounting	School Taxing Ability Protection
general sales tax	Fund
selective sales tax	income maintenance program
general business tax	public transportation service
corporate franchise tax	public health program
payroll tax	public safety program
severance tax	aid to local governments
crude oil production tax	cost of general government

Selected Readings

9.1 Health Spending Could Boost Texas's Share of Federal Grants

This reading offers a graphic example of the direct relationship between state tax effort and federal grants-in-aid. In spite of a significant increase in revenue for health services offered by the federal government, Governor Bill Clements held fast to his rigid no-new-taxes stand. He informed the 71st Legislature that he would veto any new tax, and as a result legislators abandoned the cigarette tax increase advocated by the Comptroller's Office and endorsed by their leaders.

Compared to other states, Texas gets a relatively poor return on the tax dollars it sends to Washington, and the disparity is especially dramatic in federal grants to Texas state and local government. In 1987, Texas received only $1 in grants from the federal government for every $1.41 sent to Washington. New York paid only 75 cents to get the same federal dollar. In fact, Texas ranked 49th among states in this rate of return.

Texas Not Getting Fair Share?

"Clearly, we're not getting our fair share of federal aid," said Bob Bullock, Texas Comptroller of Public Accounts. Legislative proposals by the Comptroller's Office would allow the state to capture more federal aid money for Texas' poorest citizens. These proposals would raise the state's cigarette tax and direct the additional revenue—$166 million—to the state's Department of Human Services (TDHS). This additional spending by TDHS could win Texas $274 million more in federal matching funds for vital health and social programs.

Funding Lags

One major reason for Texas' poor showing in federal grant money is the way the state funds many of its health and social programs. Unlike other states, Texas pays much of the tab for indigent health care through programs funded *entirely* by state and local dollars. This situation is largely due to the patchwork manner in which these programs evolved. Relatively little of Texas health spending is channeled

From *Fiscal Notes*, April 1989, pp. 7–9. Reprinted by permission of the Comptroller of Public Accounts.

through the state's Medicaid program and other state programs that are eligible for matching grants of federal funds.

In 1987, Texas ranked 43rd in the nation in its per capita Medicaid expenditures, at $114.90 per person. Less than 29 percent of all Texans living in poverty are covered by Medicaid. Texas is 47th among states by this measure. By comparison, California covers more than 86 percent of its poor population. Texas's Medicaid program also does not cover many types of treatment commonly provided in other states. For example, Texas' Medicaid does not cover out-patient clinic services, but 47 other states do.

Similarly, most states provide psychiatric care for children in state mental hospitals under Medicaid, but Texas pays for these types of care entirely with state dollars, through the Texas Department of Mental Health and Mental Retardation. And Texas' Medicaid reimbursement rates for doctors and hospitals—the amounts paid to health care practitioners for medical services provided under Medicaid—are so low that they strain the financial ability of some Texas hospitals to provide indigent health care.*

The Plan

Today, the Texas cigarette tax is 26 cents per pack. Twelve other states have higher rates. Under the Comptroller's proposals, the tax would be raised by seven cents, to 33 cents per pack. Some other tobacco taxes also would be increased by an equivalent amount (about 27 percent). This increase would give Texas the fourth-highest cigarette tax in the nation, about where it ranked in the 1970s. (Texas actually had the third-highest rate throughout much of the decade, and was consistently in the top five until 1982.) This ranking may be expected to fall, since at least 15 other states are currently considering raising their cigarette tax rates. The proposed increase would generate $166 million in additional tax revenue during the 1990–91 state budget period.

This additional $166 million would be directed to TDHS, for use in state programs that are eligible for more federal aid. This would bring another $274 million in federal funds to Texas during 1990–91. Essentially, Texas could more than double its money from the rate increase by taking better advantage of federal aid. This increased medical spending could partially offset the tremendous medical costs of smoking. In recent years, a number of states have attempted to estimate these costs; the Texas Department of Health (TDH) has estimated that expenditures for the prevention, diagnosis and treatment of smoking-related diseases and medical conditions exceed $1.6 billion annually in Texas. TDH also estimates that lost income and productivity for individuals who are disabled by or die prematurely from smoking totals $1.7 billion a year.

---

*Editors' note: The 71st Legislature, however, did close the Medicaid income eligibility gap by raising the income maximum from $750 per month to $1,000 per month to coincide with the federal rule. The Legislature also changed Medicaid eligibility to give more low-income, pregnant women, children, and nursing home residents access to health care services.

The Benefits

The $166 million in state tax revenue, combined with the $274 million in federal aid, adds up to $440 million in new money for health and human services. This money could be put to work in several different ways, including: changing Medicaid eligibility to give more low-income, pregnant women, children and nursing home residents access to health services; expanding Medicaid coverage to more types of treatment; raising Medicaid reimbursements to doctors and hospitals; and expanding the state's Aid to Families with Dependent Children program.

These proposals would allow the state to finance significant improvements in state health care at a relatively low price. In effect, Texas can earn nearly two extra dollars in federal aid for each dollar of additional cigarette tax revenue, and use them to benefit the state's neediest citizens.

9.2 No New Taxes

This reading presents a concise analysis of the appropriations bill enacted by the 71st Legislature. It demonstrates how the additional $3.9 billion in state general revenue spending was distributed among the state's major expenditure items.

No new taxes were needed to finance the $47.4 billion spending plan passed during the regular session of the 71st Texas Legislature for the upcoming two-year budget period that begins September 1 [1989]. In addition legislators allowed $600 million in temporary taxes to expire at the end of 1989. In 1990, taxpayers will no longer pay the 20 percent insurance tax surcharge, the $110 annual professional fee and the franchise tax surcharge of $1.45 per $1,000 of taxable capital.

The budget for fiscal 1990–91 includes substantially higher funding for public schools and higher education, health and human services, criminal justice and employee benefits. Not counting federal and other dedicated special funds, spending from the state's key general revenue-related funds will increase by $3.9 billion, or 16.2 percent more than the 1988–89 biennium's $24.1 billion, to $28.0 billion in 1990–91.

Although no new taxes were created by the legislature, some revenue measures . . . would free up money being held back for legal challenges or restore revenue otherwise lost. . . .

As always, the new budget was a major concern of the legislative session. But because of the state's expanding economy and tax base, legislators spent little time debating new taxes. In all, lawmakers weighed the merits of more than 4,900 bills and resolutions—a new record. They debated solutions to such issues as prison

From *Fiscal Notes,* June 1989, pp. 1–2, 8–9. Reprinted by permission of the Comptroller of Public Accounts.

overcrowding, reform of public school finances and workers compensation, increased funding for higher education and human services, funding for AIDS programs and pay raises for state employees and faculty. As the regular session ended, a special session was being planned for late June concerning nonbudgetary items, chiefly workers compensation.

Spending Up by $3.9 Billion

The 1990–91 general revenue-related budget is $3.9 billion more than spending for the 1988–89 budget period. Most of the increased spending in 1990–91 will go for education. State colleges and universities will have in excess of $800 million more for a 1990–91 total of $5.4 billion, or 17.4 percent above the $4.6 billion spent in 1988–89 for higher education. Public school funding will rise by $450 million, or 4.9 percent to $10.8 billion, with most of the new money aimed at helping to equalize funds for the state's 1,000-plus school districts.

Funding for health and human resources will increase by $1.1 billion, or 26.2 percent, to $5.3 billion. Much of this additional money will be used to pay for court-ordered reforms at the state's mental health and mental retardation facilities, new federal mandates in Medicaid and public assistance programs, as well as expansion of the state's Medicaid plan.

Criminal justice spending will increase by more than $500 million, or 38.5 percent, to $1.8 billion, with most of the new money used to operate new prisons, fund new community-based prison alternatives and reduce parole and probation caseloads.

Spending on employee benefits, including a five-percent pay raise and an increase in the state's contributions to group health insurance and retirement programs, will rise by nearly $500 million, or 19.2 percent, to $3.1 billion.

Finally, spending for general government programs—one of the smallest areas of the state budget—will increase by more than $500 million, or 45.5 percent, to $1.6 billion. Much of this increase will finance a $155 million renovation of the state Capitol and make larger debt service payments of about $100 million.

More Revenue

The Texas Constitution requires that the state operate on a balanced budget, so the $28 billion in general revenue-related spending for fiscal 1990–91 must be matched by a similar level of available revenues. At the beginning of the regular legislative session, the Comptroller said the state's growing economy would produce a total of $25.6 billion in available revenues in fiscal 1990–91. In January 1989, estimated sales tax revenues were revised upwards by $150 million because of strong Christmas-season sales. In April, the Comptroller added another $210 million to his estimate, mostly due to the improving Texas economy.

Legislative adoption of the Comptroller's suggested bookkeeping bill made $958 million in special fund balances available for certification by allowing the Comptroller to transfer this money to general revenue on the last day of the next budget period, August 31, 1991. (The bill also reduces 1990–91 spending by pre-paying $150 million in Foundation School Program costs in 1989 and delaying $190 million in retirement transfers until the beginning of 1992.)

Legislative actions to fix the state's embattled insurance, franchise and utility taxes and a ruling from the Attorney General also boosted available revenues by a total of $1.1 billion. A bill that added $468 million to 1990–91 revenues will replace the existing, disputed tax rate schedule for life insurance premiums with a phased-in, flat rate. An agreement with insurers on a new method to tax property and casualty premiums added another $246 million.

Another measure passed by legislators is expected to generate $290 million in additional revenue by making some technical "fixes" to the state's corporate franchise tax, which has been sharply reduced as a revenue source by a series of court decisions. Estimated revenue from the gas utility tax—another state tax under fire in the courts—was increased by $126 million due to an Attorney General's ruling that the state's potential refund liability is limited to four years, and because of a bill that increased the tax rate. This revenue-neutral bill would restore money lost when a court decision reduced the tax base.

A pair of motor fuels bills strengthening the comptroller's enforcement powers and appropriating funds to the Travis County District Attorney for the prosecution of fuels tax fraud cases will add $31 million to 1990–91 general revenue-related tax funds.

A new requirement that will speed up payments for cigarette tax stamps at the end of the 1990–91 budget period adds another $25 million to state coffers. A bill that increases the fee for a four-year commercial driver's license from $16 to $40 will bring in another $20 million.

Finally, a bill transferring enforcement of the state's bingo laws from the Comptroller to the Texas Alcohol Beverage Commission will add $15 million to 1990–91 revenues by freeing more auditors to collect the state's major taxes instead of spending their time on bingo enforcement audits which yield no money for the state. Various other revenue bills and bookkeeping adjustments added a total of $75.4 million more in available revenues for the next two-year budget cycle.

The legislature reduced 1990–91 revenue by approving $164.4 million in additional spending for 1989. Spending this money now makes less available for 1990–91. These emergency appropriations will allow the state to comply with court-ordered reforms from Mental Health and Mental Retardation lawsuits, increase funding for junior colleges, pay off bonds for the Sematech research consortium and fund other programs.

Bonds vs. Cash

In recent years, the legislature has turned increasingly to bonds rather than cash to finance construction of major capital facilities. This legislative session was no exception. Legislation signed in April authorized the state to issue $142 million in bonds for construction and repairs at state correctional facilities. (The bonds were part of a $500 million bond package already approved by the voters in 1987.) The money will be used to finance the construction of two maximum-security prison units, renovations for a prison psychiatric facility and asbestos removal at some Texas Youth Commission buildings.

In addition to appropriation from existing bond authority, the legislature agreed to put before voters more than $400 million in new bonds to finance additional prison construction and renovations at Mental Health and Mental Retardation and Texas Youth Commission facilities. Of this total, $270 million in projects are planned for 1990–91. These will be voted on November 7 by the people.

Two bond programs initially proposed by Comptroller Bob Bullock also passed. Legislators approved a bill to use up to $100 million in state bonds to provide water and sewer facilities to about 170,000 residents of 750 *colonias* along the Texas-Mexico border. Another measure sent to the governor will allow the state to issue up to $750 million in revenue bonds to make low-interest loans available to local school districts, permitting them to build and renovate classroom facilities at the least possible cost.

Selected Bibliography

Bibliographies

Cruz, Gilberto, and James A. Irby. *Texas Bibliography*. Austin: Eakin Press, 1983.

Fleischmann, Arnold, Elliott Manley Banks, Richard H. Kraemer, and Allen Kupetz. *A Bibliography of Texas Government and Politics*. Policy Research Series No. 2. Austin: Policy Research Institute, University of Texas at Austin, March 1985.

Stevens, Michael D., and Kathleen Beatty. *The Texas Constitution and Its Impact: An Annotated Bibliography*. Houston: Institute for Urban Studies, University of Houston, 1973.

Texas State Documents. Austin: Texas State Publications Clearinghouse, Texas State Library. Monthly, supplemented with an annual, two-volume *Texas State Documents: Periodicals Supplement*. Copies of reports of state agencies, state government periodicals, and other state publications are deposited in the Texas State Library in Austin and in nearly 50 public and university libraries in all regions of Texas.

Newsletters

Austin Report. Ed. Bill Kidd. Weekly. P.O. Box 12368, Capital Station, Austin, TX 76711.

Capitol Update. Biweekly. Published by Texas State Directory Press, 1800 Nueces St., Austin, TX 78701.

Quorum Report. Ed. Harvey Kromberg. Semi-monthly. P.O. Box 2675, Austin, TX 78768.

Texas Agenda. Ed. Hilary Hylton. Biweekly. Published by Decision/Strategies, Inc. P.O. Box 90422, Austin, TX 78709.

Texas Government Newsletter. Ed. Thomas L. Whatley. Weekly. This weekly two-page newsletter is designed especially for classroom use; each issue includes a summary of current developments and in-depth treatment of a selected topic. P.O. Box 13274, Austin, TX 78711.

Texas Voter. Ed. Scherel Carver. Quarterly. Published and distributed by the League of Women Voters of Texas, 1212 Guadalupe #107, Austin, TX 78701.

Texas Weekly. Ed. Sam Kinch, Jr. Weekly. 3103 Bee Cave Road, Austin, TX 78746.

The Environment of Texas Politics

Arbingast, Stanley A., Lorrin C. Kennamer, and Michael E. Bonnine. *Atlas of Texas*. 5th rev. ed. Austin: Bureau of Business Research, University of Texas at Austin, 1976.

Asayesh, Gelareh. "As Refugees Flood in, Localities Must Foot the Bill for the American Dream." *Governing* (May 1989): 23–25, 30–31.

Barr, Alwyn. *Black Texans: A History of Negroes in Texas, 1528–1971*. Austin: Jenkins, 1973.

Brock, Ralph H. "A Lawyer's Look at the Boundaries of Texas." *Texas Bar Journal*, 50 (November 1987): 1098–1100; 50 (December 1987): 1218–1220; 51 (February 1988): 136–139.

Burka, Paul. "The Second Coming." *Texas Monthly* (March 1989): 96–97, 160. Texans, under the leadership of President George Bush, have retaken Washington, D.C.

"The Chicano Experience in the United States." *Social Science Quarterly*, 53 (March 1973): 652–942. A special topical issue with 22 articles and research notes.

Chilton, Stephen. "Defining Political Culture." *Western Political Quarterly*, 41 (September 1988): 419–445.

Crawford, Ann Fears, and Crystal Sasse Ragsdale. *Women in Texas: Their Lives, Their Experiences, Their Accomplishments.* Burnet, Tex.: Eakin Press, 1988.

Davies, Christopher S. "Life on the Edge: Urban and Industrial Evolution of Texas, Frontier Wilderness—Frontier Space." *Southwestern Historical Quarterly,* 89 (April 1986): 443–554.

De la Garza, Rodolfo O., ed. *Ignored Voices: Public Opinion Polls and the Latino Community.* Austin: University of Texas Press, 1987.

Fehrenbach, T. R. *Seven Keys to Texas.* El Paso: Texas Western Press, 1983.

Fitzpatrick, Jody L., and Rodney E. Hero. "Political Culture and Political Characteristics of the American States: A Consideration of Some Old and New Questions." *Western Political Quarterly,* 41 (March 1988): 145–153.

Golden, Gayle. "Tunnel Visions." *Dallas Life Magazine* (28 February 1988): 8–10, 12–13, 16, 18, 21–23. How politicians and scientists sought the Super Collider for North Texas.

Green, Michael R. "'To the People of Texas and All Americans in the World.'" *Southwestern Historical Quarterly,* 91 (April 1988): 483–508. Concerning Lt. Col. William Barret Travis's message from the Alamo dated 24 February 1836.

Jordan, Terry G. "A Century and a Half of Ethnic Change in Texas, 1836–1986." *Southwestern Historical Quarterly,* 89 (April 1986): 385–422.

———, with John L. Bean, Jr., and William M. Holmes. *Texas: A Geography.* Boulder, Colo.: Westview Press, 1984.

Langley, Lester D. *MexAmerica: Two Countries, One Future.* New York: Crown Publishers, 1988. A study of the impact of Mexican culture on the United States.

Martinez, Oscar J. *Troublesome Border.* Tucson: University of Arizona Press, 1988. Problems of the Mexican-United States border as viewed by the governments and people involved.

"The Mexican Origin Experience in the United States." *Social Science Quarterly,* 65 (June 1984): 241–679. A special topical issue with 35 articles and research notes.

Montejano, David. *Anglos and Mexicans in the Making of Texas: 1836–1986.* Austin: University of Texas Press, 1987.

Newport, John Paul. "Texas Faces Up to a Tougher Future." *Fortune* (March 1989): 102–103, 106. The author describes Texas state government as "anything but visionary."

Pearce, James, and Jeffery W. Gunther. "Illegal Immigration from Mexico: Effects on the Texas Economy." *Southwest Journal of Business and Economics* 6 (Winter/Spring 1989): 28–38.

Penkalski, Janice. "Dual Cultures Shape Experience." *State Government* (January 1989): 16–17. Includes experiences of Texas Supreme Court Justice Raul Gonzalez and state Senator Judith Zaffirini.

Richardson, Rupert, Ernest Wallace, and Adrian N. Anderson. *Texas: The Lone Star State.* 5th ed. Englewood Cliffs, N.J.: Prentice-Hall, 1988.

Sherman, Max, ed. *The Future of Texas.* Austin: Lyndon B. Johnson School of Public Affairs, University of Texas at Austin, 1988. Thirty distinguished Texans examine current problems and issues facing the state in the 1990s.

Stephens, A. Ray, and William M. Holmes. *Historical Atlas of Texas.* Norman: University of Oklahoma Press, 1987.

The Texians and the Texans. San Antonio: University of Texas Institute of Texan Cultures, 1970–. A series of over 20 pamphlets and books, each dealing with an ethnic group—Anglo-Americans, Afro-Americans, Chinese Texans, Mexican Texans, Wendish Texans, and so on.

Whisenhunt, Donald. *The Five States of Texas: An Immodest Proposal.* Austin: Eakin Press, 1987.

Federalism and the Texas Constitution

Analyses of Proposed Constitutional Amendments Appearing on the . . . Ballot. Austin: Texas Legislative Council. Brief analysis and text of proposed amendments. Annual.

Braden, George D. *Citizen's Guide to the Proposed New Texas Constitution.* Institute of Urban Studies, University of Houston. Austin: Sterling Swift, 1975.

Braden, George D., et al. *The Constitution of the State of Texas: An Annotated and Comparative Analysis.* 2 vols. Austin: Texas Advisory Commission on Intergovernmental Relations, 1977.

Deaton, Charles. *A Voter's Guide to the 1974 Texas Constitutional Convention: A Description of the Most Important Roll-call Votes Taken During the 1974 Constitutional Convention, with the Voting Records of the 181 Legislator-Delegates Fully Shown.* Austin: Texas Government Newsletter, 1975.

Ericson, Joe E. "Origins of the Texas Bill of Rights." *Southwestern Historical Quarterly,* 62 (April 1959): 457–466.

Gantt, Fred, Jr. *The Impact of the Texas Constitution on the Executive.* Houston: Institute for Urban Studies, University of Houston, 1973.

Harrington, James C. "Once Again, a Texas Court Champions Free Speech." *Texas Lawyer* (12 June 1989): 28. Concerning Justice Raul Gonzalez's opinion in *Casso* v. *Brand,* growing out of local politics involving Othal Brand, McAllen's mayor, and Dr. Ramiro Casso, a physician and political activist.

———. *The Texas Bill of Rights: Commentary and Litigation Manual.* Austin: Butterworth Legal Publishers, 1987.

House Research Organization. *Constitutional Amendments.* Austin: Texas House of Representatives, annual. Background and analysis of proposed constitutional amendments, with supporting and opposing arguments.

McKay, Seth S. *Debates in the Texas Constitutional Convention of 1875.* Austin: University of Texas Press, 1930.

———. *Making the Texas Constitution of 1876.* Philadelphia: University of Pennsylvania Press, 1924.

———. *Seven Decades of the Texas Constitution of 1876.* Lubbock, 1942.

May, Janice C. "Constitutional Amendment and Revision Revisited." *Publius,* 17 (Winter 1987): 153–179.

———. "Texas Constitutional Revision: Lessons and Laments." *National Civic Review,* 66 (February 1977): 64–69.

———. *The Texas Constitutional Revision Experience in the '70s.* Austin: Sterling Swift, 1975.

Ponton, Arvel (Rod) III. "Sources of Liberty in the Texas Bill of Rights." *St. Mary's Law Journal* 20:1 (1988): 91–120.

Spurgin, John H. "Delegate Groups in the Constitutional Convention." *Texas Journal of Political Studies,* 1 (Fall 1978): 86–92.

Tarr, G. Alan, and Mary Cornelia Porter. "Introduction: State Constitutions and State Constitutional Law." *Publius,* 17 (Winter 1987): 1–12.

Texas Constitution Convention. *Record of Proceedings: Official Journals,* 8 January–30 July 1974. 2 vols. Austin, 1974.

Texas Constitutional Revision Commission. *A New Constitution for Texas: Text, Explanation, Commentary.* Austin, November 1973.

Vernon's Annotated Constitution of the State of Texas. 3 vols. St. Paul, Minn.: West, 1955. Vol. 3 contains texts of the early constitutions and organic laws of Texas.

Local Governments

Abbott, Carl. *The New Urban America: Growth and Politics in Sunbelt Cities.* Rev. ed. Chapel Hill: University of North Carolina Press, 1987. Detailed treatment of San Antonio.

Atkinson, Jim. "The War Zone." *Texas Monthly* (November 1988): 104–111, 172, 174, 176, 178, 180–181. A vivid description of a South Dallas area dominated by Jamaican crack pushers.

Barrett, William. "Clear as Mud." *Forbes* (15 June 1987): 96–98. Report on default of bond payment by Municipal Utility District No. 19 near Houston.

Bauman, Kit. "The View from City Hall." *D* (February 1988): 62–64, 137–138. A portrait of Richard Knight, Dallas's first black city manager.

Bland, Robert L. *Financing City Government in Texas: A Revenue Manual for City Officials.* Austin: Texas Municipal League, 1986.

Bullard, Robert D. *Invisible Houston: The Black Experience in Boom and Bust.* College Station: Texas A&M University Press, 1987.

Cole, Richard L., Ann Crowley Smith, and Delbert A. Taebel. *Urban Life in Texas: A Statistical Profile and Assessment of the Largest Cities.* Austin: University of Texas Press, 1986. Provides a yardstick for comparing the quality of life in each of the state's 52 cities with a population over 25,000 according to the 1980 census.

Davidson, Chandler, and Luis Ricardo Fraga. "Slating Groups as Parties in a Nonpartisan Setting." *Western Political Quarterly,* 41 (June 1988): 373–390. Case studies of groups in Abilene (Citizens for Better Government), Dallas (Citizens' Charter Associaton), San Antonio (Good Government League), and Wichita Falls (Committee for Good Government).

Dickson, James G. *Politics of the Texas Sheriff: From Frontier to Bureaucracy.* Boston: American Press, 1983.

Dubose, Louis. "Hispanic Power in the Panhandle." *Texas Observer* (15 January 1988): 10–12. Community politics in Hereford.

Elkind, Peter. "Cities in Bondage." *Texas Monthly* (August 1987): 104–106, 133, 149–154. How financial adviser Decker Jackson and his First Southwest Company, a Dallas-based investment firm, help cities, counties, and other units of government to issue tax exempt bonds that finance the construction of roads, schools, jails, and other public works.

Feagin, Joe R. *Free Enterprise City: Houston in Political and Economic Perspective.* New Brunswick, N.J.: Rutgers University Press, 1988.

Fleischmann, Arnold. "The Politics of Annexation: A Preliminary Assessment of Competing Paradigms." *Social Science Quarterly,* 67 (March 1986): 128–142. A study of San Antonio and Milwaukee.

Fletcher, Riley E. "Procedures for Adopting a Home Rule Charter." *Texas Town & City* (November 1986): 5–8, 10–11.

Floyd, Richard. *General Ordinance-Making Powers for County Governments in Texas.* College Station: Texas Real Estate Research Center, 1985. A review of continuing debate over the proposal.

Foley, Douglas E., with Clarice Mota, Donald E. Post, and Ignacio Lozano. *From Peones to Politicos: Class and Ethnicity in a South Texas Town, 1900–1987.* Austin: University of Texas Press, 1988.

Franks, Jeff. "High Noon or Just a Rube?" *San Antonio Monthly* (July 1987): 28–33, 88. Loss of a Democratic primary contest for constable in 1982 led to Harlon Copeland's election as the Republican sheriff of Bexar County.

Graves, Karen. "So You've Been Elected—Now What?" *Texas Town & City* (May 1989): 7, 11, 19. Tips for a newly elected city council member.

"Houston Leads Texas' Recovery." *Fiscal Notes* (August 1989): 1–9. Economic development in Texas's seven largest cities.

Hurt, Harry, III. "A Trust Corrupted, a City Betrayed." *Texas Monthly* (February 1986): 98–103, 175–181, 184, 190; (March 1986): 138–142, 208–213, 222. Hermann Hospital and the Hermann estate scandal.

Johnson, David R., John A. Booth, and Richard J. Harris, eds. *The Politics of San Antonio: Community, Progress, and Power.* Lincoln, Neb.: University of Nebraska Press, 1983.

Kincaid, John, John R. Todd, and James L. Danielson. "The Challenge of New Communities to Public Administration in Texas: The Colony as an Exemplary Case." *Texas Journal of Political Studies,* 6 (Fall–Winter 1983–1984): 3–22.

Morgan, George T., Jr., and John O. King. *The Woodlands: New Community Development, 1964–1983.* College Station: Texas A&M University Press, 1987.

Municipal Election Law Handbook. Compiled and edited annually by Glen G. Shuffler. Austin: Hart Graphics.

Murray, Richard, and Kent L. Tedin. "The Emergence of Two-Party Competition in the Sunbelt: The Case of Houston." In *Political Parties in Local Areas,* pp. 39–62. Edited by William Crotsy. Knoxville: University of Tennessee Press, 1987.

Newell, Charldean, and James J. Glass. "City Managers and School Superintendents." *The Municipal Matrix* 21 (March 1989): 1–4.

Orum, Anthony M. *Power, Money, & the People: The Making of Modern Austin.* Austin: Texas Monthly Press, 1987.

Perrenod, Virginia Marion. *Special Districts, Special Purposes: Fringe Governments and Urban Problems in the Houston Area.* College Station: Texas A&M Press, 1984.

"Planning a City Bond Election Campaign." *Texas Town & City* (March 1986): 48–53.

Rips, Geoffrey. "A Tale of Two Cities." *Texas Observer* (29 May 1987): 17–19. Two images of San Antonio.

Reinert, Al. "This Water Is My Water." *Texas Monthly* (November 1988): 128–131, 165–166, 168, 170. Conflict among counties comprising the Edwards Underground Water District.

Seib, Philip. *Dallas: Chasing the Urban Dream.* Dallas: Pressworks, 1986.

Sharp, Cecil. "Our Man Downtown." *D* (March 1988): 60–62, 106, 108, 110. Portrait of John Wiley Price, Dallas County's black commissioner.

"Texas Municipal Taxation and Debt." *Texas Town & City* (March 1989): 5, 7, 9, 12–13, 15–19, 21, 23, 25, 27–29. Results of the Texas Municipal League's annual survey provide fiscal data for 573 cities ranked by population from Houston to Quintana.

Tomsho, Robert. "Not in My Neighborhood." *Dallas Life Magazine* (8 January 1989): 8–11, 15–19. Public housing in Dallas.

Weaver, Alan. "The Briefcase Blacks." *D* (May 1989): 76–77, 87–88. Prospects for new political leadership within Dallas's black community.

Whitley, Glenna. "Duel on the Nile." *D* (February 1989): 64–67, 101–104. How Dallas beat San Antonio in competition for Egypt's Ramses exhibit.

———. "Making the Grade." *Texas Monthly* (December 1988): 116–119, 146, 148, 150–152, 154. Challenges facing Dr. Marvin Edwards, superintendent of the Dallas Independent School District.

Wilkerson, George. "Austin Community College: A Case Study in Local Politics." *3rd Coast: The Magazine of Austin* (September 1986): 48–54, 77–78.

The Politics of Elections and Parties

Bailey, Brad. "Mad, Mad Mattox." *D* (October 1989): 86–89, 99, 101–103. Political profile of Jim Mattox.

Borges, Walter. "Select Groups Bankrolled '88 Supreme Court Races." *Texas Lawyer* (24 April 1989): 1, 18–21. Includes data on leading law firms' contributions and the candidates who received the campaign money.

Burka, Paul. "Primary Lessons." *Texas Monthly* (June 1986): 104–105. Political realignment in Texas in 1986.

Citizens at Last! The Women's Suffrage Movement in Texas. Austin: Alice C. Temple, 1987. Includes introduction and an essay by A. Elizabeth Taylor, photographs, and documents.

Cottrell, Charles L., and R. Michael Stevens. "The 1975 Voting Rights Act and San Antonio, Texas: Toward a Federal Guarantee of a Republican Form of Local Government." *Publius,* 8 (Winter 1978): 79–99.

Denison, Dave. "Are We There Yet?" *Texas Observer* (13 June 1986): 6–8. Is Texas a two-party state?

———. "Election Day in Lorena." *Texas Observer* (25 November 1988): 6–8.

Donovan, Jacqueline, and Edwin S. Davis. "Trends Toward a Two-Party System in Texas: Republican Progress from 1968 to 1978." *Texas Journal of Political Studies,* 1 (Spring 1979): 77–80.

Dubose, Louis. "Invisible Army: The Christian Right at the Republican Convention." *Texas Observer* (1 July 1988): 8–10.

Dugger, Ronnie. "Ballot Security." *Texas Observer* (19 May 1989): 11–12. Attorney General Jim Mattox (Democrat) and Secretary of State Jack Rains (Republican) clash over testing the state's computerized vote-counting machines as required by H.B. 1412 enacted in 1987.

———. "Democracy in the Computer Age." *Texas Observer* (11 November 1988): 1, 6–22. Questions raised by computerized vote-counting in Texas and elsewhere in the United States.

Dyer, James A., Arnold Vedlitz, and David B. Hill. "New Voters, Switchers, and Political Party Realignment in Texas." *Western Political Quarterly,* 41 (March 1988): 155–167.

Garcia, Ignacio. *United We Win: The Rise and Fall of La Raza Unida Party.* Tucson, Ariz.: MASRC Press, 1989.

Harrington, James C. "In Praise of Willie Velasquez." *Texas Lawyer* (27 June 1988): 22.

Hart, Patricia Kilday. "Country Boys." *Texas Monthly* (July 1988): 90, 92, 94–95. Democratic party politics involved in selecting state senatorial candidate Steve Carriker to run in a special election.

———. "Getting Serious." *Texas Monthly* (September 1988): 114, 116–118. How Ann Richards used her keynote speech at the Democratic presidential convention in Atlanta to ignite her gubernatorial campaign.

Hightower, Jim. "Raising Issues, Hope and Hell." *Nation* (6 February 1989): 160, 162–164.

Hightower, Jim, and Dave Denison. "The Senate Can Wait." *Texas Observer* (27 January 1989): 6–11. A slightly edited transcript of an interview in which Hightower tells of his plans to run for another term as commissioner of agriculture.

Holcombe, John. "The 1982 Legislative Elections in Texas." *Texas Journal of Political Studies,* 5 (Spring–Summer 1983): 10–18.

Knaggs, John R. *Two-Party Texas: The John Tower Era, 1961–1984.* Austin: Eakin Press, 1986.

Lenz, Mary. "The Emerging Hispanic Vote." *Texas Observer* (20 February 1987): 11–13.

Morehead, Richard. *50 Years in Texas Politics—From Roosevelt to Reagan—From the Fergusons to Clements.* Burnet, Tex.: Eakin Press, 1982.

Murchison, William. "How to Start a Landslide: Texas." *National Review* (7 November 1988): 48–49. How George Bush went after the "Bubba vote" in Texas.

Olien, Roger M. *From Token to Triumph: The Texas Republicans Since 1920.* Dallas: S.M.U. Press, 1982.

Olson, Edward C. "Campaign Spending in Texas Legislative Elections." *Texas Journal of Political Studies,* 6 (Fall–Winter 1983–1984): 40–53.

Richards, Ann, with Peter Knobler. *Straight from the Heart: My Life in Politics and Other Places.* New York: Simon and Schuster, 1989.

Shockley, John. *Chicano Revolt in a Texas Town.* Notre Dame, Ind.: University of Notre Dame Press, 1974.

Stanley, Jeanie R. "Party Realignment and the 1986 Texas Election." *Texas Journal of Political Studies,* 9 (Spring/Summer 1987): 3–13.

Tedin, Kent L., and Richard W. Murray. "Dynamics of Candidate Choice in a State Election." *Journal of Politics,* 43 (May 1981): 435–455. Primary and general election patterns for nomination and election of the Texas attorney general.

Texas Election Laws. Compiled and edited by Glen G. Shuffler after each regular session of the Texas Legislature. Austin: Hart Graphics.

Tomsho, Robert. "The Judges Who Switched." *Dallas Life Magazine* (14 April 1985): 10–14, 16, 40, 42, 44, 46. They switched from the Democratic party to the Republican party.

Velasquez, Willie. "542 Campaigns: The Southwest Voter Registration and Education Project." *Southern Exposure* (February 1984): 46–48.

"Willie Velasquez, 1944–1988." *Texas Observer* (29 July 1988): 1, 3, 6, 13. Cover, editorial, and articles by eight authors concerning the life and work of Texas's most successful political organizer.

The Politics of Interest Groups

Allsup, Carl. *The American G.I. Forum: Origins and Evolution.* Austin: Center for Mexican American Studies of the University of Texas, 1982.

Berry, Jeffrey M. *The Interest Group Society.* Glenview, Ill.: Scott, Foresman/Little, Brown, 1989.

Borges, Walter, and Robert Elder, Jr. "Requiem for a Law Lobbyist." *Texas Lawyer* (5 June 1989): 1, 8. How Jack Sampson, a University of Texas law professor, lobbied unsuccessfully for an alimony bill in the 71st Legislature.

Curtis, Tom. "Texas' Nuclear Neighbor." *Texas Monthly* (June 1989): 70, 72, 74. Does the Waste Isolation Pilot Plant near Carlsbad, New Mexico, pose a hazard to Texas?

Denison, Dave. "An Agenda for Progess." *Texas Observer* (10 February 1989): 6–7. Based on an interview with organizer Ernesto Cortes, Jr., who directs the Industrial Areas Foundation.

Dubose, Louis. "Going Critical: South Texas Prepares for Nuclear Power." *Texas Observer* (26 February 1988): 18–20. Some criticisms of the multi-billion-dollar South Texas Nuclear Project.

Fitzgerald, Kathleen. "Bidding for Influence: Special Interests Launch a Campaign Spending War." *Texas Observer* (24 October 1987): 8–11.

Garcia, John A., and Rodolfo de la Garza. "Mobilizing the Mexican Immigrant: The Role of Mexican-American Organizations." *Western Political Quarterly,* 38 (December 1985): 551–564.

Haag, Lynn Swann. "Starting a Successful PAC." *Dallas* (April 1980): 69–73.

Harrigan, Stephen. "Worked to Death." *Texas Monthly* (October 1988): 128–133, 192–193, 196, 198–200, 207. How industrial pollution, silt, and salt are devastating marine life and vegetation in Galveston Bay.

Marquez, Benjamin. "The Politics of Race and Class: The League of United Latin American Citizens in the Post–World War II Period." *Social Science Quarterly,* 66 (March 1987): 84–101.

"The People's Lobby." *Texas Observer* (27 January 1989): 14–20. Eleven of Texas's leading public interest lobbyists outline their agendas for the regular session of the 71st Legislature.

Pickett, Sandra. "Liberty, Texas: The Case of Rose Chemical Company." *Texas Town & City* (March 1989): 24, 26, 29–30, 33. Liberty's responsibility for sharing clean-up costs for a hazardous waste disposal site operated by the bankrupt Rose Chemical Company in Holden, Missouri.

Piltz, Rick. *Hazardous Waste: Gross National By-product.* House Study Group Special Report No. 100. Austin: Texas House of Representatives, 24 February 1984.

Presley, James. "Citizens Opposing Pollution." *Texas Observer* (18 December 1987): 11–16. Resistance to Thermal Kinetic's plan for establishing a hazardous waste incineration plant at Lone Star in East Texas.

———. "Toxicana, U.S.A." *Texas Observer* (10 March 1989): 1, 8–12. Environmentalists organize to clean up Texarkana and other places afflicted with toxic waste.

Reavis, Dick J. "Unionbusters." *Texas Monthly* (June 1986): 126–131, 175–178, 180–183. Challenging the Longshoremen's Union on the Houston waterfront.

San Miguel, Guadalupe, Jr. *"Let Them Take Heed": Mexican Americans and the Campaign for Educational Equality in Texas, 1910–1981.* Austin: University of Texas Press, 1987.

Schwartz, John. "Birth of a Lobby." *Texas Monthly* (April 1985): 160, 162–165. How the Texas Computer Industry Council was organized.

Surratt, Marshall. "Utility Settlement Divides Opponents of North Texas Nuke." *Texas Observer* (30 June 1989): 1, 6–8. Citizens Association for Sound Energy (CASE) drops its lawsuit against Texas Utilities Company.

Thompson, Doug. "PAC in the Big Bucks." *Campaigns and Elections* (May/June 1988): 53–57.

Yoffe, Emily. "A Dirty, Rotten Mess." *Texas Monthly* (February 1989): 90–93, 128–133. Problems of Houston's McCarty Road landfill and other waste disposal sites in Texas.

The Legislature

Burka, Paul. "Doing the Legislature a Favor." *Texas Monthly* (May 1989): 5–6. The author argues against higher pay for Texas legislators.

Button, Betty J., and Allen J. Dietz. *Making a Difference: A Manual on Active Participation in the Texas Legislative Process.* Rev. ed. Austin: Button and Dietz, 1988.

Chafin, Tom. "Lawyer Role in Assemblies Diminishes." *Texas Lawyer* (2 February 1987): 14. Reasons why the percentage of attorneys in the Texas House of Representatives declined from 48 percent to 35 percent between 1977 and 1986.

"Communicating with Your Legislators." *Texas Town & City* (January 1989): 9–10. Tips on how to do it effectively.

Deaton, Charles. *The Year They Threw the Rascals Out.* Austin: Shoal Creek Press, 1973. Political results of the Sharpstown scandal.

Denison, Dave. "The 70th Day." *Texas Observer* (7 April 1989): 1, 3–6. The 71st Regular Legislative Session at midpoint.

———. "Flag-Burning in Texas." *Texas Observer* (4 August 1989): 1, 6–9. How the Texas Legislature responded to the U.S. Supreme Court's ruling in *Texas* v. *Johnson* (1989).

———. "Legislative Roundup." *Texas Observer* (30 June 1989): 18–21. Second part of a critique of the regular session of the 71st Legislature.

———. "The Worst Session in Memory (Almost)." *Texas Observer* (16 June 1989): 18–26. First part of a critique of the regular session of the 71st Legislature.

Dewlin, Al. *The Session.* New York: Doubleday, 1981. A novel about the Texas Legislature.

Dubose, Bert, and Glenn Utter. "Formal and Informal Rules: Regulating Public Officials' Behavior." *Texas Journal of Political Studies,* 10 (Fall/Winter 1988): 3–16. An examination of the Texas Speaker's Race Act of 1973.

Dubose, Louis. "The Din of Inequity." *Texas Observer* (16 June 1989): 26–27. Financing public education in the 71st Legislature.

Dugger, Ronnie. "Return of the Killer Bees." *Texas Observer* (19 May 1989): 7–9. Tenth-year reunion of the 12 senators who defied Lieutenant Governor Bill Hobby.

Harmel, Robert. "Minority Partisanship in One-Party Predominant Legislatures: A Five-State Study." *Journal of Politics,* 48 (August 1986): 729–740.

Harmel, Robert, and Keith E. Hamm. "Development of a Party Role in a No-party Legislature." *Western Political Quarterly,* 39 (March 1986): 79–92.

Heard, Robert. *The Miracle of the Killer Bees: Twelve Senators Who Changed Texas Politics.* Austin: Honey Hill Publishing Co., 1981. How a dozen legislators broke a Senate quorum in order to kill a bill that would have allowed conservative Democrats to vote for John Connally in a Republican presidential primary in March 1980 and then vote for conservative Democrats in a regular Democratic primary in May 1980.

Hinojosa, Juan, Jr. "The Mexican-American Caucus." *Texas Journal of Political Studies,* 7 (Spring–Summer 1985): 27–32.

How a Bill Becomes a Law: Rules for the . . . [Texas] Legislature. Austin: House Research Organization, Texas House of Representatives. Biennial.

Katz, Harvey. *Shadow on the Alamo: New Heroes Fight Old Corruption in Texas.* Garden City, N.Y.: Doubleday, 1972. About the Sharpstown scandal.

"Key Votes: A Guide to the Observer's Record Vote Count." *Texas Observer* (16 June 1989): 28–31. Floor votes during the 71st regular session of the Texas Legislature.

Kinch, Sam, Jr., and Ben Proctor. *Texas Under a Cloud.* Austin: Jenkins, 1972. About the Sharpstown scandal.

Major Issues of the . . . [Texas] Legislature. Austin: House Research Organization, Texas House of Representatives. Prepared biennially by the House Research Organization staff, this publication provides a summary of many major issues—including important bills that did not pass in a regular session and subsequent special sessions.

Member Profile Series on the Texas Legislature. Austin: Public Policy Information Fund, 1989–. Each legislator's profile provides documentation on biographical background, campaign and personal finance, legislative record, and demographics of the legislative district.

Moss, Kathryn. "The Catalytic Effect of a Federal Court Decision on a State Legislature." *Law and Society Review,* 19 (1985): 147–157. Chronicles events from *Luna* v. *Van Zandt* (1982) to enactment of S.B. 213 by the Texas Legislature (1983) requiring a mental health hearing within 72 hours after a person thought to be mentally ill has been placed under protective custody.

Pearson, William M., and Littleton Sanders. "An Assessment of Sunset in Texas: Attitudes of Three Groups." *Texas Journal of Political Studies,* 3 (Spring 1981): 20–32.

Presiding Officers of the Texas Legislature, 1846–1982. Austin: Texas Legislative Council, 1982. Provides a brief account of the life and work of each speaker and each lieutenant governor during this period.

Texas Legislative Handbook. Austin: Texas State Directory, Inc. Published biennially. Contains photos of all state legislators.

Texas Legislative Manual. Austin: Texas State Directory, Inc., 1984. Provides basic details on organization and procedures of the Texas Legislature.

Texas Monthly Staff. "The Ten Best and the Ten Worst Legislators." *Texas Monthly.* Biennial feature in the July issue following each regular session, beginning with the 63rd in 1973.

Tucker, Harvey J. "Legislative Logjams: A Comparative State Analysis." *Western Political Quarterly,* 38 (September 1985): 432–446.

———. "Legislative Workload Congestion in Texas." *Journal of Politics,* 49 (May 1987): 565–578.

Whatley, Thomas L. *A Voter's Guide to the . . . [Texas] Legislature.* Austin: Texas Government Newsletter. Published biennially since 1973, the *Voters Guide* provides a compilation and explanation of significant votes cast by senators and representatives during a regular session and subsequent special sessions.

The Executive

Buchholz, Brad. "Trucking Tug-of-War." *Texas Business* (August 1988): 49–50. About shippers, truckers, and regulation by the Texas Railroad Commission.

Case, Ken. "The Secret Life of Ruben Johnson." *Third Coast* (April 1986): 19–37; (May 1986): 20–34. A case study of banking and politics involving a former member of the Banking Section of the Texas Finance Commission.

Conason, Joe. "Robert Mosbacher's Grand Scheme." *Texas Observer* (28 April 1989): 11–15. How registered Republican Virgil Knox exposed the questionable activities of Houston's Grand Parkway Association, the Texas Highway Commission, Walt Mischer, Jr., Robert Mosbacher (secretary of commerce in the Bush administration), and others.

Crawford, Ann Fears, and Jack Keever. *John B.Connally: Portrait in Power.* Austin: Jenkins, 1973.

Davis, Edwin S. "Rule Making Activity of Selected Texas Regulatory Agencies." *Texas Journal of Political Studies,* 8 (Fall/Winter 1986): 26–36.

Davis, Mary Alice. *Disciplining the Doctors: Medical Regulation in Texas.* Austin: House Research Organization, Texas House of Representatives, 10 March 1987.

De Marco, Susan. "Home-Grown Agriculture: The Hightower Revolution in Texas." *Southern Exposure,* No. 5–6 (1986): 65–70.

Denison, Dave. "AIDS: The Task at Hand." *Texas Observer* (24 March 1989): 3–4.

———. "The Question of Impeachment." *Texas Observer* (17 July 1988): 4–5. An editorial on Governor Clements and Southern Methodist University's "play-for-pay" football scandal.

Dickson, James D. *Law and Politics: The Office of Attorney General in Texas.* Austin: Sterling Swift, 1976.

Elkind, Peter. "The Quest That Fizzled." *Texas Monthly* (May 1986): 128–131, 183–186, 188, 190–192. Academic politics and the selection of William Cunningham as president of UT-Austin.

———. "Rock Bottom." *Texas Observer* (June 1989): 84–86, 128–130. The rise and fall of Gibralter Savings and Building Association, the largest S&L in Texas.

Gantt, Fred, Jr. *The Chief Executive in Texas: A Study in Gubernatorial Leadership.* Austin: University of Texas Press, 1964.

Harris, Byron. "Break the Bank!" *Texas Monthly* (January 1988): 88–89, 134–137, 143. The boom and bust of Don Dixon and his Vernon Savings and Loan.

House Research Organization. *Vetoes of Legislation.* Austin: Texas House of Representatives, published after each regular legislative session. This biennial report lists all measures vetoed, gives the reason for each veto, and provides a response by the author of each vetoed bill or another interested person.

The Land Commissioners of Texas. Austin: Texas General Land Office, 1986.

Leavenworth, Geoffrey. "The Price of Mercy." *Texas Business* (February 1988): 34–41. How fraud, political corruption, and failures in state and federal regulation produced chaos among the savings and loan associations of Texas.

Lewis, Robert."Highway Planning in Texas—A Look at the Process." *Texas Professional Engineer* (December 1985): 18–20.

Long, Curtis J. "The Sordid History of the S&L Crisis." *Texas Observer* (30 September 1988): 11–13.

McNeely, Dave. "Prophet of the Purse Strings." *D* (July 1986): 36, 38–40. Bob Bullock's record as Texas's comptroller of public accounts.

Mason, Todd, et al. "High-Rolling Texas: The State That Ate FSLIC." *Business Week* (31 October 1988): 138–140. The staggering impact of insolvent Texas savings and loan associations on the Federal Savings and Loan Insurance Corporation.

Morehead, Richard. *DeWitt C. Greer: King of the Highway Builders*. Austin: Eakin Press, 1984.
Northcott, Kaye. "The Bonehead Business of Nuclear Power." *Texas Observer* (20 February 1987): 1, 5–7. A critique of the South Texas and Comanche Peak nuclear power projects.
Pearson, William M., and Van H. Wigginton. "Texas Legislators' Perceptions of Administrative Controls: Continued Effectiveness of Sunset." *Texas Journal of Political Studies*, 7 (Fall–Winter 1984–1985): 31–34.
Prindle, David F. *Petroleum Politics and the Texas Railroad Commission*. Austin: University of Texas Press, 1981.
Regulation in Texas. 2 vols. Policy Research Project Report No. 76. Austin: Lyndon B. Johnson School of Public Affairs, 1986.
Rutherford, Bruce. *The Impeachment of Jim Ferguson*. Austin: Eakin Press, 1983.
Slaughter, Cynthia. "Sunset and Occupational Regulation: A [Texas] Case Study." *Public Administration Review*, 46 (May/June 1986): 241–245.
Sobel, Lionel S. "The Regulation of Sports Agents: An Analytical Primer." *Baylor Law Review*, 39 (Summer 1987): 700–786. Includes analyses of the Texas "NCAA-Rule" Act (1987) and the Texas Athlete Agents Act (1987).
Weaver, Jacqueline Lang. *Unitization of Oil and Gas Fields in Texas: A Study of Legislative, Administrative, and Judicial Politics*. Washington, D.C.: Resources for the Future, Inc., 1986.
Whitford, David. *A Payroll to Meet: A Story of Greed, Corruption, and Football at SMU*. New York: Macmillan, 1989. Outlines the role of Bill Clements, Texas's two-time Republican governor.

Law, Courts, and Justice

"AIDS from a Legal Perspective." A Texas Young Lawyers Association special report composed of five articles and a selected bibliography published in *Texas Bar Journal* (February 1989): 207–225.
Alderman, Richard M. *Know Your Rights: Answers to Texans' Everyday Legal Questions*. Houston: Gulf Publishing Co., 1986.
Bailey, Brad. "Cry of Innocence." *D* (August 1989): 60–63, 75–77, 80–82. The case of convicted murderer Joyce Ann Brown. After nine years in prison, is she innocent?
Baxter, Gordon. "You Can't Do This to Me . . ." *Car and Driver* (December 1987): 28. Drinking and driving in Texas.
Brasfield, Philip. "Life and Death in TDC." *Texas Observer* (29 January 1988): 22–23. A prisoner reports on gangs within the Texas prison system.
Burch, Diane. "The Examiners: Judges with Clout." *Texas Lawyer* (16 November 1987): Sec. 3, pp. 1, 3–4. How the eight-member Board of Law Examiners and 16 appointed graders make up and grade examinations for admission to the State Bar of Texas.
Champagne, Anthony. "The Texas Judiciary: New Developments." *Texas Bar Journal* 52 (February 1989): 156–162.
Crouch, Ben M., and James W. Marquart. *An Appeal to Justice: Litigated Reform of Texas Prisons*. Austin: University of Texas Press, 1989. How the Texas Department of Corrections has been transformed as a result of *Ruiz* v. *Estelle*.
Curtis, Tom. "Making Crime Pay." *Texas Monthly* (May 1989): 88–89. On the Zavala County Detention Center, a privately financed jail that handles some prisoners shipped from Washington, D.C.
Davidson, John. "The Man Who Crushed Texaco." *Texas Monthly* (March 1988): 92–95, 138–140, 160, 167. About Houston lawyer Joe Jamail, winner of the multibillion-dollar *Pennzoil* v. *Texaco* lawsuit.

Dilulio, John J., Jr. *Governing Prisons: A Comparative Study of Correctional Management.* New York: Free Press, 1987. The state prison systems of Texas, California, and Michigan are described and compared.

Dubose, Louis. "Bankers and Judges." *Texas Observer* (5 May 1989): 16. Real estate transactions involving Charles Baker's banks and Johnson County's two state district court judges, C. C. "Kit" Cooke and John R. MacLean.

Edwards, Julie. "Controlling the Epidemic: The Texas AIDS Reporting Statute." *Baylor Law Review* 41 (Spring 1989): 399–428.

Ekland-Olson, Sheldon. "Crowding, Social Control, and Prison Violence: Evidence from the Post-Ruiz Years in Texas." *Law and Society Review,* 20: 3 (1986): 389–421.

———. "Structured Discretion, Racial Bias, and the Death Penalty: The First Decade after *Furman* in Texas." *Social Science Quarterly,* 69 (December 1988): 853–873.

Fricker, Richard L. "Crime and Punishment in Dallas." *ABA Journal,* 75 (July 1989): 52–54, 56. The Dallas district attorney's office is accused of maintaining a "win-at-any-cost" policy. Cases discussed include those of Randall Dale Adams and Lenell Geter.

Gliddens, Sally. "Mad Dog Mulder." *D* (April 1989): 62–63, 98–100, 102, 104. Profile of the Dallas attorney who prosecuted Randall Dale Adams (subject of Errol Morris's film *The Thin Blue Line*) and counseled the Rev. Walker Railey when Railey testified before a Dallas County grand jury concerning the murder attempt on Peggy Railey.

Hairston, George. "State of Texas Versus Geter/Williams." *Crisis* (April 1984): 40–47. An NAACP lawyer tells of his work on the cases of Lenell Geter and Anthony Williams.

Helms, Charles R. *Crime and Punishment in Texas.* Dallas: Associated Citizens Against Crime, 1989.

Hill, John L., Jr. "Taking Texas Judges Out of Politics: An Argument for Merit Selection." *Baylor Law Review,* 40 (Summer 1988): 339–366.

———. "A Time of Challenge: Judicial Reform in Texas." *Texas Bar Journal,* 52 (February 1989): 165, 168–170. An advocate of the "Texas Plan" comments on the recommendations of the Joint Select Committee on the Judiciary.

Keller, John. "Drinking, Drunkenness and Alcoholism: A Definition." *Texas Bar Journal,* 52 (March 1989): 278, 280, 282. One of 16 articles in this special issue devoted to alcohol and drug abuse among members of the legal profession.

Krier, Cyndi, and Claudia Nadig. "1987 Alternative Dispute Resolution Procedures Act: An Overview." *Texas Bar Journal,* 51 (January 1988): 22–23. One of several ADR articles featured in this issue.

Landis, Rebecca. *Judicial Selection in Texas.* Special Legislative Report No. 136. Austin: House Research Organization, Texas House of Representatives, 11 May 1987.

Long, Steven. *Death Without Dignity: The Story of the First Nursing Home Corporation Indicted for Murder.* Austin: Texas Monthly Press, 1987.

Martin, Steve, Jr., and Sheldon Ekland-Olson. *Texas Prisons: The Walls Came Tumbling Down.* Austin: Texas Monthly Press, 1987.

Parker, Carl A. "The Grand Jury: A Need for Reform." *Voice for the Defense,* 16 (May 1987): 5–6, 24. Written by a Texas state senator who explains that he has been "victimized," as well as served, by grand juries.

Pearson, William, and David Castle. "Attitudinal Dissonance Among Texas Judges: Rejection of Merit Selection, Acceptance of Merit Principles." *Texas Journal of Political Studies,* 10 (Spring/Summer 1988): 19–35.

Petzinger, Thomas, Jr. *Oil and Honor: The Texaco-Pennzoil Wars.* New York: G. P. Putnam's Sons, 1987.

Ramsey, Buck. "Nuremburg Defense in a Texas Court." *Texas Observer* (13 October 1989): 9–10. The trial and conviction of the "Peace Farm Three" in Carson County for a Class B misdemeanor: failure to comply with an official order to cease blocking a public road.

Reamey, Gerald S. *Criminal Offenses and Defenses in Texas.* Norcross, Ga.: Harrison, 1987.

Reavis, Dick J. "How They Ruined Our Prisons." *Texas Monthly* (May 1985): 152–159, 232–246.

Riddlesperger, James W. "Judicial Attitudes Toward Judicial Selection in Texas." *Texas Journal of Political Studies,* 10 (Spring/Summer 1988): 3–18.

Spanhel, Cynthia L. "'Typical' Texas Attorney Is Profiled Through State Bar Membership Survey." *Texas Bar Journal,* 50 (November 1987): 1124–1127. Provides data on age, gender, income, and other subjects of interest to lawyers, prospective lawyers, and social scientists.

"The Supreme Court of Texas." *Texas Bar Journal,* 52 (February 1989): 192–194. Brief biographical sketches of the nine men sitting on the court in 1989.

Taylor, Donald W. "Building New Prisons in Texas: A Project Appraisal." *Public Affairs Comment,* 34 (Summer 1988): 1–12.

Walker, Tom. "The Divorce Attorney as 'Barracuda.'" *San Antonio* (October 1988): 30–33, 56. About lawyer Eileen Flume, family law practitioner.

Revenues, Expenditures, and Fiscal Policy

Aronson, J. Richard. *Financing State and Local Government.* 4th ed. Washington, D.C.: Brookings Institute, 1986.

Brown, Stephen P. A. "The New Fiscal Environment in Texas: What It Means for State Economic Growth." *Economic Review* (January 1988): 1–9. This is a publication of the Federal Reserve Bank of Dallas.

Dauster, Nick. "Talking Sense on Taxes." *Texas Observer* (4 April 1986): 11–13.

Dubose, Louis. "To Have and to Have Not." *Texas Observer* (20 May 1988): 6–8. The issue of equitable financing of public education in Texas.

Eckhardt, Bob. "Time to Tax Corporate Income." *Texas Observer* (20 March 1987): 8–9.

"Equalizing Public School Resources." *TRL Analysis* (January 1989): 1–11.

Gold, Steven D. "A New Way to Compare States' Spending." *State Legislatures* (May/June 1989): 10–11.

Gray, Rick, et al. "On School Finance." *Texas Observer* (1 July 1988): 18–22. Edited transcript of a debate concerning the essence of the *Edgewood* v. *Kirby* lawsuit: Should tax money be redistributed among Texas's property-poor and property-rich school districts?

Haas, Debra S. "Financing Public School Facilities Under the Maximum Class Size Requirements in Texas." *Public Affairs Comment,* 34 (Winter 1988): 1–10.

Hamilton, Billy, ed. *Texas Taxes.* 2 vols. Final Report of the Select Committee on Tax Equity, 70th Legislature (Austin 1988).

House Research Organization. *State Finance Report: Writing the State Budget.* Special Legislative Report No. 71-1. Austin: Texas House of Representatives, 21 February 1989.

"How Does Texas Compare?" *TRL Analysis* (March 1989): 1–7. Comparative data on state and local government finances.

Johnson, Karl P., Jr., and Paul H. Hagen. "Texas Issues Its First Audited GAAP Financial Statements." *Today's CPA* (May/June 1989): 12–13.

Kay, Michele. "Calling the Shots." *Texas Observer* (April 1988): 28–32. A survey of Bob Bullock's public service as Texas's comptroller of public accounts.

Legislative Budget Board. *Performance Report to the 71st Legislature.* Austin, 10 January 1989.

"Legislature Considers Proposal to Pay for State Mandates." *Fiscal Notes* (May 1989): 6–9. Explains how many state laws have a significant impact on spending by local governments.

McNeely, Dave. "A Lone Star." *D* (September 1984): 67–69, 176–178. A sketch of the political career of Ann Richards, with emphasis on her first two years as state treasurer.

———. "State Funding: Apocalypse Soon." *Texas Business* (May 1986): 23–25. Prospects for an income tax in Texas.

"New Annual Financial Report Reveals State's Actual Worth." *Fiscal Notes* (April 1988): 1–4.

"Revenue Estimating for Texas State Government." *Fiscal Notes* (January 1985): 1–5.

Reynolds, Morgan O. *How Much Government Does Texas Need?* Dallas: National Center for Policy Analysis, 1989. This controversial report was written by an economics professor at Texas A&M University and published by a Dallas-based conservative think tank. It charges Texas government with gross waste and high spending.

Rips, Geoffrey. "The Lottery: Morality and Political Life." *Texas Monthly* (8 February 1985): 1–4.

Schmidt, Fred. "Make the Sales Tax Less Regressive." *Texas Observer* (24 October 1986): 11–12.

Simpson, Dee, et al. "Visions of Tax Reform: The Scholz Garten Symposium." *Texas Observer* (20 March 1987): 10–15. Transcript of an informal discussion of the prospects for tax reform for Texas.

Weiher, Gregory R. "Why Redistribution Reform Doesn't Work: State Educational Reform Policy and Governmental Decentralization in Texas." *American Politics Quarterly,* 16 (April 1988): 193–210.

Glossary

absentee voting Voting in advance by mail or in person instead of appearing at the polls on election day.

advice and consent The right of the federal or state Senate to review and approve major appointments by the chief executive.

amnesty The act of "forgetfulness" by a government for an offense, usually political, committed by a person or group of people.

answer A defendant's written statement indicating why the plaintiff is not entitled to remedy sought.

appeal A formal request to a higher court that it review the actions of a lower court; a challenge to a ruling made by a presiding officer of a legislature.

appellate court A court whose primary function is to review the judgments of other courts and of administrative agencies.

appellate jurisdiction The power of a court to review cases after they have been tried elsewhere.

at-large system An electoral system in which two or more candidates for a legislature are chosen by all of the voters of a district.

audit The final phase of the government budgetary process, which reviews the operations of an agency, especially its financial transactions, to determine whether the agency has spent its money lawfully, efficiently, and with desired results.

balanced budget A budget in which receipts are equal to or greater than outlays.

the bar The legal profession; a jurisdiction's community of lawyers.

bicameral Term describing a legislature with two houses, or chambers (e.g., House of Representatives and Senate).

bill A legislative proposal introduced in either the House of Representatives or the Senate.

biotechnology industry Enterprises that use living organisms to make or modify products, improve plants and animals, or provide treatment for human diseases.

blanket primary A primary in which voters receive a ballot containing each party's potential nominees and can help nominate candidates for all offices for each party.

block grant A federal grant distributed for use within a broad policy area, largely at the recipient's discretion.

board/commission A group charged with directing a government function; boards or commissions are used when bipartisan leadership is desirable or when their functions are quasi-judicial.

bond A certificate of indebtedness issued by a borrower to a lender that constitutes a legal obligation to repay the principal of the loan plus accrued interest.

bracket bill A bill, local in intent, that is presented as a general bill in order to avoid constitutional limitations; usually bracket bills specify a population bracket that applies to only one unit of local government.

budget A financial plan serving as a pattern for and control over future operations.

budget execution The process by which a central authority in government oversees implementation of a spending plan approved by the legislative body.

bureaucracy The totality of government offices that constitute the permanent government of a state; that is, those people and functions that continue regardless of changes in political leadership.

business tax A tax enacted as a condition to the exercise of a business.

capital felony A crime punishable by death or life imprisonment.

caption A brief written summary of the contents of a bill.

cash accounting The practice of entering expenditures into accounting logs when the money is actually paid rather than when the obligation is incurred.

casual deficit An unplanned government deficit.

categorical grant A grant that can be used only for specific, narrowly defined activities; at least 75 percent of all federal aid to states comes in the form of categorical grants.

challenge An objection to a prospective jury member; a formal legal objection to something.

chief executive The highest elected executive office in a jurisdiction, whether it be the mayor of a city, the governor of a state, or the president of the United States.

chief of state The ceremonial head of a government as opposed to the chief executive; the American presidency and the Texas governorship each combine in one office the roles of chief of state and chief executive.

citation An official summons, especially one calling for an appearance in court; a reference to previous court decisions and authoritative writings.

civil law That part of the law dealing with private, as opposed to criminal, actions.

closed primary A primary in which voters must declare their support for the party before they are given the primary ballot containing the names of the party's potential nominees.

coalition A temporary joining of political actors to advance legislation or to elect candidates; a prominent example is the conservative coalition, an informal alliance of southern Democrats and Republicans.

code A comprehensive collection of statutory laws, organized by topics for easy reference.

commission form A form of urban government headed by an elected board of commissioners, each of whom serves as administrator of a department or set of departments.

commissioners court A group of county officials comprised of the county judge, who presides, and four elected commissioners; among its policymaking functions (the court is not a judicial body) are adopting the county budget, setting tax rates, and conducting elections.

committee A subdivision of a legislature that prepares legislation for action by the respective house or that makes investigations as directed by the respective house.

common law The totality of judge-made laws that initially developed in England and continued to evolve in the United States; whenever common law, based on custom and tradition, proved inadequate, it was supplanted by statutory law.

complaint A sworn statement by a private individual claiming that another individual has committed a specific misdemeanor.

concurrent resolution A legislative action that requires the approval of both houses and signature of the chief executive.

conditional pardon A pardon that becomes effective only when the person involved meets stipulated conditions.

conference committee A meeting between representatives of the two houses of a legislature to reconcile their differences over the provisions of a bill.

consolidated metropolitan statistical area (CMSA) A megalopolitan area composed of two or more primary MSAs and with a total population of one million or more residents.

Constitution of 1876   Texas's seventh state Constitution, which remains the fundamental law of Texas; subject only to the U.S. Constitution, federal laws, and treaties, this document establishes the government, defines governing powers, and imposes limitations thereon.

constitutional amendment   A provision of a constitution adopted since its original ratification.

continuance   A postponement of a court trial date.

convention   A political meeting of the members of one party; conventions (precinct, county, district, state, national) and primaries form the temporary organizational structure of a party.

cooperative federalism   The concept that the functions and responsibilities of federal and state governments are interlocked and that nearly any governmental activity within the national sphere will reveal involvement of both levels of government.

corporate franchise tax   A general business tax imposed on corporations for the privilege of operating a business.

council-manager form   A form of urban government in which an elected city council employs a professional city manager to administer the city government.

council of governments   A multijurisdictional cooperative arrangement to permit a regional approach to planning, development, the environment, and other problems that affect a region as a whole; a COG is composed of representatives from various units of local government within each region.

county   The basic unit for administrative decentralization of state government, created by the state to serve its needs and purposes.

county attorney   A lawyer who serves as a legal adviser to county and precinct officers and who represents the state in criminal cases.

county auditor   A financial officer appointed by the district court judge(s) in a county of 35,000 or more people with a tax valuation in excess of $35 million who examines the account books and records of all officials who handle county funds.

county clerk   An elected public official who keeps records and handles a variety of paperwork (e.g., records legal documents, prepares ballots) for both the county court and the commissioners court.

county judge   An elected public official who presides over Texas's county commissioners court and the conduct of its administrative operations; the judicial duties require the county judge to preside over the county court.

county sheriff   The chief law enforcement official of a county, charged with keeping the peace of the county.

court of appeals   A court that hears appeals from a trial court; in Texas it is a midlevel court, between the trial court and the state Supreme Court or court of criminal appeals.

criminal code   Legislation that regulates individual conduct and spells out punishments for violations.

crossover voting   Voting in the primary of one party, then crossing over in the general election to vote for candidates of another party.

dealignment   A decline in political party loyalty and a rise in political independence.

death tax   A tax, usually progressive, on an individual's share of a deceased person's estate.

defendant   A person who is formally accused of a crime or is summoned in a civil suit to answer a complaint.

deficit   The amount by which a government's expenditures exceed its revenues.

direct primary   A primary election in which political party nominees are selected directly by the voting members of the party.

engrossment The preparation of an officially prescribed copy of a bill, with the text as amended by floor action.

executive branch In a government with separation of powers, that part that is responsible for applying or administering the law.

ex officio A Latin phrase meaning "by virtue of the office"; many people hold positions on boards, commissions, and so on because of another office they occupy.

felony A serious crime carrying a punishment more severe than that for a misdemeanor.

filibuster A popular tactic in the Senate that involves speechmaking to delay action on a piece of legislation.

fiscal Having to do with taxation, public revenues, or public debt.

fiscal policy That category of public policy dealing with taxes, government spending, public debt, and money management.

fiscal year Any yearly accounting period without regard to a calendar year; the fiscal year of Texas's state government begins on September 1 and ends on August 31.

foreman The person who chairs and speaks for a jury.

franchise fee A fee charged by municipalities based on the gross receipts of public utilities operating within their jurisdictions; Texas courts have held that this is fundamentally a "street rental" charge.

full faith and credit The clause in Article IV of the U.S. Constitution that requires states to legally recognize (i.e., to give full faith and credit to) the official acts, records, and civil judicial proceedings of other states.

full pardon A pardon that restores persons to their legal position prior to the crime in question.

functional expenditure A public expenditure classified according to function, e.g., education, welfare, and health.

general bill A bill that deals with general questions and that becomes a public law if passed.

general election An election held to choose among candidates nominated in a primary (or by convention or caucus) for federal, state, and local office.

general-law city A municipal area whose charter is prescribed by a general law enacted by the Texas Legislature.

general obligation bond A form of municipal bond backed by and redeemed out of a city's general revenue fund.

gerrymandering Redrawing an electoral district intentionally to benefit one particular party or group.

grant-in-aid Federal payments to states for specified purposes and usually subject to supervision and review by the federal government to ensure compliance with prescribed standards and requirements.

grand jury A group of citizens selected to review evidence against accused persons to determine whether there is sufficient evidence to bring the accused to trial.

grassroots governments Units of local government, such as cities, counties, and special districts.

high-technology industry Enterprises involved in the research, development, manufacturing, or marketing of electronic products.

home rule The ability of a municipal corporation to develop and implement its own charter; in Texas, an area with more than 5,000 people may be incorporated as a home-rule city.

hung jury A jury that is so irreconcilably divided in opinion that it is unable to reach a verdict.

ideology A consistent set of political, social, and economic values and beliefs.

Immigration Reform and Control Act of 1986 A federal statute designed to restrain the flow of illegal immigrants into the United States by penalizing employers who knowingly hire undocumented workers and by appropriating funds to provide more enforcement personnel for the Immigration and Naturalization Service.

impeachment The power of the federal or state House of Representatives to charge public officials with "treason, bribery, or other high crimes and misdemeanors."

income maintenance program A program established to provide economic assistance to the nonworking poor, e.g., old-age assistance program.

indictment A formal written accusation submitted to a court by a grand jury, alleging that a specified person has committed a specified crime.

information A formal written accusation submitted to a court by a district or county attorney, alleging that a specified person has committed a specified misdemeanor.

initiative A citizen-drafted measure that, if adopted at the polls, becomes law without approval of the Legislature.

interest group An organized body of individuals who share some goals and who try to influence public policy.

intergovernmental contracting An arrangement whereby one local government contracts with another for services that it alone cannot provide.

item veto The executive power to veto separate items in an appropriation bill; governors of many states, including Texas, have this authority, whereas the U.S. president does not.

joint resolution A legislative action that requires the approval of both houses but not the signature of the chief executive.

judgment A written opinion prepared by a judge based on a verdict; also called a decree of the court.

jurisdiction The power of a court to act on a case.

juror A person selected to determine matters of fact based on evidence presented at a trial and to render a verdict.

justice of the peace A minor judicial official, not necessarily a lawyer, who has the authority to deal with petty civil and criminal cases, perform marriages, and so on.

Kilgarlin v. *Martin* The federal district court case of 1965 that first applied the "one man, one vote" principle in Texas.

legislature The lawmaking branch of federal, state, or local government.

litigant A person who is engaged in a lawsuit.

lobbying A communication by an agent acting on behalf of an interest group intended to influence policymaking.

local bill A bill that affects only a single unit of local government, e.g., a city, county, or precinct.

magistrate A minor official with limited judicial authority, such as a justice of the peace or the judge of a municipal court.

martial law Temporary rule by the military and suspension of civil authority; martial law may be declared by the commander-in-chief of federal or state military forces (the U.S. president or the state governor) in cases of emergency.

master The judge of a trial involving alleged judicial misconduct.

mayor-council form A form of urban government with a separately elected executive (the mayor) and an urban legislature (the council) usually elected in partisan ward elections. It is called a *strong mayor–council form* if the office of mayor is filled by separate citywide elections and has such powers as veto, appointment, and removal; when the office of mayor lacks such powers, it is called a *weak mayor–council form.*

metropolitan area An urban area composed of one or more large cities and surrounding suburban communities; although socially and economically integrated, a metropolitan area is composed of separate units of local government, including counties, cities, and special districts.

metropolitan government A central government for a metropolitan area; if all existing local governments at the time of its formation are abolished, it is a consolidated government, whereas under a federated government each local unit retains its identity and some of its functions while other functions are transferred to the metropolitan government.

metropolitan statistical area (MSA) An urbanized area with a total population of at least 50,000 residents.

midnight appointment An appointment made by an out-going chief executive during the last few months of a term.

misdemeanor A crime punishable by a fine and/or jail term of one year or less.

Missouri Plan The method of judicial selection in which a nominating committee (appointed in part by the state bar, the governor, and the state's chief justice) nominates three candidates for each judicial vacancy. The governor then appoints one of them to the judgeship for a term of at least one year; at the next general election, the judge runs unopposed on a nonpartisan ballot.

multimember district An electoral district that elects more than one candidate to a legislature at the same time.

municipal annexation law A statute passed by the Texas Legislature in 1963 in response to suburbanization that allows Texas cities to annex territory beyond their corporate limits, with some restrictions.

municipal court A local government court with exclusive jurisdiction over violations of municipal ordinances.

National Supremacy clause The clause in Article VI of the U.S. Constitution that ensures that the Constitution and the laws and treaties made under it prevail over the constitutions and laws of the states.

no bill A decision not to indict made by a grand jury when it finds insufficient evidence to bring a person to trial.

nolo contendere A Latin phrase meaning no contest; a defendant's formal answer in court to a charge in a complaint or an indictment, stating that the defendant will not contest the charge but neither admits guilt nor claims innocence.

nominating petition A document signed by a required percentage of a jurisdiction's voters to place a candidate on a ballot.

notary public A semi-public official who can administer oaths, certify the validity of documents, and perform a variety of formal witnessing duties.

Ogallala Aquifer The world's largest underground water-bearing rock formation, which was formed over one million years ago by runoff from the Rocky Mountains and extends from Texas to North Dakota.

open primary A primary in which voters need not declare their party loyalty.

ordinance A statute enacted by a local government; it has the force of law but must comply with state and national laws. Texas cities, but not counties, have ordinance-making powers.

original jurisdiction The power of a court to hear a case first.

pardon An executive's grant of a release from the legal consequences of a criminal act; this may occur before or after indictment or conviction.

parole The release from prison of a convicted offender before completion of a sentence on certain conditions of behavior.

party realignment A shift in majority party status, whether of the electorate or of the parties and voting blocs in a legislature.

peremptory challenge The right of either side in a jury trial to reject a prospective juror without giving any reason.

petition Any formal request to a public agency or official; a request of a court to take some specific judicial action.

place system An electoral system in which candidates for a legislature file for a numerically designated place, and those candidates who file for the same place run against each other in an at-large election.

plaintiff The person who initiates a civil lawsuit.

plea bargaining The negotiations between a prosecutor and a criminal defendant's legal counsel over the severity and number of charges to which the defendant will plead guilty in exchange for the dropping of more serious charges or a promise to ask the court for a less severe sentence.

plural executive The structural arrangement whereby more than one individual or office shares executive powers; this arrangement characterizes most state governments, especially the government of Texas.

political action committee (PAC) An organization whose purpose is to raise and then distribute campaign funds to candidates for political office; because federal law restricts the amount of money contributed to a campaign by a corporation, union, trade association, or individual, PACs have developed into the major means by which significant contributions can affect an election.

political culture The attitudes and general behavior patterns that shape a community's politics and ultimately its policy formulation and adoption.

politics The means by which the will of the community is arrived at and implemented; the activities of a government, politician, or political party.

poll tax A tax required of voters, once used in Texas (and other southern states) to discourage blacks from voting; the Twenty-fourth Amendment to the U.S. Constitution, ratified in 1964, prohibits the requirement of a poll tax.

power linkage The linkage of activities in electoral politics to other areas of the political process; for example, the efforts of a political action committee to increase voter registration.

precinct chair The party official responsible for the interests of a political party in a voting precinct; typical duties include supervising party volunteer workers, encouraging voter registration, and getting out the vote on election day.

president of the Senate The person appointed or elected to preside over the Senate; the state Senate of Texas is headed by the lieutenant governor, a responsibility assigned by the Texas Constitution.

presidential preference primary A primary election in which the voters indicate their preference for a presidential candidate.

primary election A preliminary election conducted within the party to select candidates who will run for public office in a subsequent general election.

primary metropolitan statistical area (PMSA) An urbanized area composed of two or more MSAs and with a total population of 100,000 or more residents.

privileges and immunities The clause in Article IV of the U.S. Constitution that ensures that U.S. citizens from out of state have the same legal rights as local citizens in any state.

probate court A court that handles the distribution of a deceased person's property (estate).

probation The freedom granted to convicted offenders as long as they meet certain conditions of behavior.

progressive taxation A tax policy in which people in each successively higher income bracket pay a progressively higher tax rate.

proposition An issue, printed on the ballot, to be voted on during a referendum.

prosecutor An attorney employed by a government agency to initiate and maintain criminal (and sometimes civil) proceedings on behalf of the government against people accused of committing offenses.

public interest group An organized pressure group seeking to support causes relating to the public good, as opposed to a specific social or economic interest.

public opinion polling Private and informal surveys of public opinion or of the opinions of any group.

public policy A general plan of action adopted by the government to solve a social problem, counter a threat, or make use of an opportunity.

readings of a bill The traditional requirement that a bill be read three times before it can be passed.

recall A procedure that allows citizens to vote officeholders out of office between regularly scheduled elections.

recidivism The relapse into a former pattern of behavior, especially the return to criminal habits resulting in re-incarceration.

redistricting The redrawing by a state legislature of legislative and congressional district boundaries in response to a reapportionment (reassignment of numbers) of legislative and congressional seats among the states; this action is intended to safeguard equitable representation for the people in the face of population shifts.

referendum A procedure (not used in Texas) for submitting proposed laws or proposed state constitutional amendments to the voters for ratification.

regressive taxation A tax policy in which the effective tax rate falls as the tax base (e.g., individual income, corporate income) increases.

regular session The periodically scheduled convening of a legislature according to constitutional provision.

regulation Government intervention in the workings of business markets to promote a socially desirable goal.

reserved powers Those powers granted to states by the Tenth Amendment of the U.S. Constitution, i.e., the residue of powers not granted to the federal government or withheld from the states.

revenue bond A municipal bond whose repayment and dividends are guaranteed by revenues derived from the facility constructed from the proceeds of the sale of the bonds (e.g., toll road bond).

revenue sharing The granting of federal tax revenues to state and local governments for purposes of the recipient's choosing.

Reynolds v. *Sims* The U.S. Supreme Court case of 1964 that established the criterion of "one man, one vote" for legislative apportionment.

right A legally enforceable power or privilege.

right of association The legal power of individuals to organize into groups for political, economic, religious, and social purposes, recognized in *NAACP* v. *Alabama* (1958) by the U.S. Supreme Court.

sales tax A tax on consumption, rather than income; many states, including Texas, call for a fixed rate, ranging from 2 to 9 percent, to be charged on most purchases.

school district A special district for the provision of local public education for all children in its service area; a nonsalaried elected board, the typical governing body, usually hires a professional superintendent to administer the system.

senatorial courtesy The courtesy of the Senate, applied to consideration of executive nominations; this means that nominations from a state or district are not to be confirmed unless they have been approved by the senator(s) from that state or district.

separation of powers The assignment of law-making, law-enforcing, and law-interpreting functions to separate branches of government.

severance tax A tax imposed by about half of the states for the privilege of "severing" natural resources from the land; among Texas's severance taxes are the crude oil production tax and gas gathering tax.

simple resolution A legislative action that deals with matters entirely within the prerogatives of the House of Representatives or the Senate.

single-member district Any electoral district that elects only one candidate (chosen by a plurality) to a policymaking body such as a city council or state legislature.

small claims court A court that handles civil cases with a value under a specified limit (in Texas, usually $500 to $1,000).

speaker The presiding officer of the House of Representatives, elected by its members.

speaker pro tempore The person appointed by the speaker of the House of Representatives to serve as presiding officer in the absence of the speaker.

special bill A bill that makes an exception to general laws for the benefit of a specific individual, class, or corporation.

special committee A committee established by the Senate essentially for administrative purposes (e.g., administration committee, nominations committee).

special district A unit of government created by an act of the state Legislature or local ordinance that usually performs one function and serves a specific group of people in a particular geographic area (e.g., water district).

special election An election specially scheduled to fill an office that has become vacant before the expiration date of the term.

special fund A sum of money that must be used to finance an activity specified by a government.

special session The formal convening of a legislature, outside of its regularly scheduled meetings, at the initiative of a chief executive, according to constitutional provision.

Spindletop An extremely productive oil well that came in near Beaumont in 1901.

standing committee A committee of the Texas Senate that deals with bills within a specific subject area (called a *substantive committee* in the House).

subcommittee A subdivision of a full committee that studies legislation, holds hearings, and reports its recommendations to the full committee.

suburb A relatively small town or city, usually incorporated but outside the corporate limits of a central city.

suffrage The right to vote.

sunset laws Laws that fix termination dates on programs or agencies; implemented to force evaluation and to encourage legislative inquiry, they require formal reviews and subsequent affirmative legislation if the agency or program is to continue.

Supreme Court The highest state or federal court; in Texas the highest state court with civil jurisdiction.

tax A compulsory contribution exacted by a government for a public purpose.

tax assessor-collector An elected public official whose primary duty is to collect a county's general property tax.

tax collection The portion of the tax yield (the amount of tax that potentially could be collected) that actually is collected.

Tenth Amendment The amendment to the U.S. Constitution that pertains to the powers of state government.

Texas workers' compensation law Legislation extended in 1984 to compensate all farm and ranch laborers injured on the job.

"Third House" A derogatory term for the great number of lobbyists who seek to influence policymaking.

trade association A power group that acts on behalf of an industry.

trial court A court whose primary function is to initially hear and decide cases.

trial de novo The Latin term meaning a new trial.

trial jury A statutorily defined number of persons (usually at least six and not more than twelve) selected to determine matters of fact based on evidence presented at a trial and to render a verdict.

true bill An indictment made and endorsed by a grand jury when it finds sufficient evidence to bring a person to trial.

unicameral Term describing a legislature with one house, or chamber.

veniremen Prospective jurors or persons being considered for jury service.

veto The refusal of the U.S. president or a state governor to sign a bill into law; the federal or state legislature can override a veto with a two-thirds majority vote in each house.

voter registration The process whereby prospective voters are required to establish their identity and place of residence prior to an election to be declared eligible to vote in a particular jurisdiction.

voter turnout The number of voters who actually vote, compared to the number of voters eligible to vote.

voting precinct A local government subdivision for organizing the voting process, typically containing less than two thousand voters.

white primary A primary election in which black participation was forbidden or discouraged; common in the South in the early twentieth century, white primaries were ruled illegal by the U.S. Supreme Court in *Smith* v. *Allwright* (1944).

witness A person who has knowledge of the circumstances of a case and who may present such knowledge as evidence in a court case.

writ A document issued by a judicial officer ordering or forbidding the performance of a specified act.

Index

Adams, Randall Dale, 202
Advanced Technology Research Program, 17
Agriculture, 3–8, 18, 57, 180–182, 195–199
  cattle, 4, 5, 8, 16, 18
  commissioner, 180–182
  crops, 5, 7, 8, 16, 18
  extension program, 57
  income, 18
  irrigation, 8
  labor, 18
  land use, 20
  total assets, 18
  water resources, 4, 20, 40
  workers compensation, 18
AIDS, 165–167, 188, 239
Albert, Carl, 196
Alcoholic Beverages Commission, 247
Amarillo, 47, 94, 122, 176
Anchondo, José Jorge, 66
Andrews County, 57
Andrews, Mike, 23
Anglos, 3, 4, 11, 92, 224
  as city managers, 48
  population, 13, 14
  and voting, 76
Armstrong, Anne, 105
Arnold, Bill, 132
Austin, 8, 13, 21, 32, 33, 35, 45, 48, 102, 128–131, 135, 136, 160, 161, 165, 168, 170, 184, 191, 197, 236, 250, 256
  governing body, 49
  metropolitan area, 63
  transit system, 61
Avery v. *Midland County,* 54

Baker, James A., III, 19
Ballot forms, 80–82. *See also* Elections; Primary, party; Voting and voters
Baptist Christian Life Commission, 109, 114
Barnes, Ben, 104, 105
Barshop, Sam E., 176
Bass, Robert, 128
Bass, Roy, 99
Bates, John, 92
Baylor University, 185, 186, 232

Bayoud, George, Jr., 183
Beaumont, 6, 8, 12, 13, 19, 213
Bednarski, Richard Lee, 237, 238
Beecherl, Louis A., Jr., 176
Bee County, 57
Bell County, 57
Bentsen, Lloyd, Jr., 19, 92, 182, 183, 249
Berchelmann, David A., 214
Bernstein, Robert, 188
Bexar County, 9, 10, 57, 86, 139, 211
Blacks, 4, 11, 13, 22–24, 31, 36, 50, 153, 224
  as city managers, 48
  as Democrats, 91, 94
  and interest groups, 113
  political influence of, 49
  population, 12, 13, 22
  as Republicans, 94
  and single-member districts, 48, 49
  in Texas Legislature, 79, 89–91, 94, 141, 153
  and urban movement, 12
  and voting, 73, 76
Blackwood, Bill, 132
Blanton, Annie Webb, 93, 94
Board of Corrections, 176
Board of Human Services, 174
Board of Law Examiners, 215
Board of Pardons and Parole, 179, 227
Bonilla, Ruben, Jr., 74
Boston Globe Magazine, 195
Braden, George D., 164
Brazoria, 10
Brewster County, 54
Briscoe, Dolph, 35, 37, 104, 105
Brookhaven College, 62
Brooks, Chet, 166, 167
Brooks, Jack, 19
Brown, Reagan, 198
Brownfield, 132
Brownsville, 4, 8, 13, 18, 186, 231
Brownwood, 225
Bryant, John, 22
Budgeting, *see* County government; Fiscal policies; Governor; Legislature; Municipal government
Bullock, Bob, 16, 91, 92, 182, 183, 249

Bunton, Lucius D., 231
Bureaucracy, 183–189
Burns, John, 164
Bush, George, 19, 141, 145

Campbell, Jo, 191
Carrillo, O. P., 144
Carriker, Steve, 189
Carrollton, 129
Carter, Bill, 131–133
Cassin, William, 191
Cavazos, Lauro, 19
Cedar Valley College, 62
Christian, George, 104–106
Cisneros, Henry, 92
Citizens to Preserve the Constitution, 37
City Attorneys Association, 114
City Management Association, 114
Clayton, Bill, 116, 118, 149, 152
Cleburne, 129
Clements, Bill, 90, 92, 95, 97, 141, 152,
    163, 169, 171, 173, 176, 180, 183, 214,
    224, 230, 231, 247
  and agriculture, 182
  and appropriations, 176
  and budget, 178, 180
  campaigning, 97–99, 170, 201
  and education, 160
  and SMU scandal, 173
  and veto, 178, 181
Clemons, Billy, 166
Cobb, C. Dean, 162
Code of Criminal Procedure, 203
Code of Judicial Conduct, 237–240
Coke, Richard, 33, 171
College (Texas public junior) enrollment,
    Fall 1988, 62
Collin County, 57
Commissioner of Agriculture, 90, 108, 181,
    182. See also Agriculture
Commissioner of Health, 188
Commission on Judicial Conduct, 236,
    237–240
Common Cause of Texas, 113
Comptroller of Public Accounts, 52, 90, 92,
    160, 169, 180, 242, 247–251, 252, 256
Connally, John, 173
Constitutional revision and amendment,
    34–38, 46, 52, 58, 61, 111, 182, 221,
    224, 228, 244
  amendment process, 37, 38, 43
  Constitutional Revision Commission, 35
  legislative constitutional convention,
    35, 36

legislative proposal, 36
the people decide, 36, 37
piecemeal revision, 37
Constitution of Texas: politics of
    policymaking, 30–33, 45, 51–53, 57,
    60, 62, 75, 82, 169, 172–174, 177, 179,
    180, 210, 216, 245
  a century later, 33, 34
  drafting and revising, 30, 31, 33
  excessive amendments, 30
  a fundamental law, 20
  Preamble, 30
  structural disarray, 33
  Texas's first six constitutions, 31–33,
    181
Constitution of Texas: summary, 38–40
  Bill of Rights, 37–39
  local government, 40
  powers of government, 39
  suffrage and other articles, 39, 40
Cook, Eugene A., 215
Coppell, 63
Coronado, Francisco Vásquez de, 5
Corpus Christi, 8, 13, 48, 61, 106, 122, 186,
    191, 231
Corpus Christi State University, 154
Corsicana, 225
Councils of governments (COGs), 64, 65
County government, 4, 10, 32, 40, 43,
    53–60
  budget, 54, 56, 74, 82
  clerk, 54, 56, 74, 82
  commissioners court, 54–60, 82, 83,
    209, 210, 216–218
  county court, 209–211
  county court at law, 209, 211
  courthouse, 54, 58
  finance, 54
  metropolitan counties, 10, 11
  ordinance-making power, 59, 60
  roads and bridges, 54, 55
  sheriff, 54, 56
  tax assessor-collector, 54, 56
  treasurer, 34, 54, 56, 57
  voting registrar, 74
  see also Courts, Texas; Fiscal policies;
    Judges and justices; Spending; Taxa-
    tion
Courts, Texas, 32, 146, 172, 178, 179, 181,
    201, 204, 205, 207–215
  appellate courts, 213–215
  constitutional county courts, 33, 204,
    205, 207, 210, 211
  county courts, 209–211, 217

Courts, Texas (*continued*)
county courts at law, 204, 205, 211
Court of Criminal Appeals, 201, 202,
212–214, 221, 222, 228, 232, 237
courts of appeal, 31, 172, 207, 212, 221
district courts, 33, 204, 207, 211, 212
districts, 226, 228, 229
dockets, 228, 229
jurisdiction, 37, 39, 204, 209, 212–214,
218
justice of the peace courts, 3, 207, 209,
210, 217, 220, 221
juvenile courts, 226
Missouri Plan, 230
municipal courts, 207–209, 220, 221
probate courts, 211
small claims courts, 207, 210
Supreme Court, 59, 172, 185, 201, 202,
206, 207, 214, 215, 218, 220, 222, 228,
229, 232, 239, 240
traffic courts, 207
trial courts, 207–213
Craddick, Tom, 152
Crime control, 34
Crockett, 225
Crouch, Ben M., 232
Culver, Barbara M., 232

Dallas, 8, 10, 11, 19, 22, 33, 62, 66, 68–70,
99, 106, 108, 128, 129, 141, 176, 197,
213, 237, 239
city council, 70
city managers, 48
city planning, 68–70
ethnic minority, 12, 13, 22, 24, 48
government, 46, 49
hazardous waste disposal, 125
transit system, 61, 63
Dallas County, 9, 10, 57, 63, 86, 139, 202,
211, 213, 230
Dallas–Fort Worth International Airport,
61, 62
Dallas Gay Alliance, 240
Dallas Morning News, 34, 68, 104, 128, 176
Dallas Times-Herald, 238
Danburg, Debra, 165
Daniel, Price, Jr., 36
Davidson, David, 91
Davis, E. J., 32, 33, 171
Deaf Smith County, 122, 123
Debt, public, 254, 255
DeCluitt, Douglas, 176
Dedman, Robert H., 176
de la Garza, Kika, 19

Demarco, Susan, 197, 198
Demerson, Elisha, 94
Democratic party, 3, 72, 74–76, 78, 79, 81,
84, 86–94, 97, 100, 104, 105, 169, 183,
195, 196, 201, 231, 239
challenged by GOP, 76, 89
ethnic minority representation, 73, 74
factionalism, 86, 111
and governor, 81, 104
and new Texans, 90
one-party status, 72
position on ballot, 81
presidential primary, 87
primaries, 73, 75, 78. *See also* Primaries,
party
and realignment, 90–93
Denison, 196
Denton, Lane, 132
Denton, 94, 197
Denton County, 63
Department of Community Affairs, 174,
175
Department of Highways and Public Transportation, 247
Department of Public Safety, 176, 177,
247, 261
Dershowitz, Alan, 237
District attorney, 54, 56
Districts, *see* Special districts
Doggett, Lloyd, 90, 215
Donaldson, Nub, 130
Dye, Thomas R., 127

Eagle Pass, 12
Eagleton, Thomas, 96
Earle, Ronnie, 135
Eastfield College, 62
Easton, David, 2, 20
Ecology, 19, 20, 50, 192, 193
Economic Development Commission,
176
Economy, 4, 8, 16–18, 20, 189–192, 242,
243
of agriculture, 3–8, 16
employment, 189
influence of geography, 8
lobbying, 16
of manufacturing, 16
and politics, 16
of service industries, 16, 243, 244
in transition, 242, 243
Edgewood v. *Kirby,* 185, 243, 263
Edinburg, 186
Education, higher, 19, 20, 28, 40, 185, 186

Education, public, 4, 5, 19, 20, 28, 34, 40, 185, 186
  attendance, 33
  illiteracy, 20
  racial segregation, 33
  reform, 184, 185
Elazar, Daniel, 3, 20
El Centro College, 62
Elder, Shirley, 127
Elections, 10, 28, 33, 34, 40, 43, 46, 55, 72–83, 95, 104–106, 169, 171, 172, 181
  administration, 56, 79, 82, 83
  canvassing, 56
  county, 54
  financing, 97–102
  general, 56, 77, 79–82, 98, 100
  municipal, 46–49
  primary, 77–79, 100
  run-off, 80, 100
Ellis County, 16
Ellis County v. *Winbome,* 66
El Paso, 4, 5, 14, 16, 106
  government, 46, 47, 49
  metropolitan area, 63
  Mexican-American majority, 13
El Paso County, 10, 19, 57
Engler, Robert, 20
Evans, Jack, 70
Evans, Larry, 153
Executive department, 39, 168–199. *See also* Constitution of Texas, summary; Governor

Farenthold, Frances "Sissy," 104–106
Farmers Alliance, 5
Fayette County, 34, 57
Federal government, 26–30
  block grants, 29
  cooperative federalism, 28–30
  delegated powers, 26
  distribution of powers, 26–28
  due process of law, 27
  eminent domain, 28
  equal protection of the laws, 27
  extradition, 27
  full faith and credit, 27
  grants-in-aid, 28, 29, 48, 57, 58
  guarantees to states, 27
  interstate relations, 27
  limitations on states, 26, 27
  national supremacy, 26, 27
  privileges and immunities, 27
  republican government, 27

  reserved powers, 27, 28
  revenue sharing, 29
  state powers, 27, 28
Fehrenbach, T. R., 104–106
Ferguson, Amanda "Ma," 93, 104, 183
Ferguson, James E. "Pa," 93, 104, 172, 173
Fiscal policies, 242–249
  accounting, 248
  auditing, 248
  budget policy, 244–247
  demands for services, 243, 244
  fiscal crisis of 1980s, 242–244
  investment of funds, 247
  purchasing, 248
  spending policy, 245
  taxing policy, 245–247
Flower Mound, 63
Flynn, Paul, 66
Forshee, John, 234
Fort Worth, 8, 62, 99, 125, 128, 130, 133, 176, 230
  ethnic minority population, 12, 13, 48
  government, 49
  metropolitan area, 63
  transit system, 61
Fort Worth Star-Telegram, 165
Foster, Golda, 6
Foundation School Program, 257–259
Fox, Milton, 91
Frantz, Joe B., 11, 12
French, Kenneth, 129
Fricker, Mary, 21
Frontier experience, 3, 4, 5
Funds, 24, 25
  Available School Fund, 258, 259
  College Building Fund, 259
  Foundation School Fund, 258
  General Revenue Fund, 192, 245, 258, 259
  Permanent School Fund, 254
  Permanent University Fund, 248, 254, 259
  School Employee Retirement Fund, 248, 254
  School Taxing Ability Protection Fund, 258, 259
  Teacher Retirement Fund, 248, 254

Gainesville, 225
Galveston, 10, 13, 33, 132
Galveston County, 125
Garland, 106
Gatesville, 224

Geisweidt, Gerald, 152
General and Special Laws of the State of Texas, 203
General Land Office, 144, 181
Geography, Texas, 3–8, 9
  Big Bend National Park, 8
  Cap Rock Escarpment, 8
  climate, 3, 4
  Colorado River, 8
  Davis Mountains, 8
  and economy, 8
  and industrialization, 8
  land, 4, 5–8
  minerals, 3–7
  Ogallala Aquifer, 8
  offshore islands, 4
  Permian Basin, 6
  and politics, 8
  and population, 8
  Rio Grande, 7
  seacoasts, 4
  size, 4–6
  soil, 3, 4
  and urbanization, 8
  water, 4, 8
  see also Regions
Geter, Lenell, 202
Gibson, Bruce, 129, 130
Giddings, 225
Givens, Ron, 151
Gonzalez, Henry B., 19
Gonzalez, Raul, 92, 215
Governor, 2, 5, 32, 35, 37, 90, 92, 93, 95, 97, 104, 105, 132, 146, 147, 168–199, 201, 212, 214, 224, 228–230, 247
  compensation, 33, 171, 172
  election, 97–99, 171, 172
  executive powers, 32, 33, 37, 39, 169, 174–177, 179
  judicial powers, 178, 179
  legislative powers, 177, 178
  removal from office, 172, 173
  term, 33, 171
  and Texas Constitution, 35, 43, 177
Gramm, Phil, 90, 92, 100, 196, 198, 199
Grand Saline, 133
Granoff, Al, 129, 130
Graves, Curtis, 94
Green, Gene, 49
Gregg County, 34, 57
Greytok, Marta, 191
Grovey v. *Townsend,* 102
Guerrero, Lena, 129, 130

Hall, Anthony, 22
Hamilton, Peggy, 66
Hamm, Keith E., 164
Hammond, Bill, 128–130
Hampton, Jack, 229, 236–240
Hance, Kent, 92, 97
Harmel, Robert, 164
Harper v. *Virginia State Board of Elections,* 73
Harris County, 10, 22, 23, 54, 86, 138, 139, 141, 211
Hecht, Nathan L., 215
Hesburgh, Theodore M., 15
Hightower, Jack, 215
Hightower, Jim, 91, 108, 123, 195–199
Highway and Public Transportation Commission, 176
Hill, John, 98, 230
Hinojosa, Juan, 154
Hispanics, 11, 22–24, 74, 76, 94, 95
Hobby, William P. "Bill," Jr., 35, 37, 92, 131, 135, 145, 147, 151, 152, 167, 173, 180, 230, 244
Hobby, William P., Sr., 175
Hollowell, Bill, 133
Horton, Willie, 201
House of Representatives (Texas), *see* Legislature
Houston, 8, 10, 15, 22, 33, 66, 87, 99, 106, 108, 152, 165, 176, 191
  and ethnic minority, 12, 13, 23, 24, 48
  government, 46, 49
  Greater Houston Metropolitan Transit Authority (MTA), 63
Houston Post, 23, 42, 258
Hudspeth County, 122
Huntsville, 223
Hury, James, 132
Hutchison, Kay Bailey, 104

Immigration, 3, 14–16
  amnesty, 14–16
  employment and, 14–16
  of illegal aliens, 5, 19
Immigration Reform and Control Act of 1986, 14–16
Indians, American, 4, 11, 12
Industry, 16–18, 20, 34
  employment, 16, 17
  high technology, 17, 20
  manufacturing, 16, 17
  petrochemicals, 3–7, 16
  services, 16, 17
  see also Agriculture; Policy, public

Interest groups, 16, 75, 108–133, 174
  activities, 114, 115
  bribery, 118
  classification of, 111–114
  economic, 112, 113
  electioneering, 117
  leadership, 111
  lobbying, 16, 115–117, 174
  and PACs, 117, 118
  and political processes, 16, 108–111
  professional, 113
  public interest, 113, 114
  and public policy, 108, 119, 120
  techniques, 115–118
Ivins, Molly, 135

Jefferson County, 213
Johnson, Amy, 102
Johnson, Eddie Bernice, 129
Johnson, Lyndon B., 29, 89, 99, 105
Johnson, Sam, 132
Joiner, Columbus M. "Dad," 6
Jones, Anson, 31
Jones, Neal T. "Buddy," 129, 130
Judges and justices, 32, 37, 179, 181, 201,
    236–240
  age, 213
  appointment, 229, 230
  censure of, 229
  chief justice, 35, 54, 172, 213, 222, 229
  compensation, 209, 212, 213, 214
  constable, 54, 56, 210
  coroner, 210
  county judge, 53, 54–56, 83, 95, 218, 229
  discipline, 229
  district court judges, 54, 57, 229
  elections, 37, 229, 230
  justice of the peace, 33, 54, 56, 217, 218,
    229
  justice, court of appeals, 229
  justice, Supreme Court, 213
  juvenile court judges, 226
  magistrates, 207, 220
  misconduct, 229, 230, 236–240
  municipal court judge, 208, 209, 229
  party affiliation, 214, 230, 231
  qualifications, 213, 215
  removal of, 179, 212, 229, 237
  reprimand, 229
  retirement, 229
  selection process, 32, 33, 37, 54, 179,
    212, 213, 230, 231
  tenure, 39
  terms, 33, 54

Judicial department, 39
Judicial procedure, 218–222
  answer, 219
  appeal, 220–222
  attorneys, 216–222
  charge to jury, 219
  citation, 219
  civil cases, 218–220
  complaint, 222
  counsel, 220
  criminal cases, 220–222
  defendant, 219–221
  evidence, 221
  indictment, 216, 221, 222
  jeopardy, 222
  judgment, 219
  litigant, 218
  magistrate, 207, 220
  nolo contendere, 220
  parties, 216, 218–222
  petition, 219
  plaintiff, 219
  plea bargaining, 220
  pleadings, 219
  pretrial action, 219
  remedy, 219
  sentence, 179, 221, 222
  verdict, 219, 221
  witness, 218, 219, 221
Judicial reform policies, 227–231
  crime victims compensation, 227, 228,
    234–236
  crowded dockets, 228, 229
Juries, 216–218
  challenge, 217, 218
  charge, 219
  complaint, 217
  indictment, 216, 217
  information, 217
  jurors, 216–218
  jury, 216–218
  no bill, 217
  true bill, 217
  veniremen, 217, 218
  verdict, 219, 221
Justice, William Wayne, 223

Kamensky, John, 41
Kelley, Rusty, 130
Kenedy, Mifflin, 5
Key, Jeffrey E., 236
Key, V. O., Jr., 89, 102
Kilpatrick, James J., 196
King, Richard, 5

Kingsville, 186
Kinney, Henry Lawrence, 5
Kirby, William, 128
Knerr, Charles, 66
Kolasta, David, 258
Kubiak, L. B., 152

Labor, 36, 112, 113
  in agriculture, 18
  of aliens, 16
  right-to-work law, 36
  Taft-Hartley Act, 41
Land commissioner, 90
Laredo, 13, 14
Laredo State University, 154, 186
Lasswell, Harold, 14, 21
Law, state, 179, 202–207, 227
  capital punishment, 203, 206, 207
  civil, 202, 212, 218–220
  code, 203
  crime victims' rights, 227, 228
  criminal, 202–207, 209, 220–222
  felony, 179, 204–207, 212, 216, 223,
    225, 229
  fines, 204, 205
  jurisdiction, 203–205
  misdemeanor, 204–207, 209, 212, 216,
    217, 223, 225, 229
  penalties, 179, 203–205, 221
  reprieve, 179
  revision, 203
Lawyers, 209, 215, 216, 220, 230
League of United Latin-American Citizens
    (LULAC), 109, 113, 186
League of Women Voters, 113
Legislative Criminal Justice Board, 223
Legislative department, *see* Legislature
Legislators, 2, 5, 33, 102, 142
  age, 142
  campaign contributions, 128
  compensation, 33, 139, 140
  and constitutional revision, 35–37
  education, 142, 143
  ethnicity, 94, 140, 141
  gender, 93, 105, 140, 141
  interest groups, 110
  legislative experience, 143
  occupations, 142
  political party affiliation, 79, 89–91,
    141
  qualifications, 140
  religious affiliation, 143
  terms, 33, 137

Legislature, 2, 17, 18, 32–34, 42, 46, 57,
    58, 60, 61, 63, 64, 82, 130, 135–167,
    169, 171, 175, 183–185, 187, 188,
    192–194, 206, 209, 211–215, 218, 221,
    223, 224, 228, 229, 231, 232, 245–247,
    259
  AIDS legislation, 165–167
  campaign contributions, 101
  caucuses, 154–159
  committee system, 149–151
  control over administration, 144
  districting, 137–139, 175
  governor's influence, 159, 177, 178
  immunities, 146, 147
  impeachment powers, 144
  investigative powers, 144
  legislative address, 176
  legislative powers, 33, 145, 146, 171
  lobbying, 135, 160, 161, 174, 186
  nonlegislative powers, 143–145
  organization, 147–154
  presiding officers, 129, 147–149, 172
  procedure, 154–159
  and public policy, 2, 33, 52
  reform, 162, 163
  research, 151
  Senate Media Services, 136, 145, 153
  senatorial courtesy, 174
  sessions, 32, 33, 36, 92, 137, 178
  and Texas Constitution, 35–39, 42, 43,
    138–140, 143, 144, 146, 147, 154, 161,
    162
Leland, Mickey, 22, 23, 94
Lewis, Gib, 129, 130, 145, 149, 151, 154,
    162, 167, 230
Lewis, Ron, 131–133
Lieutenant governor, 35, 90, 104, 131, 147,
    148, 169, 172, 180, 223
Littlefield, George W., 5
Lobbying, *see* Interest groups; Legislature
Local governments, 2, 20, 29, 33, 37, 40,
    45–70
Loeffler, Tom, 131
Lohrke, Linda, 66
Loving County, 54
Lubbock, 92, 141
LULAC v. *Clements*, 231
Luna, Al, 22
Lyndon B. Johnson School of Public Affairs,
    126

McAllen, 14, 19, 154, 176
McDonald, Nancy, 166
McKenzie, William A., 176

McKinney, Mike, 166, 177
McKnight, Peyton, 37
McMullen County, 122
Madla, Frank, 132
Marquart, James W., 239
Mattox, Jim, 92, 153, 181
Mauriceville, 132
Mauro, Garry, 91, 181
Mauzy, Oscar H., 215
Mayor, *see* Municipal government
Meek, Paul, 191
Meir, Kenneth, Jr., 127
Metropolitan areas, 10, 63, 64
  CMSAs, 10
  MSAs, 10, 11
  PMSAs, 10
Mexican-American Democrats (MAD), 74,
  113
Mexican American Legal Defense and
  Education Fund (MALDEF), 113
Mexican Americans, 3, 4, 11, 13, 36, 50,
  94, 95, 186, 231
  city managers, 48
  Democrats, 91
  economic strength, 13, 95
  interest groups, 113
  in Legislature, 79, 89–91, 141, 152, 154
  political power, 13, 49, 95
  single-member districts, 48
  voting, 73, 76, 95
Midland, 6, 13, 152, 231
Minimum Foundation Program, 257
Moeller, Mike, 198
Moncrief, W. A. "Tex," Jr., 176
Montford, John, 135, 152
Moody, Dan, 178
Morehouse, Sarah M., 127
Mountain View, 224
Mountain View College, 62
Municipal government, 40, 45–53
  airports, 61
  annexation, 64, 65
  budgeting, 47. *See also* County govern-
    ment; Fiscal policies; Governor; Legis-
    lature
  city charter, 49
  city council, 45–53
  city manager, 47, 48
  commission, 47, 48, 53
  council manager, 47, 48
  election districts, 46, 48–50
  financing, 51–53
  general law city, 45, 46
  grants-in-aid, 48

  home rule city, 46, 48, 52
  Home Rule Enabling Act of 1913, 46
  intergovernmental contracting, 65
  legal status, 45, 46
  mayor, 46, 47–49, 104
  municipal charters, 45, 46
  municipal politics, 48, 49
  municipal services, 49–51
  ordinances, 46, 51
  place system, 49
  revenue, 52, 53
  services, 49–51, 53
  strong mayor-council, 46, 47
  weak mayor-council, 47

NAACP v. *Alabama,* 109
National Rifle Association, 108, 110, 117
Newell, Charldean, 66
Northcott, Kay, 165
North Lake College, 62
Nueces County, 34, 57

O'Connor, Sandra Day, 206
Odessa, 6, 13
Office of State-Federal Relations, 174
Oil industries, 3–5, 7, 16, 17, 20
Optometry Board, 176
Ornstein, Norman J., 127

Palestine, 224
Palomo, Juan R., 22
Pan American University, 154, 186, 232
Parker, Carl, 136
Parmer, Hugh, 135
Pasadena, 163
Patman, Wright, 196
Patterson, Samuel C., 14, 21
Perot, H. Ross, 243
Pettus, Beryl E., 155
Phillips, Thomas R., 215, 230
Pilgrim, Bo, 135
Piltz, Rick, 127
Policy, public, 2, 11, 19, 20, 28–30, 34, 45,
  108, 113, 183–193
  bureaucracy, 184, 193
  conservation, 192, 193
  corrections and rehabilitation, 227
  of education, 19, 184–186
  employment, 189
  hazardous waste disposal, 121–126
  health, 188
  human services, 186–188
  and interest groups, 113, 118, 119
  judicial reform, 228–231

Policy, public (*continued*)
  mental health and mental retardation, 188, 189
  reform, criminal justice system, 227, 228
  regulation of economy, 189–192
Political action committees (PACs), *see* Interest groups; Political campaigns
Political campaigns, 45, 72, 95–102, 104–106, 169
  campaign treasurer, 101
  electronic media, 98
  financing of, 97–100
  and PACs, 100
  public funding, 102
  public opinion polls, 95, 96
  regulation of, 101
  women in, 102–106
Political culture, 2, 3, 14
Political parties, 3, 77, 84–88, 169
  caucuses, legislative, 152
  conventions, 85, 86
  dealignment, 91
  executive committees, 88
  factions, 88
  gains and losses, 91–93
  permanent organization, 87, 88
  precinct chair, 86
  realignment, 90–93
  Republican inroads, 89, 90
  structure, 84–88
  temporary organization, 84–87
  Texas presidential primary, 86, 87
Politics, Texas, 2–4, 14
  of blacks, 94
  of cattle industry, 5, 16
  of economy, 5, 14, 16
  of geography, 4–8
  of interest groups, 16
  of Mexican Americans, 94, 95
  municipal, 48, 49
  of oil, 6, 16
  social forces on, 14, 16
  women in, 76, 84, 93, 104–106
Polls, public opinion, 11, 23, 96–98, 231
Population (Texas), 3, 7, 8–14, 18, 33, 45
  age, 9, 20
  county, 56
  electoral votes, 19
  ethnic groups, 9, 11–14, 22–24
  geographic distribution, 9–11, 22–24, 53
  growth, 10, 11, 19, 34, 88
  for home rule cities, 46
  and immigration, 3, 9, 10
Port Arthur, 13

Potter County, 94
Primary, party, 77–79, 86, 87, 95, 104, 169
  administration of, 79
  dealignment, 91
  financing, 79
  switching, 91, 95
Prisons, 28. *See also* Rehabilitation and corrections
Public assistance, 186–188
Public Transportation Commission, 174
Public Utility Commission, 191, 192, 262
Pyle, Jerry D., 176
Pyote, 225

Radical Republicans, 31–33
Ragland, James, 68
Rains, Jack, 183
Rangel v. *Mattox,* 231
Ray, C. L., 215
Rayburn, Sam, 196
Regions, 5–8, 9
  Big Bend National Park, 8
  Blacklands Belt, 8
  Cap Rock Escarpment, 8
  Central Corridor, 8
  Davis Mountains, 8
  East Texas Coastal Plains, 6, 8
  Gulf Coastal Plains, 7, 8
  North Central Plains, 8
  offshore, 6
  Panhandle, 4, 5, 8
  Permian Basin, 6
  Rocky Mountains, 7
  South Plains, 5, 8
  tidelands, 6
  West Texas, 8
Rehabilitation and corrections, 222–227
  boot camp, 225
  community justice council, 225–227
  drug treatment centers, 225
  institutions of correction, 226
  jails, 54, 56, 61, 223–225, 227
  juvenile facilities, 225
  pardon, 179
  parole, 179, 223, 225–227
  prison system, 222–224
  probation, 222, 225, 226
  restitution, 225
  work release, 223, 225
Republican party, 3, 33, 76, 78, 79, 81, 84, 86–94, 97–100, 104–106, 169, 201, 239
  challenge to Democrats, 76, 89
  in Democratic primaries, 79

Republican party (*continued*)
  factionalism, 86, 111
  governor, 78, 81, 95
  and new Texans, 90
  position on ballot, 81
  presidential primary, 87
  realignment, 90–93
  state convention, 87
  state executive committee, 88
Richards, Ann, 91–93, 104–106, 183
Richland College, 62
Rickman, Marilyn, 105
Rizzo, Stephen, 21
Roby, 189
Rove, Karl, 105
Rudd, Jim, 132
Ruiz v. *Estelle,* 223, 244
Rules of Civil Procedure, 218, 219, 227
Runnells, Clive, 176

Sam Houston State University, 155
San Angelo, 6, 13, 176
San Angelo Standard-Times, 32, 96, 102
San Antonio, 8, 17–19, 24, 33, 106, 191,
    239
  black population, 12, 48
  government, 49
  mayor, 92
  metropolitan area, 63
  Mexican-American majority, 13
  transportation system, 61
San Marcos, 209
Sargent, Ben, 168
Savings and loan associations (S&Ls),
    crisis in, 20
Secretary of state, 33, 43, 56, 82, 169,
    183
Select Committee on Higher Education,
    185
Senate, Texas, *see* Legislature
Senate Media Services, 49, 189
Sharp, John, 91
Sierra Blanca, 16
Slagle, Bob, 152, 230
Slater, Wayne, 128
Smith, Ashley, 152
Smith, Preston, 104, 105
Smith v. *Allwright,* 73
Southern Methodist University, 171, 185,
    186
Southwest Texas State University, 209
Southwest Voter Registration and Educa-
    tion Project (SVREP), 95

Speaker of the House, 35–37. *See also*
    Legislature
Spears, Franklin S., 215
Special districts, 54, 59–63, 65
  junior college, 61
  nonschool, 61–63
  politics of, 63
  school, 60, 61
Spencer, Thomas M., 163
Spending, 29, 50, 57–59, 255–262, 265–
    270
  for higher education, 259, 260
  for local governments, 262
  for public health, 261, 265–270
  for public safety, 261, 262
  for public schools, 256–259
  for public transportation, 260
  for welfare, 260
Spindletop, 6
State Banking Board, 183
State Bar Association, 37
State Bar of Texas, 215, 216
State Board of Education, 169, 175, 184
State Board of Insurance, 247
State Commission on Judicial Conduct,
    210, 229
State Depository Board, 183
State Highway and Public Transportation
    Commission, 99
State Purchasing and General Services
    Commission, 248
Steele, Chris, 166
Stephenville, 182
Stevens, F. L. "Steve," 176
Strauss, Annette, 49
Suffrage, 39, 40, 72. *See also* Elections;
    Voting and voters
Sunset Advisory Commission, 193
Superconducting super collider, 19
Swift, Dick, 132

Tallas, Jim, 132
Tarrant County, 9, 10, 57, 86, 213, 230
Tax and nontax revenues, 5, 33, 40, 53, 54,
    57–59, 250–253
  ad valorem, 52, 57, 58
  appraisal district, 37, 59
  business taxes, 251, 252
  death tax, 252, 253
  exemptions, 34, 58
  franchise, 52
  grants-in-aid, 253, 265–270
  for human services, 20

Tax and nontax revenues (*continued*)
  income, 28, 37, 58
  land revenues, 254
  miscellaneous revenues, 254
  rate, 54, 57
  sales, 52, 251
  tax increment financing, 52, 53
  taxpayers, 33, 50, 59
  tax reinvestment zone, 52, 53
Taylor, L. R., 68–70
Temple, 13
Terrell, Charles T., 176
Terrell, 47
Texarkana, 4
Texas A&I University, 154, 186
Texas A&M University, 11, 23, 126, 154, 186, 259
Texas Almanac, 34
Texas Association of College Teachers (TACT), 114, 117
Texas Bar Journal, 232
Texas Board of Law Examiners, 192
Texas Chemical Council, 125, 199
Texas Citizen Action, 108
Texas City, 10, 125
Texas Classroom Teachers Association, 113
Texas Code of Criminal Procedure, 227
Texas Commission on Jail Standards, 225
Texas Congress of Parents and Teachers, 109
Texas Consumers Association, 197
Texas Democratic Executive Committee, 6
Texas Department of Agriculture, 18, 149, 181, 182, 198, 199
Texas Department of Commerce, 19, 23, 192
Texas Department of Corrections, 201, 244
Texas Department of Criminal Justice, 224, 225, 227
Texas Department of Health, 188, 261
Texas Department of Human Services, 187
Texas Department of Mental Health and Mental Retardation, 188, 261
Texas Department on Aging, 188
Texas Education Agency, 130, 185
Texas Election Code, 73, 74, 78, 80, 83, 88
Texas Employment Commission, 189
Texas Farm Bureau, 108, 199
Texas Farmers Union, 109
Texas Gay Task Force, 114
Texas Grange, 33

Texas High Speed Rail Authority, 65
Texas Industrial Accident Board, 228
Texas Judicial Council, 208, 228
Texas Juvenile Probation Commission, 226
Texas Legal Directory, 232
Texas Municipal League, 114
Texas National Guard, 176
Texas Observer, 181, 198
Texas Oil and Chemical Workers Union, 113
Texas Parks and Wildlife Department, 192, 194
Texas Public Employees Association, 114
Texas Railroad Commission, 65, 92, 169, 175, 190, 197, 262
Texas Rangers, 40
Texas Research League, 170, 261
Texas Research Park, 17
Texas Society of Certified Public Accountants, 113
Texas Southern University, 232
Texas State Teachers Association, 114, 117
Texas State Troopers Association, 131
Texas Supreme Court Journal, 66, 92
Texas Tax Code Annotated, 66
Texas Tech University, 19, 232
Texas Trial Lawyers Association, 113
Texas Turnpike Authority, 65
Texas Unemployment Act, 18
Texas v. *White,* 27
Texas Water Commission, 2
Texas Water Development Board, 2, 191
Texas Women's Political Caucus, 105, 114
Texas Youth Commission, 223, 225, 226, 261
Tom Green County, 96
Toomey, Mike, 132
Tower, John, 88, 90
Travis County, 10, 55, 131, 135, 183
Treasurer, state, 90, 92, 104, 169, 183, 247, 248. *See also* Richards, Ann
Turner, Sylvester, 49
Tyler, 37, 213

University of Houston, 106, 232
University of North Texas, 197
University of Texas at Austin, 154, 172, 232, 236, 259
University of Texas at Dallas, 186
Urbanization and metropolitanization, 4, 8–11, 34
Uvalde, 104

Vela, Felemon, 231
Vertz, Laura L., 66
Vinson v. *Burgess,* 66
Voting and voters, 11, 27, 31, 33, 34, 37, 49, 57, 72–83, 94, 95, 104–106, 111
  absentee, 73, 82
  by age, sex, ethnicity, income, 73, 75–77
  apathy, 34, 59, 75
  ballots, 34–37, 56, 72, 73, 76, 80–82
  bilingual requirements, 83, 84
  and blacks, 75, 76
  on constitutional amendment, 35–37
  cost of voting, 75, 76
  counting votes, 83
  in Legislature, 35
  and Mexican Americans, 74, 76, 95
  precinct, 33, 56, 72, 82, 83
  qualifications, 40, 57, 73–75
  referendum, 45
  registration, 33, 35, 40, 56, 59, 74, 75, 77
  rights, 39, 72, 73
  trends, 75
  turnout, 76, 77

Waco, 8, 92, 213
Wagner, Fred, 2
Waldrop, Tom, 152
Wallace, Mack, 92
Wallace, Ralph, 152
Ward, Mike, 131
Warner, Ralph, 232
Washington, Craig, 22, 36, 141
Washington-on-the-Brazos, 31, 32
Water resources, 2, 191. *See also* Agriculture
Waxahachie, 19
Waybourn, William, 240
Webb, Michael, 66
West Texas State University, 186
White, Mark, 90, 92, 97, 191
  and education, 184, 243
  election campaigns, 97–99, 170
Whitmire, Kathy, 49
Wilkie, Curtis, 195
Wopner, Joseph A., 210
Wright, Brad, 166